The Complete Book of
Trains and Railways

Edited by
John Westwood

Contents

First published 1979 by Octopus Books Limited, 59 Grosvenor Street, London W1
© 1979 Octopus Books Limited
ISBN 0 7064 0939 6
Produced by Mandarin Publishers Limited, 22a Westlands Road, Quarry Bay, Hong Kong
Printed in Singapore

Introduction

This book presents a survey of past, present and future; the world's railways are passing through one of the most eventful periods of their history, a period in which it is possible to see survivals of the nineteenth century still working alongside what may be the prototypes for the twenty-first century. The conventional steam locomotive, despite its disappearance in many parts of the world, still seems likely to celebrate two hundred years of commercial service in 2012. By that year the electric locomotive will probably be the most common type; it will make great use of electronic technology, and may well be driverless.

In many countries the train will be regarded more as a passenger than as a freight facility, and on many routes passengers will be moved by fast trains which will be developments of the present Japanese 'bullet trains' and British High Speed Trains.

Even in countries where many still believe that the railway is outmoded, the passenger train is becoming faster or more comfortable. In the USA, where many (but not all) of the celebrated passenger trains have succumbed to air or highway competition, it is still possible to travel between main centres in comfortable sleeping-car trains or in fast day trains like the 'Metroliners'. That the old-fashioned overnight luxury train is not dead is proved by the Australian *Spirit of Progress*, the South African *Blue Train*, and the Russian *Red Arrow*, all of which are heavily booked.

Nor is the heroic age of railway construction quite finished. A new main line is being built across Siberia, new trunk routes are under construction in the Middle East and Asia, and the old dream of travelling by rail from Scotland to Singapore may yet be realized. Even in France, where many lines have been closed, a new high-speed railway, straight as a Roman road, is being built from Paris to Lyons. Clearly, as this book shows, railways have a future as well as a past.

Endpapers: *An iron-ore train on Western Australia's Mount Newman Railroad, a modern heavy-duty freight line.*

Half-title: *The Japanese 'Bullet Trains' still provide the world's fastest inter-city services.*

Title page: *The celebrated British locomotive* Flying Scotsman, *photographed with bell and headlamp while touring the USA.*

Contents page: *Complicated track layouts now demand equally complicated signalling and electrical installations. This photograph shows the Federal German Railways' tracks at Hamburg.*

Introduction: *On the Mount Newman Railroad in Western Australia, a train of iron ore, hauled by American-style diesel-electric locomotives, is about to leave for the coast.*

Opposite: *Modern track laid on concrete cross-ties, passing through desolate country in South Australia.*

Right: *No. 1000, a compound passenger locomotive of Britain's former Midland Railway, on display at the National Railway Museum.*

History
by John Westwood

From the earliest mine railways to today's complex national systems.

Birth and development 1830–1875

The first steps

Although the Liverpool and Manchester line in England marks the beginning of the Railway Age, it was by no means the first of the world's railways. A book published in 1550 illustrates a narrow-gauge line in the mines of Alsace, and in central Europe at about the same time there were mine wagons running with flanged wooden wheels on wooden rails. The idea of mine railways came to England from Germany, and by the middle of the eighteenth century there were about twenty such lines around Newcastle alone. Iron rails appeared in Cumberland in 1738. In 1801 the Surrey Iron Railway, near London, was opened and was notable in that it was a public railway, not confining its traffic to a particular industry. In 1807 the Oystermouth Railway near Swansea was the first to carry fare-paying passengers. In Bohemia the first section of a public railway was opened in 1827, and in the following year France's first public line, from St Etienne to Andrézieux, was formally opened after a year of unofficial operation.

In America a short wooden rail track had been laid up Beacon Hill in 1795 to transport materials for the new Boston state house. Similar lines, using horse power, were subsequently laid by several mining and manufacturing enterprises. A 14 km (9 mile) line carrying coal to the Lehigh River was opened in 1827; gravity was used for the loaded trip and mules hauled the empty cars back to the pit-head. A similar line, but of 47 km (29 miles), was opened in 1829 by the Delaware & Hudson Canal Company to its canal wharf at Honesdale in Pennsylvania. The 5 km (3 mile) Granite Railway was built in 1826 to convey granite for the Bunker Hill monument; its proprietor Gridley Bryant used iron strips to provide a running surface on his wooden rails and these 'strap rails' later became common in the USA. Iron rails did appear in America in 1831, but not all companies could afford to import these British products. Bryant also devised a primitive form of swivelling truck, or bogie, for his vehicles; his failure to patent this invention involved him in litigation with the engineer Ross Winans many years later, with the result that Bryant was ruined.

In America and most of Europe, steam locomotives were not used on these early railways, the horse being the preferred tractive power. Although steam locomotives had been successfully used in British mining railways since 1812, it was not until 1825 that Colonel John Stevens built and operated a small demonstration locomotive on a circular track at his estate in New Jersey. Then in 1829 the Delaware & Hudson tried the British-built *Stourbridge Lion* over its track but found that it was much too heavy for the wooden rails. In continental Europe, France was the first to try steam power when in 1828 the engineer Marc Seguin imported Stephenson locomotives from Britain to be operated on the St Etienne to Andrézieux railway.

The first public steam railway was the Stockton & Darlington, surveyed and built by George Stephenson at the request of mine owners needing a cheap way of taking coal to the wharf. Although at the hilly inland end haulage was by cables powered by stationary steam engines, the remaining 32 km (20 mile) stretch was operated by locomotives (for freight) and horses (for passenger services). The line proved successful both commercially and technically, and inspired the merchants of Manchester to promote their own line to the sea. Outside Britain, the citizens of Baltimore began a railroad towards the interior

Previous pages: Although it was a very early example of steam-locomotive design, and technically primitive, Hedley's Puffing Billy was evidently well-built, for it had a surprisingly long working life. This picture shows it at Wylam Colliery, Northumberland, probably in 1859.

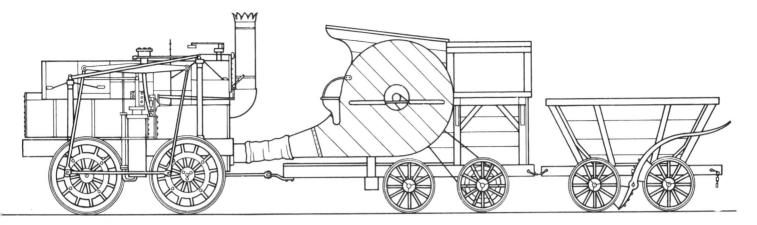

The French quest for original solutions was demonstrated right from the start of the Railway Age. This is Marc Seguin's locomotive which hauled the first French steam train in 1830 on the St Etienne–Lyons Railway. Though similar in most respects to British locomotives, its fire was enlivened by a forced draught made by an axle-driven fan mounted in a special wagon next to the engine.

in 1828, and in the summer of 1830, apart from the Liverpool & Manchester Railway, three other notable public lines were opened. One was the short Canterbury & Whitstable, a partly locomotive- and partly cable-worked line in Britain; another was the first section of the St Etienne–Lyons Railway in France, whose engineer Marc Seguin had designed two steam locomotives to supplement the horses, and the third was the first 21 km (13 mile) section of the Baltimore & Ohio Railroad.

The Liverpool & Manchester Railway is regarded as marking the beginning of the Railway Age because it brought to public attention the potentialities of inter-city steam-hauled rail transport. It was engineered by George Stephenson, who after making an unsatisfactory survey redeemed himself by successfully passing the line over the formidable Chat Moss bog, laying it on massive piles of brushwood and hurdles. The promoters of the line were largely businessmen who wished to break the monopoly of the existing Manchester to Liverpool canal, which they believed was hindering their business. The project naturally met great opposition from the canal and coaching interests and, as would happen with many subsequent railways, this opposition held up for some months the passage of the necessary railway bill through Parliament. Stephenson also had to struggle with those who preferred to run trains by cable haulage, powered by a succession of stationary steam engines, and it was only the Rainhill Locomotive Trial of 1829 that finally settled this question in favour of the steam locomotive. The 50 km (31 mile) line was opened by the Duke of Wellington in September 1830 and quickly proved a success. Contrary to expectation, passenger traffic was more important than goods; the speed and cheapness of the new form of transport was such that not only did all passengers desert the road coaches but additional passengers, who otherwise would not have travelled at all, flocked to the railway stations. The financial success of the line inspired projects elsewhere and promoters used the statistics, such as they were, of this railway to produce estimates of revenue for their own projected railways. It became apparent that railways were a 'good investment'.

The expansion of railway construction

The Railway Age arrived in Britain and America before their governments had found a railway policy. Thus in Britain there was no government guidance to encourage promoters to build lines in accordance with a thought-out plan of construction. The early railways were usually promoted by local interests for the benefit of their trade; the Bristolians' support for the Great Western Railway between Bristol and London is an obvious example. After the Liverpool & Manchester Railway had begun to pay good dividends, other railways were promoted as investment opportunities. These, too, naturally tended to be built where there was a good demand for railway service. But when the funds seeking investment outpaced the promotion of feasible projects the result was a proliferation of schemes which could never pay a good dividend, or even make a profit. Those of this latter group which passed parliamentary scrutiny and survived to become unprofitable parts of the big railway companies certainly benefited their localities but were, in effect, subsidized by more profitable areas. Railway promotion was so rapid in Britain that by 1840 the shape of the future main lines was clearly discernible. The London & Birmingham had been finished, and Birmingham was connected to the Liverpool & Manchester Railway by the Grand Junction Railway; three companies (which in 1846 would amalgamate to form the London & North Western Railway) thereby collectively provided a London to Lancashire main line. Bristol was about to be joined to London by the Great Western Railway and to Exeter by the Bristol & Exeter. The London & Southampton Railway, the nucleus of the future London & South Western, was being finished and the shape of the future Midland Railway was discernible in the companies that had laid lines connecting Gloucester with Birmingham, Birmingham with Derby and Nottingham and Derby with Leeds and York. Further north the Edinburgh and Glasgow and the Newcastle & Carlisle railways were almost complete. By 1875 England, and central Scotland and south Wales, were covered with a dense railway network that included many miles of line that would always run at a loss.

USA

Railway construction in the USA was similarly unplanned, and with similar results. That is, railways were built fast where they were needed but wasteful competition and duplication, together with lack of co-ordination, were a high price to pay. After the Baltimore & Ohio, the South Carolina Railroad from Charleston was the next common carrier railway and was the first to use steam traction in daily service. Both these lines had experimented with sails, and with self-propelled vehicles powered by horses working treadmills, but both soon opted for steam. The Baltimore directors had been impressed by the one-tonne *Tom Thumb,* which its builder, Peter Cooper, had demonstrated on their tracks in 1830. Their first regular locomotive was the *York* of Phineas Davis, which won a locomotive contest they staged. The South Carolina's first locomotive was the *Best Friend of Charleston*, built in New York. This locomotive soon came to a violent end, after its fireman had discovered the labour-saving advantages of holding down its safety valve.

Expansion was rapid after 1830, although for the first decades it was achieved by a large number of very small and sometimes under-capitalized companies. Thus it was possible to travel from Washington to New York in 1838, but only by changing from one railway to another at frequent intervals. By 1843, apart from the ferry crossing of the Hudson, there was a continuous line from Boston to Buffalo formed by the end-on linkage of nine companies. The first single-company link between the Atlantic and the Great Lakes only came in 1851 with the broad-gauge New York & Erie Railroad. Chicago's first train, over a 14 km (9 mile) length of what would later be the Chicago & North Western Railroad, ran in 1848 but it was not until 1854 that a railway traveller, with numerous changes of train and company, could move from the eastern cities to Chicago.

In other parts of the USA isolated lines were being built which would later be absorbed in the big companies. The 8 km (5 mile) Pontchartrain Railroad at New Orleans had a British locomotive in service from 1832. The Pennsylvania Railroad had a line from Philadelphia to Pittsburgh completed in 1854. The first railway in Texas was opened from Harrisburg in 1853, and the first in California, the Sacramento Valley Railroad, in 1856. Such early lines were promoted and financed locally by businessmen confident that traffic would be forthcoming. Gradually, however, railways began to be regarded less as an enhancement of existing commercial activity than as a means of developing and settling virgin territory. Such lines could hardly be financed by local businessmen, so banks began to act as railroad financiers, collecting money from investors with which to buy shares in railways that looked promising. The Federal government also helped. Anxious especially to develop the West, it gave loans to new railways (thereby sparing them the high rates of interest expected by normal investors) and also made grants of land along the projected routes of new railways. These land grants could be used by the railways as collateral for loans while the lines were being built, and could be sold cheaply to settlers afterwards. Between 1850 and 1872 the Federal government and nine states gave land grants equivalent to the combined area of Britain, Spain and Belgium.

Europe

France, which was well advanced in steam railway technology, might well have followed the British and American example and created an unplanned railway system. But the parliament intervened; it allocated money for a study of railway problems, decided that its own as well as the king's consent was required for the granting of concessions to build railways, and in 1833 launched itself into a series of debates which eventually resulted in the first nation-wide railway plan, embodied in the Railway Law of 1842. This specified that Paris would be the railway centre, with lines radiating to Calais and Lille, Strasbourg and Nancy, Toulouse and the Spanish frontier, Bordeaux and the Spanish frontier, Rouen and Le Havre, and Nantes and Brest. Only two cross-country lines were envisaged, from Marseilles to Bordeaux and from Dijon to Mulhouse. The government was to provide the land and build the infra-structure (track foundations, bridges and tunnels), while private companies would lay the track and operate trains. The government would supervise rates and safety, and would have its own representatives on company boards. Although the plan was long thought-out, its implementation took even longer. Many companies were formed but most were soon in financial difficulty. The state began to guarantee a minimum rate of interest to faltering companies and to operate certain lines for which viable companies could not be found, but by mid-century only about 3,200 km (2,000 miles) were open. The only sparkling results came from the Nord Railway which was making a success of the Calais and Lille lines. The success of the Nord prompted Napoleon III's government to encourage, by amalgamation, the formation of similarly big companies. Six companies, each with a territorial monopoly, emerged from this process: the Nord, Est, Ouest, Paris–Lyon–Méditerranée, Paris–Orléans, and Midi companies. All except the last-named (which served the south) radiated from Paris. Helped by government guarantees of interest, the new companies completed their main lines and began to build secondary routes, so that by 1870 the network was largely complete.

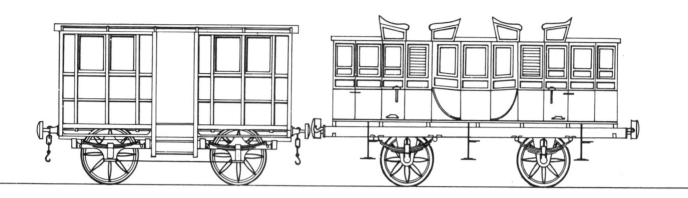

The boldest of the European railway plans was that of Belgium. Having won her independence from Holland in 1831, she was only too willing to assert her national spirit by investing in a symbol of a bright future. The commercial basis of the plan was the reward which would be reaped if Belgium could capture the international transit traffic. This she did with her first two lines: a north–south line from Antwerp through Brussels to the French frontier and an east–west line from Ostend through Louvain to Germany. These two state-owned lines, completed by 1844, crossed at Malines where the workshops were built. A few more lines followed and then the new organization rested on its laurels; private companies built most of the remaining lines, so that by 1870 the state railways owned less than 900 km (560 miles) of the network of 3,000 km (1,850 miles). The most unusual of the companies was the Société Générale d'Exploitation. This owned rolling stock but no track, and hired locomotives to companies unable to afford their own.

In neighbouring Holland there was very little planning. Dutch capitalists were not keen to invest in railways; in the 1830s the king felt obliged to give a personal guarantee of interest on the shares of a proposed railway. The first line was from Amsterdam to Haarlem, over which a Stephenson locomotive, *Arendt*, hauled the inaugural train in 1839. Further progress was slow, largely because canal and coastal shipping already provided a good service (this was one reason why freight revenue was proportionately less important than on other railways; the Netherlands Central Railway never possessed a freight locomotive). The first cross-frontier lines, to Aachen and Antwerp, did not at first link up with the Dutch system; the first main line across the frontier was the Rhenish Railway's line from Amsterdam to Emmerich. A Franco-Belgian company, the Netherlands Central Railway, opened its Utrecht to Zwolle main line in 1864 but was a financial failure. Eventually railways were concentrated, with government encouragement, into two enterprises: the private Holland Railway Company and the Netherlands State Railway. The latter operated mainly in the south and bought most of its locomotives from England whereas the former preferred to use German equipment.

The guarantee system was extensively used by the Russian government to attract both foreign and domestic capital to railway building. The first railway, from St Petersburg to Tsarskoye Selo, was opened in 1837. It was 23 km (14 miles) long, privately built, and intended to attract support for railway construction. Tsar Nicholas I, partly for strategic reasons, did decide to start a carefully planned network; lines from St Petersburg to Moscow, St Peters-

By the late 1830s railway passenger cars were breaking away from the stage-coach tradition, although a vestige of the latter can be seen in the right-hand vehicle shown here, where the central (first class) compartment has been deliberately styled to resemble a stage coach. Second-class passengers in this vehicle, owned by the Paris to Versailles Rive Gauche Railway, travelled above the wheels, while the third-class passengers sat on the roof. The left-hand drawing shows a Belgian first-class carriage, which offered two 9-seat compartments.

burg to Warsaw, and Warsaw to the Austrian frontier had first priority. The St Petersburg–Moscow line, opened in 1851, was state-built to very high standards. Under the general direction of the American railway engineer Whistler, Russian army officers had directed the forced labour of thousands of serfs. However, the state could never find the capital for all the railways it planned and many of the subsequent lines were constructed by private companies.

Spain was unique among the European powers in that its first railway was a colonial line, built in Cuba as early as 1837. George Stephenson visited Spain in 1845 to study railway prospects there and wrote a 29-word report for his British clients: 'I have been a month in the country, but have not seen during the whole of that time enough people of the right sort to fill a single train.' So the first railway in Spain, the Barcelona to Mataró line of 28 km ($17\frac{1}{2}$ miles) was opened in 1848 thanks to Spanish businessmen. Because of the mountainous interior and the lack of traffic, railway building in Spain was really beyond the resources of private companies, although they built some substantial early lines (Madrid to Alicante in 1858, Madrid to Barcelona in 1860, Madrid to Cadiz and to Lisbon in 1866). In 1866, following the French example, the government in return for financial aid required companies to amalgamate into larger and more viable concerns.

After the 1840s, British participation in the financing and building of Europe's railways diminished; opportunities seemed more inviting in the British Empire and America. French banks and French engineers began to replace the British, so that by mid-century and for long afterwards it was French capital, French locomotives and rolling stock, and French structural engineering that were dominant in many countries. Two French houses struggled for supremacy in this new kind of empire-building: the Rothschilds and the Pereires, the latter usually acting through their Crédit Mobilier. It was the Pereires who, while the French parliament was endlessly debating how to plan the future railways, decided to speed up the process. They had studied the results of the Liverpool & Manchester Railway and were convinced both of the profitability and the usefulness of railways. Anxious to invest in this promising business, they obtained permission to build a railway right under the noses of the parliamentarians, from Paris to the nearby town of St Germain. This St Germain line, opened in 1837, was very successful and helped to stimulate railway construction elsewhere so that when the 1842 Railway Law was passed there were already in existence, on routes which would obviously be a part of the final plan, some 600 km (370 miles) of track already laid. In the following years the Pereires controlled or dominated the Midi, Est and Ouest systems, while their rivals the Rothschilds gained the Nord, Paris–Orléans and PLM. This balance of power pleased neither group, and each sought to extend its empire abroad. Crédit Mobilier involved itself in building Russian railways and struggled against the Rothschilds to control lines in Austria, Spain, Switzerland and Italy. In this period, European railways were a prototype of the multinational business.

It was the Rothschilds who had gained the concession for the first Austrian steam railway. This was the Vienna to Brno line, which they cunningly named the Kaiser Ferdinands–Nordbahn, thereby associating the royal name with their enterprise. But the Austrian government decided to build further lines from its own resources, which it did until it found it had no resources left. It then turned back to private enterprise, and the Pereires scored a great victory by forming a new company which bought up most of the state lines; this

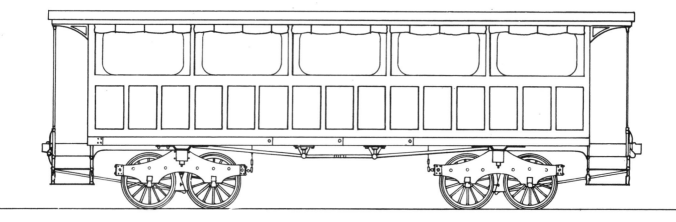

company, which was managed by French officials and directed from Paris, was called, with misleading delicacy, the Austrian State Railway Company. It was an immediate success; French private enterprise did at least drive out the lethargic, bribe-taking Austrian bureaucracy. Although it was national-ized in 1909 it had a Pereire on its board until Hitler annexed Austria. The Rothschilds counter-attacked in the 1850s, gaining control of the Milan–Venice railway in Austria's Italian territory, of the Sudbahn (linking Vienna with Trieste over the Semmering Pass), and of the Franz Josef Railway from Vienna to Budapest and Belgrade. These acquisitions, with the Roths-childs' other railway interests, meant that that family controlled a sizable railway territory embracing Austria, Hungary, Bohemia and parts of Germany.

In Italy, because of the fragmented political structure, only short lines were built at first. The Kingdom of the Two Sicilies gained the credit for the first Italian railway—an 1838 line skirting the Bay of Naples. Tuscany later built some lines radiating from Florence, and the liberalizations achieved by Pope Pius IX included railway-building in the Papal States: Rome's first railway, to Frascati, was opened in 1856. Piedmont was perhaps the most advanced of the Italian states, and its 166 km (103 mile) line from Turin to Genoa was opened by King Victor Emmanuel II in 1854.

In nearby Switzerland—forbidding terrain for early railway builders—there was a surfeit of promising projects but little willing capital. Before the new constitution of 1848 the powers of the cantons made it almost impossible to obtain agreement on long routes. Even when the 1848 reform gave more power to the central government, railway building was still considered to be mainly canton business. Nevertheless the first train between Zurich and Baden, hauled by the 'long-boiler' locomotive *Limmat*, ran in 1847. By 1855 there were three large companies and several smaller. All were short of funds, the target of takeover bids by competing French banks, and crippled by the demands of the different cantons. Costs were high, revenues were low, shares were down. The larger companies eventually agreed to co-ordinate their activities in 1861 but in 1897 they were nationalized. About half the invest-ment in Swiss railways by that time was French; for the Swiss it had been money well spent, because although the railways had not paid high dividends

Some early European passenger cars were built to what was later regarded as the standard American 'day coach' plan, with centrel aisle and cross seats. This design dates from the early 1840s and was used by the Strasbourg to Basle and the Vienna to Brno railways. The use of two four-wheel trucks foreshadowed later decades, although in this instance there was no swivel action.

they had produced enormous benefits for the Swiss economy.

Another nation fragmented by political boundaries was Germany, and here railway building followed a different course. At first the state governments showed little enthusiasm for railways; roads were still very poor and it was thought that they should have priority of investment. However, King Ludwig of Bavaria was a railway enthusiast and sent men to investigate the British and French railways. It was to his persistence that the first German railway was due. This was the line from Nuremberg to Fürth, 8 km (5 miles) long and opened with the Stephenson locomotive *Adler* in 1835. Another proponent was Friedrich List, who enthused about railways after a visit to America. In 1833 he published a pamphlet that foresaw very accurately the future German main-line system and created enough support to launch a line from Leipzig to Dresden. This important and prosperous inter-city railway was opened in 1839. The largest of the German states, Prussia, was cool towards railways, but Crown Prince Frederick William used his influence to permit private ventures to go ahead. The first result was the Magdeburg–Leipzig line in 1840, soon followed by two lines from Berlin. By then the Prussian government was less suspicious and not only offered guarantees of interest but also bought shares, and even began to construct its own state lines. A railway plan was drawn up and by 1860 5,600 km (3,500 miles) had been opened. States which decided to build their own railways rather than rely on private enterprise included Hanover, Württemberg, and Baden. Even Bavaria turned towards state lines for a decade after private companies faltered. Thus, after a later start, Germany was ahead of France by mid century. This lead was maintained and would have its appropriate result when France and Prussia went to war in 1870.

Other countries

Outside Europe and America, early short lines began to appear around mid century, usually in colonial possessions. First of these railways was Spain's 1837 venture in Cuba; the first British line was in British Guiana, opened in 1847. The beginnings of India's substantial network came in the mid 1850s with the opening of the first line of the Great Indian Peninsula Railway's route from Bombay, and of the East Indian Railway's from Calcutta. In Australia, Victoria's line from Melbourne to Port Melbourne opened in 1854, followed by New South Wales' Sydney to Paramatta line in 1855 and South Australia's Adelaide to Port Adelaide line in 1856. New Zealand's first railway, a 900 mm (3 ft) gauge mining line at Nelson, was opened in 1862. Canada's first railway was opened in 1836 from La Praire (near Montreal) to St Johns. Although early Canadian locomotives were British, the trend soon turned towards American-style equipment and operation. In South Africa, apart from an earlier short line at Durban, the first railway was from Cape Town to Wellington, opened in 1863 and destined to become part of a busy main line. In Argentina, no colony but strongly influenced by Britain, the first railway, from Parque to Floresta, was opened in 1857. It was built to the 1,680 mm (5 ft 6 in) gauge because, it was said, its first locomotive had been intended for India. Other colonial powers were not slow to build railways. The Dutch began to construct the first line of the subsequently well-developed network in Java in 1864. Among French colonial lines, the Algiers to Oran line, opened in 1871, was interesting in that it was owned and operated by the Paris–Lyon–Méditerranée Railway; a somewhat analogous position was won by Britain's London & North Western Railway in 1873, when it opened its Dundalk, Newry and Greenore Railway in Ireland.

Railways at war

The brisk course of American railroad development was enlivened by the Civil War, in which railways played an unexpectedly large role. This was not the first use of railways for military purposes. The Liverpool & Manchester Railway had once been used to accelerate the dispatch of troops from Manchester to a troublesome Ireland, and Tsar Nicholas had used his Warsaw–Vienna line to send troops to help the Austrian emperor defeat the revolutionaries in 1849. A really crucial role had been played by railways in the campaign by the French and the Piedmontese against Austria in 1859. The Paris–Lyon–Méditerranée Railway brought French troops to Marseille for embarkation, and when they landed in Genoa they were moved into action by Piedmont's railways. The rapid switching of Piedmontese and French troops by rail enabled them to outflank the Austrians and defeat them at the Battle of Magenta. In the postwar settlement France received Savoy, on the French side of the Alps, and the Savoy lines of the Piedmont railways were sold to the PLM. However, Piedmont gained control of most of the Milan–Venice line because the frontier with the Austrian Empire was pushed back to Verona. This line had merged with the Austrian Sudbahn in 1859, and after hostilities the commercially amalgamated but politically split concern was controlled by an Italian management west of Verona and by the Austrian management elsewhere; these two managements reported to a suitably neutral board in Paris.

In the American Civil War the North relied heavily on its more mature railway network, and soon found that it had to give railway officials freedom from military interference in the war zones, for officers had little understanding of transport organization. Its creation of the US Military Railroads to administer the northern lines, staffed by professional railwaymen holding military rank, largely achieved this. The South was handicapped because most of the locomotive works and rail factories were in the North, so it tried to capture Northern equipment. In the raid on Harper's Ferry it not only destroyed 42 Baltimore & Ohio locomotives, but carried away an additional 14, as well as 58 km (36 miles) of rail. The US Military Railroads succeeded in passing supplies to Sherman's 100,000-man army over a single-track railroad which passed through 580 km (360 miles) of nominally enemy territory. But this achievement was always overshadowed in the popular mind by the 'Great Locomotive Chase' in which the Confederate locomotive *General* was captured by Northern raiders, and then recaptured after a chase of some 160 km (100 miles).

After the Civil War the greatest American railway project could go ahead. Previously, although the idea of a transcontinental railroad had fired many imaginations, a stumbling block had been the insistence of the Southern States that the terminus should be in a city such as New Orleans or Memphis. The Pacific Railway Acts of 1862 and 1864 authorized the Union Pacific Railroad to build westwards from Omaha, and the Central Pacific (later the Southern Pacific) to build eastwards from Sacramento. The latter line faced the worst physical obstacle, the Sierra Nevada Range, which was eventually crossed with the help of specially imported Chinese manual labour. The Union Pacific had no mountain ranges to cross but was hindered by Indian attacks. In 1869 the two lines met in Utah. This, the first of the world's great transcontinentals, had been largely financed with loans and land grants by the Federal government. In terms of American development as a nation and as an economic system it was money well spent.

Locomotive manufacture outside Britain

Meanwhile the technical lead enjoyed by Britain was being eroded by the rise of locomotive builders in other countries. Sometimes, as happened typically in America, British-built locomotives would be the basis on which local mechanics designed their own engines. In other cases overseas mechanics would be sent to Britain by their governments or their employers in order to acquire the new knowledge. Among such mechanics was the Russian serf Cherepanov, who in 1833 would build a Russian steam locomotive at his Urals metal works. Cherepanov spoke no English, and his first locomotive was a remarkable effort, being built on the basis of observation and memory. Another visitor to Britain was Johann Schubert, who in 1839 would produce his locomotive *Saxonia* for the Dresden–Leipzig Railway. Schubert was also of very humble origin but, anticipating the academic trend in German locomotive design, he had become a professor in the local technical school before venturing into steam-locomotive construction. Elsewhere in Europe former employees of British locomotive builders were hired by new locomotive works. Among these men was the Scotsman Haswell, who for 45 years would design and build locomotives for the Austrian railways, and would introduce the heavy 0-8-0 freight locomotive to Europe. Another was Joseph Hall, who left the employ of Robert Stephenson in 1839. He then travelled abroad to Germany and in 1841 designed and built the first locomotive of the celebrated firm of Maffei in Munich.

The first locomotive-building concern in continental Europe appeared as early as 1831 at Mulhouse in Alsace; founded by Meyer, it later became the celebrated Koechlin Works. In the USA, Matthias Baldwin began to build locomotives at Philadelphia in 1831, at first using British models but later developing his own ideas; his firm, the Baldwin Locomotive Works, eventually became the world's largest. Another influential American was Isaac Dripps, the master mechanic of the Camden & Amboy Railroad, who in 1831 played the leading part in puzzling out the assembly of Stephenson's *John Bull*, which had arrived in a dismantled state. Later he fitted a two-wheel leading truck or bogie to this engine to help guide it round the tortuous curves of his railway and to push away errant cattle (the cowcatcher part had to be altered after an obstinate bull had been speared by its projecting rods). Dripps also experimented with a spark-catching chimney and in 1836 built a locomotive, appropriately named *Monster*, that had eight driving wheels divided into two groups connected by gearing.

One of the best-known of the early American locomotive engineers was Horatio Allen. Allen was sent to England by the Delaware & Hudson Company to acquire locomotives. The *Stourbridge Lion* was one of his purchases and he drove this on its test trip in 1829, the first run of a steam locomotive on a commercial American railroad. He later helped in the design of the *Best Friend of Charleston* for his South Carolina Railroad. In 1832 he built three articulated machines for the same railroad. These 2-2 + 2-2 engines with two pairs of narrow boilers back to back, with each pair supplying one cylinder, were by most definitions the world's first articulated locomotives.

German engineers

British engineers still went to work abroad, but their influence became gradually less important as other locomotive-building countries produced their own designers. Nor was this movement entirely one-way. From Dresden came Karl Beyer (later Charles Beyer) to join the British locomotive builder

Sharp, Roberts as a draughtsman. The sturdiness of his locomotives, and their bold outline with large rounded domes, set a standard for British-built locomotives, and his influence continued after he founded his own company—Beyer, Peacock—in 1853. Other Germans, who stayed at home, were laying the foundation of the German railway industry. Max von Weber, son of the composer, developed a locomotive speedometer in the hope of reducing accidents to enginemen. His concern for his men was also expressed by providing them with generous protection from the wind. Joseph Trick, an engineer at the Esslingen Works, built the first locomotive specifically for hill-climbing in 1849. He also invented the Trick Port, a supplementary channel for steam entering the cylinder, which in some conditions made efficient valve design easier. In Berlin August Borsig built his first locomotive in 1841, and by the time of his death in 1854 had built 500 more. At first he used British and US models; his first locomotive was based on Norris's type and his most successful series was a 2-4-0 of British inspiration. However, in later years the Borsig Works followed its own course and became one of the world's greatest builders of locomotives. But possibly the most significant German contribution to locomotive technology came from the Krupp Works, where steel locomotive tyres were manufactured from 1851. The use of steel for this purpose enabled greater axle loads to be used without running the risk of wheel breakages.

The Golden Age 1876–1914

Economic and social effects of railways

By 1870 the main lines of the European networks were almost complete, although secondary lines were still being built. In Europe, Britain had the greatest mileage—24,500 km (15,250 miles)—but Germany was catching up fast with 19,500 km (12,100 miles). France and Russia had about 17,000 km (10,500 miles) each, followed by Spain and Italy with about 6,000 km (3,700 miles) each. Belgium had 3,000 km (1,850 miles) and Holland and Switzerland 1,400 km (870 miles) each. Belgium was the country best served by railways, its 3,000 km (1,850 miles) being spread over a small area. Thanks to its early and rational plan of construction, it had also been the first to reap massive economic benefits. Because of the railways, its exports of cast iron rose by 800 per cent between 1836 and 1845, while coal production doubled. Other countries could show similar results later; not only did the railways cheapen transport but by widening the market for the goods they carried they stimulated greater production. At first passenger traffic developed faster than freight; the railways were so much faster, cheaper and safer than the road coaches that they not only took all the highway passengers but also carried people who otherwise would not have travelled. With freight traffic, it took time to persuade shippers to change their mode of transport, and because canals still gave a good service the railways never grasped the entire freight market.

The benefit brought by railways was especially dramatic in Switzerland because transport costs previously had been so high. There, the price of wheat in the cities fell by one third after the railways came. Coal prices fell by a half, and coal consumption increased by more than one hundred times. The tourist trade grew spectacularly. New, high-quality industries were established to serve a European-wide market, and the resulting increase in urban wages persuaded many country dwellers to move to the cities. Europe was beginning to function as a single economic unit; the Pyrenees had been crossed at each end, and the Alps had been penetrated through the Mont Cenis Tunnel and over the Brenner Pass. Work started on a third transalpine route, the St Gotthard Tunnel, in 1872, and German exporters were already looking towards northern Italy as a great potential market for rail-borne coal. Only two countries seemed to be lagging behind in western Europe. In Spain the railways passed through a land that was still not capable of originating much traffic, and in Italy railway construction had been bedevilled by political considerations; it seemed that only the French could build successful railways in Italy, and as soon as the Italian nationalist politicians discovered this they took measures to drive them out.

In the USA there had been a burst of railroad building, in the decade preceding the Civil War, that had almost quintupled the mileage, and further increases brought it to 84,000 km (53,000 miles) by 1870. Apart from easing and cheapening transport in the eastern states, this brought into the American economic system the new lands of the Middle West. Illinois, Indiana and Wisconsin became the leading wheat-growing states after the railroad had opened these virgin territories to settlers and given their crops access to eastern USA and European markets. Later, as the rails continued west, the same process would open up new lands all the way to California. At the same time, the railroads had become the major market for many industries. It was on the basis of demand for rail that the US iron, and then steel, industry turned over to mass production. By widening the market for manufactured goods, the railways enabled other industries to turn over to mass-production methods, thereby initiating the era of large-scale production and consumption.

In America and Europe the social effects of cheap fast passenger transport were felt as people began to move around both for business and pleasure. In so doing they became conscious of belonging to a nation, rather than to a state, province, or township. By 1875 a New Yorker could take a job in Boston or Chicago knowing that he would be only eight hours or thirty hours distant from his family. A Scotsman could seek his fortune in London, knowing that if he failed a train could take him back to Edinburgh in $9\frac{1}{2}$ hours.

Scandal and fraud

Despite Federal and state assistance, nine-tenths of US railroad construction was financed by the private investor. Never before had so much money sought investment, and many profited from this fact. Some of these profiteers made their own contribution to growth, but others simply milked the railroads and the investors. In the first category comes the New York Stock Exchange, which rose to pre-eminence among financial institutions because it became the main market place for railway shares at a time when such shares were dominating the market. Also, perhaps, on the creditable side were speculators like Vanderbilt and Hill who, unscrupulous profiteers though they were, had the vision to build up big railway systems that would serve the country well. Vanderbilt, by astute stock manipulation, created the New York Central System from a multiplicity of shorter lines, while the Canadian James Hill before the end of the century succeeded in organizing the two northern transcontinentals, the Northern Pacific and the Great Northern, and in providing them with a big feeder system by adding the Chicago, Burlington & Quincy Railroad to his empire. Other men, men such as Jay Gould and Jim Fiske, simply grabbed and stole and left nothing worthwhile behind them. Among Gould's exploits were stock manipulations which enabled him several times to

Cornelius Vanderbilt
(1794–1877)

buy Erie Railroad shares cheap and sell them dear. He used his profits to buy control of the Union Pacific and contrived that the UP should pay dividends far higher than its revenues warranted. This raised the market price of UP shares, and he thereupon sold his shareholding at a great profit, using the money to buy the insolvent Kansas Pacific and Denver Pacific railroads. Having done this, he went through the motions of getting the Kansas Pacific to extend its line westwards, threatening massive competition for the UP. To protect itself, the UP had to buy up the Kansas Pacific at an inflated price. The many-times-enriched Gould then left to start a new game elsewhere. Gould was only one outstanding example of a whole tribe of parasites whose activities eventually aroused the farming and industrial interests, the interests most badly damaged by the side effects of these proceedings. Government intervention became more frequent and effective, resulting in the railroads as a whole being burdened with so many state and Federal regulations that their competitive strength in the next century was seriously damaged.

Among the earlier scandals that had aroused public concern was the Crédit Mobilier affair. This was really only a single example of a widespread practice in which financiers and speculators would form a construction company to build a particular railway. Some of the participants would be directors of the railroad and would arrange a contract whereby the construction company would start building the line in exchange for an immediate payment made in the form of that railway's shares. They then used these shares as collateral to raise the money needed for the construction. At the same time, the shares gave them a controlling interest in the railway, so they could progressively raise the price paid to the construction company until the railway went bankrupt. The Crédit Mobilier was deeply involved in the first transcontinental line, and its insalubrious dealings, which included this kind of fraud, were revealed only in 1872, after it had been found distributing some of its shares as bribes to Congressmen. In general, it was genuine shareholders, and local interests which had supported particular railways, that were the losers in these transactions. The speculators and promoters usually died rich.

Europe was not without its scandals but they never seemed quite so blatant and large-scale as in the USA. Jay Gould's blackmailing of an established company by means of a threat to build a competing line had several parallels in the old world. Thomas Brassey was the most successful and publicly respected of the British contractors (he built 11,200 km, or 7,000 miles, of railway, including the British Grand Junction, the French Paris–Rouen, and the Canadian Grand Trunk), but he did not consider it dishonest to inspire and build the 'Direct Portsmouth' line in England, and then successively offer it to the three companies already struggling for the Portsmouth traffic, each of which dreaded the possibility of its competitors acquiring a shorter route. Brassey, of course, had not broken the law, and in this he was unlike George Hudson, the most celebrated of British 'railway kings' (for some reason such men were called 'railway kings' in Britain, but 'robber barons' in America). Hudson, a York draper who had been enabled by a legacy to buy his first railway shares, rose by astuteness and lack of scruple in the years of the British 'Railway Mania', in the early 1840s, when both speculators and confused private investors were recklessly buying railway shares. By exploiting quarrels between competing railways, by judicious share purchases and sales, and by a certain degree of manipulation both of people and of share prices, Hudson bought himself control of railways in the north and centre of Britain. He enriched himself, and ruined many better men, but at least he created one of the greatest of the big British companies, the Midland Railway. He was eventually brought down when he opposed interests more powerful and no more scrupulous than his own.

Hudson's great enemy, the Great Northern Railway, was damaged in 1857 when it was revealed that the company's registrar had robbed it of almost a quarter of a million pounds. Such frauds were not uncommon. The railways were the world's first big business, and ways to supervise employees and executives were not easy to find; never before had so much money been placed in the hands of so many persons under such little immediate supervision. A similar scandal rocked Italy in 1861, when the vice-president, a banker, of the Roman Railway Company was arrested for fraud.

Continental contractors had no more scruples than their Anglo-Saxon brothers, as Portuguese experience demonstrated. Portugal had been rather slow to build railways, partly because there were several interests zealously squashing any projects other than their own. The French, in particular, wanted to link Portugal with Spain and thus with France, thereby breaking Britain's trading monopoly; in this endeavour Spain was not co-operative, and its adoption of the 1,680 mm (5 ft 6 in) gauge, imitated by Portugal, was a blow to the French government. Nevertheless, the first railway in Portugal was a French company. It ran from Lisbon to Cintra and it was inaugurated by the King of Portugal in 1856; unfortunately the ceremonial train broke down and the king and his entourage did most of their inaugurating on foot. The biggest of the railway companies was the Royal Portuguese Railway Company, which in 1859 had secured a concession to build from Lisbon to the Spanish frontier, with a second line to Oporto. Its promoter was a Spanish contractor, José de Salamanca. Salamanca contracted through a second company to complete and operate the line within three years, and received a government subsidy on the strength of this. He pocketed this subsidy and kept up the railway share prices by paying dividends out of capital. Construction was still unfinished in 1865, by which year Salamanca and his friends had unloaded their shares in the French Bourse where they steadily fell to a low of 145 francs per 500 franc share. The cost of the line built by Salamanca the contractor was double the price originally agreed by Salamanca the promoter, but even so the quality was poor. The promised bridge over the Douro was not delivered, so inhabitants of Oporto until 1878 had to cross the river and go out of the city in order to reach the terminus. Still, thanks to Salamanca, Lisbon was in circuitous and expensive rail communication with the rest of Europe by 1866.

As time passed, the activities of the various railway swindlers diminished. Partly this was because railway construction slackened, but mainly it was because investors and governments became less easy to defraud, having learned by hard experience. Closer government supervision, though it led to railway speculators seeking ways to influence government and judges by bribery, was important. Also important were house-cleaning measures by financial and business circles seeking to restore respectability to private enterprise. In the USA the investment banker J. Pierpoint Morgan was the most prominent of several bankers who plainly put their investor-clients first. Morgan refused to invest the funds entrusted to him in doubtful railway enterprises. Moreover, when the fierce railway competition of the 1870s and 1880s brought many railroads to bankruptcy, it was Morgan who was often asked to reorganize them. Thus began the era of railroad consolidation, as men like Morgan, powerful because they were honest, forcibly joined smaller lines to the larger systems. In 1885 Morgan visited Europe and discovered that British investors, who had placed much money in American railroads, resented the expensive competition between trunk lines; at that time the so-called Nickel Plate Railroad was being built solely for the purpose of blackmailing the New York Central, while another was being built eastwards from Pittsburgh with the sole object of blackmailing the Pennsylvania Railroad. Inviting the builders of these and other lines to his yacht, Morgan would apply a mixture of threats and promises to force them to agree on sensible settlements. In helping other ailing companies, including the Baltimore & Ohio, and the Philadelphia & Reading, Morgan established syndicates to provide capital, while insisting on the appointment of competent and honest management. Another important work of Morgan was the creation in 1894 of the Southern Railway. He had a strong and beneficient influence in New England and in the two northern transcontinentals, the Great Northern and the Northern Pacific. His closest imitator in railroad reorganization was Edward H. Harriman. In 1897 he re-organized the weak Union Pacific, restoring branch lines it had lost, paying off its debts and buying a line to give it access to southern California. He relaid its main line with heavier rail, eased its curves and relocated a section so as to save 64 km (40 miles); in 1900 the UP once more paid a dividend. He then proceeded quietly to buy the shares of the Southern Pacific, which owned the line to San Francisco from the UP's western terminal at Ogden. Having gained control he reconstructed its main lines, and the two great systems, which were naturally complementary, were then linked both by ownership and by technical standards. But the nineteenth-century behaviour of big monopolies like the railroads had by that time created a hostile attitude among the public, the legislators and the courts; in 1913 the UP and SP combination was broken up, having been adjudged contrary to the recent anti-trust laws.

In general during the last quarter of the nineteenth century, the private railways in America and Europe became more stable and service-conscious. Facing little real competition except that of their own making, they settled down to make profits from providing useful services at a fair price. Conscious that their public image had suffered during the years when anarchic competition in some areas had co-existed with grasping monopoly in others, they sought to impress the public by new fast trains that would symbolize speed, safety and luxury. In this aim they were helped by the continuing improvement of the railway track and its structures.

The permanent way
The coming of the steam locomotive had coincided with the replacement of the old brittle cast-iron rails with the more durable rolled rails. Further resilience had soon been obtained, both in America and Europe, by the substitution of wooden cross-ties (sleepers) for the old stone blocks on which early rails were laid. In the 1830s two schools of rail design emerged. The British civil engineer Joseph Locke, the brain behind several main lines, perfected the double-headed form of rail, which had a cross-section resembling the figure 8. This rested in chairs fixed to the cross-ties and was secured with wooden wedges. The intention had been to reverse the rail after the top surface was worn, bringing the lower head to the top. This was not successful because after a few months the bottom surface was indented by the chairs. However, Locke's rail had many virtues and became the 'bullhead' type favoured in Britain and many other parts of the world. In the USA the flat-bottom rail, of inverted T section, became standard. This seems to have been invented by Colonel Stevens during a visit to Britain. Not liking the complication of

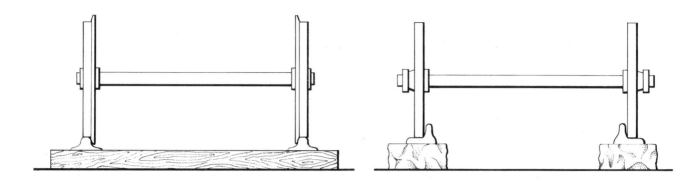

A cross-section of early English railway track. The iron rails (left) *are laid on wooden sleepers, or cross-ties, and the wheels have guiding flanges on their inner faces. This concept soon became the standard for all railways, superseding the older plateway idea* (right) *in which flanges on the rails performed the guiding function. The plateway shown here, laid on stone blocks and with a gauge of 1,524 mm (5 ft), was built in the late 18th century at an English colliery.*

chaired bullhead rail, Stevens devised a rail that could be held in place by a simple spike driven in by a hammer. The bullhead rail maintained its popularity in Britain until the mid-twentieth century, but eventually even the British decided that flat-bottomed rail was less complicated and therefore cheaper.

Contemporary prints of the early British railways show gaily painted toy-like trains passing over massive engineering structures. This adoption of structures many times bigger and stronger than what was needed, of earthworks and tunnels designed to keep gradients moderate, and of curves with a radius as large as 1.6 km (one mile), was a characteristic of British railways rarely found elsewhere, except in that second British railway network constructed in India. In the beginning it was probably uncertainty over safety margins and over the future amount of traffic, plus professional pride on the part of the engineers, that set this pattern of construction. One of its consequences was that British railways were heavily capitalized; in 1850 it was estimated that, on average, British railways had cost £35,000 per mile, as against £11,000 in Germany. But another result was that after nearly one and a half centuries Robert Stephenson's bridges and viaducts were still in use, carrying locomotives six times heavier and three times faster than those of 1840. In America the approach was entirely different. Tracks were laid as cheaply and as quickly as possible. The intention was for a railway to pay dividends without delay. Only when traffic reached a volume which the line could no longer handle would there be money for upgrading: for strengthening bridges, laying heavier rails, improving drainage, replacing grade crossings by bridges, replacing timber viaducts by masonry or steel, and realigning difficult sections to ease the gradients and curves. This was the favoured approach, too, of many colonial railways. In Europe, there was a mixture of British and American practice. The early German railways followed the US model but those of France approached British standards. Indeed, the Paris–Rouen–Le Havre line, one of the first, was engineered by Locke and built by Brassey with all the features of a British main line, including tall viaducts made of local materials. This line was to some extent imitated by other French railways, although it was not long before a definite French style of building began to emerge. In Russia, as in many other countries where there was alternation of state-built and privately-built railways, and where the available capital fluctuated, there was a corresponding alternation of engineering standards. The early St Petersburg–Moscow Railway, though supervised by an American railway engineer, was very British in its standards: it was double-track, easily graded, dead straight for most of its length and very expensive. The subsequent Trans Siberian, on the other hand, was built as a frankly 'pioneer' line, its upgrading to main line standards being postponed to subsequent decades.

The most important advance in track standards came with the introduction of steel rails, which spread over most of the world's main lines in the last quarter of the century. Large-scale production of mild steel first became possible in 1855, and as early as 1857 the Midland Railway in Britain relaid a short section of track at Derby, where exceptionally heavy traffic had meant the replacement of rails several times each year; after relaying with steel rail, no replacement was needed for 15 years. In Britain, by the late 1860s, steel rail was being introduced as fast as it could be afforded. It not only saved expense in the long run but it also contributed to safety, for breakages of iron rails were quite common. Elsewhere in the world steel rails came later. Some US lines had always been somewhat conservative in this matter, probably fearing that investment in new types of rail would cut into immediate dividends. The old strap rail, lethal when the iron strip became detached under a passing train, was used as late as 1848 by the Galena & Chicago Union. The first Bessemer steel rails were rolled in the USA in 1865, but in 1880 less than a third of the country's trackage used them. However, by the turn of the century the iron rail had virtually disappeared. In Europe progress was usually faster than in the USA. Even in Russia generous hidden subsidies were paid after 1875 to domestic rail producers who changed over to steel. The use of mild steel for bridges came concurrently. Here Britain lagged behind, largely because her bridge inspectors regarded the new material with great caution. Steel made it easier to pass hitherto uncrossed water barriers. The great Forth Bridge, with its two 520m (1,710ft) spans connecting Edinburgh with north-eastern Scotland, was opened in 1890. A year earlier a more modest but nevertheless important structure at Hawkesbury had at last provided a direct rail link between Sydney and the north of New South Wales. In the USA the first use of steel in a railway bridge was at St Louis in 1874; this crossed the Mississippi and gave St Louis direct access to the eastern states. The first bridge with an all-steel structure came in 1879, crossing the Missouri at Glasgow. The era of the steel railway bridge would continue into the twentieth century, with such structures as the 1932 Sydney Harbour Bridge, used by a new electric commuter railway; the 7km (4½ mile) Huey Long Bridge, opened in 1935 and carrying the tracks of three railroad companies into New Orleans; the 1935 Little Belt Bridge on the main line from Esbjerg to Copenhagen, and a more recent Baltic bridge over the Fehmarn Sound in Germany, opened in 1963.

The gauge problem

A seemingly imperishable question, the gauge problem, entered a new phase in the late nineteenth century. George Stephenson, whose railways and locomotives had such an initial influence on railways throughout the world, had chosen a distance of 1,422mm (4ft 8in) between the rails, and most of the early railways had copied this. However, this was not so much a conscious choice by Stephenson as an absence of choice; he merely stayed with the existing gauge of his colliery line. Some later engineers questioned the wisdom of this and made claims for other dimensions. A broad gauge was claimed to give extra stability and to accommodate more powerful locomotives, while a narrower-gauge line was much cheaper to build and could be laid on sharper curves, making it suitable for mountainous terrain. It later emerged that broader gauges, if they carried bigger freight vehicles, also produced lower costs per ton-mile. In the early decades of railway construction there were divergences from the 'standard' of 1,435 mm (4 ft 8½ in; Stephenson on second thoughts had added half an inch to his original specification). Such divergences were towards a broader, rather than a narrower gauge. Especially notable was the 2,140 mm (7 ft 0¼ in) of Britain's Great Western Railway.

It soon became evident that 1,435 mm (4 ft 8½ in) was not the ideal gauge, if such an ideal gauge existed. Most engineers, if given a choice, would have preferred a wider gauge. However, as railways grew it became clear that standardization of gauge was more important than choosing the theoretically ideal gauge. Through running of trains was impossible where adjoining railways had a different width between the rails. This soon became evident in England, where there needed to be an inconvenient and expensive tranship-ment of passengers and freight at the break-of-gauge stations where the Great Western Railway (GWR) connected with other lines. Public outcry was orchestrated by the GWR's rivals, who wished to inflict a grave blow on that company, and resulted in parliamentary intervention in the 1840s. The Gauge Commission, which Parliament established, staged trials which did show that the broad gauge was technically superior. But because the standard gauge was already preponderant the Commission recommended that no more broad-gauge mileage be built, except in Ireland, where 1,600 mm (5 ft 3 in) would remain the standard. So for the next decades the Great Western comprised old broad-gauge and new standard-gauge lines, with the former gradually becoming mixed gauge until finally, in 1892, the GWR became an entirely standard-gauge railway. Other countries faced similar problems, but usually dealt with them earlier. In Holland the 1,940 mm (6 ft 4⅜ in) gauge of the first railways became 1,435 mm (4 ft 8½ in). In southern Germany there was a similar early abandonment of broad gauge. In Spain a Royal Order of 1844 established six Castillian feet as the standard (this was 1,672 mm, a little less than the 1,676 mm of the 5 ft 6 in gauge chosen by British engineers for India and elsewhere). Although this did not prevent Spain's second railway, a mineral line, from adopting 1,435 mm (4 ft 8½ in), the Spanish main lines, as well as those of Portugal, were built to the 1,676 mm (5 ft 6 in) standard. In Russia the first railway was 1,814 mm (6 ft), but the second, from Warsaw to the Austrian frontier, was 1,435 mm (4 ft 8½ in) so that it could connect with an Austrian railway. For the third line, the standard-setting St Petersburg to Moscow Railway, Tsar Nicholas I was persuaded by his American adviser Whistler that 1,524 mm (5 ft) would be enough, and 1,524 mm thereby became the Russian standard. The Canadian government withdrew its approval of the 1,676 mm (5 ft 6 in) gauge in 1870. In the USA there was a great diversity of gauge in the early years, as there was little co-ordination, or expected co-ordination, between the railways of different states. Because the South Carolina Railroad was of 1,524 mm (5 ft) gauge, this became the standard of most lines in the South until 1886. The Camden & Amboy chose 1,473 mm (4 ft 10 in) and this for decades was the standard for New Jersey and for Ohio; some railroads built freight cars with wide wheel treads, the so-called compromise cars, which could run on both standard and 1,473 mm (4 ft 10 in) tracks. The world's first international railway—from Portland, Maine, to Montreal, Canada—chose 1,676 mm (5 ft 6 in), and the Erie Railroad opted for 1,814 mm (6 ft). From 1865 to 1871 the 1,814 mm gauge of the Erie formed part of a group of lines offering carriage from New York to St Louis by what they proudly advertised as 'The Great Broad Gauge Route'. In 1871 there were 23 different gauges in the USA (the twenty-fourth and widest appeared on an Oregon lumber railroad in the 1880s; this was 2,440 mm, or 8 ft). The first transcontinental line was intended to be 1,524 mm (5 ft), but the final bill that authorized its construction specified 1,435 mm (4 ft 8½ in). This bill was something of a milestone towards eventual gauge standardization, a goal seen to be increasingly urgent as the different states were tied into one great economic system. By 1887 all the important broad-gauge lines had changed to standard gauge.

It might have been expected that the British, having had such early experience of different gauges and their problems, would have avoided similar difficulties in their later railway building. To some extent they did, because narrow-gauge lines never took a great hold in Britain; the Light Railways Act of 1896 allowed local railways to economize not by choosing a narrower gauge but by adopting lower technical standards in conjunction with a low speed limit and other regulations. However, when the British built railways overseas they usually became entangled in gauge difficulties. For example, they built the first railway in South Africa to 1,435 mm (4 ft 8½ in) gauge but, when this reached the mountains, their engineers decided that 762 mm (2 ft 6 in) would be better; from the resulting political and technical debate emerged the compromise 1,067 mm (3 ft 6 in) which became the standard in British Africa. In South America, the railways built by the British in Argentina were marked by a diversity of gauges which still persists. In Australia they made a great effort to standardize the gauges when Victoria, New South Wales and South Australia began to build railways at about the same time. But owing to an unfortunate difference of opinion involving an Irishman, a Scotsman and an Englishman, these good intentions came to naught, and subsequent generations of Australians found that to travel from Brisbane to Perth involved travel by 1,067 mm (3 ft 6 in) gauge trains in Queensland and Western Australia, by 1,600 mm (5 ft 3 in) in Victoria and South Australia and by 1,435 mm (4 ft 8½ in) in New South Wales and across the desert.

When the first Indian railways were planned the governor-general was Lord Dalhousie, who earlier had played a prominent part, with Gladstone, in regulating the British railways of the 1840s. Dalhousie emphatically forbade the existence of more than one gauge in India and 1,676 mm (5 ft 6 in) was chosen. But in the last decades of the century, long after Dalhousie had left, new Indian gauges appeared. Because so many areas needed railways, especially for averting local famines, and because such areas were too poor to warrant broad-gauge lines, it was decided to establish a secondary network of cheaper metre-gauge lines. At first it was not intended that these should be other than short lines, but soon metre-gauge main lines appeared. By the time the British left in 1947 there was as much metre-gauge mileage as broad-gauge. Not only this, but the success of the metre gauge had opened the way for even smaller gauges of 610 mm (2 ft) and 762 mm (2 ft 6 in).

What happened in India was really only a repetition of what was happening elsewhere. In the second half of the nineteenth century those countries which had more than one gauge were either acting, or discussing how to act, in order to establish a single, uniform gauge. But in those parts of the world that had hitherto been blessed with a single gauge, various interests were promoting the introduction of a second gauge which, in one way or another, was claimed to be more suitable for certain purposes. The success of the 600 mm (1 ft 11½ in) gauge Festiniog Railway in Wales after it introduced steam traction in 1863 was an inspiration for proponents of narrower gauges. Many foreign officials visited it, among them a delegation from Russia which on its return recommended the adoption of a second, narrower, standard gauge. Russian narrow-

The crest of the Festiniog Railway, an adaptation of the Prince of Wales' cipher.

gauge lines duly appeared in the 1870s; at first they were 1,067 mm (3 ft 6 in) but eventually 750 mm (2 ft 5½ in) predominated. By 1913 there were 2,900 km (1,800 miles) of them. They had been built to narrow gauge mainly to economize, and when a few of them developed a heavy traffic there was not always enough money to convert them entirely to 1,600 mm (5 ft) gauge. Thus the narrow-gauge line to Archangel, only six years after its completion in 1899, was being converted to mixed gauge in order that its narrow-gauge locomotives might haul broad-gauge trains.

A similar process took place in western Europe. Local metre-gauge lines, independent of the big companies, were encouraged by the French government. Portugal built metre-gauge lines, especially up rural valleys but including some heavy-traffic lines around Oporto. In Germany narrow-gauge railways were largely of 750 mm (2 ft 5½ in) and metre gauge. By 1909 there were 2,200 km (1,340 miles) of such lines in a total network of 60,000 km (36,500 miles). Both in Germany and France such lines had little pretence to main-line status although some networks were quite extensive. In Belgium, a separate state company was set up, the National Company for Local Railways (SNCV), whose shareholders were largely the central and local governments. This company built and operated an extensive and continuous network of metre-gauge light railways, built very often along the roads and totalling 3,200 km (1,950 miles) by 1908. In Switzerland a multitude of metre-gauge railways were built, usually promoted or financed by towns or cantons requiring services that the main-line companies would not provide. These lines varied from rack railways climbing to mountain tops for the tourist trade, to quite sizable systems like the Rhaetian Railway; this line, beginning as a 13 km (8 mile) railway initiated by the town of Davos, grew to a 410 km (250 mile) electrified system serving the winter resorts of eastern Switzerland.

State and private railways
After a referendum the main Swiss railways were nationalized in 1902. The new Swiss Federal Railways, however, did not embrace all the Swiss railways. Others were absorbed later while many, like the Rhaetian Railway, still remain outside the state system. The question of state versus private ownership of railways had been raised in almost every railway-building country at one stage or another, and in the half-century preceding World War I it became a hot issue in many countries. There were a number of good arguments for taking a vital public service into public ownership and control, but in this period Britain and the USA remained staunchly on the side of private enterprise even though one of America's greatest railroads, the Pennsylvania, had its origins in a line built by the State of Pennsylvania. But in continental Europe many governments at an early stage had been obliged to build, or to take over, railways when the task of constructing them had proved to be beyond the means of private companies.

In France the railway companies after 1870 were held in low esteem. The war against Prussia had been lost partly because the Prussian army made better use of railways, and this misfortune was laid at the door of the railways rather than of the French army. Railway rates were a constant source of complaint by constituents to deputies of the parliament. When the Paris–Orléans Railway asked for a government guarantee of interest if it took over the running of some unprofitable secondary lines in the south-west, the chambers refused, and the state itself took over 2,600 km (1,580 miles) of lines in the west and south-west. This Etat railway became a system lying in the

Bordeaux–Nantes–Tours triangle, with access to Paris by running powers over the Paris–Orléans and Ouest companies. Meanwhile the chambers had enthusiastically voted for 8,800 km (5,350 miles) of new line to be added to the 1870 network, and most of the new lines became the responsibility of the state, since few companies were willing to risk their capital on them. This was a crippling burden on state finances, and in 1883 there was an agreement by which the companies took over most of the state secondary lines, with the companies retaining the right to receive government money in years in which revenue was insufficient to cover dividends. By 1905 only the Ouest was still making use of that government guarantee, and it was bought up by the state and incorporated into an enlarged Etat system. Thus when the war came the French main-line railways were divided into the Est, Nord, Paris–Lyon–Méditerranée, Paris–Orléans and Midi private companies, and the Etat state-owned company.

In Belgium there had been much French capital invested in private railways, and the threat to the country's neutrality during the Franco-Prussian War raised doubts in Belgian minds about the wisdom of having so many railways in foreign hands (a similar argument would be used in Japan after the war of 1904–5, culminating in the nationalization of Japanese Railways). Belgium thereupon began a gradual process of buying out the companies and adding their mileage to the State Railways. The latter began to show the kind of commercial enterprise that many did not expect to see from a state corporation. In particular, its rewarding experiments with cheap passenger fares were studied by other railway administrations and sometimes copied.

Bismarck would have preferred to nationalize the railways of the new German Empire, but in that Empire there were powerful states apart from Prussia. Bavaria, especially, wished to preserve its independent railway system. However, the Prussian State Railway grew with the incorporation of Hanover, Hesse, and Nassau, and with the acquisition by conquest of the Alsace–Lorraine Railways. Its head office in Berlin was almost next door to the new Imperial Railway Office which had been established to co-ordinate the railways of the Empire. In Prussia, moreover, Bismarck was able to take over most of the remaining private lines. By 1914 the Prussian State Railway owned about two-thirds of the Empire's network, and could usually get its preferred policies adopted by the remaining one-third. Of the other imperial railway systems, that of Russia veered between state and private ownership according to the availability of capital; at one point the government even sold Alaska and its St Petersburg to Moscow Railway in order to raise money for more state lines. By 1914 most of the Russian private railways had been taken over by the state. In Austria, the great reorganization would take place after the war. In the meantime the Austrian State Railway, privately owned by mainly French interests, continued to dominate, except in Hungary, where its lines were nationalized. In Italy, as in Hungary, railway nationalization was largely a nationalistic gesture and brought no real benefits. It began in the 1860s and continued sporadically into the late 1880s. But since the state railways were so obviously inefficient they were handed back to new companies (for operation, not for ownership) before being renationalized in 1905.

Transcontinental travel

The successful completion of America's first transcontinental railway soon inspired other projects. Several more lines would span America within a few decades. Among them were the Northern Pacific and the Great Northern to

Seattle, the Southern Pacific's line from New Orleans to Los Angeles and, a latecomer, the Chicago, St Paul and Milwaukee's 2,300 km (1,385 mile) extension to Seattle. The last-mentioned line was undertaken simply for competitive reasons; the Milwaukee Railroad felt it was in danger of being squeezed out of business by the James Hill combination of the GN and NP which naturally routed their western traffic over the Milwaukee's rival, the Burlington Railroad (also a Hill line). Thanks to modern construction methods, the new line was completed in three years and opened in 1909. By 1916 710 km (438 miles) of it had been electrified. But this line never paid; there were too many lines between the Midwest and Seattle, and the opening of the Milwaukee route coincided too closely with the opening of the Panama Canal, which took freight traffic from all the transcontinentals.

Perhaps the most ambitious transcontinental project was that for the Canadian Pacific Railway. Even more than the first US transcontinental, this line had major political objectives. At the time it was by no means certain that British Columbia would remain in the British Empire; it was isolated from the rest of Canada and close, geographically and commercially, to the northwestern states of the USA. The confederation of the Canadian colonies was seen as a way to retain British Columbia, and a railway from the older colonies of Ontario and Quebec to the Pacific was part of the price which British Columbia exacted for joining the new federation. It was a very difficult line to build, for not only were the Rockies an obstacle but there was also the swamp and muskeg territory around Lake Superior to be conquered. The project nearly failed through crises of confidence and of finance, but it had strong political support in London and Canada, financial backing from the rich Hudson's Bay Company, and the dauntless American contractor, Van Horne. The line was completed in November 1885 and the first through train to the Pacific left Montreal in July 1886 and arrived 139 hours later.

Two decades later another Dominion-binding transcontinental was opened: this was the Trans-Australian Railway, begun in 1913 and finished in 1917. Built largely across featureless and waterless terrain this 1,700 km (1,051 mile) standard-gauge line linked the railways of the isolated state of Western Australia with those of the eastern states.

The Canadian Pacific inspired the Russian government to build its Trans Siberian line. This aimed to develop the economy of Siberia, to support a Russian fleet on the Pacific, and to extend Russian commercial and political influence in China. Part of it, the Chinese Eastern Railway, passed over Chinese territory, where it soon sprouted a branch line to Port Arthur, the South Manchurian Railway, whose purpose was frankly military and expansionist. It is hardly surprising that the completion of the Trans Siberian route coincided with the Russo-Japanese War, which resulted in Russia losing the South Manchurian Railway.

The Chinese Eastern Railway was by no means the only new line with expansionist motives. The never-to-be-completed Cape to Cairo project was to provide an all-British route from top to bottom of Africa; and the German-financed Baghdad Railway from Turkey to the Persian Gulf was regarded as a threat to British influence in that sensitive region.

The new transcontinentals regaled their wealthiest passengers with trains of great luxury, at the same time providing trains of great austerity but tempting cheapness for immigrants. The Trans Siberian Express, though slow, had a lounge car complete with piano, and a bathroom with a marble-tiled shower. In the 1920s the thrice-weekly Trans-Australian train between Port Augusta and Kalgoorlie also provided a piano, even though the journey took only 37½ hours compared to the nine days of the Moscow–Vladivostok journey. The US transcontinental lines relied on Pullman to provide fitting accommodation for sleeping, dining, and lounging passengers and were not disappointed.

In Europe Pullman was emulated by a Belgian, Nagelmackers, who on a visit to the USA had been impressed by Pullman cars and in 1869 endeavoured to start a similar service in Europe. Although Belgian railways were sympathetic, most of the other continental systems at first were not. After a number of false starts and failures he eventually scored a great success with his Paris–Vienna service, and this was the real beginning for his *Compagnie Internationale des Wagons-Lits*. He not only provided in his cars luxurious sitting, sleeping, and dining accommodation, but also arranged for the traditionally tedious frontier document and baggage examinations to be carried out on board the moving train. Like Pullman, he provided the cars and expected the railway companies to haul them; the railways received the first-class fares while Nagelmackers' Wagons-Lits received the passengers' supplementary fares. In 1883, after lengthy negotiations between Nagelmackers and seven railway companies, the first of 'The Great International Trains' began to run; this was the Orient Express, providing a service between Paris, central Europe and Turkey. It captured the public imagination, brought in profits at least for the Wagons-Lits company, and was followed by many other similar trains, including the Trans Siberian Express. In the meantime, all over the developed world, railways were operating faster and more comfortable trains. In America, competition for the New York–Chicago traffic resulted in the Pennsylvania and the New York Central railroads introducing amid great publicity a series of fast luxury trains, culminating in the *Broadway Limited* and the *Twentieth Century Limited*; in 1914 these covered the distance in 20 hours, requiring an average speed of 77 km/h (48 mph) from the *Twentieth Century Limited*. In Britain the 'Races to the North' of 1888 and 1895, in which two rival associations of railways, making up respectively the West Coast and the East Coast routes to Scotland, tried to outpace each other, gave way to a more sedate competition. But in 1914 the Great Western Railway could offer two 95 km/h (59 mph) services from London to Bath (174 km or 107 miles), and the North Eastern had a train covering 71 km (44 miles) in 43 minutes.

Braking systems

Although the increasing comfort of passenger vehicles was perhaps the most noticeable improvement in rolling-stock design in the half century before 1914, the more fundamental changes concerned safety in operation. In particular, the period was marked by the advent of reliable braking systems and of safer couplings. The USA led the world in both these fields, possibly because the USA had the most alarming accident rate. On average, in America in the 1850s, the railways killed one passenger in every 200,000 compared to one in 1,700,000 in France and one in 6,680,000 in Britain. What railways the world over needed above all was a brake that could be operated from the locomotive yet act all down the length of a train (that is, a 'continuous' brake), and that would apply itself automatically in case of failure, especially after a train had split in two. There were a number of brake systems in existence but none of these quite met the need for an automatic and continuous brake, and in any case they were only applied to passenger trains. Freight trains had hand brakes; in the USA these were applied by brakemen running along the roofs of

*George Westinghouse
(1846–1914).*

the cars and screwing down the brake handles. In Britain and elsewhere there were brake levers operated from ground level; before descending a steep gradient a train had to be halted for its brakes to be pinned down. For stopping a freight train in motion there were only the locomotive brakes and the brakes operated by the train's guard in the rear brakevan. Naturally enough, with such inadequate brake power fatal runaways were common. The American George Westinghouse produced his automatic brake in 1872. This used compressed air supplied by a steam pump on the locomotive. All the vehicles had compressed-air reservoirs which applied pressure in the brake cylinders to keep the brakes off. Brake applications were made by releasing this pressure, which meant that in the case of a train breakage the broken air pipe would allow pressure to drop and thereby stop both halves of the train. By 1885 nearly all American passenger trains used this brake, but with long freight trains the brakes at the rear tended to come on much later than those near the locomotive. However, in 1887 Westinghouse had alleviated this latter defect.

Train couplings on most US railroads were of the link-and-pin type, in which a man had to stand between the two vehicles as they met and drop the pin in the coupling at precisely the right moment. Many fingers, arms, and lives were lost in this process until in 1863 Ezra Miller invented the Miller Hook, which enabled cars to couple automatically by engaging movable coupling hooks. However, this device was only suitable for passenger cars. But in 1868 Major Janney invented the Janney coupler, the forerunner of most automatic coupling systems, which was a central movable-jaw coupler robust enough to take both the tractive pull and also the buffing stresses. This 'buckeye' coupler was followed by a marginally improved version, the Willison coupler, in which instead of the movable jaws of the Janney an arrangement of fixed jaws with movable locking jaws was used. It has been calculated that in the 1880s there were almost 40 different types of coupler used in the USA, and a large number of braking systems. The existence of good systems did not guarantee that all companies would use them, especially in view of the high cost of installation. It was only in 1893 that the American railways agreed to standardize the Westinghouse brake and buckeye coupler, and then only because the federal Interstate Commerce Commission, which was already closely supervising railroad behaviour, secured the passage of the Railroad Safety Appliance Act which enforced this standardization. In Europe, Westinghouse brakes (or in some countries, especially Britain, the new automatic vacuum brake) were introduced in due course, but not always full-heartedly. The British railways were especially casual in their approach, and for their freight cars continued both with archaic chain couplings and hand brakes. Even with passenger vehicles, some British lines showed scant regard for safety. The aggressive management of the London & North Western Railway was particularly nefarious in this regard. The chief mechanical engineer of this company was drawing good patent royalties from the somewhat mediocre brake designs he had devised for his vehicles, and was accordingly reluctant to introduce the Westinghouse system. Only when the British government compelled them did some British companies fit continuous automatic brakes to their passenger stock. However, British lines did adopt the buckeye coupler for certain of their passenger trains and because it was strong it often held a train together in derailments. In western Europe automatic couplers for freight work were not fitted, partly because the existing screw coupler, though time-consuming, was otherwise very satisfactory, and partly because, with vehicles being constantly interchanged over frontiers, it would have been necessary to obtain the agreement of all the western European railways to make the change at the same time. The Willison coupler, however, was adopted by a few of the world's railways including those of the USSR.

Freight cars everywhere became larger during this period. The standard American vehicle was the eight-wheel box-car destined to be built right up to the present in steadily increasing sizes, and used for traffic that in Europe would often have been carried in specialized cars. However, in one specialized field America did lead the way. This was the use of refrigerator cars. Although milk had been carried into New York in primitive ice-packed cars as early as the 1840s, it was really the Chicago meat-packer Swift who developed this technique. Sending cattle to the eastern markets on the hoof resulted in loss of weight, so the concept of slaughtering animals in Chicago and packing the meat in refrigerator cars had obvious attractions. The success of this venture soon led to imitation by the fruit growers of California and elsewhere, and it was not long before trains of refrigerator cars (owned not by the railroads but by specialized companies) were plying over US railroads. In later years a feature of these trains was that they left the fruit-growing areas with no fixed destination; only as they approached the eastern cities did their operators specify a destination in accord with the current pattern of demand for fruit. Outside the USA a somewhat similar fruit-handling operation was soon organized to take Spanish fruit to northern destinations; in due course these refrigerator trains were fitted with vehicles whose gauge could be changed en route from the Spanish 1,676 mm (5 ft 6 in) to the standard European gauge.

Safety

Many railways did not appear to place safety at the top of their priorities. From time to time important advances in signalling were devised, applied by some companies, but ignored by others until a bad accident or government intervention (and often the one followed by the other) caused them to change their minds. In the last decades of the nineteenth century railway safety improvement generally took the form of widespread application of advances first made in earlier decades.

The first serious railway accident occurred just six weeks after the Battle of Waterloo; this was a boiler explosion in Britain, a type of mishap quite frequent during the early decades of the steam locomotive, even after most governments had established their own inspectorate. However, the most frequent serious accident was collision, and in time a complex system of devices was brought into use for the control of train movements. On the first railways train movements were regulated by 'policemen', who would require a time interval between successive trains, using sand-glasses to measure the interval and hand signals to instruct locomotive crews. But this did not prevent rear-end collisions if, for some reason, a train broke down *en route*; what was needed was a space interval, not a time interval. Such a space interval became possible with the telegraph, first used by Britain's Great Western Railway in 1839. With this it was possible to report back down the line when a train had cleared the intervening section of track. This was the origin of the block system, later applied almost universally on double-track routes, whose principle was that no train could enter a given section between two control points (usually stations or signal cabins) until the previous train had cleared it. British companies often seemed somewhat reluctant to introduce the telegraph for this purpose but changed their minds when they discovered that they could make good money by offering a public telegraph service at the same time. Meanwhile the railway policeman had been replaced by various types of mechanical signal operated from the control points. In Britain and many other countries the semaphore signal became popular, thanks to its good visibility and simplicity. France was one of a number of countries that favoured discs and boards in addition. There developed a divergence between countries like Britain and Germany, whose signals were so arranged as to indicate at junctions the route for which points and switches had been set, and countries like France where, instead, the signals gave an indication of the maximum speed limit, corresponding to the route that had been set up.

In America, long double-track sections were infrequent, and before the telegraph came traffic moved according to strict schedules which stated where opposing trains would cross. But if one train was late the crew of the opposing train sometimes decided to push on to the next crossing station; indeed they had no way of knowing whether their opposite number was merely delayed, or completely broken down and cancelled. In these conditions horrifying head-on collisions, known popularly as 'cornfield meets', did happen. Only after Samuel Morse had devised his version of the telegraph could the American lines reorganize their train control. Dispatchers, equipped with telegraph machines, were housed in offices at passing stations and could hand written orders to the crews of trains whose original instructions needed to be changed.

It was often a bad accident that persuaded companies that new procedures were needed. In France, an 1842 collision on the Paris to Versailles line at Meudon, which was followed by a fire and the incineration of many passengers including the famous Admiral Dumont d'Urville, persuaded the French railways that locking passengers into their compartments between stations, a practice regarded as a safety measure, was not so very safe after all. The introduction of the block system to America came in 1865 after a lethal rear-end collision of two troop trains in New Jersey. In 1874 a fatal collision of two British trains at Norwich made it clear that the telegraph alone was not a foolproof safeguard on single track, and four years later Tyer introduced his electric token machines. Tokens were a locoman's authority to proceed on a single-track section and Tyer's machine ensured that only one token could be in use at any given time. A frequent cause of accident, the setting of signals to give clearance to two conflicting trains at the same time as well as the setting of signals in conflict with the setting of points and switches, began to be eliminated by mechanical interlocking machines. These prevented signals from being cleared until conflicting signals and switches were set in agreement. The first such interlocking gear seems to have been that at Bricklayer's Arms, near London, in 1856. This was designed by Saxby who became one of the world's best-known names in train signalling apparatus. In 1889 the Regulation of Railways Act made interlocking compulsory on British main lines. An advance made in America was the use of compressed air in interlocked signal and switch control. This first appeared in 1890, and similar pneumatic interlocking was soon adopted in Britain after a delegation from the London & South Western Railway had made a visit to the USA and had been impressed by this apparatus. Electric track circuiting, which indicates the presence of a train in a given block section, was also in use on a few lines by the end of the century. With power signalling (pneumatic was followed by electric operation) and track circuiting, it was a short step to automatic forms of train control, notably automatic signals and automatic train control ('cab signalling'). Automatic train control, as it emerged from the experimental stage in America and

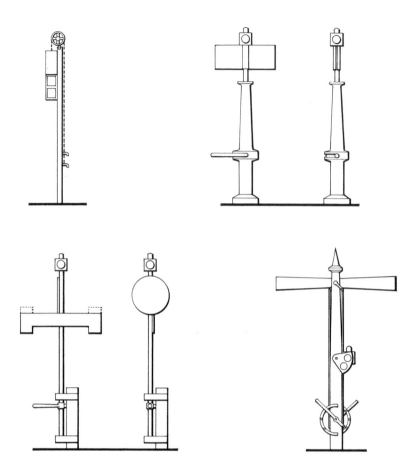

Early British railway signals. Above left: *For night operations the Stockton & Darlington Railway used this early example of the colour-light signal, a sliding shutter being raised or lowered in front of red and green lamps.* Above right: *A board signal, operated by handle. This showed a full board and red light as a stop indication, and a board edge and white light for all-clear.* Below left: *An improved board signal which showed a disc in the all-clear position. Upper or lower projections on the arms showed whether the signal controlled the up or down direction.* Below right: *A three-position semaphore, with one arm for each direction of travel. For all-clear, the arm fell into a slot in the post, and caution was indicated by a 45 degree inclination.*

Europe, applied a train's brakes automatically when the signals were set against it, if its driver had neglected to do so, and gave an indication in the locomotive cab of the signal's aspect. This was not only intended to eliminate the very occasional but sometimes lethal accidents caused by the misreading of signals but also to permit near-normal speeds in foggy weather. Perhaps this was why the Great Western Railway in Britain was one of the most advanced in this technique. Automatic signalling, in which the trains themselves actuate the signals, was also available at the end of the century; one of the first lines to use it was the Budapest underground railway opened in 1896.

Different countries were individualistic in their signalling arrangements. Semaphore signals could be of various shapes, positions, and colours, and many railways, as in France, liked to use rotating discs, diamonds, checker-boards and other indicators. Many countries continued to use white as the all-clear light long after Britain and other countries had changed to green. In central Europe, signals were more rarely encountered; the custodian of the clock telegraph at a station would stand on the platform as an indication to a passing train that all was well, a practice that has still not quite disappeared. But despite individualism in choice of indicators, good ideas spread fast. Taking one country as an example, Italy installed its first Saxby interlocking frame in 1874, and this was quickly followed by others. But Italian railways seem to have been first to use yellow as a colour indicating caution, and also made early use of the telegraph and telephone. The first use of the latter in signalling was probably the 1882 connection between the Turin stationmaster and a nearby Saxby signal cabin.

Indian Summer 1914–1945

Railways in World War I

However much the course of World War I may have confounded the military prophets, in at least one respect it did come up to expectations: this was very much a railway war. The gradually increasing role of railway transport in nineteenth-century conflicts had not been unnoticed by the general staff of the military powers, and by 1914 they were not only well prepared but had actually based their strategies on the potentialities of railways to shift and to maintain armies of a size never before seen. It was the Germans who were best prepared. In their wars against Denmark (1864) and Austria (1866) the Prussians had gained much experience which they put to good use in the subsequent Franco-Prussian War (1870–1). In the American Civil War (1861–5) a successful general, who relied greatly on rail transport, had spoken some immortal words about the importance of 'getting there firstest with the mostest'. In accordance with this advice, it had been a Prussian priority to build as many railways as possible to the frontiers so that in the event of war it would be Prussian troops who would be in position first. This policy brought dramatic benefits in the victorious war against France.

The Prussians had also trained several railway-operating battalions. In this they were not alone but they were exceptionally thorough in their training; they had even built a railway that was operated by railway troops in peace-time, handling mainly civilian traffic. In this war the importance of rail communication was emphasized by the French *francs-tireurs*, who attacked Prussian trains in the occupied zones; the Prussians showed that they agreed that their trains were important by executing as many *francs-tireurs* as they could capture, for which they were duly accused of barbarism. After the war Bismarck, largely for military reasons, wanted to nationalize the German railways but never quite succeeded. However, the German, and especially Prussian, railways already had a certain military aspect. A German historian described the railway and postal services as 'merely the civil sections of the army' containing 'three-quarters of a million men who stood stiffly at attention when their superiors spoke to them'. Railway directors were often generals and strict military-style discipline was enforced. All this, apart from its military significance, helped to give German railways a reputation for smart railway operating and also stifled the emergence of strong trade unionism.

After the Franco-Prussian war, it was clear to the staffs of the European powers that in the next war it would be fatal to lag behind the enemy in mobilizing and deploying the troops. Year by year new mobilization plans were drawn up in accordance with the latest changes in army strength and availability of railways. Moving massive reserves in a couple of weeks to the frontiers was a complex operation, for those men (and their horses) had also to be fed. Thus mobilization plans were weighty documents composed by special mobilization staffs. Individual army units and railway stations would be issued only with those sections of the plan that concerned them. These were secret documents and stationmasters were usually provided with a safe in which to lock them up until mobilization was declared, when they were to unseal them and discover what they were required to do.

Those powers fortunate enough to be surrounded by water barriers took matters a little less seriously, but for the Continental powers there was constant worry and agitation about the sufficiency of existing railways in an emergency. New lines began to be built for purely military reasons. Germany, facing the prospect of war on two fronts, built an exceptionally dense network of lines and this alarmed France and Russia, which to a certain extent tried to keep pace. A railway race was part of the arms race. Russian railway building was badly distorted by military requirements. Around the end of the nineteenth century Russia had been feverishly building railways in the west and south-west in anticipation of war against Austria or Germany. But when war came in 1904 it was against Japan, and the Russian army had to be served by the rickety single track of the hardly finished Trans Siberian Railway. After this unsuccessful war Russia began to strengthen her railways in the east, in the expectation of another conflict with Japan. And when the next war came, it was against Austria and Germany.

When mobilization was declared, the railways of Germany, France, Russia and Austria cancelled most civilian trains in order to free resources for military movements. All countries deployed their troops according to plan and usually a day or two ahead of schedule (probably because railway officials, being railway officials, had left themselves hidden reserves, 'recovery margins', when they informed pre-war military planners of their lines' capacities). In Russia, where despite double-tracking of strategic lines there was still a lack of line capacity in certain frontier areas, military trains moved so smoothly that civilian freight, hastily dumped at the line-side when the crisis began, was picked up and dispatched even before the fifteen days of initial mobilization were completed.

In France mobilization also went well but the early retreat to the Marne put a strain on transport from which the French railways never really recovered. Much rolling stock was lost (British railway companies made good part of this loss by sending spare locomotives to the Western Front), and plans were disrupted by the unexpected change of traffic flows caused by the redeployment of masses of troops to positions in what was once regarded as the rear. One handicap borne by the French railways was a lack of standardization, making it difficult to shift equipment from one railway to another that was more hard pressed. Prussia and Russia had long ago solved that problem by standardizing locomotives and equipment. Thus in Russia there was a standard 'government' 0-8-0 locomotive numbering more than 8,000 units and used by most of the different companies. It was this engine that was most frequently transferred from one railway to another (even the initial two weeks of the Russian mobilization plan had envisaged the transfer of 1,360 locomotives from the rear railways to those closest to the frontiers).

As the war developed, the demands on rail transport grew. In 1914, on average, the Anglo-French Western Front required 80 military trains each day but in the final hectic months, from March to November 1918, there was an average daily requirement of 74 trains for shifting reserves and 217 for moving supplies. At the peak of operations 198 trains in one day were run to move troops and 424 to transport supplies.

Most of the belligerents divided their railways into war and civilian zones, with military control dominant in the war areas and often in the rear areas too. Co-ordination of military demands and railway operating requirements was difficult and was never achieved perfectly. Possibly the Germans did best in this; there was strict military control over all railways but the civilian railwaymen were quite happy to work under military dictation. The Russians were the least successful in solving this problem. Indeed they got themselves into the same kind of situation that Abraham Lincoln had encountered in the Ameri-

William Hedley's Puffing Billy *of 1813. Used for half a century at a Northumberland colliery, this locomotive is now at the Science Museum in London.*

Left: *Britain's railways were solidly built from the start. This painting shows a bridge of the Stockton & Darlington Railway, with the inaugural train of September 1825.*

Below: *An early Stephenson locomotive, the* Invicta. *Rather similar to the* Rocket, *this machine was supplied to the Canterbury & Whitstable Railway and is now preserved at Canterbury.*

Coaches &c. employed on the Railway.

T.T.Bury, del.   H.Pyall sculp.

Nº 1. The Northumbrian, Steam-Engine, &c.   2.3.5. Carriages for Passengers.   4. Private Carriage.   6.7. Carriages for Cattle.

London, Published Feby 1831 by Ackermann & Cº. 96 Strand.

Above, far left: *An early scene on the Liverpool & Manchester Railway, showing the station and offices at Crown Street, Liverpool.*
Far left, below: *Passenger cars and cattle trucks of the Liverpool & Manchester Railway.*
Above left: Hardwicke, *a 2-4-0 passenger locomotive of the London & North Western Railway.*
Centre left: *No. 1000, a Midland Railway compound 4-4-0 of the early 20th century.*
Below: *Brunel's broad-gauge Great Western Railway passed along the coast in south Devon, and from time to time trains were brought to a halt by breaches in the sea wall.*

For much of the 19th century the
4-4-0 'American' type locomotive
was dominant in the USA. Used
for both passenger and freight
work, it was characterized by
outside cylinders, bar frames and
ornate finish.

WM. R. LENDRUM
BUILDER
SCRANTON, PA. U.S.A.

can Civil War: a peremptory and uncomprehending attitude towards railway-operating men on the part of army officers entrusted with transport arrangements. The Russian railways were divided into those serving the frontiers ('the railways of the military zone') and those which were far in the rear. Co-operation was lacking and this showed itself most damagingly when the military authorities began to hoard rolling stock 'in case of need'. The civilian railway authorities were unable to get these valuable freight cars released, with the result that vital materials (as well as bread for angry citizens) became unavailable where they were needed. One crisis led to another; coal mines closed, crowds rioted, and 1917 arrived. At one stage a desperate government halted passenger trains on the key St Petersburg to Moscow route for a week so that grain could be taken to the capital.

Railway-operating battalions, which had existed in most of the big armies since the nineteenth century, had to be rapidly expanded during the war. This expansion was largely achieved by allocating former railwaymen to them, but in all armies there were examples of skilled railwaymen being drafted as cooks, officers' orderlies or infantrymen. Some belligerents, notably Britain and Russia, had to recall railwaymen back to civilian life when labour shortages developed on the home railways. One important task was the operation of narrow-gauge trench railways, which plied between the main-line railheads and the front line. Here again Germany was perhaps the best equipped, but it was France that had done most to develop this technique; Paul Décauville in 1876 had introduced his 'portable railway' mainly for agricultural use, but then found that among his best customers were the war departments of several military powers. The British government, presumably anticipating yet another war on India's North-West Frontier, had even ordered a Décauville kit with a locomotive divisible into two sections for transport by elephant.

Another task of the railway battalions was the restoration of lines damaged by a retreating enemy. When the Germans advanced into Russia they had the additional task of converting the Russian 1,524 mm (5 ft) gauge to the European standard. Up to the middle of 1916 they had so treated over 7,500 km (4,700 miles), mainly in Russian Poland. The method was to shift one rail by 80 mm ($3\frac{1}{2}$ inches), which was not difficult with wooden cross-ties. In favourable conditions a railway troop detachment (two NCOs and about 34 men) could convert 1,200 metres (1,300 yards) in one day's work, but this fell drastically when there was snow on the line. The Russians also damaged the track by, typically, blowing up every second rail joint. Later they developed the technique (imitated by the Germans in World War II) of dragging a heavy hook behind a locomotive to break the cross-ties and distort the rails.

Physical damage to the railways was much less than in World War II. The worst war damage was caused by scorched-earth tactics; hence the areas most affected were north-eastern France, Poland and Belgium. In the last-named it was only in 1930 that the last of the temporary bridges erected by the British army's Railway Operating Division was replaced by a permanent structure. Damage by shellfire was noticeable in certain hard-fought areas, Verdun being an obvious example and northern Italy another. Damage from bombs was slight; bombing did sometimes disturb supply depots and transhipment points close to the front, but material damage was slight. However, London's Waterloo Station was one victim, receiving a bomb on an empty passenger car. Venice Mestre station was also badly damaged by bombing. German railways and stations, however, escaped fairly lightly, since little actual fighting took place inside the country's frontiers.

Above left: The world's most numerous passenger locomotive type was the Prussian State Railways P8 4-6-0, of which about 3,500 units were built. This example was photographed in West Germany, near Stuttgart, in 1970. The type no longer works in Germany but some survivors of the class linger on in Romania and Poland.
Left: The type 141R 2-8-2 was built in America to French design, and became the basic SNCF locomotive in the difficult postwar years. Well over a thousand units were supplied, and they lasted until the end of steam traction. Most were used for freight, but some fast and secondary passenger trains were also regularly entrusted to them. The picture shows one of the class at Le Mans with a Paris to Quimper train.

In Britain and America the war situation was different as there were no frontiers to be fought over. At the outbreak of war the British railway companies were taken over by the government's Railway Executive, composed of leading railway managers. These handled the task of carrying changed traffic flows so well that their work did much to prepare public opinion for the elimination of the old railway companies, which when contrasted with the work of the Railway Executive seemed hopelessly uncoordinated and wasteful. In fact, the Railway Executive had an easy job, but this was not realized at the time; it could enforce much-needed inter-company co-ordination, and the government ensured that it was not troubled by profit-and-loss considerations.

When the USA entered the war in 1917 there was an immediate build-up of traffic, which the railways soon seemed incapable of handling. Much of the trouble was in the dock areas, where loaded freight cars were held for weeks awaiting a suitable berth. But part of the problem was caused by the persistence of old habits. Notable among these was the practice of sending freight by roundabout routes so that it would register the biggest possible mileage (and revenue) on the originating railway. At the end of 1917 President Wilson took control of the railways under his emergency powers, paying each company a rent for its services. This control, exercised through the United States Railroad Administration, succeeded in transferring much traffic to shorter routes, avoided routing traffic through congested terminals, cut out other wasteful manifestations of competition, and reduced passenger-train mileage by about one-sixth. It also introduced standard 'USRA' designs for locomotives and rolling stock, and many of these items were produced for various railroads. Apart from the changes brought by the USRA, the war did not affect American railroading to the same extent as in continental Europe. Exports of US-built locomotives did take a different pattern, however. To France, America sent narrow-gauge trench-railway locomotives and also, later, some main-line freight engines to meet urgent French requirements. To help beleaguered Russia obtain supplies from the west via Siberia, many hundred units of a 2-10-0 locomotive, jointly designed by a Russian railway mission and US locomotive builders, were exported. Because of the Russian Revolution some of these locomotives remained in America, and most of those that reached Russia arrived too late to help the Allied cause in World War I, even though they lasted long enough to serve the same purpose in World War II.

Many of the world's railways not directly involved in the war nevertheless suffered from the unavailability of new equipment traditionally bought from one or other of the belligerents. Most of the railways of the British Empire additionally endured deferred maintenance, and some of them had sent some of their railway equipment overseas: Indian railways sent metre-gauge locomotives and track to supply British troops fighting the Turks in Iraq, and some double-track lines in western Canada were singled in order to obtain rails for France.

Postwar reorganization

Thus for one reason or another, the immediate postwar years were difficult for most of the world's railways. But these were temporary difficulties; only the far-sighted visualized the more permanent problem which would arise during the 1920s and 1930s, namely the competition of the internal-combustion engine. In the meantime many countries were reviewing the way in which their railways were organized, and in particular they were asking themselves if privately-owned railways were really necessary.

Europe

In 1918 the railways of different countries could be divided into those that were wholly state-owned, those that were privately owned, and those in which some were private and some state-owned. The last category was the largest. It included most countries of western Europe, in which the state at an early stage, in order to speed up construction of railways, had taken a share in building and running them. Sweden is a good example, for her first private railway and her first state railway were opened in the same year of 1856. The western European countries already envisaged the eventual takeover by the state of all lines, and this was often written in the charters of the private companies. Thus in 1938 the French state took over the French private main-line companies and joined them to the state-owned lines to form the French National Railways (SNCF). In Belgium and Italy a similar process had been virtually complete before 1914. In some countries, including Sweden and Switzerland, the process of nationalization has not yet been completed, although the state railways of both these countries have a greater share of the mileage. A feature of Swedish policy has been the steady nationalization of the narrow-gauge lines, followed by their conversion to standard gauge. In Holland the coexistence of a large private system with an equally large national system ended only in 1938 when the Holland Railway Company and the State Railway Company were amalgamated to form the Netherlands Railway Company (NS), in which all shares were held by the state. But before that, in 1919, the two companies had at last come together to make a working agreement to standardize their practices. One big difference had been that the State Railway had located its signals on the left side of the track, even though it had right-hand running; this was because it had bought its locomotives from England, where a left-hand driving position was normal.

In three west European countries, Britain, Spain and Germany, the situation was exceptional. In Spain, the private railways continued, but in 1924 the Spanish government introduced a statute by which it shared in the financing, management and profits of the railways. However, this arrangement was overtaken by the Spanish Civil War and in 1941 the war-ravaged railways were nationalized to form the Spanish National Railways (RENFE). In Britain, government control ended only in 1921. In the meantime there had been a big railway strike in 1919, even though a few months previously the government had conceded an eight-hour day for railwaymen. There had also been much discussion of how the railways should be organized, as there was a general reluctance to return to what was regarded as the wasteful and over-competitive multiplicity of private companies. Many expressed a preference for nationalization, on the familiar grounds that railways were too important a national service to be left in the control of dividend-seeking companies. The government, however, rejected nationalization. In 1920 it published very advanced proposals which suggested the amalgamation of the old undertakings into six new big companies, each with a territorial monopoly and including separate companies for Scotland and for London. It also proposed that manual workers should have a place on the boards of the new companies. However, combined opposition from those who wanted outright nationalization, with scant regard for the shareholders, and those who rejected any form of government intervention at all, encouraged the government to abandon these proposals. Instead, the Railways Act of 1921 compelled the 123 companies to form four new large enterprises, each with a territorial monopoly. Of the old companies only the Great Western survived, absorbing sundry Welsh companies to cover the western part of England, with Wales. The three new companies were the Southern, the London Midland & Scottish (covering the Midlands, the north-west and part of Scotland) and the London & North Eastern (covering eastern England and part of Scotland). There was no worker participation in this new organization but the railways were compelled to negotiate with the unions on wages and conditions—a radical imposition.

In Germany, the break-up of the old Empire necessitated a reorganization of the railways; with the end of Bismarck's imperial dream came, paradoxically, the realization of his unfulfilled hope for a completely unified railway system. The Deutsche Reichsbahn (DR) was set up as a national railway company, incorporating all the main-line systems of the individual states. It naturally had its headquarters in Berlin and was really the old Prussian State Railway writ large. As would happen when British railways were finally nationalized in 1948, the biggest of the former companies became dominant and imposed itself, with results good and bad, on the new enlarged organization. One of the bad results was that many good administrators outside the Prussian system lost the chance to employ their talents for the general good. The first years of the Reichsbahn were exceptionally difficult; although war damage was small, the reparations demanded by the victorious western powers had included the handing over of 5,000 locomotives and 150,000 freight and passenger vehicles. Moreover, when in 1923 it became obvious that Germany could not pay the crushing reparations indemnity, the 'Dawes Plan' included a provision that the railways were to be independent of the German government and for five years the Reichsbahn had to include foreign specialists in its management.

North America

The US railroads were released from wartime government control in 1920, after several years of debate as to their future. However, the feeling against the company structure was not as strong as in Britain, and the companies resisted government intervention more actively than did the British companies. In the end President Wilson's Transportation Act of 1920, which returned the railways to company control, merely strengthened the power of the Interstate Commerce Commission; in particular, the Commission could henceforth set minimum as well as maximum rates in order to prevent the kind of ruinous rate-cutting wars that had so damaged the railroads and their clients before the war. The ICC did try to persuade the railroads to merge into large units but without success.

In Canada, however, the railways were in a state that made any return to the old ways highly unwelcome, if not impossible. When the very successful Canadian Pacific transcontinental line was finished in 1885, Canada possessed, apart from this private company, the Intercolonial Railway and the private Grand Trunk Railway. The former had been built largely to persuade the Maritime Provinces to join the Canadian Federation. With a main line from Rivière du Loup to Halifax, this well-built line was finished in 1876, two years after it had been decided to entrust it to the Department of Public Works of the Canadian government. The Grand Trunk included the earliest public Canadian railway, which connected Montreal with Portland in the USA; the lines of the former Great Western Railway, which connected Toronto with the US railways via Windsor and Sarnia; and the Grand Trunk proper, whose main line from Montreal to Toronto was built by British capital to British constructional standards. The Grand Trunk also ran eastwards as far as Rivière du Loup to connect with the Intercolonial.

Canadian Pacific's first crest, used from July to December 1886.

Government influence on Canadian railway-building in Canada has usually been more enthusiastic than rational, with the result that at almost any given time every railway management has been either anticipating, or participating in, or recovering from a Royal Commission of enquiry into the railways. It was a Royal Commission that in 1851 recommended that all new lines receiving financial assistance should be of 1,676 mm (5 ft 6 in) gauge, and this provision for three decades did much to hinder the interchange of traffic with the US lines. In the years before World War I, for reasons that are even harder to justify, or even discern, the government approved the building, simultaneously, of not one, but two, new transcontinentals. One was the private Canadian Northern Railway, which from small beginnings in Manitoba expanded by 1918 to a coast-to-coast route, constructed very cheaply and with one exception to low engineering standards, but adequate for the underdeveloped territory through which it mainly passed. The exception was a substantial tunnel under Mount Royal at Montreal, which did much for the development of the northern suburbs. The third transcontinental was a combination of the private Grand Trunk Pacific and a government-built line from Moncton in New Brunswick, through Quebec City and on through the wilds to Winnipeg. The latter was the National Transcontinental Railway, built to exceptionally high engineering standards with moderate gradients and curves; British-style in engineering, it was also mainly British-financed. At Winnipeg it joined the new Grand Trunk Pacific. This company, sponsored by the Grand Trunk, was also to be responsible for the operation of the National Transcontinental Railway. That is, it was to operate the whole route which, measuring 5,700 km (3,543 miles) from Moncton to its terminus at Prince Rupert on the Pacific, was finished in 1914. The Canadian Northern's line to the Pacific at Vancouver was finished the following year. Both these new and hostile lines used the Yellowstone Pass through the Rockies, where their single-track lines were so close that most casual observers thought that this was one double-track railway.

Such blatant duplication of lines was evident elsewhere in Canada. The Canadian Pacific had also been expanding. It provided a second route from Montreal to the Atlantic, and also duplicated the Grand Trunk's line from Montreal to Toronto with its own single track, which for miles ran side by side with the Grand Trunk's double track. These obvious deficiencies of the existing company structure were made intolerable by the financial difficulties in which the railways found themselves. The Canadian Pacific was generally profitable, but the rest were not, and were heavily over-capitalized. The Grand Trunk, managed in London, was not administered well, partly because its board was more interested in dividends than in maintaining its property.

By 1919 the Grand Trunk directors warned the Canadian government that they would have to default on bond interest payments, but the government refused to help. The directors then refused to continue to operate the Grand Trunk Pacific, whereupon the government put the company into receivership and then bought it up. One of the final acts of the British board was to vote itself five years' salary, and a year's salary to its top officials, the funds coming from the company's fire-insurance fund. Eventually in 1923 a new government-owned company came into being, Canadian National Railways.

Canadian National Railways, the biggest and uniquely state-owned North American railroad, included not only the Grand Trunk, but also the Canadian Northern, Intercolonial, and other lines in financial trouble; it was virtually all the main Canadian companies except the Canadian Pacific. Thus Canada found itself with two railway companies of approximately equal size, one profitable and self-confident, and the other an amalgamation of 149 demoralized and mainly unprofitable enterprises. But so intelligent and energetic was the CNR's first president, Henry Thornton, that by the end of the 1920s the CNR had become a coherent enterprise, capable of making an operating profit, and already outpacing the Canadian Pacific in quality of service. This spectacle of a state company threatening to excel over a private company was not pleasing to many, and after Thornton retired in 1932, no man of similar calibre was ever appointed as president. Quite the contrary, in fact.

Australia and New Zealand

In another British dominion, Australia, the question of railway nationalization was still premature, as the different state governments would refuse on principle to transfer to the Federal capital their authority over the state railways. It would not be until the 1970s that some Australian states, unwilling to bear any longer the financial burden of their ill-managed railways, would forget earlier principles and hand over their railway systems to Canberra. In the meantime, however, the nucleus of a state railway organization already existed in the Commonwealth Railways, organized to run the new Transcontinental line, the line from Port Augusta to Alice Springs, and also the hopelessly unprofitable and isolated line to Darwin. The Transcontinental could also be regarded as the first step in Australian gauge standardization, for it was a 1,435 mm (4 ft 8½ in) gauge line, implying that if there were to be any conversion, it would be to, and not from, the standard gauge of New South Wales. The next gauge move, though not really a conversion, came when the New South Wales Railway was connected by a new line to South Brisbane in Queensland, bringing standard gauge into that state. In 1962 a similar standard-gauge extension in Victoria would at last make it possible to travel from Sydney to Melbourne without the need to change trains at Albury, where the NSWGR and the Victorian Railways joined.

In New Zealand, where the 1870s had been the great railway-building years, the 1,600 mm (5 ft 3 in) gauge had not long survived the government's decision to standardize 1,067 mm (3 ft 6 in). The choice of this narrower gauge was in keeping with the 'American' style of New Zealand railway construction: the building of the greatest mileage for the least capital, upgrading the lines only when increasing traffic should justify the expense. As for nationalization, most of the railways were government-built, and the few large private lines had been absorbed into the New Zealand Railways before World War I.

The growth of motor transport

A feature of World War I had been the great use which the belligerents made of motor transport and of the aeroplane. The development of these two technologies was thereby accelerated, bringing closer the day when their civilian application would present a damaging, perhaps mortal, threat to railway transport. To a certain extent the railways had already suffered from one kind of competition before the war, that of the electric streetcar. But except in America, where the streetcar's enlargement into the interurban electric car had robbed the main-line railways of some useful traffic, the electric vehicle had only taken away traffic that because of cheap fares and short distances had never been really profitable.

When the war ended, many soldiers had been taught to drive motor trucks, and many motor trucks were sold by the various armies to the public at giveaway prices. The subsequent transformation of demobilized soldiers into one-man motor-haulage businesses was hardly surprising, and some of these enterprises survived to grow into serious transport undertakings. In few countries was motor transport regulated by the government, and road hauliers were free to set their own prices for each operation (unlike the railways in most countries) and to take or reject traffic offered to them according to its likely profitability (again unlike the railways, which were common carriers, bound to take all traffic that was offered and, in many countries, to charge each client the same price). Moreover, road transport used 'permanent way' that was paid for, maintained, and policed by public authorities, whereas the rates charged by the railways had to cover the cost of their tracks and installations. These 'unfair' advantages of the motor truck were backed by some real technical benefits. A shipper might find that he could get faster service from a motor truck; whereas a freight car would wait around until enough cars had been assembled to form a train, the truck could leave as soon as it was loaded. Also, for all except large enterprises, which might have their own private railway siding, the motor truck eliminated transhipment; goods did not need to be taken down to the railway freight station and transhipped into a railway car, with a reverse process, time-consuming and costly, at the other end. Thus many shippers, who could enjoy the 'unfair' advantages of the cheap rates that could be offered by the motor transport firm, and faster door-to-door transit too, were inclined to abandon the railways in favour of the roads. In addition, there was another and rarely mentioned reason why shippers might prefer the road haulier; from a small and insecure haulage company they received personal and helpful attention, whereas from a big and long-established railway they all too often did not.

In most of Europe and America, the share of the railways in total freight traffic began to decline after about 1920, due partly to highway competition (which took away mainly those items of freight for which the railways charged high rates), and to industrial depression (which reduced those low-value, low-rated, bulk traffics for which railways were more suited than road vehicles). Added to these problems were higher wage and fuel costs. In the USA and Britain the wartime government controllers had granted wage increases which, left to themselves, the companies would have been very unwilling to accept. Parallel processes took place in other countries and were especially marked in Germany, where the railwaymen were actually willing to consider strike action after 1918.

In the 1930s, with the Great Depression, the railways' situation worsened. In most countries the railways' reaction was policies designed on the one hand to restrain highway competition, and on the other to make the railways' own services more attractive. Action on the political and publicity level did help to persuade governments to introduce regulations which it was hoped would enforce 'fair' competition on the road operators. These regulations varied from country to country. In the USA the railways received little help in this respect, but in western Europe various licensing restrictions were imposed on road-transport firms. Such regulations were strong in France and Germany, where it was realized that if motor trucks 'skimmed the cream', that is, took the most profitable traffic from the railways, then the railways would no longer be able to perform the vital public service of carrying the less profitable traffic. But the road operators were never required to pay their fair share of highway costs, and because they were such small and numerous businesses, it was impossible to supervise them in the same way that railways were supervised.

Measures to make railway service more attractive included acceleration of freight trains, and especially the introduction of fast freight trains running on regular timetables at passenger train speeds, guaranteeing a next-morning delivery between cities up to 500 miles apart. In the USA, the first of these services was the Cotton Belt's *Blue Streak*, introduced in 1931. New types of freight cars were designed to suit special traffic which it was considered worthwhile to retain or win back. In order to provide the same door-to-door service offered by motor trucks, the demountable container was used by some European railways. This was virtually a freight car body which could be easily transferred from a railway flat car, used over the long haul, to a flat motor truck for the pick-up and delivery sectors of the trip.

The crest of the St Louis Southwestern Railroad, operator of the Blue Streak.

Passenger traffic declined slower than freight in most countries, though there was a deep trough during the Depression. In most countries the railways themselves attempted to exploit the motor bus by acquiring vehicles which they used to operate feeder services to their stations. This was a sensible method of co-ordinating the 'retail' advantages of the motor vehicle with the long-haul 'wholesale' advantages of the train, but in some countries it was stopped on grounds of so-called monopoly. In Britain the railways, apart from operating motor buses, also organized successful internal air services. In the meantime railway passenger services were greatly improved. The highly-publicized streamline train aroused public enthusiasm, and the passenger train was still considered to be a natural form of long-distance transport, even though motor-car ownership, despite the Depression, was increasing rapidly.

In some countries, especially those that had undergone revolution, different processes took place. In Russia, where war, civil war and revolution had left railway transport in a sad state, the industrialization plans led to great increases of traffic, which the government at first attempted to carry without a corresponding capital investment in railways (even though, mistakenly, a disproportionate amount of capital and labour were expended to improve canal and river transport). In the early 1930s it was obvious that the Russian railways could not cope, and recourse to executing railwaymen on charges of 'sabotage' and 'wrecking' did not help. Eventually, realistic resources were allocated to help the railways and there was much construction of new lines, double-tracking, and modest starts in electrification and dieselization. In Turkey and Iran, where new leaders had taken over after revolutions, railway-building was initiated as a kind of nation-building exercise. The Trans-Iranian Railway, from Bandar Shahpur on the Persian Gulf to Teheran and Bandar Shah on the Caspian, was finished in 1938, being the first major railway in Iran.

On the whole, railway managements in the twentieth century were conservatives, not innovators. But when railway companies tended to be small and numerous there were usually, apart from the mass of unenterprising railways, one or two that would take the risk of putting new ideas into practice. When railways became larger, often becoming the sole railway in a given country or territory, it was natural that they should settle complacently into old and well-tried routines; indeed, it seems fairly clear that it was only the new difficult conditions that made technical, commercial, and operating changes seem acceptable. In America and western Europe, at least, railway improvements over the past half century have been due not to the inventiveness and energy of service-conscious railway administrators, but rather to the pressures put upon them by competing forms of transport, and by the rising costs of their traditional inputs, coal and labour.

Railways since 1945

Postwar gloom

In World War II most of the belligerents had repeated the railway organizational measures of World War I. An exception was the USA, where the railways were not taken under government control but merely co-ordinated in a semi-voluntary way. Physical destruction was much greater than in World War I, thanks to the development of the bomber. The main effect of bombing was in the disruption of railway work rather than in the damage caused. In Britain, less than 1,000 railwaymen and passengers were killed by bomb attack. The most war-damaged railways were those of France, Holland, Russia and perhaps Italy. In the two first-named, the railways were bombed by both sides and sabotaged by their own resistance movements. In Russia the ebb and flow of the struggling armies was accompanied by the thorough destruction of railway facilities by each side in turn as it retreated. Traffic increased greatly everywhere partly because of the demands of war and partly because the railways' competitors, motor transport and coastal shipping, were seriously restricted by fuel shortages and enemy attacks. Traffic reached a peak in 1944 in North America which in the case of passenger traffic would never be surpassed. In the USA, 1944 freight traffic was 82 per cent greater than in 1918 and passenger more than double. As elsewhere during the war, the fastest trains were withdrawn from American railroads, and passenger services were not expanded to handle the increased traffic. The result was overcrowding and slow transits which had a bad and long-lasting effect on the public's opinion of railway travel.

In North America, congestion was less severe than in World War I, partly because lessons had been learned and partly because the inter-war technique of Centralized Traffic Control (CTC) was applied to lines facing wartime pressure. CTC is the control of train movements over perhaps hundreds of kilometres of track from one central office, whose personnel operate all signals and switches by remote control and can see train movements presented as lights on a panel. This technique makes it easy to arrange train meets on single-track line; in fact these meets are timed so accurately that sometimes both trains can reach the double-track crossing station simultaneously, and pass without either stopping. One key line on which CTC was installed early in the war was the Canadian National's single-track line from Moncton to the main wartime port of Halifax. This line was Halifax's only rail connection with the rest of Canada and the USA, and after the installation it could handle 50 trains each day. Such a capacity was certainly needed, for one sailing of the troopship *Queen Elizabeth* would require 28 special trains.

In Europe there were wholesale transfers of rolling stock. The Hungarian State Railways, for example, became a key link between the Axis powers and the Russian Front, and to help it handle the extra traffic the Italian Railways handed back locomotives of Austrian, and therefore familiar, construction which had been transferred as reparations after World War I. Special wartime locomotives were also designed and built in large numbers. Most numerous of these was the German *Kriegslok* 2-10-0, built in thousands in Europe and left behind on the railways of countries which had been occupied by the Germans. After the invasion of Normandy, the US standard wartime 2-8-0 and the British 'Austerity' 2-8-0 were used in large numbers by continental railways, and some, especially the *Kriegslok*, are still in service.

Of the German-occupied territories, eastern France and the Netherlands were possibly the worst damaged; so damaged in fact that the Dutch and French railways often found it possible after the war to make a clean start and, rather than spend resources on the restoration of old facilities, build completely new installations. When Holland was liberated the railways were left with 334 locomotives, 80 electric multiple-unit trains, 36 diesel electric trains, 233 passenger cars, and 1,073 freight cars, compared to the 1939 stock of 865 locomotives, 430 electric trains, 82 diesel trains, 1,908 passenger cars, and 30,453 freight cars. Much of the missing equipment was eventually returned from Germany but by no means all and by no means promptly. Destruction of facilities, especially workshops, was on the same scale, and much catenary and substation equipment had also been taken by the Germans. Maintenance of Dutch railways had virtually ceased in 1944 when, after a message from London, Dutch railwaymen ceased work, leaving the German army to operate the railways. In the first postwar months a few new steam engines of pre-war design were acquired, and great use was made of British 2-8-0 'Austerity' locomotives, but in the long run advantage was taken of the destruction to electrify far faster than would have been the case otherwise. In some fields, like car building, modernization began simultaneously with restoration, with all-steel vehicles becoming standard.

Elsewhere in formerly occupied Europe, restoration had top priority; highway vehicles had almost disappeared in many countries so the railways had an even greater burden of responsibility. Trains were infrequent and confined to really essential traffic required to avert famine and to restart basic industries. Improvization was essential; so, for example, Chapelon's celebrated 4-8-0 passenger locomotives could be seen hauling heavy coal trains in northern France. In Central and Eastern Europe the Germans left behind large numbers of their *Kriegslok* 2-10-0 and these formed the basis of railway operation in some areas, notably Austria. However, those *Kriegslok* units left in Eastern Europe were largely appropriated by the Russians. The Russians also removed much of the railway equipment they found in their zone of Germany (subsequently known as the German Democratic Republic). A complete electrified system was taken, on double-track lines one track was removed so that the rails could be sent to rehabilitate Soviet railways, and some single-track lines were lifted entirely for the same purpose. Workshop equipment was also taken. Single-track main lines can still be seen in the GDR, the missing track never having been restored; however, with CTC some of these singled sections have been found adequate.

In western Germany the advancing Allies were able to make almost immediate use of the railways, for the Germans left their locomotives behind them when they retreated. Locomotive power had not been scarce in Germany during the war and many new locomotives had been put into store for future use. The cab-sides of most engines were plated with 15mm ($\frac{5}{8}$in) steel as a protection against low-flying aircraft attacks. Apart from clearing up rubble and restoring damaged installations, the Allied railway battalions were not worked hard, for it was found that German railwaymen carried on their duties quite contentedly under military supervision. However, various shortages meant that only really essential trains could be operated. In the following years, when the Germans recovered direction of their railroads, they too began steadily to increase the mileage worked by diesel and electric traction, although there was not, nor could there be, a premature scrapping of steam locomotives. The division of Germany into two republics meant great changes in the direction of traffic flows, the east–west lines naturally losing much of their importance. However, German railways, partly for strategic reasons and partly because of the pre-1918 independence of the various states, had never been based on the capital in the same way that French main lines radiated from Paris, so it was not hard to adapt to the new traffic flows. West Germany's main lines became the Hamburg–Bremen–Rhineland–Munich and the Hamburg–Hanover–Munich routes.

Railways all over the world faced difficult times in the postwar years. In the more developed countries it was the re-emergence of a strengthened competition which was the main threat to the railways' future. The motor truck, which now tended to be less a one-man enterprise than a part of a big trucking company, took from the railways much of their most profitable traffic: high-value manufactured articles for which railway freight rates were high. However, it is true that the trucks also took traffic which was unprofitable for the railways: short-distance and small-size consignments. A rational division of traffic would have been achieved if the trucks had been confined to the latter kind of business, allowing the railways to concentrate on the business for which they were most fitted—the carriage of large shipments over long distances. To some extent this did happen, but to very different degrees in different countries. Some European countries legislated to prevent trucks from taking an excessive bite from the railways' traffic, but found it technically or politically impossible to do what was economically rational, that is, to levy on trucking companies a fair charge for highway and policing services. Truckers received these free while the railways paid about a fifth of their income on track and signalling. In America any legislation tended to favour the trucking industry rather than the railroads; the latter were not even free to regain business by lowering their charges.

In many countries, especially the USA, the Netherlands, Germany and Japan, the long-haul and bulk traffic, for which the railways were very suited, was attacked from a different direction, by coastal and inland shipping. Here geography was the deciding factor and there was little competition which the railways could describe as 'unfair'; at least not until they made efforts to recapture that traffic, when shipping interests sometimes succeeded in preventing them from reducing their rates. In the passenger field there was a divergence between what happened in the countries of great distances, like North America and Australia, and what happened in Europe. In the big countries the aeroplane had begun to erode the railways' passenger traffic well before the war, ever since Douglas had introduced the DC-3 aircraft in the mid 1930s. However, it was precisely in these long-distance countries that passenger services were least profitable for the railways, partly because the traffic flows were not dense and partly because long-distance trains with their sleeping, lounging and dining accommodation carried fewer passengers than shorter-distance trains. So it was not long after the wartime peak of passenger traffic that the railways began to lose passengers and to withdraw passenger services. Attempts, sometimes successful but more often not, were made to retain certain services with new rolling stock, and the long-distance passenger train still exists in America and Australia, but most travellers move by automobile or aircraft. In the European countries, however, the picture was different. Faster and more comfortable trains, and skilful public relations, enabled most systems to hold their passengers; some railways even achieved an increase, and Europeans in general never came to regard train travel as something old-fashioned or eccentric, as happened in America.

What was particularly worrying for railways was the declining share of freight traffic which they carried. In the postwar decades there were some railways, the British, for example, whose freight traffic declined absolutely (British railways carried 303 million tonnes in their peak year of 1923, 268 million in 1948, but 202 million in 1969). There were other railways, like those of North America, in which freight traffic increased but at a much smaller rate of increase than the total freight traffic carried by all forms of transport (in Canada, for example, railway freight tonne/miles doubled between 1913 and 1970, but the Canadian economy developed much faster than that). Moreover, the traffic left to the railways was usually the low-valued (and therefore low-charged) traffic; freight revenues therefore suffered more than freight traffic. However, this gloomy picture was not universal. There were still countries like Russia, China and India where economic development was still at a state when ever-increasing amounts of bulk traffic were requiring carriage and when road transport was still insignificant. The railways of these countries faced a more palatable kind of difficulty, that of handling fast-increasing traffic with a minimum of resources.

In the western world the railways could be further divided into those which in the three postwar decades seemed to cope with their problems and create modern systems organized and operated on rational principles, and the railways of Britain and America which, for a time and each in their own characteristic way, became travesties of competent railway management. In Britain the railways and road-haulage firms in 1948 joined the airways as nationalized corporations. There were many good arguments for railway nationalization: Britain's railways were run-down and needed massive capital investment which could only be supplied by the state; competition between rail and road needed to be supervised so that each form of transport would be used for those tasks for which it was most fitted; railway transport was perhaps too important a social service to be in private hands, and bringing the railways into one organization promised further economies of scale, as, for example, through standardization of equipment. In general, most of the hopes placed in nationalization were disappointed. The new undertaking was only ostensibly subject to the much-vaunted 'public accountability' while at the same time it was vulnerable to government intervention, which became progressively more frequent. The government appointed a top management which was undistinguished, and then discouraged the rare initiatives of this management by a series of controls and imperatives which, taken together, were unworkable. It was two decades before clear minds were applied to railway problems. In those 20 years British Railways was organized and reorganized, centralized and decentralized, as successive governments came to power with new policies. Trains were painted in a variety of exciting new colours. Capital was wasted on a new and unnecessary range of standard steam locomotives. Co-ordination of rail and road not only did not take place, but was avoided; in Britain the first major railway electrification and the first motorway were undertaken simultaneously and ran parallel, and sometimes in sight of each other. While large sums of public money were invested unwisely, good capital investment projects were started, halted, and restarted because the government would sanction capital expenditure only on a one-year basis. Finally, as on many US railroads, management decided on dieselization, undoubtedly advantageous, as a cure-for-all-ills, which it could never be.

In the USA government intervention was never quite the problem which it became for British Railways, but it was nevertheless damaging. Enterprising

The British Transport Commission crest, first appearing in 1956, for motor and main-line coaches.

railway management was rare in the USA, and it was all too often discouraged by bureaucratic intervention. For example, the control over railway rates exercised by the Interstate Commerce Commission meant that a railroad which introduced more efficient equipment might be prevented from reducing its freight rates accordingly, on grounds of 'unfair' competition. Railways which wished to withdraw unprofitable passenger services were prevented from doing so; where high taxation levied by a state made passenger services impossibly costly, the same state could refuse to permit the railroad to withdraw them. In the meantime the Federal government built a network of superhighways that enabled truck operators to offer faster services at lower cost, US Army engineers installed lock systems, dredged and otherwise improved inland and coastal waterways, and both Federal and state governments financed the building of city airports. These handouts of the taxpayers' money to the railways' competitors were accompanied by high taxation of railway property. It could happen that a city or state would agitate about the need for a smart new railroad station which, when it was built by the railroad, would be taxed at a higher valuation by the same local authorities. However, the greatest harm caused by outside intervention was to labour relations.

Reductions in the labour force
Developing railway technology in the first half of the twentieth century had made it feasible to reduce the labour force. This did occur; indeed, from 1940 to 1975 the US railroads cut their labour force from one million to half a million, even though freight traffic increased during that period. However, there was scope for much greater reduction than this. But the railway trade unions, able to influence the votes of hundreds of thousands of workers in elections, particularly local and state elections, had much greater political power than railway managements. Many states were induced to pass 'full-crew' laws, which in effect meant that railroads in those states were required to employ far more men than were really necessary. In general, railroad managements were reluctant to face the strike action entailed by a confrontation with the railway unions. The latter, apart from successfully insisting on high levels of manpower, also were able to impose high wage rates. When strikes did occur, or were threatened, the Federal government intervened to impose settlements which would only damage the railroads' commercial prospects; in the 1946–1952 period, because of labour troubles, the US government three times took over the railroads under its emergency powers, the duration of one such takeover being almost two years. The big test came with dieselization and the railroads' wish to dispense with locomotive firemen as steam engines were phased out. From 1959 to 1963 there was argument, threatened strike action, congressional and court intervention until in 1964 an arbitration award permitted the elimination of firemen on most non-passenger trains. However, it was not long before the dispute was rekindled and many railroads were forced to reinstate their firemen.

The firemen issue did arouse public interest, and the accusations of 'featherbedding' levelled at railroaders did intensify public antipathy towards the railroads. Featherbedding indeed there was, and examples were not hard to find because they were universal. Here is just one: to run a fast passenger service from Denver to Chicago (1,670 km or 1,034 miles) on a $16\frac{1}{2}$ hour schedule, eight locomotive drivers and eight firemen had to be employed, with crew changes about every 100 miles. Moreover, with what was called 'overtime', these eight crews collected $10\frac{1}{2}$ days' basic pay. In olden times 100 miles had been an average day's work for a locomotive crew, and in the mid 1970s, when trains might cover that distance in less than a couple of hours, it was still regarded as the standard distance entitling the men to one day's pay.

In the post-authoritarian age, there was a genuine problem in ensuring that railway workers would put into society as much as they drew out of that society. In America there was little attempt to solve this problem because too many influential interests refused to acknowledge that it existed. In continental Europe, especially in those countries which had known the psychological shocks of defeat and destruction, railway workers were less distrustful of managements and more willing to sacrifice today's possibility for tomorrow's prosperity. There were, it is true, frequent railway strikes in some countries, notably Italy and France, but these were short and almost ritualistic. Between strikes railwaymen worked hard with an apparent pride in their job.

Even in Britain, where labour relations were generally poor, unions did not push their demands to a point which would bring railroads to bankruptcy, as happened in the USA, where the first Class I railway to go out of business (the Ontario & Western) did so in the mid 1950s. In Britain, the railway unions extracted conditions and wage rates which did at certain periods mean that the money paid out in wages was not fully returned by the value of the work performed. But in general the self-interest of railway union leaders was not unenlightened. When in the early 1960s the British taxpayer began to resent the never-ending government financing of the railways' deficits, at a time when British Railways' revenue was in decline, the unions did not obdurately oppose economies in the use of manpower. It was clearly seen that rational use of labour was necessary for the railways' survival and unions acquiesced in an orderly reduction of manpower in exchange for a share in the financial gains of such a rationalization. It was not until the mid 1970s, partly because there were several competing railway unions, that pay claims sometimes became unreasonable in relation to the work done and to the railways' revenues.

The delicate question of the number of men required to operate a non-steam train gave some insight into the rational use of manpower by different railways. In the USA even a locomotive moving without a train was required to take a 5-man crew with it. In Britain a fireman was no longer required outside the small hours unless the run was longer than two hours or 100 miles. On the SNCF 2-man locomotive crews were required by the unions but railcars and multiple-unit electric trains could be operated with one man in the cab plus a train conductor with access to the driver's position. Switching locomotives within station limits could also be single-manned. In Germany all trains except those with an average speed of more than 90 km/h (55 mph) could be driven by one man, provided the conductor had the means to stop the train in emergency. In Ireland there was one-man operation. Italian State Railways were equipped for one-man operation but two were used 'as a step to reduce unemployment'. In Spain there were two men in the cab. In the Netherlands only one man was required in the cabs of electric passenger trains. In Sweden, short trains could be crewed by one man.

In countries of the Soviet bloc the railway trade unions co-operated fully with government policies. Their task was largely that of explaining such policies to their members and ensuring that the latter conformed. This sometimes meant that working conditions, including safety measures, were not always commendable. On the other hand, it gave Soviet and eastern block railway managements greater freedom of management than their British or American counterparts.

The growth of diesel and electric systems

During the first postwar decade, when railway service in most countries of Western Europe seemed so slow to rise from its wartime trough, one of the few sources of optimism was France, where the SNCF was steadily electrifying its main line south from Paris through Lyon to the Mediterranean. Work started as early as 1946, literally when the rubble was still being cleared, and electric services from Paris to Lyon were inaugurated in 1952. France had extensive experience of electrification before the war with, in particular, two electrified main lines from Paris to the south-west. These had been converted at 1,500 volts dc, and the same system was chosen for the first postwar project. Power for the Paris–Lyon scheme came from hydro-electricity generated in the Alps. Sub-stations were remotely controlled and placed (according to the capacity of their rectifiers) at intervals of 9 km (5½ miles) or 14 km (9 miles). One result of the electrification which captured the public eye (and not only in France) was the acceleration of passenger trains, but the more important benefits were less obvious except to railwaymen. Under steam traction there had been speed and load restrictions west of Dijon because of long gradients. This had, in effect, meant a restriction of line capacity with much through freight traffic being passed over the parallel but less suitable secondary main line through Nevers. Electrification, with the provision of locomotive power which could be relied on for consistent hill-climbing capacity, eased this problem, and a further innovation, *banalisation*, finally eliminated it. *Banalisation* was a train-control technique, permitting both tracks to carry traffic moving in the same direction. Thus at peak periods, when there was usually a definite one-way trend of traffic, the underemployed track would be changed to what was formerly called 'wrong-line working' for a period. Technically, there was nothing spectacular in this procedure, which could be described as treating a double-track line as consisting of two single track lines under Centralized Traffic Control. Operationally, however, this was a great step forward, and avoided the need to convert double-track to quadruple-track. Meanwhile, as the electrification was carried out, other improvements were made. Centralized Traffic Control enabled signal boxes to be reduced from 39 to 19, flyover junctions were built to speed the entry to Paris and the passing of Dijon and Macon, and alignment was improved to permit higher maximum speeds. Taking advantage of electrification work to make other improvements would be a regular feature of future electrifications, in France and elsewhere. Electrification therefore came to mean not simply a new method of traction but almost the provision of a completely new railway.

It was the diesel locomotive, however, which made the most dramatic progress in the postwar decades. By 1957, only one of the Class I US railroads, the coal-hauling Norfolk & Western, still made great use of steam traction, and even the N & W would shortly change over to diesels. Most North American railroads dieselized faster than consideration for optimum advantage would have warranted. Sometimes the wish to appear progressive, to be able to announce an 'all-diesel' railroad was responsible for this haste; sending almost-new steam locomotives to the scrap-heap could seem very progressive and decisive to those who did not stop to ask themselves how much those steam locomotives were worth. However, this should not be regarded as a criticism to which only railroad managers were liable, for airline managements behaved in precisely the same way when the time came to consider a changeover from propeller to jet propulsion. In general, the world's railways could be divided into those which for one reason or another eliminated their steam fleet as soon as possible, once the decision to dieselize was taken (these included most of the North American railroads, Britain and the USSR) and those which slowly dieselized, retaining the newer steam locomotives in the meantime (France, Germany and Italy were prominent among these). Among the advantages of the latter policy were the avoidance of premature writing-off of steam locomotives, the maintenance of a stable diesel-locomotive industry with a steady stream of orders, rather than inflicting a boom-and-slump sequence generated by a rushed dieselization scheme, and the opportunity of learning from mistakes in time to avoid really large-scale blunders.

Time was certainly needed to consider the optimum mix of electrification and dieselization; while electrification was best fitted for heavy-traffic lines, which could justify the heavy capital expenditure on lineside equipment, the exact division between electrification and diesel territory depended very much on a careful study of local circumstances. What happened on the best-ordered railways was that the obvious candidates for electrification were converted first and the first diesel locomotives were allocated to lines which would be electrified later. When this second group of lines were electrified, the diesels would be sent to the next most heavily-trafficked lines. With variations, this process was adopted in France, Germany, Italy, Russia, India, South Africa, and several other countries where, for the most part, it is still continuing; India and South Africa still operate many steam locomotives, and so, to a limited extent, do other countries. In North America the diesel had very little competition from electrification; in fact the advent of the diesel persuaded some companies which had electrified difficult sections to replace electrics with diesels. British Railways' motive-power policy was eccentric. After nationalization in 1948, its new management decided to introduce a completely new range of steam locomotives and then, a few years later, decided to dieselize rapidly and completely all lines not electrified.

The postwar years witnessed the granting of independence to several former colonial territories. Of these, India was the biggest and the only one to have a really substantial railway network. Although run down during the war, Indian railways were remarkable among colonial lines for their high engineering standards, and when India embarked on her five-year industrialization plans the railways could rely heavily on this built-in reserve capacity to handle the increased traffic flows. After a period during which Indians appointed to the highest managerial positions were to some extent learning their jobs, various improvements were introduced. Some of these were technical and others social. Among the latter were the progressive introduction of fast third-class-only long-distance passenger trains, and the opening (sometimes more ostensible than real) of railway operating jobs to all, irrespective of caste. Among the technical innovations was the introduction of a new standard range of more powerful locomotives. (Under British rule there had been fairly strict standardization. The new locomotives carried this further with, basically, just four types: a passenger and a freight design for each of the two main gauges.) To ensure that the railways, with little investment in double tracking and new lines, could carry the increasing traffic in coal and minerals, new high-capacity 4-axle freight cars were introduced. In subsequent decades electrification of some main lines was carried out and, more recently, a start has been made in converting narrow and metre-gauge routes to broad gauge—a very long process. After starting with a big steam-locomotive works in the late 1940s, Indian Railways have since provided themselves with further production units and now build their own electric and diesel locomotives as

The crest of Indian Railways (Hindi version).

well as passenger and freight cars. Their steam-locomotive works eventually changed to diesel- and electric-locomotive production but steam engines are expected to remain in service well into the next century.

Another colonial territory with a developed railway network was Java, the most prosperous of the former Dutch possessions in the East Indies. As the most developed part of the new republic of Indonesia, Java witnessed much capital investment of which by no means all arrived at the intended destination. During the Japanese occupation and the subsequent liberation war, the railways suffered badly, even though by some kind of gentlemen's agreement the opposing Dutch and indigenous forces sometimes allowed trains to run unhindered between their respective zones. Rehabilitation of the railways was patchy. The main lines received German 2-8-2 steam locomotives and, later, German and American diesels, together with all-metal passenger cars. However, the secondary lines are still operated on rather less than a shoestring, with old and badly-maintained rolling stock running over threadbare track. The war did eliminate one difficulty, however, for the Japanese solved the Javan gauge problem by transferring all the 1,435 mm (4 ft 8½ in) gauge equipment to China, leaving 1,067 mm (3 ft 6 in) as the standard gauge.

Another big territory which could almost be described as ex-colonial was China, whose first railways had been built by foreigners in search of 'spheres of influence'. After the Chinese revolution of 1911, itself partly incited by controversy about who should own and operate China's railways, there was a disturbed period of gradual nationalization, civil war, Japanese occupation, and civil war again. Finally, in 1949, a strong government was installed, committed to massive economic development. With its emphasis on basic industries this economic policy assured the Chinese railways of an important role. At first there was much Russian assistance; the Chinese Eastern Railway through Manchuria, once part of the Trans Siberian, was operated by Russia until 1952, and served as a training ground for Chinese railwaymen learning from Russian example. The Russians also assisted in setting up railway workshops; a steam locomotive of essentially Russian design is still being built in China. After the Russians left, the Chinese were able to carry on alone, building their own diesel and electric locomotives and laying new track.

In the USSR railway development was held at a level somewhat behind the rate of industrial growth. This meant that traffic density was high; by the early 1960s the Soviet railways, possessing about only one tenth of the world's railway mileage, carried half of the total freight traffic moved by the world's railways. The first postwar five-year plan was largely devoted to repairing wartime damage and neglect, but in the 1950s there was opportunity for improvement. However, not all opportunities were taken. Like railway managements elsewhere, the Russians did not see why methods which had worked before the war should not be continued after it. But unlike western managements, they lacked the spur of competition to force them to look around for better ways of performing their tasks. Highway transport had been neglected in the Soviet Union, where there were few hard-surfaced roads, and the inland waterways were a hindrance only insofar as they absorbed capital investment which would have been better utilized by the railways. In any case, at a time when the main problem was not finding traffic, but in handling it, waterway 'competition' was not competition at all, but useful load-shedding. So the Soviet railways handled their growing traffic, not so much by electrifying or dieselizing, but by building enough steam locomotives to provide two engines for the heavier main-line trains. This, even in Russian conditions, was not the most economical solution of the problem, but it was not until after the death of Stalin that out-of-date concepts could be safely abandoned. Then, basing itself largely on French experience, the Soviet Ministry of Transport embarked on large-scale electrification of main lines. At the same time, using at first designs based on American practice, there was a really massive production of diesel-electric locomotives. A Soviet passenger train was soon listed among the world's fastest; this was the *Avrora* between Moscow and Leningrad which covered 318 km (198 miles) of the journey at 138 km/h (86 mph). Thus, at a time when in many developed countries doubts were being cast on the railways' ability to survive even as freight carriers, in Russia, China, India and other countries committed to rapid growth, the railways evidently had a future as well as a past.

Towards a new railway system

The inability of many railways to make a profit in the face of new competition meant that by the mid 1950s it became fashionable to predict an early end of railway transport; the steel wheel running on the steel rail was condemned as obsolete. Over the past two decades, however, there has been a change of attitude. This stems from two new factors: there were technological advances in rail transport which promised to do much to provide better service and reduce costs and, secondly, it was realized that the elimination of railways would create enormous problems, so governments began to examine transport problems and decided to make it easier for railways to perform those tasks for which they were best suited.

Typical of the new attitudes was the so-called Beeching Report on British Railways, published in 1963 and acted upon in subsequent years. Among its recommendations was that the railways should be allowed to shed loss-making operations, such as the running of stopping passenger trains and the maintenance of branch-line services. By cutting out loss-making activities, there would be more resources available for improving those services which had a promising future, particularly longer-distance freight and passenger services. By reducing the railway mileage to about 12,800 km (8,000 miles) a much better-utilized network would be created. The network in fact was only reduced to about 17,700 km (11,000 miles) because line closures aroused great opposition, especially when it was realized that the British Railways management was not always correct in its assessments of which lines were the least promising. Subsequently British Railways received greater freedom in fixing its charges; it could, within limits, actually bargain with individual shippers to obtain higher revenue. In the late 1960s however, it became clear that most of the economies obtained from withdrawal of services were absorbed by rather higher wages. The concept of 'cost-benefit' then came to the fore; it meant that a railway line's viability was no longer to be judged by its profitability but by its financial result taken in conjunction with the value of the benefits it conferred on society. This opened the way for subsidy of loss-making services maintained for social reasons. Commuter services were a first beneficiary of this attitude, and financial responsibility for some was taken over by local authorities.

Each in their own way, the railways of other western countries benefited from similar changes of government attitude. In Canada there was the inevitable Royal Commission, which decided that it was unfair for Canadian railways to carry on loss-making service without public subsidy, while the government of Ontario decided to halt the building of a new expressway into

Toronto and instead to institute its own commuter rail service over the tracks of the Canadian National Railways. In France, 1971 saw the amendment of the 1937 agreement which had led to the formation of the SNCF. From 1971 the French National Railways were to have freedom of management, especially in financial matters, and equality of opportunity was to be imposed on all forms of transport (a provision which benefited the railways, which were more regulated than other forms of transport). In 1973 the governments of both Britain and Germany admitted that if railways were to provide the required level of service they could hardly make a profit, and therefore sums had to be made available to them for investment.

In the USA, events took a different course. There was a trend, encouraged by the government, towards the merger of railways. The Chesapeake & Ohio took over the Baltimore & Ohio and the Western Maryland, the Norfolk & Western absorbed the Nickel Plate and the Wabash railroads, and the old James Hill empire was reconstituted when the Great Northern, Northern Pacific, and Burlington united to form the Burlington Northern. These three amalgamations produced stronger and bigger companies which were allowed by the labour unions to eliminate some, but by no means all, of the duplication of facilities in their territories. Other very desirable mergers did not take place, however, sometimes because labour pressures made the potential economies seem unattainable, or because the partners could not agree on terms. In the eastern states, where there was a long-standing duplication of railway lines and very strong competition from the air and highway, individual railroads seemed likely to follow the path into insolvency taken by the Ontario & Western in 1957. In 1961 the New Haven Railroad, connecting New York and Boston, went bankrupt and was absorbed into the Pennsylvania Railroad. The Erie and Lackawanna railroads merged in the vain hope of avoiding bankruptcy, and so did the two one-time trend-setters of the American railroad industry, the New York Central and the Pennsylvania, forming for a time the Penn Central Railroad. But these changes were insufficient. Freight services remained very vulnerable to highway competition, even though for the most part they ran over distances which in European conditions would have made them the undoubted preserve of rail transport. Freight trains were delayed where they passed from one system to another, and the high cost of labour made it essential to run as few trains as possible; the resulting long trains meant that services were infrequent and facilities such as yards were of excessive size and even then could not handle traffic efficiently. In 1970 Penn Central went bankrupt, as several other eastern railroads had done already.

This railroad crisis was one which the government could not ignore, and the eventual result was the creation of Conrail (Consolidated Rail Corporation) which was essentially a nationalized railway even though every effort was made to hide this fact from a public long schooled to regard the word 'nationalization' with suspicion. Conrail united into one organization the seven eastern railroads: Penn Central, Boston & Maine, Erie-Lackawanna, Lehigh Valley, Central of New Jersey, Reading, and the Lehigh & Hudson River. In order to provide some competition, two profitable railroads, the Southern and the Chesapeake & Ohio, were invited to take over 3,200 km (2,000 miles) of track formerly belonging to the bankrupts. However, because of a dispute over work rules, the SR and C & O only accepted this offer under pressure. Conrail's prospects were hopeful; elimination of duplication would be feasible over the long term though, in the short term, it was not possible to reduce the labour force to a size (about half) which railway technology really warranted.

Great Railways

by John Westwood The history and present state of twelve notable railways and railway systems.

The Great Western Railway (Britain)

In 1923 the numerous British railway companies were amalgamated by act of parliament to form four large concerns. Only one of them retained its identity in this reorganization. This was the Great Western, which before grouping was the largest of the railways and which afterwards was still the third largest, having absorbed in 1923 the railways of south and central Wales. Not many railways have had such a long life, from the passing of its parliamentary bill in 1835 to the formation of British Railways in 1948. But this was not the only reason why the company had such an unusual place in the affections of those interested in railways. Its essential appeal was that it was highly individualistic, and made a success of this individualism.

With Brunel in charge of the construction of its main line from London to Bristol, it early distinguished itself by adopting the 2,134 mm (7 ft) gauge and by aligning its route to achieve the gentlest of gradients. By virtue of these two advantages its trains were the fastest in the country, a fact which stood it in good stead when the first of the parliamentary enquiries was made into the desirability of converting the railway to the standard gauge used by other railways. In the end, though, this was an occasion when being different did not pay, because despite the technical advantages of the broad gauge the existence of two gauges in one small country had grave inconveniences, and parliament finally required a change to standard gauge. For many years much of the GW mileage had a third rail, thereby creating a mixed gauge, until in 1892 the last broad-gauge train left the company's terminus at Paddington for Penzance.

The company seemed to lose much of its zest during the period of the mixed gauge. The appointment as chairman in 1865 of Daniel Gooch, once Brunel's locomotive superintendent, did much to steady the GW's fortunes without, however, restoring the earlier vitality. One of Gooch's projects was the Severn Tunnel, built at great cost in money and worry from 1873 to 1886 to shorten the distance to south Wales. Unanticipated trouble from deep springs was one of the great difficulties encountered in building this 7 km ($4\frac{1}{3}$ mile) underwater tunnel. Two decades later the company began to build more cut-off lines: a route through Newbury to shorten the distance to Devon, and another to provide a direct line from London to Birmingham enabling the GW to compete with the London and North Western Railway for traffic between London, Birmingham and Liverpool.

It was also in competition with the London & South Western for the traffic from Devon, a competition which was symbolized by the competitive timings of the two companies' Ocean Mail Specials from Plymouth to London. Having competitors on its two peripheral main lines, but a virtual monopoly of Bristol and south Wales traffic, the GW was in the position of having a stimulus to do better as well as a sense of security. Perhaps it was this, together with its feeling that ever since the gauge dispute other railways regarded the GW with either hostility or envy, that enabled the company to thrive so distinctively in the 20th century.

Externally, the GW had its own 'house style', exemplified in the design of stations and fixtures. Its locomotives, too, were distinctive and could be divided into two groups. Some were highly traditional in outline, being improvements on old designs which had done good work in the past. Tall copper-capped chimneys and shiny brass domes and safety-valve covers were the trimmings of these locomotives, which reflected the conservative side of

Previous pages: Tracks at the approach to London's Waterloo Station.

the company's character. Even after the 1948 nationalization, the GW works at Swindon continued for a time to produce the most numerous and traditional GW locomotive type, the 0-6-0 pannier tank locomotive. The other group of locomotives, developed in the 20th century by the distinguished locomotive engineer Churchward, were horrifying to traditionalists when they first appeared. Gaunt, with domeless tapered boilers, prominent outside cylinders and driving wheels which somehow seemed indecently exposed, they remained unusual even after they had been enlarged to create such successful machines as the King and Castle classes. They burned Welsh coal, so were usually smokeless, and were painted Brunswick green with highly polished brass fittings. A GW passenger train, painted chocolate and cream and hauled by such a locomotive, was a sight which many found stirring and reassuring. Such trains included the *Cornish Riviera Limited*, and the *Cheltenham Flyer* which, by covering the 124 km (77 miles) between Swindon and Paddington in $56\frac{3}{4}$ minutes, broke a world speed record one day in 1932.

Conservative in many ways, the GW was innovative in others. It introduced corridor trains as early as 1892. Alone among the four inter-war British railways, it made a great success of diesel railcars. After World War II it experimented with gas-turbine propulsion. More important, it had by far the best safety record of British railways, largely because it adopted and steadily extended its system of automatic train control in which a train was automatically brought to a halt if its driver ignored signals at danger.

The North Eastern Railway (Britain)

In 1922, just before it became the most substantial constituent of the new London & North Eastern Railway, the North Eastern Railway possessed 2,800 km (1,750 route miles) and was reckoned to be the fourth largest railway in the kingdom. It was also one of the very best, an innovating line which at the same time had a reputation for steadiness and reliability. It tended to be underestimated outside its own region. This was partly because it did not touch London, and partly perhaps because many preferred to ignore it. It was too solid a refutation of the prevailing ideology that monopoly was bad, for the NER was a clear-cut monopoly and yet it provided an excellent service to the public.

Born by the amalgamation of three companies in 1854, the NER succeeded in keeping its territory to itself. It did this by absorbing possible rivals, like the Stockton & Darlington Railway, or by promising to build lines which were proposed by rival concerns. Only once did it fail to block a rival. This happened in its southernmost district when the city of Hull encouraged the building of the Hull & Barnsley Railway. But the competitive rate-cutting between the two railways and the docks which they owned ended in the victory of the NER. The Hull & Barnsley continued to exist, but relations were fairly amicable, and indeed finally culminated in a merger.

The main line of the NER formed the central part of the East Coast route to Scotland. It began at Doncaster, where there was an end-on junction with the Great Northern's main line from London, and went north through York and Newcastle to Berwick where it joined the North British Railway's line to Edinburgh. From the main line extended a network of secondary lines, many of them tapping the coal and ore resources whose traffic was the basis of the Railway's financial success. Its main line boasted some of the finest bridges of the railway age. The Royal Border Bridge south of Berwick and the High Level Bridge at Newcastle were both designed by Robert Stephenson and opened by Queen Victoria in 1850. The King Edward VII Bridge over the Tyne was opened by that king in 1906.

The Railway was the country's biggest dock-owner and its ports were largely occupied with the export of coal which it brought down from the mines. The efficient working of the coal traffic was its main concern. On the locomotive side, this culminated in the building of a very capable outside cylinder 0-8-0 freight locomotive. On the rolling-stock side, the NER pioneered the use of high-capacity coal cars. Whereas the standard British coal wagon carried eight or ten tons of coal, the NER from 1902 was using 20-tonne vehicles. This change was facilitated by the fact that the NER, unlike other railways, owned the coal wagons; elsewhere it was the collieries that provided the rolling stock. Thus the NER was in a strong position to persuade the collieries to redesign their coal-loading facilities to accept the bigger cars, and thereby solved a problem which elsewhere in Britain persisted for many decades.

Because Britain's first railway museum was founded at York, a good selection of NER locomotives has been preserved. There was little that was remarkable about the company's locomotives, apart from their all-round excellence. They were long lasting, cheap to build, and easy to handle. The freight engines were powerful and the passenger engines fast. One NER 4-4-0, No. 1621, is preserved at York by virtue of its performance in the 'Race to the North' in 1895: it ran the 200 km (125 miles) from Newcastle to Edinburgh in 113 minutes. The flat, straight stretch of line between Darlington and York was the scene of many high-speed runs and in 1914 a train which was scheduled to run its 71 km (44 miles) in 43 minutes was the fastest train in the British Empire.

Other achievements of this company include the first main-line electrification, 30 km ($18\frac{1}{2}$ miles) of mineral line between Newport and Shildon. There was also a mechanical cab-signalling apparatus installed on the main line to help drivers in foggy weather. The NER was also the first railway to recognize trade unions when in 1889 the management agreed to discuss working conditions with a trade-union official as well as with 'representatives of the men'. A year earlier the company had agreed to submit a local labour dispute to arbitration. In those days such concessions were regarded by many as monstrous but today it can be seen that here, as in other things too, the NER was just a little in advance of its contemporaries.

The Midland Railway (Britain)

In 1923, when the Midland Railway was merged with others to form the London Midland and Scottish Railway, it was the third largest of Britain's railways, after the Great Western and London & North Western. It possessed over 3,300 km (2,000 miles) of route, owned a railway in Ireland, was part-owner of several joint lines and maintained a steamer fleet. Unlike the GWR and the LNW it had never indulged in spectacular exploits, yet in its own quiet way had done much to benefit both its clients and its shareholders. It gave the impression of a carefully managed and carefully designed railway.

Its very origin was unspectacular. It did not begin as a main line linking London with some other great city but was an amalgamation of three Midland lines which together connected Leeds, Nottingham, Derby, Leicester and

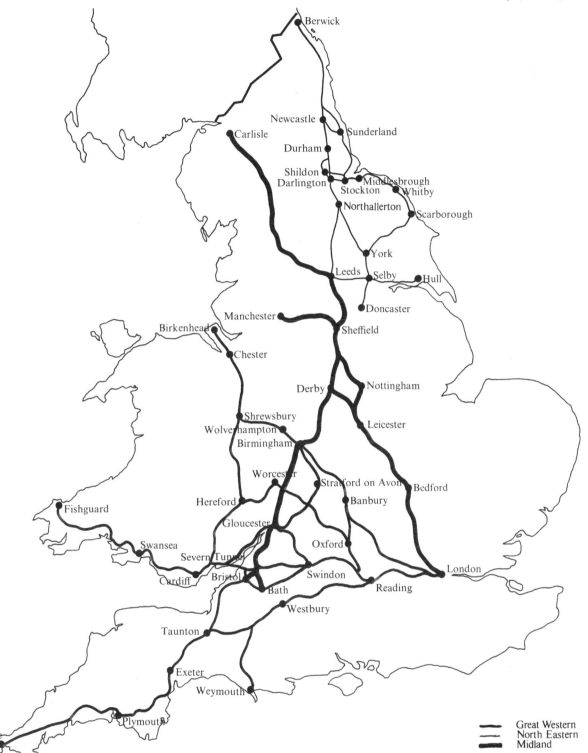

The main lines of Britain's Great Western, North Eastern and Midland Railways.

Birmingham. These three formed the Midland Railway in 1844 and were soon joined by the Birmingham and Gloucester. Later construction and acquisitions enlarged the MR so that it had its own line southwards to London (where it commissioned the finest of the London termini, St Pancras); northwards beyond Leeds through forbidding terrain over the Pennines to Carlisle, and south-westwards to Bristol, which became the southern end of Britain's most important cross-country route, through Birmingham up to Yorkshire.

In its early days the MR was part of the first Anglo-Scottish main line, because it connected the London & North Western at Rugby with the York

Newcastle & Berwick at York. This arrangement did not last long because the West Coast route and the East Coast route were soon completed, but the MR became a serious competitor for this traffic when its London–Carlisle route was complete. It never tried to rival the East and West Coast routes in terms of speed and stayed out of the glorious but rather useless 'Races to the North' but it did attract passengers by its comfort and reliability.

In 1873 George Pullman was invited to build some of his celebrated sleeping, parlour and day cars for the MR, and to operate them at his own risk and profit. Made in the USA but assembled at the MR works at Derby the first car, built of oak and mahogany, was a sleeper. A number of runs for the press were made and then this car, in company with others, was put into service on the London to Yorkshire run. These sleeper and parlour vehicles were very popular among those who could afford to pay the supplement. They were also remarkably well built, remaining in service for many decades. The day coaches, for second- and third-class passengers, offered unheard-of luxuries to British travellers. No longer did they need to rely on footwarmers in winter, for the vehicles had central heating, and they all had access to a toilet. And yet, perhaps because the day cars were so unfamiliar, the public did not like them, and they were soon withdrawn.

In 1875 the MR's management abolished second-class passenger accommodation, thereby transforming the situation of the ordinary railway passenger. For competitive and public-relations reasons the other British railways were forced to follow suit. The essence of the change was that all former second-class vehicles became third class, and the old and rather primitive third-class cars were withdrawn. Moreover, the Midland promised that all future third-class vehicles would have upholstered seats and that the compartments would be larger; already, since 1872, third-class accommodation had been provided in every train. Thus was born the British tradition of comfort and speed for the lowest class of passenger, a tradition which still persists. The final chapter of this initiative came in 1956 when, after many decades in which the British lines provided just first class and third class, the BR management abolished third class by retitling such accommodation second class.

For much of its revenue the company relied on the coal traffic from the Midlands to London. To handle the coal trains much of its main line was quadrupled, with two lines reserved for freight. Even so there was growing congestion and one of the MR's contributions to railway operating technique was its pioneering of centralized train control. With controllers located at key points, supervising operations over a large area and in telephonic touch with other controllers, train movements could be better co-ordinated.

Throughout its eight decades the MR had only four chief mechanical engineers, so there was a continuity in locomotive design. Kirtley, its first locomotive engineer, built very sturdy locomotives, some of which lasted until the 1950s. Johnson, his successor, not only introduced the only family of compound locomotives to be a real success in Britain but also, thanks to his application of steam sanding gear, was able to reintroduce the single-driver locomotive for fast trains. Johnson's successors of the twentieth century left less of a mark, and really developed rather than enhanced the Midland tradition. In its last decades the MR was a railway of small locomotives; it relied on the 0-6-0 for freight and the 4-4-0 for main-line passenger work, and doubleheading was frequent. Indeed, the coal trains to London were entrusted to a pair of 0-6-0s as regular practice.

It was Johnson who introduced the so-called Midland Red colour scheme. Applied to both locomotives and passenger coaches, it created an impression of dignity and luxury. To achieve the particular hue, locomotives were turned out with twelve coats: two coats of grey, four of purple brown, a top coat of crimson lake with some purple brown mixed in, and then five layers of varnish. The effect was unsurpassable, and has presented problems in recent years to owners of preserved MR locomotives. Johnson's locomotives were meticulously designed and engineered, with great care being taken to impart a beauty of line achieved largely by the use of a flowing curve wherever a straight outline was not essential. Care of detail was not confined to locomotives. Midland stations were tastefully designed with light and airy awnings of gabled glass supported by graceful cast-iron columns. Station nameboards were so designed as to be easily read from trains moving in either direction. Many examples of MR design can still be seen, even the characteristic wooden fencing, and of course the magnificent terminus and hotel at St Pancras.

The Nord Railway (France)

When the French railways were amalgamated in 1937 to form the SNCF the Chemin de Fer du Nord could claim to be the oldest of the constituent companies for it was formed by a royal decree in 1845. Its debut marked the beginning of the era of big companies, and also the emergence as railway magnates of the Rothschild family which was granted the concession. The oldest line of the new company had been built nine years earlier, and by the time of nationalization the company possessed about 3,850 km (2,400 miles) of line, not including its mileage in Belgium nominally owned by its Nord-Belge Railway.

Three years after its incorporation the company was overtaken by the 1848 revolution. Much of its property was damaged by saboteurs; these were frequently its own employees, who were demanding higher wages and the

The main lines of France's Nord Railway.

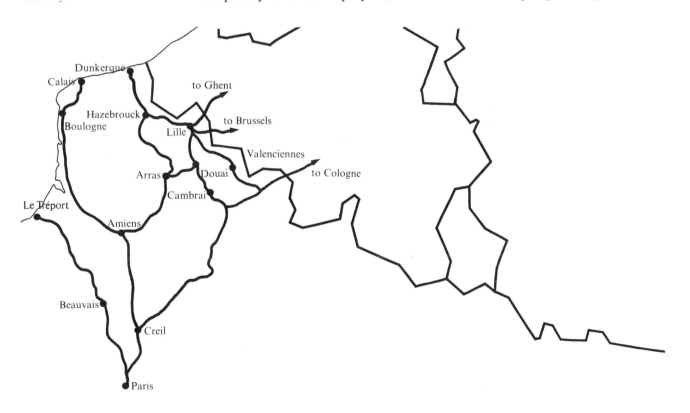

expulsion of foreign (mainly British) railwaymen. However, the revolution was followed by the long reign of Louis Napoleon, a man who appreciated railways but who also regarded them as servants of his state. The example of the Nord was soon followed elsewhere, as the smaller companies joined to form five big companies in addition to the Nord and each of these had a territorial monopoly. In the case of the Nord, this monopoly was in the segment of territory extending north-eastwards from Paris. The Nord's main lines were from Paris to Calais, from Creil (51 km or 32 miles north of Paris) to the Belgian frontier at Jeumont, and from Longeau (near Amiens on its Paris–Calais line) to Lille and Belgium. Secondary and branch lines criss-crossed between these main lines so that the Nord's network was unusually dense for France. The Railway was also very compact, for its territory hardly exceeded 330 km (200 miles) in any direction. Because it served an area which was agriculturally rich, well endowed with industry and coal, and fairly densely populated, the traffic density and the revenue per kilometre were also higher than the French average. Thanks to this, when in the 1880s the private companies were under political attack, the Nord could boast that it had never claimed a centime from the state under the terms of its concession (in which the government had guaranteed to support a dividend in years when the company might make a loss).

After the Est Railway, the Nord suffered most from the three wars with Germany. Damage in the Franco-Prussian War was not great, although the company's prestige was damaged by the general failure of French railways to carry out their military tasks; however, after the politically-inspired criticism had died down it was realised that it was not the Nord and Est railways which had failed but the military control under which they had been placed. World War I was, for four years, largely fought over the Nord's territory. The Railway lost much of its rolling stock in the German advance of 1914, and this was partly compensated for by drafting equipment from other railways; some British locomotives were also sent, as one of the Nord's tasks was the supply of the British Expeditionary Force. Some locomotives of Nord design were also built in British workshops. Later in the war some of the company's lines were carrying twice as much traffic as in pre-war times, and occasionally a line would be required to pass 120 trains daily. However, at the end of the war many lines which had been under occupation were systematically destroyed by the retreating German army. After the war the Railway was kept going with the help of British and American freight cars, and subsequent German reparations were also important.

Like the other French railways, the Nord made losses in the inter-war years, and its absorption into the new SNCF was therefore probably fortunate both for its shareholders and its clients. In retrospect, it was perhaps the most distinguished of French railways. British commentators regarded it as the only French company to provide passenger schedules worthy of comparison with those of Britain. Heavy 600-ton international trains were already run from Calais docks before 1914, and regularly surmounted the formidable Caffiers Bank (11 km or 7 miles of 1 in 125 (0.8 per cent) grade south of Calais) at up to 40 mph (65 km/h). A tradition of individualistic locomotive design was the foundation of this sturdy running. Starting with the Grands Chocolats (brown-painted compound locomotives), designers like the celebrated du Bousquet built some of the finest of the world's steam locomotives, usually on the de Glehn compound system which found its first applications on the Nord.

The Royal Prussian State Railways (Germany)

When in 1924 the German state railways were amalgamated into the Deutsche Reichsbahn, the Prussian State was by far the biggest of the constituent railways with almost three times as much mileage as the second biggest, the Bavarian State Railway. In terms of labour, the Prussian State was a dominant employer, having 485,000 workers in 1908 (compared to the 55,600 of the Bavarian and the 45,000 of the Saxon State Railways). However, Prussia had not been the first of the German states to build railways. Her first short line, from Berlin to Potsdam, was opened in 1838 by which year both Bavaria and Saxony already had their first lines. Railway construction in Prussia did not go ahead very rapidly since the government was at first indifferent to the various proposals put forward. For many years the military authorities could not see the strategic value of railway communication, while the post office department, having established a thorough and complex mail delivery based on the highways, was reluctant to change its plans. However, the Prussian railway law of 1838 at least did not oppose railways in general, and this was sufficient encouragement for a number of promoters to organize companies.

Although as the years passed the government began to help the companies, often by buying their shares, it was not until 1850 that the state built its own first railway, the first line of the Royal Prussian State Railways. In subsequent decades the state and private railways coexisted in Prussia with, in principle, private companies building lines of good commercial prospects and the state

The main lines of Germany's Royal Prussian State Railways.

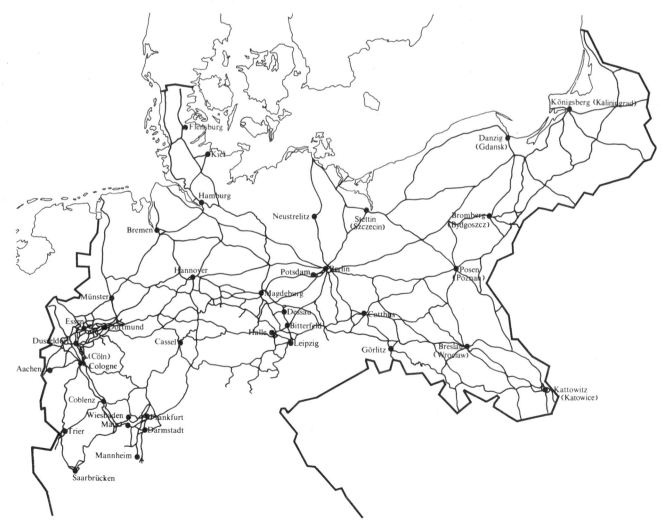

building those which were considered desirable but not commercially viable in the short run. Of the latter the most important was the Ostbahn, running from Berlin to the East Prussian capital of Königsberg and the Russian frontier. This was very much a strategic railway, even though it did much to help the economy of East Prussia.

By mid-century the Prussian generals had a sound appreciation of what railways could do for German defence. Other railways were built to and along the frontiers with France and Russia, while a military training railway was established at Berlin. The Prussian railways, both state and private, did fairly well in the Franco-Prussian War; at least they brought up reserves faster than the French railways brought up French reserves, and that is what counted. The establishment of the German Empire after this war, and the predominance of Prussia, might have been expected to begin the unification of all German railways with the Prussian State Railways as the leading constituent. In fact this did not happen because some states, Bavaria in particular, jealously defended the independence of their railway systems; Bismarck's dream of a unified German system could not be realized. However, he did begin to nationalize the big private Prussian railways, thereby expanding the state system. Expansion had already resulted from the absorption of the Hannover State Railways when Hannover united with Prussia. In 1896 the Prussian State Railways had also been joined by most of the Hessian lines; and was renamed the Preussisch–Hessichestaats Eisenbahnen. By 1909 the State Railways had 37,400 km (23,190 miles) of line, and there were only 2,900 km (1,800 miles) of private line left in Prussia.

Foreigners were often impressed by the businesslike efficiency of the Prussian State Railways. Lloyd George, when President of the Board of Trade, said in 1906 that he believed that Germans were very satisfied with their railway system and he was going to find out why. Prussian railwaymen believed that their calling was the most dignified of all labour, after service in the army. In fact there was a military atmosphere surrounding the whole railway. The idea of the railway as the third armed service was widely held, which was perhaps why a Prussian railwayman stood smartly to attention when addressing a superior official, and why he would never dream of going on strike. Much of the praised efficiency of the Prussian system was in fact merely the visible aspect of an authoritarianism not practised on other European railways. The Railways' clients had their rights, but they were limited and not negotiable. Services were provided and the clients could use them on a take-it-or-leave-it basis. In this way the Railways could impose efficiency, but only at the expense of flexibility; one symptom of this was the periodic shortage of rolling stock, when farms were not able to ship their produce, nor mines their coal.

Nevertheless the Prussian State Railways did provide a steady, reliable service at an economical cost. There was little waste of money on public-relations gestures. As might be expected, there were few really high-speed passenger services; the best trains in 1914 took $8\frac{1}{2}$ hrs between Berlin and Cologne (591 km or 367 miles) and $3\frac{1}{4}$ hrs from Berlin to Hamburg (286 km or 178 miles). The Prussian school of locomotive design built engines which were less powerful than those of other countries but which were long lasting and easy to maintain. It was this Railway, too, which first made a success of the locomotive superheater, thereby producing a great economy in fuel consumption. The Railways' diesel locomotive trial was not successful but it was a rare attempt, in the years before World War I, to apply diesel traction in railway service. Electrification came in 1903 with the suburban Berlin–Lichterfelde scheme, followed in 1911 by the first section from Dessau to Bitterfeld, of the main-line Silesian electrification. It is said that Kaiser Wilhelm II opposed electrification on the grounds that electrified lines were too vulnerable in wartime, which is why the Railway did not plan to carry electrification too close to the frontiers.

Because this Railway was so predominant in Germany, many of its practices were adopted by the other state railways as a matter of operating convenience. It was the Prussian State which introduced the D-train to Germany, a vestibuled corridor train for which a supplementary fare was payable. After 1924, when all the state railways were merged, it was natural that a preponderance of high posts should go to former Prussian State officials and from this it followed that, at last, Prussian practice became German practice. The DR (Deutsche Reichsbahn), and later the DB (Deutsche Bundesbahn) in West Germany and the DR in East Germany, are very much descendants of the Prussian State Railways. That system, however, has not only disappeared as a corporation but its once unified system is now divided between two Germanies, Poland and the USSR.

The Trans Siberian Railway (Russia)

The longest of the great continental railways is the Trans Siberian, built to connect the railways of European Russia with the Pacific coast of the Russian Empire. It was begun in 1891 when the imperial heir, the future Tsar Nicholas II, laid the foundation stone at Vladivostok. Built and opened in sections, the through route was open by 1904, although initially Lake Baikal was crossed by train ferry. The line owed much to the enthusiasm of the Russian Prime Minister, Witte, who had started his career as a railway administrator. It was regarded both as a strategic and as a colonizing line. Strategic because it would supply the Russian naval base at Vladivostok, thereby assuring a Russian naval presence in the Pacific, colonizing because the vast lands of western and central Siberia were only awaiting an influx of peasants from the overcrowded steppes of European Russia in order to become a vast new producing area.

Although the Trans Siberian Express started from St Petersburg (now Leningrad) and Moscow, the Trans Siberian Railway proper began in the Urals at Chelyabinsk. It was single track and built to 'pioneer' standards for the sake of speed and cheapness of construction. It was not expected that it would need upgrading for some years, as initial traffic was expected to be small. However, the Russo-Japanese War of 1904–1905 proved too much for the railway: enough troops and supplies to match the Japanese armies in Manchuria could not be transported. Emergency measures were taken, like the provision of extra passing loops so that traffic capacity was about doubled, and the train ferry was made superfluous by the construction of a difficult line along the cliffs of Lake Baikal. But it was too late; Russia had to accept peace terms just as her forces began to accumulate behind the war zone. The next task was to bring the discontented troops home again. But the line could not handle this traffic as fast as the soldiery wished, with the result that troops in trains along the line mutinied. For some days the line was in the hands of mutineers and rebels, and order was only restored by sending two punitive trains of loyal troops from each end of the line.

Part of the Trans Siberian route passed through Manchuria because by

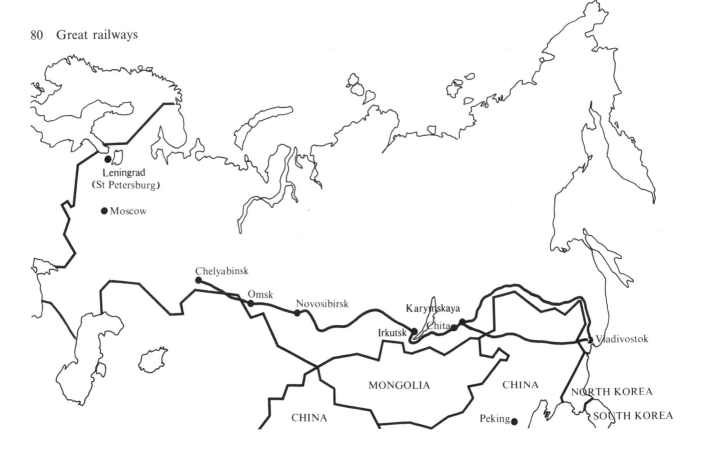

Leningrad
(St Petersburg)

Moscow

Chelyabinsk

Omsk

Novosibirsk

Karymskaya

Chita

Irkutsk

Vladivostok

MONGOLIA

CHINA

NORTH KOREA

CHINA

SOUTH KOREA

Peking

The Trans Siberian Railway. (The largest land area shown is that of the Russian Republic, part of the USSR.)

virtue of a treaty imposed on the weak Chinese government Russia had built a nominally independent line, the Chinese Eastern Railway, as this link of its transcontinental route. However, in the expectation of a future war against Japan it was decided to build another line to replace the Chinese Eastern. This new line, which was longer but ran on Russian territory throughout, was completed during World War I. During the Russian Civil War the line was fought over, and for a time was once again in the control of rebels—in this case Czechoslovak soldiers, former prisoners of war—who mutinied when they were being transported eastwards. For the first post-revolutionary years the line was in a run-down state; as early as 1917 American railway engineers had been called in to reorganize the line, but they left before they could achieve very much.

However, when the Soviet Union began to industrialize, parts of the line in Central and Western Siberia began to carry very intensive traffic. Despite subsequent construction of supplementary lines the section between Omsk and Novosibirsk is now probably the world's busiest railway in terms of freight; so much so, that Soviet Railways prefers to keep the number of passenger trains to a minimum. The line is now double track, and the original flimsy bridges and structures have long since been replaced. The line is electrified as far as Karymskaya; Moscow–Karymskaya is the world's longest electrified railway at 6,150 km (3,820 miles).

In its first decade the Trans Siberian certainly did much to create a new and prosperous Siberia. Peasant settlers poured into the region in the fourth-class passenger cars operated for the immigrant traffic and, a few years later, were exporting their butter and meat to the markets of Europe using the special trains provided to carry this traffic to the ports. Internationally the so-called Trans Siberian Express was quite celebrated, for it not only provided the world's longest train ride but did so with an abundance of luxury. With rolling stock and facilities provided by the International Sleeping Car Company, the

International train (so called to distinguish it from the more mundane, yet still excellent, train provided over the same route by the state railway administration) offered such luxuries as carpets throughout and marble-tiled bathrooms.

Passenger traffic of this type was quite small; the state railway's Trans Siberian train was normally of only four cars (two second class, one first, and a combined restaurant, kitchen, bathroom and luggage vehicle). Mallet-type locomotives were used in large numbers, their flexible wheelbase being very suited to the poorly-laid track of the early years. In 1914 a weekly service from Moscow to Vladivostok was introduced, which took nine days to Vladivostok. It was possible for a passenger from London or Paris to travel to Moscow by the Nord Express and then continue to Tokyo, which could be reached in just eleven days from Moscow.

Although, with the approval of Soviet Railways, most long-distance passengers on this route now travel by air, one of the USSR's most comfortable trains still plies this route between Moscow and Vladivostok. This is the *Rossiya* which takes seven days and two hours for the 9,297 km (5,777 miles). Another train, the *Baikal*, goes as far as Irkutsk. In addition, services from Moscow to Peking use this route between Moscow and Lake Baikal. It was Chinese crew members of the Peking–Moscow train who, a few years ago, were accused of dropping defamatory leaflets from the train as it wended its way through Siberia. The Trans Siberian is not by any means an ordinary railway.

The New South Wales Government Railways (Australia)

The NSWGR, recently reorganized as part of the New South Wales Public Transport Commission (NSWPTC), is the busiest of the Australian railway systems. The first line in the state, a 22 km (14 mile) line from Sydney to Parramatta, was finished in 1855 by the government, which had taken over construction from the previous private company. Another company, the Hunter River Railway, met a similar fate and it became obvious that if New South Wales were to have railways they would have to be state railways, for investors had more promising uses for their capital. However, private enterprise in its short life had left the legacy of gauge differences in Australia, for it was the vacillations of the Sydney Railway Company, manfully supported by the vacillations of the NSW government, which ensured that the NSW gauge, though standard, was not adopted by Victoria and South Australia.

During the first decade of railway construction the beginnings emerged of the three main lines from Sydney to the west, north and south. Up to 1914 there were only five single years in which no new line was opened; the network steadily increased until the two main lines reached the Queensland and Victorian borders, while the western main line was scheduled for early completion to Broken Hill. Subsequent important lines have included the North Coast Line from Newcastle to the Queensland border, subsequently extended to Brisbane. In the meantime a network of secondary lines was laid. Optimism about agricultural prospects, together with political pressure, resulted in many new lines through areas of potential rather than actual prosperity. Only in the western parts of the state was railway transport lacking. A feature of this railway building was the large-scale application of the light

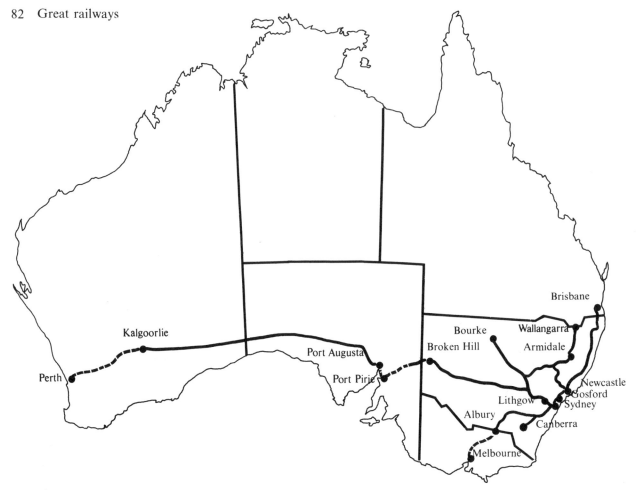

The Trans-Australian Railway and the main lines of the New South Wales Government Railway.

railway, called in Australia the pioneer railway. Such lines could be regarded as substitutes for narrow-gauge railways. They were of standard gauge and could therefore use the normal rolling stock but were built very cheaply. Special rules were applied to their working and a low speed limit was imposed. These pioneer lines served their purpose admirably. The most successful were later upgraded to main-line standards while most of the others served their localities for decades; it is only in the past few years that the state government has begun to close some of them.

With several wide rivers, as well as the table-lands and the Blue Mountains to negotiate, the NSWGR had several noteworthy engineering features. The western main line climbed the Blue Mountains near Lithgow by the famous 'Zig Zag' route; trains were hauled and pushed up by several locomotives through a series of reverses. This switchback alignment with its grades of 3 per cent (1 in 33) was eventually replaced by the present route, a six-mile deviation with grades of 1.1 per cent (1 in 90). The bridge over the Hawkesbury River on the busy Sydney to Newcastle line was, until the building of the Sydney Harbour Bridge, the largest in Australia and was also claimed to set a world record for the depth of its foundations, 162 ft below water level. The Sydney Harbour Bridge is itself a railway bridge as it carries the double track of the NSWGR's north shore suburban line.

The Railway has one of the world's biggest suburban networks around Sydney. Electrification of these lines began in 1926 and now covers almost the entire suburban area as well as the western and northern lines as far as Lithgow and Gosford; electric locomotives are used on long-distance trains passing through these two points. Steam traction came to an end in 1972, being replaced by Australian-built versions of American diesel locomotives.

For most of its history the Railway used steam locomotives designed by the British firm of Beyer, Peacock, some units of which were built in local workshops. Most impressive of the Railway's steam locomotives were postwar 4-8-4 + 4-8-4 Beyer-Garratts, by some parameters the biggest Garratts ever built, and the Class 38 Pacifics, designed by the Railway and built locally during the 1940s.

Among the unique features of the Railway are its footwarmers, still in use on some trains because steam locomotives were replaced by diesels lacking steam-heating apparatus. It is also the only railway to include dog cars in its passenger stock. These vehicles, designed for the transport of racing greyhounds, are passenger coaches in which the passenger seats have been replaced by boxes. Less quaint are the very comfortable doubledeck stainless steel electric multiple unit trains for outer suburban service, and the equally fine trains which the Railway operates in conjunction with other railways—trains like the *Southern Aurora* night service to Melbourne and the *Indian-Pacific* to Western Australia. Freight traffic, once almost entirely agricultural, has long included heavy coal traffic to the docks at Newcastle. This traffic is expected to grow as exports to Japan develop and the Railway has recently ordered 100-ton freight cars for coal, 200 of which are, very unusually, to be built of stainless steel. Some passenger services are being improved: the Sydney–Canberra service is being reduced from a 4 hr 49 min schedule to 3 hours and some 160 km/h (100 mph) multiple-unit trains have been ordered.

The Trans-Australian Railway (Australia)

The last of the great transcontinentals, the Trans-Australian Railway, was opened in 1917 providing the first overland link between the state of Western Australia and the eastern states. It is 1,691 km (1,051 miles) long, and passes for almost all its length over the flat, waterless and treeless waste known as the Nullarbor Plain. Its eastern terminus was at Port Augusta, which had a 1,600 mm (5 ft 3 in) gauge connection with Adelaide by the South Australian Railways, and its western terminus was at Kalgoorlie, connecting with the 1,067 mm (3 ft 6 in) gauge line of the Western Australian Government Railways.

The construction of the railway met no great physical obstacles. The line is very flat (which is why heavy passenger trains can nowadays be entrusted to a single diesel locomotive) and there are no sharp curves. In fact for 480 km (300 miles) the railway is absolutely straight. Obtaining fuel and water was the main problem which the railway builders could often only solve by transporting these requirements over long distances using horses and camels. Drinking water is still delivered to some stations by railway tank car. So desolate is the territory through which the line passes that it was not regarded as a means of opening up new land; it was, and remains, a purely transit line.

Of the line 965 km (600 miles) is in South Australia and 724 km (450 miles) in Western Australia. It was not, however, built or operated by the railways of these states. It was an all-Australian railway, the biggest undertaking of the federal Commonwealth Railways, recently renamed Australian National Railways. Its gauge, 1,435 mm or 4 ft 8½ in, reflected the federal government's intention that that gauge should one day be standardized throughout Australia. This meant that there was a break-of-gauge at each end, which raised the cost of freight transport over the line. In fact, freight movement was not large, certainly not large enough to bring Western Australia fully into the eastern markets. Passenger travel developed slowly, accompanied by grumbles as through travellers between Perth and Sydney found that they had to change gauges at Kalgoorlie, Port Augusta and Albury. Those travelling to eastern Australia from Europe could save two days by disembarking at Fremantle and finishing their journey by rail across Australia. But it was only the well-off and fairly adventurous who used the transcontinental trains. Few families were split between eastern and western Australia, and tourist traffic between the two regions was small. In 1925 the Railway operated only 24 sleeping cars, plus four second-class vehicles. These had been specially built for the line with bodies and underframes of Australian timber. The first-class cars each provided only 20 berths, while the second class had 36. Trains also included a dining car and a parlour car. By the standards of the time, the trains were among the world's finest. Typically they consisted of seven corridor vehicles. The parlour car provided a piano, writing tables and books, and was divided into smoking and non-smoking sections. First-class passengers had the use of a shower, and the dining car could seat 40 passengers at one sitting. Each such train could accommodate 120 passengers, although the year-round average complement was 78. A crew of twelve manned the train. A feature of this service was that passenger fares included the price of meals as on a liner, and this still applies today. The journey from Port Augusta to Kalgoorlie took $37\frac{1}{2}$ hours, implying an average overall speed of 45 km/h (28 mph).

Some of the intermediate stops were quite long, not because any passengers left or joined the train, but because locomotives had to be changed or serviced. Because of the infrequency of trains, the lack of water, and other limitations, effective utilization of locomotives was difficult, and successive changes were made in the pattern of locomotive movements. At one stage only two locomotives were used for each passenger train, each running more than 800 km (500 miles) before being changed. In the mid 1920s, however, there were still four traction sections, the longest being the 487 km (303 miles) from Cook to Rawlinna; the engine crews were changed more frequently, but even so spent a third of their working time waiting for a return train. Locomotives were of standard New South Wales designs, a 4-6-0 for passenger and a 2-8-0 for freight.

From 1937 more powerful locomotives were in service, permitting improved schedules. By that time the eastern terminus was at Port Pirie, 89 km (56 miles) nearer Adelaide. The coming of the diesel locomotive in 1951 radically reduced the working costs, thanks to its independence of water supplies. Then, in 1968, a new standard-gauge line linked Kalgoorlie with Perth, and a year later the eastern terminus of the line was joined by a standard-gauge line from Sydney via Broken Hill. All this transformed the traffic prospects, and freight traffic has developed very well. A container 'land bridge' service has recently been introduced between Perth and Sydney, supplementing the piggyback service already provided for truck companies. Meanwhile, the *Indian Pacific* train—covering the 3,968 km (2,461 miles) between Perth and Sydney in $65\frac{3}{4}$ hours, and providing sleeping, lounging and eating facilities perhaps unrivalled elsewhere in the world—has been so popular that its frequency has been increased from thrice to four times weekly. Apart from this train, there is still the traditional Trans-Australian service between Perth and Adelaide. Conveyance of passenger's cars by Motorail is also offered. Over the last decade the Trans-Australian Railway has changed from a railway serving mainly political ends to one of increasing economic importance.

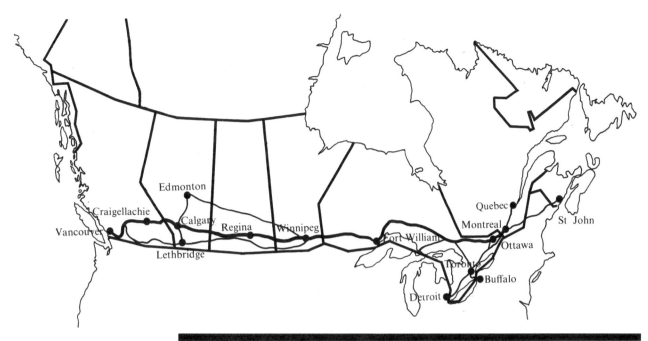

The Canadian Pacific Railway (Canada)

The Canadian Pacific Railway. The heavy line indicates the original route and the light lines show the additional main routes operating today.

The Canadian Pacific is one of the world's best-known railways. This is partly because of its genuine political importance and constructional triumph, and partly because it has always had the benefit of an astute management well aware of the value of good publicity. Thanks to this publicity some Canadians, and most outsiders, believe that the CPR is Canada's oldest and biggest railway whereas it is neither. Indeed, nowadays railway transport is only a secondary interest of the Canadian Pacific, which has been cynically described as a public-relations company with interests in transport, hotels and telecommunications. All the same, both in real terms and in folklore, the CPR has been one of the most formative enterprises in the history of Canada.

The company was formed in 1881 with the purpose of finishing the transcontinental railway linking eastern Canada, via the prairies, with the Pacific. This was in accordance with the promise made to British Columbia when that colony agreed to join the Canadian Federation as a province. Very careful surveys of the possible routes had already been made, although the actual choice of the final route had been subject to political pressures. In fact, political pressures had bedevilled the whole project, so much so that a Royal Commission had been appointed to sort things out, a sequence of events which was to become traditional in Canadian railroading. Some construction of western railroads had already been started, notably at Winnipeg and British Columbia. The acceptance of the Canadian Pacific Company as builder of the railway was just one more move to achieve the completion of the line despite shortage of capital, forbidding terrain and general pessimism.

The terms on which the company agreed to build the line were, however, exceptionally generous. Vast tracts of land were granted; lines already built by the government were to be handed over to the new company; materials were to be imported duty-free; there was to be a government cash grant of £25 million, and for twenty years there was to be freedom from most taxes and from new competing railways. Despite this government generosity, during construction the company was several times on the verge of bankruptcy but was saved by the determination of its engineers and promoters and by the inflow of additional capital from London. The first sod was turned in May 1881 and the final spike, joining the line built westward from Montreal with the line eastward from the Pacific, was driven at Craigellachie in November 1885. In June 1886 the first through train left Montreal for the Pacific.

The building of this 4,656 km (2,893 mile) line was one of the greatest engineering achievements of its time. Not only were the Rocky Mountains crossed through the difficult Kicking Horse Pass, but the less spectacular but equally forbidding section passing to the north of Lake Superior was achieved. Here it was not so much a question of mountain obstacles but of mile upon mile of deep, wet swampland, and bitter winter blizzards. In later years the route through the Rockies was improved. The 'Big Hill' through the Kicking Horse Pass, with its 11 km (7 miles) at a gradient of 4.5 per cent (1 in 22) was eased by the building of two spiral tunnels, which brought the gradient down to 2.2 per cent (1 in 45). Later the Connaught Tunnel was built to ease the gradient over Roger's Pass, and to protect the line from avalanches.

Meanwhile the CPR, as befitted an enterprising private company, was building lines elsewhere in Canada, so that by 1923, when most of its competitors were amalgamated to form Canadian National Railways, the CPR had almost as much mileage as the new government railway and served much the same places. In fact on the highly competitive Montreal–Toronto route the CPR single line and the CNR's double line ran side by side for many miles. Competition between the two companies tended to be wasteful and there were some sporadic, although usually ineffective, efforts towards co-ordination. One of the few such measures actually taken in the 1930s was the pooling of passenger train services on the busy Quebec–Montreal–Toronto and Ottawa–Toronto routes. One result of this pooling was that the smartest CNR train, the *International Limited*, departed from the CPR station in Montreal.

At its Angus Workshops at Montreal, the CPR was one of the few American railways to design and build its own locomotives. Some very distinctive types were built in the last decades of steam traction. With grey boilers and maroon side panels, the Selkirk 2-10-4s, designed for the Rockies, and the Royal Hudson 4-6-4s, used on heavy passenger trains, were very impressive machines, while the high-speed 4-4-4 type was a unique attempt at achieving high average speeds with light trains over winding track.

The transcontinental passenger trains were the CPR's advertisement, and *The Canadian*, a stainless-steel dome train with diesel traction, introduced in 1955, was merely the finest service in a long tradition. It was also the final train of this tradition, for by 1978 neither the CNR's *Super Continental* nor the CPR's *The Canadian* could attract sufficient traffic to make their continuation acceptable. Although not everywhere profitable, CPR freight traffic will probably develop further in many areas. Container freight has been doing well, while the prospect of ever-increasing shipments of coal and grain over the Rockies to the Pacific ports has already brought unit trains into use and made electrification a real possibility.

The New York Central Railroad (USA)

Thanks partly to bold publicity gestures around the turn of the century, the New York Central became one of the best known of American railways. It was created in 1853 when 10 railroads, that together provided a somewhat uncertain service between Albany and Buffalo, decided to join forces constituting an 872 km (542 mile) enterprise of 150 locomotives, 300 passenger cars and 1,700 freight cars. In 1867 Commodore Vanderbilt, who had by various manipulations acquired control of two railroads running north along the Hudson from New York, joined these two to the New York Central, of which he became president. Further purchases took the NYC on to Chicago.

As president, Vanderbilt was characterized by foresight, dishonesty and drive. As an economy he directed that all NYC locomotives should be black, with no fancy brasswork, while at the same time he created new shares in the company which he presented to himself and his friends. But even on the watered-down capital of the company he was able to pay good dividends. The eastern states between New York and Chicago were destined to become a fiercely competitive region as half-a-dozen railroads struggled for the traffic, and Vanderbilt was an excellent leader in this kind of warfare. This did not prevent him, however, from occasionally being worsted. When in a rate war with the Erie Railroad he lowered the cost of shipping cattle from Buffalo to New York to just $1.00 per head, far below real cost, the president of the Erie bought up all available cattle in Buffalo and sent them to New York by NYC.

Following for much of its way the valley of the Hudson, the NYC soon began to advertise its main line as the 'Water Level Route' and its posters, showing a smooth 4-track line, seemed to suggest that on the NYC at least the sleeping-car passenger would have a smooth and quiet ride. The Railroad's passenger agent towards the end of the century, Daniels, was one of the early masters of bold public relations. When he introduced the *Empire State Express* between New York and Chicago he persuaded the locomotive superintendent to build a special high-speed engine to haul it over one section. Buchanan, the Scottish superintendent, obliged with No 999, which was said to have exceeded 160 km/h (100 mph) on this run. It probably did not quite reach that speed, but the Railroad's publicity ensured that every full-blooded American should believe that it did. In 1902 the *Empire State Express* was supplemented by the even more glorious *Twentieth Century Limited*, which did the New York to Chicago run in just twenty hours. An all-Pullman train, it was distinguished, at its daily afternoon departure from New York, by a 79 m (260 ft) red carpet rolled down the platform for the benefit of its passengers, and by the promise to pay every passenger a refund in case of late arrival.

When in 1913 the NYC's third and final Manhatten terminus, Grand Central Terminal, was opened, with two levels of electrified underground tracks and magnificent concourses above, the NYC was at its prime. But it was only after World War II that the company encountered real difficulties. In the inter-war period, although it felt the new highway and airline competition, it managed to make a living while presenting its old image of dignified competence to the public. After 1945 it spent $56 million on new passenger cars, and then was among the first to introduce containers for its merchandise freight. Its Flexivan system was more economic than the 'piggyback' systems favoured by most other companies, although it suffered somewhat from its non-standard status, limiting it mainly to NYC territory. In co-operation with the Santa Fe Railroad, a train of these Flexivans was sent from New York to Los Angeles in just over 54 hours; this was only an experimental run, but it foreshadowed the introduction by US railroads of accelerated container and piggyback trains.

Partly because of the burden of passenger services, whose clients had taken to the highways and airways, and partly because of inefficient use of highly paid labour, the railroad encountered severe financial troubles. Managerial changes, introduced with great flourishes, did not radically change the situation. Passenger trains were withdrawn where possible, but usually government intervention prevented such withdrawals. Finally, in 1968 the NYC merged with its greatest competitor, the Pennsylvania Railroad, to form the Penn-Central System. This marriage of convenience ended unhappily. The two companies had widely different philosophies; they had promised that no labour would be made redundant by the merger; their working methods were different; their computers and electronic gear were incompatible, and their locomotives used different types of cab-signalling. Possibly, given time, the two partners would have settled down fruitfully. But time was not given, and in 1976 Penn-Central became the largest constituent of Conrail, a quasi-governmental railroad corporation combining several of the main-line eastern railroads.

The Illinois Central Railroad (USA)

Years before the Union Pacific and Central Pacific railroads were attracting worldwide attention with their transcontinental railway project, the Illinois Central Railroad was already practising the techniques for building long lines through promising but uninhabited terrain. Incorporated by the state of Illinois in 1851, it was the first railroad to be financed by a large grant of federal land. It agreed to build 1,125 km (700 miles) of line by 1857 and to pay the state seven per cent of its gross earnings. Despite its possession of federal land as backing, the Railroad had great difficulty in raising capital, much of which eventually came from Britain; William Gladstone and Richard Cobden were among the company's shareholders. Nevertheless, by the stipulated date and at the cost of many labourers' lives, the first 1,125 km (700 miles) were completed. There was a main line southwards from the border with Wisconsin to Cairo, where the rivers Ohio and Mississippi converge, and there was a so-called branch line from a point halfway along the main line, Centralia, to Chicago. Subsequently, mainly by purchase of smaller lines, the main line was extended southwards to New Orleans and other lines were built to Birmingham, Louisville, St Louis and Omaha. By 1956 the company, which liked to style itself 'Main Line of Mid America', possessed over 10,460 km (6,500 miles) of route in fourteen states.

It was the IC which set the style for the colonizing activities of the later transcontinental railways. Finding that tracks and trains were not enough, it made a determined effort to draw people to its territory. Advertisements of the endless possibilities of settlement in Illinois and elsewhere began to appear on the sides of New York streetcars. Emissaries from the company visited eastern cities and states to persuade farmers to move west. A special effort was made to attract immigrants, and the company's agents began to visit Europe in search of likely settlers. Much of the publicity literature was, even for that time, wildly misleading, for the land served by the Railroad was certainly not the land of milk and honey portrayed. Still the effort was very successful.

Eventually this mass migration paid off, because the land served by the Railroad did become the USA's great food-producing area. But in the short run many settlers could not pay the instalments on the land they had purchased from the Railroad, and this was perhaps the root cause of the unpopularity which the IC experienced in the 1870s among its farming clientele. But in fact the Railroad hardly deserved this unpopularity as it was, and is,

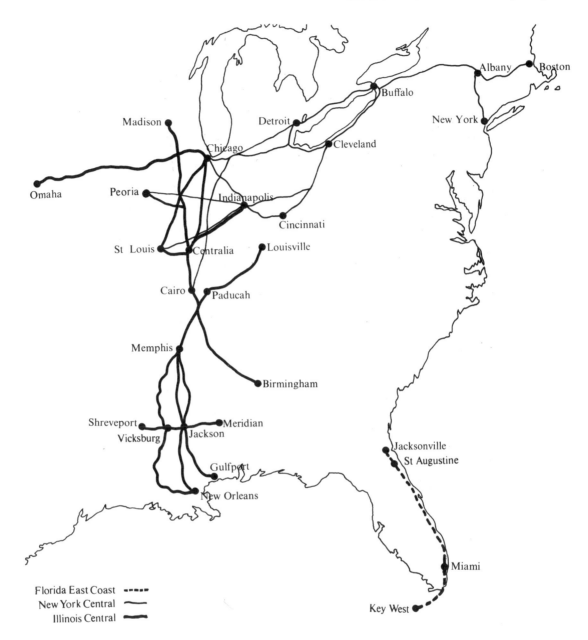

The main lines of the New York Central, Illinois Central and Florida East Coast Railroads.

more responsive than most to public opinion. It is probably the only railway to gain fame, as opposed to notoriety, from a fatal accident: the ballad about Casey Jones was written by a negro labourer in the IC roundhouse at Canton who knew Casey Jones and his engine and how Jones met his death in a collision on 30 April 1900.

One of the biggest of US railroads, the IC has often set standards for other lines. In 1856, before the advent of Pullman cars, it introduced sleeping cars. In 1881 it showed what could be done to end the inconvenience caused by the different railway gauges in the USA. Its southern main line, 880 km (547 miles) stretching south from Cairo to New Orleans, was by careful planning converted from 1,524 mm (5 ft) to standard gauge in just half a day. During World War II, finding that a quarter of its labour force had been taken into the forces, it began to recruit sixteen- and seventeen-year-olds, to whom it successfully entrusted responsible jobs like those of firemen and brakemen. In 1967, in the interest of more efficient train control, it began to instal microwave radio links all along its 1,567 km (974 mile) main line. Also in that year, impressed by the achievements of unit trains for coal traffic, it introduced what it called rent-a-train facilities for its grain shippers. Unit trains were formed exclusively for grain, with low rates charged, in a largely successful effort to bring freightcar utilization well above the rather low American norm. About the same time it offered its 'Hustler' fast freight service, in which shippers were promised a refund of the premium payment if the goods should arrive later than promised. More recently it has had some success in persuading labour unions to relax full-crew rules, making it possible to operate shorter but more frequent piggyback trains. Its workshops at Paducah have been reconstructing diesel locomotives not only for itself but for other railroads too.

Until Amtrak days, the IC ran a distinguished if diminishing number of smart passenger trains of which the *Panama Limited* was the best known. When the Depression hit the Railroad this train was one of the victims, along with the Railroad's workers, whose wages and numbers were reduced. However, in 1934 the IC felt strong enough to reintroduce the *Panama Limited*, this time with new all-Pullman air-conditioned rolling stock. It covered the 1,485 km (921 miles) from Chicago to New Orleans in 18 hours. It still operates, but is now under Amtrak auspices. As early as 1936 the Railroad introduced its first diesel streamliner, the *Green Diamond*, between Chicago and St Louis.

Like several other large US railroads, the Illinois Central is now part of a conglomerate, Illinois Central Industries, which has substantial interests in manufacturing and property. Since 1972 a new member of the conglomerate has been the IC's former competitor—the Gulf, Mobile & Ohio Railroad—which also had a main line from Chicago to New Orleans. The combined railroad, now known as Illinois Central Gulf, has 14,800 km (9,200 miles) of line and seems likely to profit from national energy policies; coal, hauled in unit trains from on-line mines, is already its most important traffic.

The Florida East Coast Railroad (USA)

American railways have tended to live through more dramatic ups and downs than their European counterparts, but exceptional even in the USA is the Florida East Coast Railroad. Conceived and built by Henry Flagler, a partner of John D. Rockefeller, the line originally ran from Jacksonville to a new hotel built by Flagler at St Augustine. This was the first, and somewhat premature, effort to develop a mass tourist trade in Florida. The line was later continued south along the eastern shore of the peninsula until Miami was reached in 1896, but the so-called Florida Boom did not start until 1924. However, Flagler was a rich and optimistic man and in 1912 he really put the FEC in the headlines with his extension to the naval base of Key West. For 206 km (128 miles) the line could call itself the 'Seagoing Railroad' because Key West was an island and the railway was built across the sea on a succession of islands, bridges and embankments over shallow water. One bridge, the Little Duck Viaduct, was 11 km (7 miles) long.

When the Florida Boom arrived, more traffic was offered than the Railroad could handle, and there was an immediate investment in double tracking the Jacksonville–Miami main line and in new locomotives and cars. This investment was completed just as the Boom collapsed, just before the Depression, just before Florida's main crop—citrus fruit—was assailed by the fruit fly, and just before a rival railroad, the Seaboard, entered Miami. In 1931 the FEC declared bankruptcy and was in the hands of the receivers until 1961. The Key West extension was converted to a highway.

Release from receivership did not imply prosperity. Receiving from other railroads at Jacksonville its daily procession of passenger trains, the FEC had an air of streamlined, dieselized modernity, but in reality it was poverty-stricken. When a national agreement on a pay rise was made between the American railroads and the unions the FEC said it could not comply. The result was one of the most protracted strikes in railroad history. Rather than submit, the FEC operated a reduced service with supervisory personnel, non-striking workers and new recruits, and soon discovered that it had suddenly become a more efficient and profitable railroad. Although the strike lasted 13 years, in the sense that it was not formally concluded until 1976, the strikers lost as soon as it became apparent that sabotage was failing to change the Railroad's attitude. This sabotage included the dynamiting of several trains, and pot-shots at train crews and passenger trains. President Kennedy urged the Railroad to give in, and neither the local police nor the FBI, according to the management, seemed to be very keen on investigating sabotage cases. All this changed when two trains were blown up when President Johnson was in the vicinity. For the sake of presidential dignity at least the FBI was compelled to intervene more actively, and sabotage came to an end.

The FEC no longer runs passenger trains. Its last service, on its daily run, was preceded by an inspection car, and its passengers, peering from behind cracked or holed windows, had their names and addresses taken by the conductor in case they were blown to pieces. The danger of passenger operation made it fairly easy for the FEC to discontinue this side of its business.

Alone among the big American railroads, the FEC runs its trains in clear disregard of the work rules laid down by the unions. One result is that to run a freight train between its two termini at Miami and Jacksonville it now uses a two-man crew, who work from about eight to eleven hours. In 1976 its crew wages for this run were $152.00. Before the strike, work rules would have obliged the company to use three 5-man crews for this train, because of the minimum-crew law and the requirement to change crews twice during the run. The corresponding wage-bill (expressed in 1976 prices) would have been $1,022.

Owned by a paper company that regards the Railroad as an investment that must pay a good dividend, the economies resulting from its independent stand have been largely ploughed back into capital investment. It has improved its track standards by widespread use of concrete cross-ties, heavy rail, and closer spacing of cross-ties. It has also abandoned the American practice of laying track with staggered rail joints. These are now in alignment, European-style, so that mechanical track laying, using pre-assembled rail and cross-tie assemblies, can be used. Because train operating costs are so reduced it has become possible to abandon the American practice (adopted mainly because of high labour costs) of running a few very heavy trains in preference to a larger number of smaller ones. This improved frequency of service has been well received by shippers and extra traffic has resulted. There has also been an improvement in freightcar utilization; the FEC freightcar averages more than 128 km (80 miles) a day compared to the US average of less than 96 (60).

With a fairly short average length of haul, and serving a region where there is little heavy industry, the FEC—if it were run like other US railroads—could be expected to be in a serious financial situation. Because it is not operated normally, only rationally, it is profitable.

Steam Locomotive Development

by J.T. van Riemsdijk
From the first locomotives of the 1800s
to the articulated locomotives of the 1950s.

Though steam locomotives have varied enormously in size, detail of design and construction, all orthodox ones have been variations on a basic pattern which took shape with the *Rocket* in 1829. The frames of the locomotive rest upon the axleboxes, or bearing blocks, of the wheels with springing provided by laminated plate or coiled springs of steel. The frames have slots in which the axleboxes can move vertically, called 'horns' or 'pedestals', and the springs of different axles may be connected by pivoted levers to 'equalize' the suspension. All locomotives have relatively large wheels, between about 1,219 mm (4 ft) and 2,133 mm (7 ft) in diameter on standard gauge, driven by the cylinders via connecting rods, wheel pairs being connected together by coupling rods. These wheels are fitted directly in the frames and provide the rigid wheelbase (small sideplay is sometimes allowed for). Most locomotives have additional carrying wheels of smaller diameter, which are not driven, and, if the loco-motive has more than six wheels, carrying wheels are arranged in a subframe providing considerable sideways movement on curves. Two-wheel subframes are arranged to swing sideways with a radial movement, with a real or theo-retical pivot nearer the centre of the locomotive. A four-wheel subframe, or bogie, can rotate about an approximately central pivot and is also provided with sideplay. These subframes are arranged with centring springs, or an equivalent device, to bring the locomotive to a central position over the track at the end of a curve, and to cushion the shock of entry into a curve so that this is not wholly borne by the leading wheels of the rigid wheelbase. All carrying wheels assist in bearing the weight of the locomotive through springs.

Most locomotives have two double-acting cylinders, which drive one pair of wheels directly, and others of the same diameter indirectly by coupling rods. The two cylinders may be outside, which means that their connecting rods work upon crank pins set in the wheel bosses, or they may be inside, in which case the driving wheels are mounted upon a cranked axle. The drive is hori-zontal or nearly so, so that the thrust is taken on the horns and does not disturb the springs. Locomotives with three or four cylinders have two outside, and one or two inside. In such cases the drive may be concentrated on one wheel pair or divided, with the inside cylinders driving a crank axle the wheels of which are coupled to those driven by the outside cylinders.

In the cylinders, steam is admitted to and exhausted from each side of the pistons in turn, by valves controlled by the valve gear. The valves may be flat 'slide' valves, working on a flat portface, or cylindrical 'piston' valves work-ing within a cylindrical portface. Both these types of valve reciprocate at the same rate as the piston, though with a smaller travel. Poppet valves rising and falling upon seatings, usually four per cylinder, are sometimes found in modern locomotives. The valve gear makes it possible to change the valve timing for reversing, and also for early cut-off of the steam supply, to allow it to do work in the cylinder by expansion, which is essential for economical working. Each cylinder has a 'steam chest' within which the valves work.

The boiler has a horizontal barrel and is supported upon the frame. At the rear end is the firebox, which is within the boiler, surrounded by water walls, with a grate at the bottom and an ashpan provided with air inlets and dampers below. The firing hole, in the boiler back, is covered by a firedoor. The front upper part of the firebox is a tubeplate, from which some 200 tubes lead the fire forward through the barrel to the smokebox. Between the fire itself, on the grate, and the tubeplate, the firebox is divided by a brick arch extending about two thirds of the way to the back of the box, and sloping gently upwards. The fire has to pass round this to reach the tubeplate, and this equalizes the draught

Previous pages: *Despite early electrification, Switzerland has a flourishing locomotive industry and an individual style of design. Some representatives of this style can still be seen in active service on special excursions or on the several Swiss steam tourist railways. The picture shows locomotive No. 1 at work on the Sensetalbahn near Laupen, where steam traction may be seen twice a month during summer.*

in the tubes, improves combustion by turbulence, provides for mixing in of extra air from the firehole, and takes the flames close to the walls of the box. The water walls of the firebox are prevented from bursting under pressure by a large number of stays joining the inner and outer plates.

In the smokebox, the exhaust pipe (or blastpipe) stands upright below the chimney, and each blast of exhaust produces a partial vacuum which draws the fire through the boiler. There is also a 'blower', usually a ring of fine steam jets surrounding the blastpipe, which can be used to draw the fire when the engine is standing, or running with steam off.

In a superheated locomotive, steam from the boiler is passed through a number of small tubes lying within extra large boiler firetubes known as superheater flues. The steam reaches the cylinders at a higher temperature than possible within the boiler at its correct working pressure, and this results in important economies in fuel and water. Locomotives without superheaters use 'saturated' steam.

The controls of a steam locomotive are the main steam valve, or regulator (throttle), the valve gear control and the brake. In addition there are boiler fittings, such as live and exhaust steam injectors, or a feed pump, for maintaining the water level; water-level gauges; the blower; safety valves, and other valves used in connection with boiler cleaning. Pressure gauges are provided for boiler pressure and sometimes for steam-chest pressure. They are also needed for the brakes and the steam heating apparatus for the train, if fitted. Lubricators are fitted at various parts of the locomotive, and those for the cylinders are sometimes in the cab, under the driver's eye. The brakes may be steam, air or vacuum operated, or a combination. Steam brakes are only applied to the wheels of the locomotive, but air or vacuum may be used in the train as well. The brakes are cast-iron (in early days, wood) blocks pressed against the wheel treads.

Tank locomotives carry supplies of fuel and water on the main frame. Other locomotives have separate tenders coupled more or less permanently to them carrying larger supplies to give them a longer range or a longer period of continuous working.

The steam locomotive is unlike any other machine in one remarkable respect. Its various elements all interact, rather as they do in the body of an animal. The performance of the engine affects that of the boiler, via the action of the blast; with the result that the same boiler will perform differently when mounted on a chassis of different design. The engine part directly affects the behaviour of the locomotive as a vehicle on the track; and behaviour on the track has an influence on performance of the boiler, by the degree of disturbance produced to the fire. It is impossible, therefore, to determine the performance of the various elements by testing them separately. This interaction makes locomotives more powerful when running on the track than when running on rollers in a testing plant. In a diesel-electric locomotive, the diesel engine, generator, and traction motors can all be tested independently. Their performance is not affected by their combination in a moving vehicle.

Some of the many important details of the steam locomotive should be briefly described. The two most important types of valve gear are Stephenson's link motion and Walschaert's valve gear. In the link motion, much the more common before 1900, each valve is controlled by two eccentrics whose movements are combined by a slotted link, from a point on which the drive to the valve is taken. By moving the link relative to the die block (which actually takes the movement to the valve), forward or reverse running is possible according to which eccentric is more influential. Intermediate positions give advanced timing and reduced valve travel to bring about earlier 'cut off' and more economical working at speed. Walschaerts valve gear, a Belgian invention, uses one eccentric (or, if outside, an equivalent 'return crank') which oscillates a centrally pivoted slotted link, from either end of which the drive to the valve can be taken. This drive is combined with a movement derived from the piston to provide a constant advance of the timing independent of the shortening of the valve travel at the link, necessary for early 'cut off'.

Feeding of water into the boiler is usually continuous. Originally done by axle-driven pumps, it was later most commonly achieved by injectors, either using live steam from the boiler or exhaust steam extracted from the blastpipe. The injector is a system of cones through which steam and water pass in a continuous stream. It was invented by Henri Giffard in 1859 and has been greatly developed subsequently. Its operating principle is a matter of advanced physical science and cannot be briefly summarized. It involves conversion of the latent heat of steam into kinetic energy by condensation. Steam-operated feed pumps were used in recent years on most European and American locomotives, in conjunction with feed water-heaters deriving the heat from exhaust steam. Generally, these produced only marginally greater savings than exhaust steam injectors but they were rather more dependable.

For high-powered locomotives, hand-firing of coal is not practicable. Mechanical stokers were, therefore, adopted in America and for the largest locomotives in Europe and elsewhere. Most types were of American design. Coal was moved, usually by a screw conveyor, from the tender to a platform within the rear of the firebox, from which it was directed on to the grate by steam jets adjustable by the fireman. Oil firing, using jets of oil atomized by steam, was also common in the United States and Russia, and other countries where oil was cheap. Wood, for so long the staple diet of early American locomotives before 1880 was always hand-fired. It remains in use in a few places as do a variety of waste materials which can be economically burnt in a locomotive firebox on industrial or agricultural railways.

The steam locomotive required vast quantities of water, delivered to its tender or tanks through large standpipes or water cranes. In Europe and especially in Britain (where, curiously, the world's longest non-stop run of nearly 400 miles (640 km) was daily performed by Gresley's LNER Pacifics), water was picked up at speed by a scoop dipping into a trough between the rails. The quality of water available on various routes was a very important factor in boiler design. Water-softening plants were often necessary, and the French railways adopted a continuous water treatment system on the locomotive itself.

The first steam locomotive

Penydarran, produced by Richard Trevithick in 1804, was his second engine and the first to pull a train successfully. His subsequent experiments ended with *Catch me who can*, which pulled a coach on a circular track in North London in 1808 and gave, for the first time, the opportunity of buying a railway ticket to ride behind a locomotive. As railways, using horses or steam power with cable traction, were already fairly commonly found at the beginning of the 19th century, on private industrial sites, somebody was bound to produce a self-propelling steam engine for them before long. However, Trevithick had introduced the use of 'strong' steam (steam at a pressure well above that of the atmosphere—in fact, as much as four times as

The last operator of the large Mallet-type articulated steam locomotive was the Indonesian State Railways. With its high power, flexible wheelbase and moderate axle weight it was very suitable for the long mountainous branch lines of southern Java. No. CC5017 is a 2-6-6-0 built in Germany to an American Design. Here it is shown near Tjitchalenka with a mixed train.

SUPERHEATED STEAM LOCOMOTIVE
Sectioned diagram of Southern Railway (UK) 3 cylinder Schools class 4-4-0 locomotive

The source of power is the fire burning on the grate (**43**). Air for combustion enters the ashpan (**44**) through damper doors (**42**). Coal is fired (by hand shovel in this small locomotive) through the firedoor (**23**) which also admits a little warmed air. A deflector plate (**21**) prevents cold air entering the tubes when the door is open.The fire passes round the brick arch (**16**) and through the fire tubes (**10**) and superheater flues (**9**), drawn by the suction effect of exhaust steam passing from the blastpipe (**3**) to the chimney. If the engine is not working, steam jets from the blower ring (**4**)

produce the suction. The firebox crown sheet (**15**) and other flat surfaces are tied to the boiler shell by stays (**18**) and the whole boiler is lagged (**11**). The regulator handle (**22**) operates the main steam valve (**12**) in the dome. There is a 'steam stand' or 'fountain' (**20**) supplied by a collector pipe (**14**), from which steam is taken for auxiliaries, such as the injector (**48**) for feeding water to the boiler, and the vacuum brake ejectors working the locomotive brake cylinder (**47**) and the train brakes via the train pipe connections (**1**) at both ends of the locomotive. Steam is also taken for train heating via a reducing valve, to heating hose connectors (**24**) at both ends, and for the whistle (**19**). There are two safety valves (**17**).

When the locomotive is working, steam from the regulator valve (**12**) passes to the saturated or 'wet' steam header (**7**) of the superheater, then through numerous small pipes or 'elements' to the superheated

water

saturated steam

superheated steam

exhaust (expanded) steam

steam header (**5**). In each element, the steam makes four passes along the flue, the element having three 'return bends' (**8, 13**). A 'snifting valve' (**6**) on the wet steam header allows the elements to be cooled by air drawn in when the engine is coasting with the regulator valve shut.

Steam enters all three cylinders (only the middle one is shown) via two-headed piston valves (**26**) moved backwards and forwards by the Walschaert valve gear, which derives its motion from a single eccentric (**38**) and the crosshead (**33**), which is the junction of the piston rod (**30**) and the connecting rod (**39**) and is guided by slide bars (**32**). The connecting rod drives a crank (**41**) incorporated in the driving axle (**40**). The motion from the eccentric is taken forward by the eccentric rod (**37**) to the expansion link (**36**) which is pivoted in the middle. From this the radius rod (**34**) takes a movement variable in amount and also

reversible, because its connection to the slotted link can be shifted up and down by the driver, via a lifting link and a 'weightshaft' (**35**). The radius rod movement is combined with that of the crosshead by a combination lever (**28**) connected through the union link (**31**). The resulting movements of the valves allow the running in either direction and for expansive working. Valve and piston rods enter steam chests and cylinders through steamtight glands (**27**).

The brake shoes (**45**) are connected to the brake cylinder (**47**) by beams and rods, known as brake rigging. The driving and coupled wheels are sprung with laminated plate springs (**46**), while the bogie has coil springs (**25**). In addition to pivoting at its centre, the bogie can move sideways controlled by transverse springs (**29**).

Deflector plates (**2**) at the front of the locomotive help to lift exhaust steam clear of the cab windows.

hot gases, smoke etc.

air to grate

CITY OF CARLISLE

46238

Above: *The front end of one of the New South Wales Government Railways' class 38 Pacifics. These locomotives, designed and built in Australia, hauled the main passenger trains until dieselization.*

Below: *A class 051 locomotive near Neuenmarkt in West Germany. The 2-10-0 was a favourite wheel arrangement for German freight engines, and many examples of the type are still used in East Germany.*

Below: *Narrow-guage 0-8-0 locomotives can still be seen in the Gmünd area of Austria.*
Bottom: *On the Indian metre gauge a 4-6-2 and 2-8-2 halt in Agra while their train is watered.*

great). This made it possible to dispense with condensing, without which Newcomen- or Watt-type engines could not operate. This, in turn, made the engine lighter, as did the high pressure in itself, and opened the possibility of the self-propelling machine, which Trevithick quickly exploited.

The Penydarran locomotive proved able to haul 25 tonnes along a 14 km (9 mile) railway and back again without taking water on the way. It could climb the 1 in 36 gradient on the line and normally ran at 8 km/h (5 mph). It had a single, double-acting, cylinder driving the wheels on one side through gearing giving a slight reduction of wheel speed. The boiler was cylindrical, with a single U-shape flue having the firegrate in one end and the chimney at the other. Trevithick found that when the exhaust (which passed through a silencer) was turned upwards in the chimney, it made the fire burn harder, and this observation was of the highest importance, because virtually every subsequent successful steam locomotive depended on this effect.

In 1812, the first commercially successful locomotives were constructed by Matthew Murray for John Blenkinsop, to work on the Middleton Railway near Leeds. Blenkinsop felt that a proper grip for traction was possible only if the rails had teeth and the locomotive had a gearwheel engaging with them. The four locomotives originally built were the forerunners of the many rack locomotives used on mountain lines all over the world. They were also the first to have two double-acting cylinders driving cranks phased at 90 degrees to ensure positive self-starting—always the most common arrangement for steam locomotives. They could haul 100 tonnes at 5–6 km/h (3½ mph), replaced fifty horses and put 200 men out of work. The last went in 1834.

William Hedley, viewer (or manager) of the Wylam colliery on the Tyne, built *Puffing Billy* in 1813 after experiments carefully planned to establish whether a smooth wheel on a smooth rail would provide sufficient grip to enable a locomotive to haul a train on all but the severest gradients. *Puffing Billy*, with the similar *Wylam Dilly* and *Lady Mary*, were the first successful adhesion locomotives and remained in service until 1861. They had Trevithick-type boilers, and their two cylinders drove the wheels through beams, rods, cranks, and gearing of considerable complication. Perhaps their low-operating speed (walking pace) and moderate loading (50 tonne trains) contributed to their remarkable longevity. Two are preserved in museums in Britain.

George Stephenson's first locomotive, the *Blucher*, appeared in the middle of 1814. It had vertical cylinders, set one behind the other in the boiler, their piston rods working upwards to connecting rods down each side of the engine. The final drive from the cranks to the wheels was by gearing. Though very like Blenkinsop's engines in general layout, it was an adhesion machine and at one time had a chain drive to the front tender wheels to increase its grip. Stephenson experimented a great deal in the next ten years. In fact, almost all the work of developing the steam locomotive to a thoroughly practical machine was done by Stephenson in this period. He experimented with coupling the wheels by chains, conceived inside crank axles and inside coupling rods, and eventually adopted the outside coupling rods later standard on steam and many electric and diesel locomotives. He built perhaps a dozen locomotives and was established as the leading railway engineer by the time the Stockton & Darlington Railway was proposed.

The Stockton & Darlington was a public railway, surveyed and built by Stephenson, which used steam locomotives for some of its traffic from the beginning. Its opening in 1825 is commonly regarded as the beginning of railways as a public transportation system. The locomotive *Locomotion* built

One of the final haunts of steam traction in South America, the Salta to Socompa line in northern Argentina is a winding and mountainous route. Part of the General Belgrano Railway, it is metre gauge and runs through the Andes to the Chilean border. The picture shows a 2-10-2, of a class built in the USA and Czechoslovakia, making a sturdy effort with a freight train.

by Stephenson for the opening was distinguished by the use of outside coupling rods, but was otherwise much like most of its predecessors, with rather elaborate driving gear, the cylinders being sunk in the boiler top as in the Middleton engines. It had a single flue, not doubled back. It was essentially a freight locomotive: such a boiler could not generate steam fast enough for rapid travel. Stephenson himself was, by this time, more concerned with the civil engineering of railways than with locomotives, and recommended Timothy Hackworth, who had helped to build *Puffing Billy*, for the job of looking after the Stockton & Darlington locomotives, while his own son, Robert Stephenson, took a major part in the development of locomotive building for other lines.

The *Rocket*

The *Rocket*, built by Stephenson, was the successful entry in the Rainhill trials held in 1829 prior to the opening of the Liverpool & Manchester Railway.

The *Rocket* incorporated a boiler proposed by Henry Booth, secretary of the Liverpool & Manchester company, having 25 small firetubes instead of one large one. (At the same moment in history, Marc Séguin of the St Etienne to Lyon railway in France was fitting a boiler with a large number of small fire-tubes to a locomotive of earlier Stephenson type and, thereby, enormously increasing its steam-raising capacity.) The *Rocket* had an external firebox at the rear of the boiler barrel, with water-jacketed sides and top. The fire was drawn through the tubes by the action of the exhaust steam—following Trevithick—the two upturned blast nozzles in the base of the long chimney having slight constrictions to increase the intensity of the action. This feature may have been copied from Hackworth's *Sans Pareil*.

Another distinguishing feature of the *Rocket* was the direct drive from two outside cylinders on to crankpins in the wheels. All the essentials of the later steam locomotive were there, and the proportions of boiler, cylinders and wheels were notably good, so that this engine could reach 58 km/h (36 mph) in its original form and over 80 km/h (50 mph) when the cylinders were lowered to a less steeply-inclined position.

The frames of *Rocket* consisted of a few iron bars and the cylinders were 'outside' and inclined. These features were to become characteristic of the first successful and distinctly American type, the 4-2-0, especially as built by Norris of Philadelphia, and bar frames, in a highly developed form, were to remain standard practice in America throughout the history of the steam locomotive. Their derivation from *Rocket* may be traced through the designs of Edward Bury and his partner, Kennedy. Bury was engineer to the London & Birmingham Railway in the late 1830s and early 1840s. In 1830, he and Kennedy had built a four-wheeled coupled engine named *Liverpool* which had a cranked axle and inside cylinders and, therefore, a firebox overhanging at the rear. It also had bar framing. The firebox was more or less a vertical cylinder joined to the barrel at right angles. It was not wholly circular in plan, because it was flat at the front to accommodate the firebox tubeplate. It was sur-mounted by a hemispherical top which acted as the steam dome—not at all an easy thing to make in those days.

After his appointment in 1837 to the London & Birmingham Railway, Bury populated that line with his small four-wheel types with bar frames, 'haystack' fireboxes (that is, D-shaped fireboxes with hemispherical casing and top), and a tight coupling between engine and tender to counter the inherent unsteadiness of a four-wheel vehicle. These locomotives were really too small both for the

*George Stephenson
(1781–1848).*

*Edward Bury
(1794–1858).*

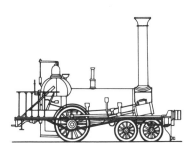

Top: *Stephenson's* Rocket *of 1829, with its wooden tender. Wood was also used for other parts, including the boiler lagging and buffer beam. Outside cylinders and bar frames were used.*
Centre: *Early examples of the inside-cylinder layout were the small bar-framed engines built by Edward Bury for the London & Birmingham Railway in the late 1830s. The raised, so-called 'haystack', firebox was another feature of these machines.*
Bottom: *The Norris 4-2-0 of 1839 showed the influence of Stephenson and Bury, but was nevertheless an original concept. It did well in its native America, and was also built for some European railways.*

London & Birmingham and for other lines which bought them, and a 'battle of the wheels' ensued as Bury's competitors advertised the advantages of their more advanced six-wheel designs. On the London & Birmingham, Bury had often to use three or four of his locomotives to haul one train, and once used seven (but that, he claimed, was in a strong wind). Bury's factory was noted for its fine workmanship, and this reputation helped to maintain the success of its undersized 2-2-0 passenger and 0-4-0 freight locomotives for several years after they were outclassed by competing designs.

It was Bury's locomotives exported to the USA which popularized the bar frame in that country; in Britain the bar frame was abandoned after the 1860s and had never been widespread after the early years. The British regarded the bar frame as technically inferior to the plate frame. It lent itself less easily to the attachment of cylinders, buffer beams and cross-bracing. But plate frames demanded a higher level of engineering skill, and this was not available in mid-century America. Iron bars resembled timber beams and were therefore more easily understood by American workers. Moreover, American rolling mills were capable of rolling bars, but not plates of the large size required. American technicians of that time worked to standards of accuracy that were insufficient for the precise erection of plate frames. It seems likely, too, that Bury's bar frames responded more favourably to the rough track of the American railroads.

The Norris locomotive, which for a time had great success not only in its native America but also in European markets, was virtually a Bury locomotive in which the cylinders were placed outside the frames and in which a leading four-wheel truck replaced the leading axle of the Bury design. The Norris 4-2-0 locomotive was even ordered by a British company, the Birmingham & Gloucester Railway, which used several units on its main line over the celebrated Lickey Incline. This did not please Bury, who in 1841 personally drove one of his own locomotives up the Lickey in competition with a Norris machine. In this contest the American locomotive came out well ahead, and Bury made loud accusations of foul play. These accusations were probably justified, for the Norris brothers were known to operate their locomotives in excess of their rated boiler pressure.

Early American locomotives

Although for a time the Norris factory, founded in 1830, was the most prolific American locomotive builder, the Norris brothers were hardly pioneers. They had been preceded by several less successful builders in the USA. Some of these built one experimental locomotive and then disappeared from view while others finished their careers as locomotive engineers with the new railway companies. The Americans, like the French, imported a few locomotives of the pre-*Rocket* type from England, but then began to produce their own designs. The first full-size American locomotive was the *Tom Thumb*. This was constructed by Peter Cooper, a Baltimore merchant who was a devoted champion of the steam railway. It had one cylinder, and a vertical boiler whose firetubes were musket barrels. It could produce $1\frac{1}{2}$hp, and was intended to demonstrate to the infant Baltimore & Ohio Railroad that steam traction was practical. The B & O tried it, and a race was organized against a horse. The horse won, but the Railroad's directors were nevertheless persuaded that steam had a future. In 1831 the Railroad organized a steam locomotive contest, and the winner was the *York*, built by a Pennsylvanian watchmaker, Phineas Davis. This locomotive had a large vertical boiler, weighed $3\frac{1}{2}$ tonnes, and ran on four wheels of 762mm (30in) diameter.

The first US locomotive to operate on a regular schedule was *The Best Friend of Charleston*, another vertical-boiler design, built in 1830 for the South Carolina Railroad by the West Point Foundry of New York. The design was largely the work of Horatio Allen who, earlier, had visited England as chief engineer of the Delaware & Hudson Railroad. In England he bought several locomotives, of which one, the *Stourbridge Lion*, was the first steam locomotive to run on a US commercial railroad. This was in 1829, when the machine was driven by Allen himself. However, Allen discovered that he had purchased a machine far too heavy for the wooden rails of his line, and for this reason the *Stourbridge Lion* was not a success. Allen was also, apparently, the first engineer to attempt a locomotive headlight; up to 1837 trains did not move at night in the USA, but in that year Allen placed a flatcar in front of one of his locomotives, on which a bonfire was kept brightly burning. The previous year he designed three articulated locomotives for his South Carolina Railroad. These were 2-2 + 2-2 machines with two pairs of narrow boilers back-to-back, each pair supplying one cylinder and having a common firebox and smokebox.

Lack of manufacturing capacity as well as the need to acquire the latest technology caused the USA to import over 100 locomotives from Britain between 1829 and 1841. In 1831 the Stephenson locomotive *John Bull* arrived for the Camden & Amboy Railroad, being re-assembled by Isaac Dripps. From his experience with Stephenson technology, Dripps went on to innovate on his own account. He successfully experimented with spark-arresting chimneys, so necessary with wood-burning locomotives in summer and autumn operation. In 1836 he built a massive 0-8-0, aptly named *Monster*, whose coupled wheels were in two groups connected by gearing.

The re-assembly of *John Bull* had been observed by Matthias Baldwin, a former jeweller of Philadelphia, who built his own locomotive, *Old Ironsides*, in 1832 for the nearby Germantown and Norristown Railroad. *Old Ironsides* was based on a more up-to-date Stephenson design but due to Baldwin's lack of experience, and the primitive manufacturing conditions, it was not a complete success. However, it did work, and made money for its owners. Baldwin received orders from other railroad companies that were starting to operate, and in due course the Baldwin Locomotive Works became one of the world's best-known locomotive manufacturers. The one-time chief competitor of Baldwin, the Norris Works, went out of business in 1869. The Norris brothers had always been more interested in making fast money than in perfecting technology, and the few innovations they introduced tended to be superficially attractive without adding much of value. Moreover, their manufacturing standards were not high, and their locomotives were frequent victims of boiler explosions. Baldwin, on the other hand, introduced several manufacturing innovations which improved the constructional standards of his locomotives. So although his design innovations were not very significant, his products were both cheap to build and of reliable construction.

Stephensons, having constructed a few locomotives like *Rocket*, but with more and smaller boiler tubes, enlarged the type slightly and incorporated the water-jacketed firebox within the boiler shell, producing the *Northumbrian* type. They then adopted inside cylinders, in the bottom of the smokebox, driving on to a cranked rear axle just ahead of the firebox (the *Planet* type), and expanded this into a six wheeler by adding an extra axle behind the firebox. Four- and six-wheel engines of this type were exported to America where most were eventually rebuilt. The short-wheelbase engines were perfectly satisfactory on the finely-engineered railways of Britain, where tracks were well aligned and supported, but they rode very badly on the light and usually irregular metals of the undercapitalized American pioneer railroads. These inside-cylinder engines did not have the bar framing of *Rocket*, but a much more rigid system of plate and wood beam frames, generally six in number— outside the wheels, inside the wheels, and inside each crank of the driving axle—to give the maximum support to the crank axle, which was liable to fracture. The rigidity of such machines proving unsuitable for American conditions, the American solution was the 4-2-0.

The first 4-2-0 was designed by John B. Jervis and built at the West Point Foundry in 1832. Originally planned as an anthracite burner, and unsuccessful in that respect, it was soon altered to burn wood, and in that form it had a boiler of Stephenson type, inside cylinders in the bottom of the smokebox (which was widened to accommodate them because they were spread as wide apart as possible) driving a cranked axle at the rear of the firebox. The connecting rods passed on each side of the firebox. The front end of the engine was carried on a pivoted bogie having four wheels. The long wheelbase and three-point support enabled the engine to ride steadily on twisting track, and the rotating bogie allowed it to take sharp curves easily. It was a success. Many of the imported engines were rebuilt to a similar plan. The one weakness was lack of weight on the driving wheels and this was remedied in the classic design by bringing the driving axle ahead of the firebox, but, as the cylinders were outside, the driving axle did not need to be far forward to provide clearance for the cranks and big ends in front of the firebox.

The 4-2-0 type was an excellent machine of robust and simple construction and was soon being exported to Europe. The reign of this wheel arrangement was short. These engines weighed between 7 and 10 tonnes, which soon proved insufficient. Around the year 1840, two-thirds of all locomotives in America were 4-2-0s; a couple of years later they ceased to be built, having given way to the 4-4-0. The first American 4-4-0, by Henry Campbell of the Philadelphia, Germantown & Norristown Railway, was completed in 1837. It was nothing more or less than a Stephenson *Patentee* type 2-2-2, but with the rear axle coupled to the driving axle and a four-wheel swivelling truck in place of the leading axle. While it enjoyed the advantage of extra weight on the drivers, it was still almost as rigid as the English engines and was apt to derail. The true American 4-4-0 appeared in the next two years and was essentially the 4-2-0 with a second coupled axle behind the firebox. The suspension of the four driving wheels was equalized—a vital feature for American tracks—due to the work of Eastwick and Harrison though its origins were in England. This preserved the three-point support of the 4-2-0s. The leading coupled wheels were without flanges because the bogies could only rotate and had no side play.

These early 4-4-0s mostly had Bury- or Stephenson-type boilers, inclined cylinders and short-wheelbase bogies. They were very lightly built, weighing between 15 and 25 tonnes, but the suspension and perhaps the none-too-smooth surfaces of the iron rails and tyres enabled them to pull very heavy loads at low speeds. The early ones were known to pull 400 tonne freight trains at 16 km/h (10 mph) or thereabouts, as well as light passenger trains at 30 to 50 km/h (20 to 30 mph). This versatility ensured a very long life for the 4-4-0 type in America and it undoubtedly remained numerically predominant throughout the 19th century, though progressively superseded for freight work from about 1870. Around 1850, the type changed considerably in appearance. The cylinders came down to a horizontal position, and the bogie in consequence was greatly lengthened, while the boiler barrel became sharply tapered at the rear to fit a greatly enlarged or 'wagon top' firebox.

William Mason of Taunton, Mass., did most to bring the American 4-4-0 to its classical perfection. Beginning in 1853, he constructed a long line of 4-4-0s that were meticulously designed and built. Components were planed and shaped so that they would fit snugly without caulking. Boring was so exact that bolts fitted tight and stayed tight. Leading trucks were of lengthened wheelbase, contributing to stability and appearance. Cylinders were mounted horizontally. Boilers were attached to cylinders and frames by means of his smokebox saddle. Although the American 4-4-0 survived beyond the mid-twentieth century, its finest moment was perhaps the exploit of No. 999 of the New York Central Railroad. This machine, built by the Scotsman William Buchanan, had 7 ft 2 in (2,184 mm) driving wheels and in 1893 won fame by hauling the *Empire State Express* at a claimed speed of 112 mph (180 km/h).

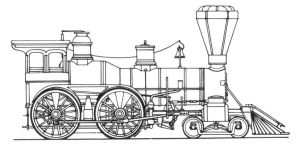

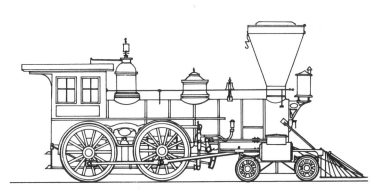

Top: *An early example of the American 4-4-0, which became popular in the 1840s. Tall spark-arrestors were a feature of American locomotives, which usually used wood fuel.*
Centre: *A later development of the American type. This locomotive, built by Danforth Cooke in 1857, has the longer wheelbase for the leading truck, first introduced by the Rogers Works. This arrangement allowed the culinders to be lowered and fixed horizontally. A 'wagon-top' boiler is also fitted.*
Bottom: *Also built in 1857 was this 4-4-0 for the Toledo and Illinois Railroad, which retains the parallel boiler.*

Stephensons' *Patentee* and long-boiler designs

The Stephenson *Planet* type and its 2-2-2 derivative, the *Patentee*, were enormously influential in Britain. Locomotives with framing outside as well as inside the wheels continued to be built for something like 70 years, and even longer on the Great Western. In the middle of the 19th century, 2-2-2s of *Patentee* type, built by British or Continental builders, were found all over Europe.

The double-framed six-wheel engine was not only built as a 2-2-2. Coupling the last pair of axles produced the 2-4-0, originally built for freight work, but later very popular as an express engine. The 0-4-2 was an alternative for slow service, and the 0-6-0 was soon preferred for the heaviest freight. All these types were really the same, with cylinders under the smokebox driving on to a central cranked axle, the motion work occupying the space between the

frames in the front half, while the space between the second and third axles was occupied by the firebox.

Perhaps the greatest exponent of this type of machine was Matthew Kirtley of the Midland Railway, who steadily developed it from the mid 1840s to the 1870s. In this period the quality of iron improved and, in the end, steel began to be available, both for the locomotive and for the track. Kirtley's designs were subtly improved to exploit the better materials and in his last express 2-4-0s he finally dispensed with the outside frames: he felt that the crank axle was at last wholly dependable. To Kirtley also must go the credit for the simplest provision for burning coal instead of coke as previously preferred in locomotive fireboxes. Under his direction, Charles Markham evolved the brick arch in the firebox and the extra supply of air via the fireman's door (additional to that coming through the grate) which were copied universally.

The double-frame 2-4-0 was provided with a leading bogie in a few cases, though the general popularity of the 4-4-0 in Britain came after the heyday of double framing, at a time when engineering materials made it unnecessary. Large numbers of such 4-4-0s were exported to Holland, and were excellent machines which lasted till the end of steam; Holland even saw the ultimate extension of the type into a 4-4-2. The Great Western Railway prolonged the type as a result of the broad gauge of 2,133 mm (7 ft) which Brunel had adopted and which lasted into the 1890s. For this gauge, Stephensons had built a large *Patentee* named *North Star*, the best of the early GWR engines. When Daniel Gooch took charge of the locomotive affairs he built a class of enlarged *North Stars* and then, from 1847, produced a very remarkable 4-2-2 version.

In 1841 the Stephenson Company patented its 'long boiler' locomotive. Although the name only refers to the boiler, this type was totally different from

In the mid-19th century a specifically French style of locomotive design emerged. A well-known example is the 'single' type designed by Polonceau for the Paris–Orléans Railway in 1854. Fast, yet substantially built, some of these engines lasted into this century.

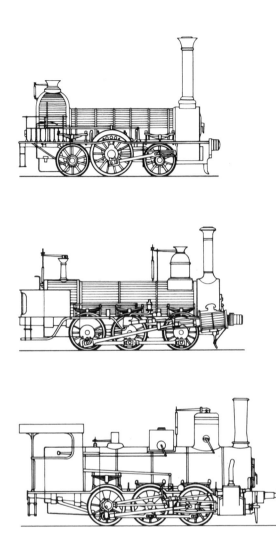

Top: *Stephenson's 'long boiler' type appeared in the early 1840s. This had the firebox and smokebox overhanging the rather short wheelbase, causing some instability at high speeds.*
Centre: *A French example of the 'long boiler' type, this was built for the Paris–St Germain Railway in 1849. Although designed for comparatively slow freight service, this design evidently suffered from stability problems, for in due course a pair of trailing wheels was added, changing it from an 0-6-0 into an 0-6-2.*
Bottom: *A later and more sophisticated version of the 'long boiler' freight locomotive was this 0-6-0 designed by Gölsdorf for Austrian railways. Intended for slow services over hilly and curving track, this locomotive's short wheelbase was an advantage on the more tortuous sections and little handicap at the speeds demanded by freight operations.*

their previous productions in other important ways. The long-boiler barrel lay above all three axles, with the firebox overhanging at the rear as in Bury's locomotives and the Norris 4-2-0. The smokebox was well forward at the front, in line with the cylinders which were outside and drove on to the central wheels. Although some were built with inside cylinders, the true long-boiler type was not, and in the absence of a crank axle inside plate frames sufficed.

The reason for this design was to absorb more of the heat of the fire in the long firetubes. The short-barreled *Patentee* type, when worked hard, was known to throw flames from the chimney, and often ran with the lower part of the smokebox front red hot. The short wheelbase and the large overhang of the weighty firebox at one end, and the cylinders at the other, made this design unstable at speed, and as a 2-2-2 it enjoyed a very short vogue. But as a six-coupled freight engine it became immensely popular on the continent of Europe. Usually known as the 'Bourbonnais' type, because of its particular early association with one route in France, it proved the ideal freight engine of the mid-19th century, and many lasted till the end of steam because they were able to negotiate sharp curves in factory or dockland goods yards. In Britain, the long wheelbase 0-6-0 was preferred.

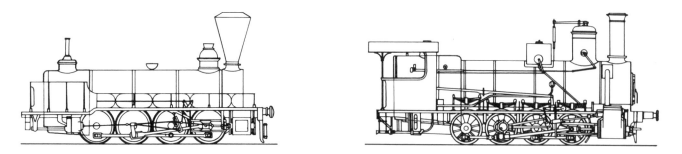

There were two notable Continental derivatives of the six-wheel long-boiler locomotive. One was the equivalent 0-8-0 of which the first example was the *Wien Raab* built at Vienna by John Haswell, one of the most distinguished of the British expatriate engineers who developed railway systems overseas, exhibited in 1855 and bought by the French Midi Railway. This was the prototype of the classic European heavy freight loco. Another was the long-boiler 2-4-0, which was especially popular in France, and as speeds increased evolved into a 2-4-2. Many French 2-4-2s were large and powerful machines, and the type was the mainstay of the express services of the Paris, Lyon & Méditerranée, and of the Paris–Orléans railways for many years.

The finest were undoubtedly the PO engines designed by Victor Forquenot, some of which were still working light fast trains in the early 1950s, when around 80 years old. Their outside cylinders had slide valves on top, worked by external Gooch link motion, which gave unusually regular and precise valve timing. Some of these engines were rebuilt as two-cylinder compound 4-4-2s, involving provision of a leading bogie, and the long-boiler concept must be considered as underlying the development of the 4-4-2 or 'Atlantic' type, which appeared in Europe with a narrow firebox at about the time of its emergence in America in the middle 1890s.

Another British development of the locomotive which achieved greater success on the Continent than in Britain was T. R. Crampton's high-speed design, in which the large driving wheels were placed at the rear, their high axle being behind the boiler backplate. Unlike the original Jervis 4-2-0 it had cylinders outside and valve gearing worked by eccentrics mounted on the crankpins. The front of the engine was carried on four, or, in a few cases, six smaller wheels and the whole wheelbase was rigid. The idea was that in this arrangement the boiler could be placed very low down, to the benefit of stability. The weakness of the design was the small proportion of total engine weight that could be borne by the driving wheels.

By the 1870s, the essential features of American locomotive design had long been stabilized along the lines described above. On the continent of Europe, there was some following of British patterns but for the most part outside cylinders and inside frames were preferred. The French favoured the long-boiler pattern and its derivatives. The Germans made great use of the 2-4-0 for passenger service in a layout combining outside cylinders overhanging the front wheels and a long coupled wheelbase embracing the firebox.

In Britain, inside cylinders were almost the rule. Two of the greatest designers, William Adams and Patrick Stirling, did persist with the use of outside cylinders for the largest locomotives until they both retired in the middle 1890s. Their locomotives, moreover, were probably the best in the country and Adams especially can now be seen as a truly progressive designer. The

Above left: *The large freight locomotive was introduced to Europe by John Haswell, a Briton employed at the Vienna railway workshops. His prototype, soon imitated by other railways, was this long boiler 0-8-0,* Wien Raab, *which he built in 1855.*

Above: *Fifteen years after the appearance of* Wien Raab, *the Austrian workshops were building much larger derivatives of the design. This example was typical of the large European 0-8-0 of the late 19th century, some of which survived into the 1950s.*

Top: *An early German example of the 'long boiler' type, built at Hannover in 1848. Of the 2-4-0 wheel arrangement, this was also an early example of the 'mixed traffic' locomotive, suitable for both freight and passenger trains of moderate speed. Apparently at the speeds then current this design was not troubled by stability problems.*

Centre: *Adding an extra axle was an obvious solution for the stability problems of 'long-boiler' locomotives. The British designer Robert Sinclair chose to add a pair of carrying wheels beneath the firebox in this passenger locomotive he built in 1860 for the Grand Luxembourg Railway. The 2-4-2 wheel arrangement later became very popular in some countries, especially France.*

Bottom: *Also in the 'long boiler' line of development was this 2-4-0 fast passenger design by V Forquenot of the Paris–Orléans Railway. However, the design was soon modified, becoming a 2-4-2 which was oustandingly successful and which was still in service after World War II.*

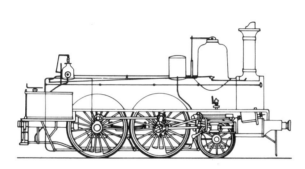

earlier tradition of Crewe design was due to W. Buddicom, who later worked in France, and involved the use of outside cylinders fixed between the plate frames in which the driving axles were located, and outer plate frames carrying the axleboxes of the small leading wheels. Later Crewe-built 2-2-2 express engines with outside cylinders, Ramsbottom's *Lady of the Lake* or *Problem* class, had single inside frames, but Crewe abandoned outside cylinders, except for the long series of Webb compound locomotives, after Webb succeeded Ramsbottom in 1871.

Between the complete multiple-frame arrangement, as exemplified in Kirtley's Midland Railway engines, and the single inside-frame arrangement, there were various mixtures of style. The most important style was one in which driving wheels were located in inside frames, and carrying wheels in outside frames. Though originated by one John Gray, this style was first notably used by David Joy in the *Jenny Lind* 2-2-2s, built by E. B. Wilson of Leeds and supplied first to the London, Brighton & South Coast Railway, and subsequently to many others. The four carrying wheels having the axleboxes outside made the engines very stable while the inside axleboxes of the driving wheels ensured good compliance with variations in track levels. A high centre of gravity could safely be allowed such engines. The type remained popular because there was scope for fitting quite large boilers.

Probably the finest development of the type was to be seen in Patrick

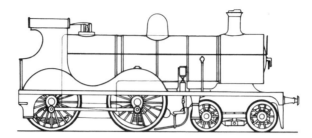

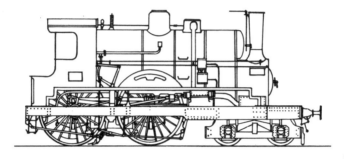

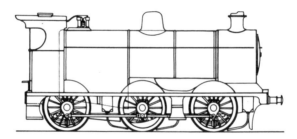

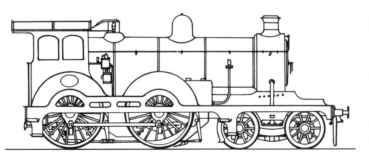

Top: *The inside-cylinder 4-4-0 became the classic British passenger locomotive of the late 19th century. This is one of the most elegant examples, the class E of the South Eastern & Chatham Railway. Built in 1908, the design is attributed to the Chief Mechanical Engineer of that Railway, although it is more likely the work of his chief draughtsman.*

Second from top: *This French 4-4-0 of the Est Railway was originally built as a 2-4-0 in 1878. With another engine of the same class it was fitted with a double boiler to the design of that Railway's chief engineer, Flaman, in 1891. Probably to help support the extra weight it was fitted soon afterwards with a leading four-wheel truck.*

Centre: *The classic British freight locomotive for almost a century was the inside-cylinder 0-6-0, whose design hardly changed over the decades. This example was built by the Midland Railway, and similar units were built by its successor, the London Midland & Scottish. From 1911, and for three decades, this class was built until a total of more than 700 were at work.*

Second from bottom: *A late and larger example of the British 4-4-0 was the 'Claud Hamilton' class of the Great Eastern Railway, introduced in 1900 and in operation for six decades.*

Bottom: *This 4-4-0 was built for the Prussian State Railways in 1893. The outside valve gear was easily accessible for adjustment and reflected that Railway's quest for low maintenance costs. Simplicity of detail and fairly low boiler pressures were additional Prussian characteristics, and had the same aim.*

Top: *The 2-4-2 wheel arrangement was not popular in Britain, except for tank locomotives. It was fairly easy to modify a 2-4-0 tender engine design by adding a coal bunker and water tanks at the rear, with an extra supporting axle; that is how this suburban tank locomotive of the Great Eastern Railway originated. Introduced in 1884 for London commuter services by T. W. Worsdell, it was virtually a re-design of the same engineer's 2-4-0.*

Centre: *In Britain the 2-4-2 tank engine was soon outnumbered by the 0-6-2, which provided the extra traction of a third driving axle. Suitable for both passenger and freight work, it was especially popular on railways with heavy short-distance traffic, like the coal lines of south Wales. This example, however, was built for the Furness Railway of northern England. It dates from 1905.*

Bottom: *Another British railway with a short main line was the London, Brighton & South Coast, and for its fast London–Brighton service D. E. Marsh designed this 4-4-2 tank locomotive, class 13. These were fast and convenient locomotives and in 1910 one of them, fitted with a Schmidt superheater, demonstrated the advantages of that device with a 25 per cent decrease in coal consumption.*

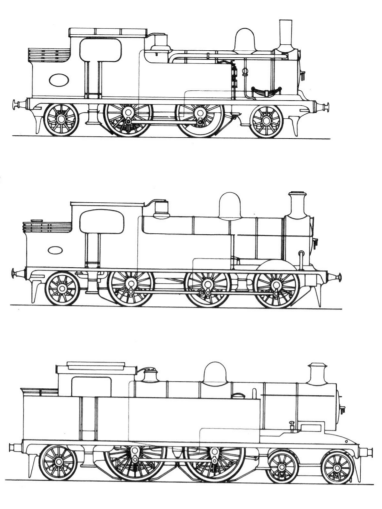

Stirling's Great Northern 2-2-2s with 2,286 mm (7 ft 6 in) driving wheels, which were virtually as fast and powerful as his better known 2,438 mm (8 ft) wheel outside cylinder 4-2-2s. Also with 'mixed' frame arrangement were most of the larger 2-4-0 locomotives built well into the 1890s including Kirtley's last Midland engines, many Great Western standard-gauge ones, the Fletcher and Tennant 2-4-0s of the North Eastern, the Great Eastern 2,133 mm (7 ft) and 1,727 mm (5 ft 8 in) driving-wheel engines and many others.

Inside frames and the evolution of the British 4-4-0

In the first years of the 20th century, every major British railway was working express trains with inside-cylinder inside-framed 4-4-0s—except the Great Western, where the 4-4-0s had double frames, and the Great Northern, which used 4-4-0s for less important trains and preferred 4-4-2s for heavy trains and Stirling's 'single drivers' for the lighter ones. The universal goods and mixed traffic engine was the 0-6-0, again with inside frames and cylinders. Indeed, this type was certainly the largest numerically, and probably earned more revenue than any other in the whole history of steam traction in Britain— 0-6-0s were built new till 1940.

In addition to these two versions of the standard British layout, in which a cranked axle lies in the middle of the engine with the cylinders and motion work ahead of it and the firebox behind, there were essentially similar 4-4-2, 0-6-2, 0-6-0, 2-4-2, and 0-4-4 tank engines; and 2-2-2, 2-4-0, 0-4-2, and 4-2-2 tender engines. All these types had the characteristic short boiler barrel and, usually, deep firebox. In such a great range of types, built over so long a period, it is difficult to select examples for special mention, or to present a clear story of development, but there is one continuing line which may be judged to be the most important and which, perhaps, produced the finest examples of this basic type, and this line starts with William Stroudley.

Stroudley began his carrer with the Highland Railway, where his sole but significant innovation was a very small 0-6-0 tank in which the pattern was established. Moving to the London, Brighton & South Coast Railway, he slightly enlarged this machine and produced the well-known 'Terrier' in 1872. He also built 0-6-0 goods engines, 0-4-2 mixed traffic engines, and 0-4-2 and 2-2-2 express engines. His mantle fell in effect on the shoulders of Dugald Drummond, who followed him from the Highland to be works manager at Brighton, and who later became locomotive engineer of the North British, where he produced enlarged versions of some Stroudley designs and also encountered the 4-4-0 engines of Thomas Wheatley—these engines were the first, rather primitive inside-framed inside-cylinder 4-4-0s in Britain.

After Drummond, Lambie and then J. F. McIntosh developed the Caledonian 4-4-0 into a truly formidable machine for its size, McIntosh, in particular, paying attention to the design of the boiler to enlarge the passage for the gases through the tube bank and eventually adding a superheater. The succession of McIntosh's Dunalastair classes, from the first to the fourth and finally superheated, provided as fine a 4-4-0 as any of the inside-cylinder type.

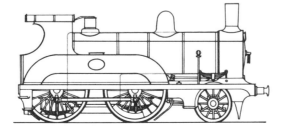

Above left: *The single driving-axle locomotive lasted longer in Britain than elsewhere, being regarded as a very free-running machine; it was only when trains became so heavy that a pair of driving wheels was inadequate to start them without slipping that the type became obsolete. This example was built by William Stroudley in 1881 for the London, Brighton & South Coast Railway.*
Left: *The 2-4-0, with driving wheels up to 2,134 mm (7 ft) in diameter, was the mainstay of fast passenger services on many British railways in the late 19th century. This example was introduced on the Great Eastern Railway in 1882 and was designed by T. W. Worsdell.*

Drummond joined the London & South Western Railway in 1895. He brought what by then might be regarded as the Scottish tradition with him and built excellent locomotives until he attempted ten-wheelers. His design innovations were failures and, in this, he was not alone: the challenge of the ten-wheeler defeated many British designers at this time. Only two designers built large numbers of 4-4-0s to a wholly different pattern: David Jones of the Highland, who perpetuated the old Crewe type of framing in a long series of passenger locomotives of undoubted effectiveness and Adams, who started with 4-4-0 tanks on the North London and, after a spell on the Great Eastern, produced a long and distinguished series of locomotives for the London & South Western.

Adams was one of the greatest of 19-century locomotive engineers; it was with the ideas of Adams, rather than those of Stroudley or Drummond, that the future of the steam locomotive lay. On the North London he found some 4-4-0 tanks with inside cylinders and equalized coupled-wheel suspension, and this experience led him to produce the first bogie with sideways movement. He soon added side control springs, at first of rubber and later of steel, and so created the locomotive bogie in its definitive form.

Next he adopted outside cylinders provided with unusually large capacity steam chests, well designed passages and large valves. The absence of a crank axle made possible some enlargement of the grate without lengthening the wheelbase. He standardized equalized suspension for all his subsequent 4-4-0s, giving them the three-point support which had proved so important in North America, but with the refinement of the Adams bogie. Plate frames, as in all British 4-4-0s, permitted the usual deep firebox and he paid particular attention to draughting by providing an annular blastpipe arranged so that the hollow centre of the exhaust steam cone drew on the lower tubes of the boiler. This equalization of the draught over the tube bank was of particular importance, because most contemporary locomotives drew mainly on the upper tubes with the result that the lower tubes were rapidly blocked with ash and steaming of the boiler was impaired. The annular blastpipe was the only effective improvement on the plain version before the introduction of double chimneys, but was more copied abroad than in Britain.

This development took place in the 1860s and 1870s, and Adams went on enlarging his 4-4-0 until his retirement in 1895 by which time his locomotives were certainly the best in England.

Right: *One of the later generation of British 'single' locomotives, H Pollitt's design was for the Great Central Railway in 1889. Larger than its predecessors, it had an extra axle, making it a 4-2-2. The leading truck enabled it to ride well at high speeds, while the introduction of steam sanding apparatus helped it start heavy trains. Engines of similar characteristics were built by several other British railways at this time; the Midland Railway, in particular, made a great success of the 'single', and one of its 4-2-2 engines is now preserved.*

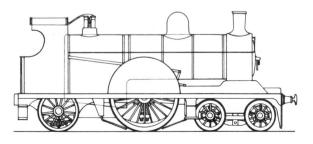

Early compound locomotives

In the whole history of the steam locomotive only two major variations from the *Rocket* concept have been of lasting importance. One is the articulated locomotive and the other is compound expansion, in which the steam is used in a high-pressure cylinder first and then further expanded in a low-pressure cylinder of greater volume. There have been many types of articulated locomotive, but only two have been of worldwide importance, and of those two one was built in far greater numbers than the other. This was the type evolved by Anatole Mallet, originally as a compound design, in 1885. Anatole Mallet was also the first to build a practical compound locomotive of any sort, and his first was a small 0-4-2 tank engine for the Bayonne–Biarritz Railway in southern France. It first ran in 1877.

This first engine was a two-cylinder compound and to ensure self-starting, had to be worked as a simple-expansion engine for the first few revolutions of the driving wheels. This was achieved by admitting boiler steam to the intermediate 'receiver'—in communication with the low-pressure steam chest—at a reduced pressure, while the high-pressure cylinder exhaust was diverted directly to the blastpipe. More complicated starting devices were contrived by other engineers but this was all that was needed.

The two-cylinder compound possessed some advantages over the two-cylinder simple-expansion locomotive, but one especially received attention—the more economical use of fuel and water. It soon became popular on many European railways. The very large Prussian system, under the technical guidance of August von Borries, built over 6,000 saturated-steam locomotives of this kind, in sizes varying from the small 2-4-0 to the 0-8-0 freight locomotive. Other countries followed suit and in England the North Eastern built many 0-6-0 goods, 0-6-2 tank, and 4-4-0 and 4-2-2 passenger engines, which did very well.

It should be recorded that one of the large compound 4-2-2 engines produced over 1,000 horsepower at 138.4 km/h (86 mph) when hauling a load of 270 tonnes inclusive of the tender. For a 40-tonne locomotive in the year 1890 this was outstanding. In later years, two-cylinder compounds were built with engine weights to about 90 tonnes. The large ones were mostly in North and South America: there were saturated 4-6-2s in the United States before 1900, superheated 2-8-2s and 4-8-4 tanks in Argentina, and, in fact, the two-cylinder compound was common in much of Latin America. In Europe its most permanent footing was in the east, notably in the many designs of the great Karl Gölsdorf for railways of the Austro-Hungarian empire, many of which remained at work until very recently.

The enlargement of the type was of course limited by the size to which a single low-pressure cylinder could be allowed to grow. It is also significant that, because of the emphasis on the economical advantage of the compound, it was considered worthwhile by the two European designers whose simple engines were already outstandingly efficient—William Adams in England and Victor Forquenot in France—both of whom converted individual locomotives to the compound system with inconclusive results.

Three-cylinder compounds were never very numerous. In England, F. W. Webb (one of the most eminent of engineers on the largest and most influential English railway) tried for 20 years to build good compound locomotives with very little success. His three-cylinder system involved two outside high-pressure cylinders of small diameter and one inside low-pressure cylinder of very large diameter. The logic of this lay in the restricted width of LNWR locomotives, affecting the outside cylinders, and the greater ease of accommodating adequate bearings for a single-crank rather than a double-crank axle.

Most three-cylinder compounds had the obvious arrangement: one high-pressure cylinder inside and two low-pressure ones outside. Optional working as a three-cylinder simple on heavy gradients was provided for in the designs of Adolf Klose for the Württemberg Railway in the 1890s and copied elsewhere. The more usual arrangement, in which low-pressure cylinder volume is greater to provide for compound working under all conditions except the moment of starting, originated with a 2-6-0 locomotive built to the design of E. Sauvage for the Nord Railway of France in 1887. Though very successful, this very advanced design was overshadowed almost at once by the four-cylinder compounds of that railway, which were to prove so influential.

Only two really numerous classes of three-cylinder compound seem to have been built well into the 20th century. For the Jura-Simplon and, later, the Swiss Federal railways, Weyermann's 2-6-0 with divided drive was built in over 170 examples from 1896. Some of these were sold to Holland in 1945 and continued to give good service for several more years. In 1901, the first of the Midland compounds was built at Derby in England, to the joint design of Smith (of the North Eastern Railway) and Johnson (of the Midland). Of these there were eventually 245, building continuing through the 1920s.

Compound locomotives with four cylinders, two high-pressure and two low-pressure, were the most numerous and, as will be detailed later, eventually developed the greatest power to weight ratio, the greatest thermal efficiency, and some of the longest and most trouble-free lives of any steam locomotives. In these best locomotives, the drive was usually divided: the high-pressure engine working one axle and the low-pressure another, the axles being, of course, coupled. This arrangement was evolved in France. In 1886, at the invitation of Gaston du Bousquet of the French Nord Railway, A de Glehn of the Alsatian locomotive works produced an experimental engine using a standard Nord boiler. Like Webb's first three-cylinder engine two years earlier, this had no coupling rods, but did have four cylinders, the LP ones outside. Du Bousquet exchanged the positions of the HP and LP cylinders, and provided coupling rods in his 4-4-0 version which appeared in 1891, and this engine established the form of many thousands of French and other locomotives built in the next half-century. Typical of these engines was the longitudinal separation of HP and LP cylinders, which went some way to equalizing the connecting rod lengths of the two sets. In the PLM (Paris, Lyon & Méditerranée Railway) system, which evolved at the same time, the four cylinders were all in a line across the engine, even though the drive might be divided. Although the PLM used the du Bousquet layout in some of its most successful earlier 4-4-0s and 4-6-0s, it returned to the all-in-line layout for its larger engines in the 20th century.

A number of two-crank four-cylinder compound arrangements enjoyed some popularity. Tandem cylinders, in which high-pressure and low-pressure cylinders were in line and worked the same piston rod, were much used in Russia and Eastern Europe around the turn of the century and were favoured by the US builder Brooks. 'The Most Powerful Locomotive in the World'—a frequently-transferred title—was for a time a 2-10-2 tandem compound of the Santa Fe railway. More numerous in America, and easier to maintain, were the Vauclain compounds, a speciality of the Baldwin locomotive works under Samuel Vauclain in which HP and LP cylinders were placed one above the other on each side of the locomotive, with separate piston rods driving a common crosshead.

The well-known Mallet articulated locomotive was conceived as a compound. In this type the boiler is rigidly attached to a two-cylinder chassis at the rear end, while the front end is supported on another two-cylinder chassis coupled to the rear one, but able to swing sideways on curves, boiler weight being carried on a sliding saddle. Flexible steam connections are required for the front engine and also flexible exhaust pipes. In the compound Mallet, the rear engine received boiler steam and the front engine received the steam exhausted from the rear engine. The flexible connections were therefore not subject to full boiler pressure. The first engines of the type appeared in 1889, on an exhibition railway of 600 mm (1 ft 11⅝ in) gauge (a gauge which the Decauville company had chosen for light railway products of all kinds, and which is still the normal small contractor's railway standard. The first Mallet locomotives were commissioned by Decauville). The enormous development of the Mallet type for railways with sharp curves and steep gradients all over the world resulted mainly in large and powerful compound tank locomotives. In America, the type was adopted in the 20th century for main-line freight work. So enormous did these machines become that eventually it was impossible to accommodate low-pressure cylinders of sufficient diameter within the moving load gauge. The Virginian Railroad double ten-coupled Mallets of the early 1920s had the largest LP cylinders, of 1,219.2 mm (48 in) diameter. Beyond this power, four-cylinder simple expansion became necessary and, in the advanced state of technology at this period, there was no problem with high-pressure flexible steam joints. It was also found that the simple engines ran more freely because the valve design associated with very large LP cylinders was not really adequate. Henceforward, the simple-expansion Mallet became popular in America, but in fact compound Mallets were built until 1952.

The compound locomotive can have certain advantages over a simple, assuming equally good design in both cases: the compound uses less fuel and water, produces a more even drawbar pull, is capable of better sustained acceleration, is more powerful for a given weight, and rides better on the track. Against this, the compound is usually more expensive (though commonly longer lasting) and requires a more highly-trained driver. The compound has generally been most successful in countries where educational standards are high.

The big-engine era

Around the turn of the 19th century, there was a worldwide increase in the weight of passenger and freight trains. Locomotive design standards evolved in the second half of the 19th century soon proved incapable of further enlargement. These classics, aptly symbolized by the British and the American 4-4-0 were still built but began to be relegated to secondary services by many of the larger companies.

In North America, there seems to have been little difficulty in designing and building larger locomotives. This was because the greater height of the loading gauge permitted higher-pitched boilers, and because the use of bar framing had long resulted in the practice of having the grate above the frames in 4-6-0 and 2-8-0 locomotives. The fireboxes of such engines were wider than could be accommodated between the plate frames which were almost universal in Europe. In smaller-wheeled locomotives the grate could be placed above the

Top: *In the USA the 4-4-0's role as a freight engine was challenged by the 2-8-0 on some lines, especially on railways which found that heavier trains were more economic to operate. This is an early example, built for the Lehigh Valley Railroad in 1886 and incorporating a leading truck of the type developed by Levi Bissell in 1857.*

Centre: *Another replacement for the 4-4-0 was the Mogul, or 2-6-0. This was never as numerous in America as the 4-4-0, but was often favoured by short lines for mixed traffic service. This example was built by Brooks in 1877.*

Bottom: *A natural development of the American 2-6-0 was the 4-6-0, or Ten-wheeler. In a sense it was a passenger variant of the 2-8-0 and several builders built 2-8-0 and 4-6-0 engines which were of the same design, apart from the chassis. This example was built as a mixed traffic locomotive for the Atchison, Topeka and Santa Fe Railroad in 1900.*

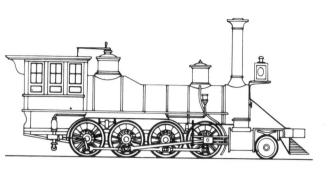

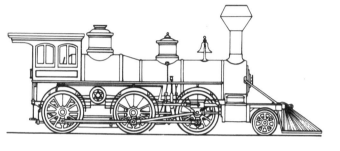

wheels, and in some 4-6-0s it could be fitted above the trailing wheels with some extension of the rear axle spacings.

In Britain, the progression from 4-4-0s and 0-6-0s to ten wheelers was not easy. The main trouble was the high rear axle of a 4-6-0, which resulted in a long, shallow firebox, to which the crews were not accustomed and which could be difficult to fire, because a shovelful of coal thrown to the front of the box sometimes hit the brick arch and fell in the middle. The rear axle usually interfered with the ashpan with the result that part of the grate became blocked quite early on a long run.

Ivatt produced Britain's first Atlantic in 1898. It was mechanically much like the Stirling '8 footer' 4-2-2, with outside cylinders, and the low rear axle made it possible to fit a deep firebox which, though longer than that of the Stirling engines—over 2.41 sq m (26 sq ft) in area as against 1.86 (20) in the last few singles—was easy to fire and could have a satisfactory ashpan. Four years later, Ivatt produced the first of his very numerous large Atlantics, identical except for their wide fireboxes and large boiler barrels. However, these engines only became outstanding performers after superheating. Aspinall pursued a similar policy, but as the existing locomotives were 4-4-0s with in-inside cylinders and 2,210 mm (7 ft 3 in) coupled wheels, he perpetuated these features in his Atlantics, which were extremely tall and most unusual machines but also successful.

Most designers attempting the 4-6-0 type failed to produce engines which were noticeably more powerful than the 4-4-0s, and either adopted the Atlantic or reverted to an enlarged 4-4-0 when stronger track and the advent of superheating made this possible. There were some inside-cylinder 4-6-0s, among which S. Holden's engines stand out as easily the most successful and long lasting.

There were, however, two successful early designs of saturated express 4-6-0 engines with outside cylinders, which appeared almost at the same moment in 1902. These had more in common than is generally recognized. One of these designs was by Churchward of the Great Western, a great engineer whose work was extremely influential in Britain. His design was strongly influenced by American practice, though not to the extent of using bar framing. He adopted a raised Belpaire (square-topped) firebox and a tapered boiler barrel. The valves were on top of the cylinders and driven by inside link motion, and he paid particular attention to the detailed design of the piston valves, cylinder passages and valve gear. The boiler was pitched very high and the ashpan was effectively in two parts, one ahead and one behind the rear axle. The competence of the Churchward 4-6-0 was never in doubt.

The other successful 4-6-0 was designed by James Manson. The Manson engines were restricted in weight, but incorporated many of the good features of the Churchward engines, plus the advantage of an increased rear-wheel spacing allowing a fairly deep firebox. There was a marked resemblance between the Manson engines and the numerous standard 4-6-0s for the Indian broad gauge. These began to appear from the same works at the same time, and were built for some 45 years in large numbers. It was in Scotland that the first British 4-6-0 had appeared: David Jones' *Big Goods* on the Highland Railway in 1894, and the Manson engines, while not outstanding, were the first express locomotives in an important modern Scottish design development.

The eight-coupled heavy goods loco did not present the problems at the firebox caused by a high rear axle, and from the beginning of the 20th century many British railways built 0-8-0s with inside or outside cylinders, and the 2-8-0 type followed quickly. Of the latter, the best were again Churchward's on the Great Western, which, like some other 2-8-0s, had the same boilers, cylinders, valve gear and other components as 4-6-0 express engines.

When in 1923, the British railway companies were formed into four groups, the East Coast group (LNER) used very competent Atlantics of the Great Northern, North Eastern and North British Railways on its long-distance expresses between London and Scotland and other important routes. Eight-coupled heavy freight engines of Great Northern, North Eastern and Great Central types, and innumerable 0-6-0s, handled the goods traffic. The West Coast group (LMS) used mainly 4-4-0s of which the best were the Midland compounds and the superheated simples of the London & North Western. There were also several hundred 4-6-0s which were less satisfactory, and double-heading of heavy trains was common. There were numerous eight-coupled goods engines, mainly ex LNWR—including Webb compounds with three and four cylinders. The Great Western remained substantially unchanged, with Churchward's standard types fully capable of doing all the duties required of them. The Southern group only had ten-wheel express engines in small numbers: Atlantics substantially of Great Northern design on the Brighton, and 4-6-0s on the London & South Western. These last included some of Drummond's unsuccessful four-cylinder machines, but also a number of modern-type two-cylinder simples with external Walschaerts valve gear designed by Urie.

Local services on all groups were mainly in the hands of inside-cylinder tank engines, but there were exceptions to this on the Great Western, which had numerous 2-6-2 tanks, and on what had once been the London, Tilbury & Southend, which had used outside-cylinder 4-4-2 tank engines since 1880. Locomotives with more than two cylinders, for any service, were in a very small minority. The first three-cylinder engine of modern type was a 0-10-0 tank of the Great Eastern, built in 1903 to demonstrate acceleration superior to that obtainable with electric trains. Three-cylinder drive then became a speciality of the North Eastern, and later the Great Northern, and was to play an important part in locomotive designs of the London & North Eastern.

The first British four-cylinder simple-expansion locomotive (again, apart from some very early experiments) was built by Manson for the Glasgow & South Western in 1898. It had a long life but remained unique on that system. More important were three French compound Atlantics bought by the Great Western, which gave rise to the highly satisfactory four-cylinder simple 4-6-0s of the Star, Castle and King classes, and eventually, through those, to the Pacifics of the London, Midland & Scottish Railway.

Four-cylinder designs on the LNWR, LYR and the Great Central were less successful. Three and, even more markedly, four cylinders improve the balance of a locomotive. If all four drive on the same axle there is no 'hammer-blow' on the track, because the reciprocating parts are working as opposed pairs and rotating weights in the wheels are not needed to balance them. Manson and others hoped, therefore, to be allowed to increase axle loading but were usually opposed by the civil engineers.

The early years of the 20th century saw the development of a practical system of superheating for locomotives by Dr Wilhelm Schmidt. The Schmidt system, like its derivatives known by the names of other engineers, involved the passage of the steam, after it had left the inside of the boiler, through a large number of small tubes inserted within enlarged boiler flues. The extra heat content reduced condensation losses within the cylinders and increased the power output or, alternatively, reduced fuel and water consumption. In England, the virtues of the system were first strikingly demonstrated by a large 4-4-2 tank engine of the Brighton Railway, class 13, which proved able to handle a 250 tonne express over a distance of 145 km (90 miles) without taking water en route and running mostly at over 80 km/h (50 mph), doing round trips of 425 km (264 miles) on one heaped bunkerful of coal—some $3\frac{1}{4}$ tonnes. Comparative running with one of the excellent LNWR unsuperheated 4-4-0s so convincingly favoured the Brighton engine that the LNWR proceeded to build a superheated 4-4-0, the *George the Fifth*: the first of a class which proved capable of power output greatly in excess of expectations based on its dimensions.

In Britain, superheating improved many existing classes, especially the larger and newer engines which had not yet produced power commensurate with bulk. There were disappointments: the rearrangement of boiler tubes sometimes resulted in poor steaming; the high steam temperatures led to lubrication difficulties; and, when piston valves were adopted in place of slide valves, less clear steam paths, often blocked by carbonized oil, as well as leaking valves caused locomotives to deteriorate rapidly after overhaul. These problems were resolved by the development of superior lubricants, by the use of narrow rings on the piston valve heads, and the increasing adoption of easier steam paths and long-travel long-lap valves. Eventually, high superheat played a vital role in outstanding performances from such different types as Ivatt's Great Northern Atlantics, Chapelon's compound locomotives in France, and the great North American locomotives—of which one engineer once remarked that he liked the steam so hot that the piston rod came blue out of the stuffing box on the rear cover!

Large American locomotives in the 20th century

The distinguishing feature of the large American locomotive was the wide firebox at the rear of the main framing—with a trailing truck beneath—with two or, from the middle 1920s, four wheels. The first form of wide firebox to receive much use was the Wootten type for burning anthracite. This appeared in 1877. Wide fireboxes for burning low-grade coal appeared early in Belgium. There were other European examples but the normal modern type first became current in America in the early 1890s.

It was above all the Atlantic (4-4-2) type which demonstrated the advantages of this type of boiler; some of the best express trains running in the United States were pulled by the Vauclain compound 4-4-2s of the Atlantic City Railroad, first built in 1896. For competitive services, the Pennsylvania Railroad also used the Atlantic type, and the evolution of these locomotives on the Pennsylvania eventually resulted in the E6 class of 1910, which in its superheated condition was capable of developing 2,400 hp in its cylinders and had an engine weight of some 110 tonnes. This was undoubtedly one of the finest American locomotives, and one of the finest Atlantic designs in the world—with a power-to-weight ratio only surpassed slightly by the Atlantics of the French Nord Railway in their final form and nearly equalled by the Ivatt Atlantics with the large superheaters of the British Great Northern. Both these European types were, of course, much smaller machines.

The E6 class were two-cylinder simples, as were the vast majority of non-articulated American locomotives. The growth to enormous size in the 20th century did not change this state of affairs. American locomotive engineers were extremely practical and their situation was one in which thermal efficiency was altogether less important than the ability to run long distances with minimum attention and to haul enormous loads. Locomotive crews were expected to show courage and physical strength rather than intellectual quality. Physical strength of a high order was required to fire a Pennsylvania Atlantic, and even more, a 'Pacific', of the earlier series, before the mechanical stoker took over in the 1920s.

The Pacific type proper, with a wide firebox, was named after some small engines of the Missouri Pacific Railroad, which appeared in 1902. It was simply an enlargement of the Atlantic, with six-coupled wheels, and as often happened when extra wheels were added the coupled wheels were smaller than those of Atlantics. The first American Pacifics retained the traditional inside-link motion-driving outside valves through pendulum levers of rocking shafts—so long a feature of all American designs. The trailing wheels mostly had inside bearings. But by about 1910, external Walschaerts gear came into use, and the trailing truck had outside bearings giving greater freedom for a capacious hopper-style ashpan. There were innumerable American Pacifics. When hand-fired, they were probably the hardest locomotives in the world to work. Their true potential was realized only in the 1920s and 1930s with mechanical stoking. It is again to the Pennsylvania Railroad that we must turn for the finest examples of the type—the series which culminated in the K4s class of 1914. The earlier ones were, at one time, the most powerful locomotives in the world on a horsepower basis, and the last, with poppet valves—certainly the most powerful Pacifics—having developed 4,250 hp on test in 1942. This was slightly less than the maximum obtained from the French Chapelon 4-8-0 class four-cylinder compound at about the same time. The French locomotives were rebuilt from Pacifics with about three-quarters of the weight of the Pennsylvania engine.

This comparison is not one of merit: both American and French designs were of the very highest quality, and each perfectly adapted to the conditions of use. But it does illuminate the very different problems facing locomotive designers: the Americans were able to use high axle-loadings and cheap fuel and catered for long distances and high speeds; the Frenchmen had to work within weight and loading-gauge restrictions which required the use of four cylinders and eight-coupled wheels. The French had to reduce fuel consumption to the minimum.

The two equivalents of the Pacific type were the 2-10-0 and the 2-8-2 (or 'Mikado'), both of which could use the same boiler as the Pacific, the small wheels of the 2-10-0 permitting the wide grate to pass above them. The 2-8-2 is perhaps the most typical American locomotive of this whole period. Not only was it built in large numbers for American home railroads but it was also the most extensively-exported type. American Mikados of all gauges were to be found all over the world, their capacious fireboxes burning all sorts of fuel, their simple and robust mechanism defying the worst of maintenance and the most gruelling operating conditions. Moreover, the basics of American design, evolved when track was bad, made the Mikados well able to keep their feet on badly-maintained and severely-curving and graded routes—because of fully equalized suspension of driving wheels and trucks.

Apart from articulated locomotives, dealt with in a separate section, the culmination of the American single-frame locomotive was the type with a four-wheeled truck under the firebox, first introduced by the Lima locomotive works in 1925 in the form of a 2-8-4, closely followed by a 2-10-4. The idea was to increase the steaming capacity sufficiently to enable a high tractive force to be developed at relatively high speeds. The once popular criterion of starting tractive effort (unrelated to boiler capacity) became insignificant. This philosophy, applied to the Pacific type, gave rise to the 4-6-4 (or 'Hudson') and the 4-8-4 was an enlargement of this. The 4-8-2 had never been regarded as a high-speed locomotive and was never built with very large coupled wheels, but this did not apply to the 4-8-4. Many of these types were given boosters in their early days. These were small steam engines driving two wheels of the trailing truck, to assist in starting, but able to be disconnected for running at speed. Their use was a result of the new locomotives replacing older ones with more coupled wheels, many of them Mallets.

The most famous of the 4-6-4 and 4-8-4 types were probably the Milwaukee Hiawatha 4-6-4s, the Santa Fe 3776 class 4-8-4s and those of the New York

Central Railroad. These great locomotives habitually sustained very high speeds with very heavy loads—the Niagara 4-8-4s built in 1945 could manage 1,000 tonnes at 160 km/h (100 mph), and the whole class averaged a monthly mileage of 16,000, some regularly reaching 24,000 where the rosters permitted. In the final phase of American steam power, extraordinary attention was paid to ease and rapidity of servicing. In freight service, locomotives were often serviced without leaving their trains, during relatively short stops, and this was a vital factor in the achieving of large mileages. A Hudson had a maximum sustained cylinder hp of 4,700 on test, for an engine weight of about 160 tonnes. The Niagara 4-8-4 could sustain 6,600, with an engine weight of about 210 tonnes. For comparison, Chapelon's three-cylinder compound 4-8-4 could sustain 5,500 hp, with an engine weight of about 145 tonnes.

American and other articulated locomotives

If we exclude some primitive experiments, the history of the articulated locomotive can be taken as starting with the Semmering trials of 1851, the object of which was to find a type suitable for working the severe Semmering incline in Austria. Of the four competing machines the *Weiner Neustadt* fore-shadowed the Meyer articulated locomotive in having two bogie engines beneath a long but fairly normal boiler. Another, the *Seraing* (named after the Cockerill works in Belgium), had two bogie engines beneath a double boiler arranged firebox to firebox, with chimneys at the extremities, and so was an example of what later was known as the 'Fairlie' type after a later patentee. Both Meyer and Fairlie locomotives were successfully built in small numbers, and some still exist in running order, but these types are totally outweighed in importance by the Mallet and the Garratt arrangements.

It has already been pointed out that the Mallet was conceived as a compound and was built extensively for some 30 years before being adopted in America. Until the Americans started building them, Mallets with separate tenders were rare, but some of the tank locomotives were very large for their time. The Gotthard 0-6-6-0 of 1890 weighed 85 tonnes, and the Belgian engine of similar wheel arrangement, used for banking up the Liège incline, weighed 110 tonnes. Perhaps more typical were the numerous Mallets constructed in Europe for service in the Dutch East Indies: the 2-6-6-0 tanks of 1902 weighed some 60 tonnes, which was quite large for the gauge of 1,067 mm (3 ft 6 in). Some of these are still in service. The Mallet was always regarded by Europeans as a 'colonial' or a mountain-climbing type, and most of the very numerous European-built examples were for service on narrow-gauge lines. In the 20th century, and perhaps with the American example, many large Mallet tender locomotives ran on 'colonial' railways—some built in America and to cite the former Dutch colonies again, there were double eight-coupled locomotives of American and European build, followed by Swiss-built 2-6-6-0s in the late 1920s, some of which were running in 1976.

The first American Mallet was an 0-6-6-0 built by the American Locomotive Company's Schenectady works in 1904 for the Baltimore & Ohio. It was a banking loco, and replaced two 2-8-0 locomotives showing nearly 40 per cent reduction in repair costs and achieving something like 85 per cent cent availability in its first few years of service. As the builders had never constructed anything like this before, this must be taken as a remarkable tribute to the excellence of American design and construction, but the smoother operation of a compound locomotive, and the more rigid articulation of the two power units, as compared with two ordinary locomotives coupled together, must have helped a great deal. This was a 152 tonne engine, and its success led to an immediate popularity of the Mallet which was soon extended beyond banking to line freight work, and even in a few cases to express passenger haulage.

The ultimate in size of the compound Mallet was reached in 1920 with the 2-10-10-2 locomotives of the Virginian Railway, in which the low-pressure cylinders were of 1,219 mm (48 in) bore, adhesion weight was 280 tonnes and the horsepower developed at the slow speed of about 40 km/h (25 mph) (for which the locomotives were intended) amounted to nearly 7,000. There were also a few triple eight-coupled Mallets, with driving wheels under the tenders, on the Virginian and Erie railroads, but although the total adhesion weight reached some 350 tonnes, the power, and therefore the speed, was less than in the 'double Decapods'. Yet one worked a train weighing 16,300 tonnes at 24 km/h (15 mph).

As already pointed out, the size of the low-pressure cylinders and the difficulty of providing adequate valves to deal with enormous volumes of low-pressure steam led to progressive replacement of compound by simple Mallets, by rebuilding and by new construction, but this was not without exceptions. Probably the last Mallets built were compounds of the Norfolk & Western class Y6b. Eighty Y6 locomotives were built between 1936 and 1952, the last being Y6b. They were 2-8-8-2s, capable of working 7,000 tonne trains on easily graded routes at speeds up to 80 km/h (50 mph). Their boiler pressure was 300 lb/sq in, driving wheels were 1,524 mm (5 ft) in diameter and weight was 270 tonnes.

The use of simple expansion obviously made higher powers possible within the permissible width over the cylinders of the front engine. The large Mallet had improved control of the lateral movements of the front engine. It was in this way that the largest and most powerful of all steam locomotives were constructed, and here it must suffice to cite the Union Pacific 'Big Boy'

A 'Big Boy' articulated locomotive of the Union Pacific Railroad. The Mallet type locomotive reached its highest stage of development in the USA, and especially on the Union Pacific, which found the type ideal for hauling heavy trains over the foothills of the Rockies. Of the 4-8-8-4 wheel arrangement, the 'Big Boys' were the Railroad's final Mallet type, and by several parameters may be regarded as the world's largest-ever steam locomotives.

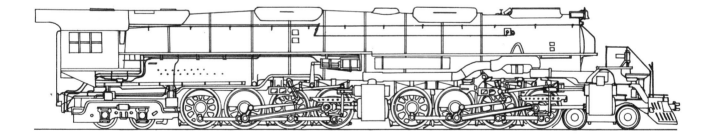

4-8-8-4s, and to give their particulars for comparison with the more modern but smaller compound Y6b class. The boiler pressure was the same at 300 lb/sq in, but the driving wheels were 228.6 mm (9 in) larger in diameter. Weight was 350 tonnes (without tender) as against 270. The firegates of these enormous locomotives were roughly 6,096 mm (20 ft) long and 2,743 mm (9 ft) wide, the firebox being extended forward in a combustion chamber and provided with water tubes supporting the brick arch. Used mainly on heavily-graded routes, they could develop 7,000 drawbar hp at low speeds—a remarkable figure because steam locomotives reach their maximum output when running relatively fast—and were able to run at 112 km/h (70 mph) with 3,000 tonnes on the level. Happily, many of these great engines are preserved in the country that was created by the railroad.

The Garratt locomotive was conceived by Herbert Garratt and became the speciality of Beyer, Peacock & Company of Manchester, England. It was never built in the quantities of the Mallets, of which over 3,000 were built in the US alone, and more in Europe. There were certainly less than 2,000 Garratts in all but most of these were large machines. In this design, the boiler is carried on a cradle slung between two engine units and has no wheels beneath it. This is the great virtue of the layout; the barrel can be of large diameter and relatively short, and the firebox, almost always of the wide, square-topped variety, can be deep, with a deep ashpan, and simple in shape (and therefore cheaper and more easily designed to keep maintenance costs down, with simple direct staying of the water spaces around the fire).

The first Garratts were built in 1908 for Tasmania. They weighed only 33 tonnes and had four-wheeled engines pivoted to the central cradle, with, as in all Garratts, water and fuel supplies on the engine units. One engine was worked at high pressure, and the other at low, this first type being compound, though almost all later Garratts were simple-expansion machines. The type progressed slowly until 1921, when a 134 tonne 2-6-0 + 0-6-2 was built for trials on the 1,067 mm (3 ft 6 in) gauge South African Railways. Compared with a British-built compound Mallet weighing, with tender, 180 tonnes, the Garratt proved faster with the same load and burned less fuel. It also rode very much better, thanks to the wide spacing of the pivots of the boiler cradle, which lie within the coupled wheelbase in Garratt locomotives to ensure that the weight of the boiler is well balanced on the engine units. On sharp curves the front end of a Mallet boiler swings outwards and the inertia of this can be detrimental to good riding.

The Garratt proving the better engine on all counts, South African Railways adopted Garratts for new construction, and because this railway system

The Beyer-Garratt type of articulated locomotive was especially popular in southern and eastern Africa, where it is still in use. South African Railways were the largest purchasers of the type, both for 1,067 mm (3 ft 6 in) gauge main-line use and for the 600 mm (2 ft) narrow-gauge lines. This drawing shows a large 4-8-2 + 2-8-4 type, imported from Manchester in 1929 for main-line service.

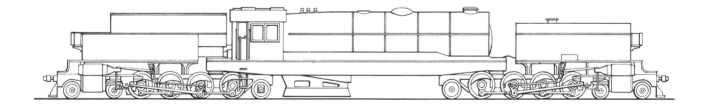

enjoyed a high prestige among engineers other railways made increasing use of the type. In South Africa, the narrow gauge does not involve a small loading gauge, and does not preclude very heavy loads and speeds up to 88 km/h (55 mph)—indeed some steam 4-6-2 locomotives had 1,829 mm (6 ft) diameter driving wheels. To this day, the South African system is one of the most modern and efficient, and Garratt steam locomotives, though in diminishing numbers, work it.

While the Garratt (or Beyer Garratt as it later became known) was predominantly found in English-speaking countries, or those where British engineers and businessmen ran the railways, it was also used elsewhere and built under licence by Continental builders. Some remarkable machines were made, of which the fastest were the 4-6-4 + 4-6-4 locomotives of the PLM Algerian system, which proved able to run with perfect steadiness at 136 km/h (85 mph). Among the last built were 42 4-8-4 + 4-8-4 for the standard-gauge New South Wales Railways in Australia. Like the last Y6b Mallets they appeared in 1952, their total weight (being tank engines, like all Garratts) of 260 tonnes being closely similar to that of the Y6b without tender. The Garratt was found all over the world, except in North America, but it was above all the continent of Africa that depended most heavily upon them, and still does. From the express Garratts of Algeria, right down the continent, east and west, to Cape Province, this long, powerful and flexible machine worked many of the heaviest trains, passenger and freight.

The last development of European steam locomotives

No comprehensive survey can be attempted here but certain important lines of development can be traced. It was the appearance of the French Nord Atlantic at the turn of the century, and its remarkable feats of speed and load haulage, that really set the style for most subsequent French steam locomotives, and many British and German ones. In France, only the PLM kept to its own style of four-cylinder compound, while the British derivatives were four-cylinder simples.

The Nord Atlantic of G. du Bousquet was a narrow-firebox engine, with some 2.69 sq m (29 sq ft) of grate, and the cylinder arrangement described under early compound locomotives above. On its first trials it developed 1,440 hp and in later saturated condition these engines produced some 1,600 in the cylinders, equally divided between high- and low-pressure groups. For a weight of only 69 tonnes, this was a standard not bettered anywhere and probably not equalled, and was the result of a careful study of steam flow in the pipes and valves of the whole double expansion system. Similar but larger engines, weighing some 77 tonnes, were built for the Paris–Orléans Railway and these, again in fully-developed saturated condition, could be relied on to produce 1,800 hp and reached nearly 2,000 hp on test.

Many French railways built 4-6-0s inspired by these engines. Superheating improved the Nord Atlantics, which were to remain on fast luxury trains of 350 to 400 tonnes weight until the late 1930s. A 4-6-0 version proved even more potent, thanks to a further review of what has since become known as the 'steam circuit', and, still weighing only 70 tonnes, these engines could be relied on to produce 2,000 hp without falling pressure or boiler water level. They first appeared in 1909, received superheaters before many had been built, and improved blastpipes and chimneys in middle life. They lasted till the end of steam, thereby proving that continual very hard work need not wear out a locomotive. The Nord 'Super Pacifics' of the 1920s and 1930s were derived from them and had narrow fireboxes of great length. Though they were lighter than other French Pacifics they were the most powerful, producing some 2,700 hp, until the Chapelon rebuilds came into service on the Paris–Orléans Railway.

The Paris–Orléans Pacifics were the first in Europe and dated from 1907. They were scarcely more powerful than the Atlantics and superheating did little to improve them. The maximum horsepower that could be obtained was about 2,200 and this was largely because their steam circuits were constricted. André Chapelon, perhaps the greatest locomotive engineer of the 20th century, examined their design critically and decided that it was not fundamentally bad, but required detailed improvement in several ways—no single remedy would transform them.

He rebuilt one with greatly enlarged steam passages; poppet valves worked by the original Walschaerts gear but giving much larger openings to steam and exhaust; enlarged steam chests to reduce the drop in pressure during admission to the cylinder (due to that fact that flow during admission greatly exceeds average flow in the superheater and steam pipes); he increased the superheat to avoid condensation in the low-pressure cylinders, and devised a double blastpipe and chimney incorporating the Kylala exhaust splitter and petticoats at three levels to guide the steam, even when the blast was very soft, into the chimney and to even out the draught at different heights in the smokebox. The increased pumping efficiency of the 'double Kylchap' exhaust greatly reduced the back pressure on the pistons. As a result, the power of the locomotive was raised to 3,400hp and a whole series was subjected to modification.

Later, further detailed improvements and an increase in diameter of the low-pressure cylinders raised the horsepower of a subsequent batch to 3,700. Finally in this particular development, the rebuilding of some of the small 1907 Pacifics into 4-8-0s, with the Nord type of long and narrow firebox, exactly doubled their output, from 2,000 to 4,000hp, with a grate area of no more than 3.44sqm (37sqft) and an engine weight of some 105 tonnes. Later rebuilds of this type produced 4,400hp for an engine weight of nearly 110 tonnes, and this power-to-weight ratio has never been improved upon in a steam locomotive. Moreover, these later, strengthened engines did not wear themselves out, because the blast arrangement produced a very even pull on the fire, further assisted by the relatively long cut-offs at which compound locomotives work even when achieving a high overall expansion ratio. The long cut-off also results in a more even turning moment and drawbar pull, both conducive to reduction in the wear of the mechanism. To crown all this, these Chapelon locomotives produced the best figures for thermodynamic efficiency, i.e. fuel and water economy, of any steam locomotives, achieving a best figure of 12.8 per cent utilization of the calorific value of the fuel.

Chapelon principles were eventually adopted by other railways and other countries, and were found to improve simple-expansion locomotives as well. In France, most of the larger locomotives were more or less altered and some of the Etat and PLM Pacifics were totally treated to achieve Chapelon-type results. There was also new construction of old designs modified according to these principles, notably of over 300 mixed traffic 2-8-2s (Class 141P) redesigned by Chapelon, which proved similar in power to the 4-8-0s, and of 35 4-8-2s (Class 241P) of PLM design, much transformed to be able to develop nearly 5,000hp. There was also a unique 4-8-4, rebuilt by Chapelon as a three-cylinder compound, which achieved 5,500hp, remarkably evenly divided between the three cylinders, for a weight of some 145 tonnes. This great machine was the experimental prototype for a series of three-cylinder compounds of 6,000hp, planned to be built largely on American lines, with cast-steel engine beds (the ultimate development of the bar frame in the USA). Unhappily, these were never built, but the performance of the 4-8-4 caused a rapid redesign of the electric locomotives then being planned for electrification of the PLM main line.

Preference for compound locomotives in Europe was severely upset by the invention of a practical system of locomotive superheating by Dr Wilhelm Schmidt in the first ten years of this century. In many tests superheated simples were found to be more economical than saturated compounds. In further tests, superheated compounds were found to be more economical still, but this did not prevent a complete change of policy on the Prussian State Railway (probably the largest single transport undertaking in the world), where Robert Garbe, the locomotive engineer, worked closely with Schmidt in the production of a large series of superheated simples which dominated the working of all traffic except the fastest passenger trains within a few years. These engines were of superb mechanical design but low power-to-weight ratio, a combination which ensured long and trouble-free lives. Built in thousands, they were spread across Europe as reparations after both world wars, and their design principles were perpetuated in the standard loco-motives of the Deutsche Reichsbahn, which were also superbly built, totally reliable in service, and rather undistinguished in performance.

The other German railways generally preferred compounds up to the time of their amalgamation into the Reichsbahn in 1920. The Bavarian system used numerous engines built by J. A. Maffei and designed by the firm's engineer and director A. Hammel. These were remarkable machines, many of which were exported to other European countries. They were four-cylinder com-pounds with the drive concentrated on one axle, and they had bar frames. The Bavarian Pacifics in this style were perpetuated in new engines by the Reichs-bahn in 1930, because its engineers were at the time unable to produce a simple expansion engine which was suitable for either the light, fast *Rheingold* express, or heavy work on steeply graded south German routes. The Würt-temberg and Saxon systems also used large compounds, of which the most noteworthy were the Württemberg 2-12-0 freight locomotives, designed by Eugen Kittel and built by Esslingen, which found their way to many steeply-graded routes in Central and Eastern Europe after World War II, including the famous Semmering route which had prompted the trials of 1851. It was perhaps because the Prussian system was relatively flat that the simple engine was preferred there.

The railways of the Austro-Hungarian empire, and of the Eastern European countries which resulted from its disintegration, were for long dominated by the numerous locomotive designs of Karl Gölsdorf.

From the 1800s onwards he produced a great number of different designs for the greatly varying conditions of major and minor routes, but all were characterized by the need to keep axle-loading down to very low figures for the sort of powers that were required. His designs were compounds, with two or four cylinders, and their appearance and construction were very different from any other designer's ideas. The framing was light and box-like, running plates and splashers over the wheels were largely suppressed, and boilers were tapered to reduce weight at the front, while working pressures were relatively low to enable thinner plates to be used.

Gölsdorf was undoubtedly a genius, and many of his locomotives survive even today as proof of their durability and suitability. Perhaps his most cele-brated express engine, and certainly his largest, was a 2-6-4 with enormous firebox, which was long associated with the *Orient Express*. A single equiva-lent 2-12-0 was highly successful; among smaller machines, numerous Atlantics, 4-4-0s, and small compound tank engines gave long service, while the two-cylinder compound 0-10-0 was still to be found working recently in

France and Italy as well as on more familiar ground.

In Britain, after grouping of the railways in 1923, the enlarged Great Western continued Churchward's designs with small additions, especially in the four-cylinder 4-6-0 type. The numerous Castles and the fewer Kings had the highest power-to-weight ratio of any British locomotives until the middle 1930s. A King weighing 89 tonnes could develop 2,000 hp (which was better than an unrebuilt Paris–Orléans Pacific but not as good as a Nord 4-6-0 in power-to-weight terms).

London & North Eastern locomotive affairs were in the hands of the imaginative Sir Nigel Gresley, whose three-cylinder simple expansion Pacifics, first built for the Great Northern, were progressively improved until one of them, the streamlined *Mallard* with a double Kylchap exhaust, achieved the world speed record for steam in 1938, at 202 km/h (126 mph). These engines could develop 2,700 hp in the cylinders, with a weight of just over 100 tonnes, which equates with the Nord Super Pacifics in France. Gresley used three-cylinder propulsion for almost all his designs, from 4-4-0s to 2-8-2s.

Three cylinders were also used in the Southern Schools class 4-4-0s of which 40 were built from 1930. These were the last and most powerful European 4-4-0s, weighing 67 tonnes. Later, when O. V. S. Bulleid joined the Southern from the LNER, three-cylinder Pacifics based on Gresley's type but with many novel features were added to stock. The London, Midland & Scottish had inherited a very heterogeneous locomotive stock, without a single reliable large passenger engine. Although excellent mixed traffic 2-6-0 and 2-6-4T locos were produced, and large numbers of small reliable engines of pre-grouping design, it was eventually necessary to build a class of large three-cylinder 4-6-0s, the Royal Scot type, from 1927. But it was not until W. A. Stanier, from the Great Western, took charge that wholesale building of new standard designs began. Among these were a mixed traffic 4-6-0 and a heavy freight 2-8-0 with many parts in common, both excellent machines based on Churchward principles, with taper boilers. Stanier also produced four-cylinder simple Pacifics, based at first on the Great Western King class 4-6-0. The later examples, the Duchesses, were the most powerful class of British locomotive, one having developed 3,300 hp.

Locomotives for export
The countries which played the greatest part in the development of the steam locomotive were Britain, France and the United States. Germany contributed superheating, and Belgium contributed the most widely-used valve gearing and possibly the much favoured square-topped firebox. The emphasis in this account has been confined to the main development and most countries simply cannot be mentioned. These are those whose locomotives were built by, or inspired by, the great locomotive-exporting countries. Many were colonies of those countries but others were not. In Europe there was no native loco-motive style in Spain or Holland, or many other countries. Countries not hitherto mentioned which had a native style and a substantial export trade were Switzerland and Czechoslovakia. The Swiss built very fine compound locomotives for their own system, until they decided to exploit their own water power rather than import coal, and so adopted large-scale electrification. They had a considerable export trade in steam locomotives, as they now have one in electric traction. The Czechs built what were probably the finest European simple-expansion locomotives since the last war, and their exports were also to be found all over the world.

The main exporting countries were the United States, Britain, France and Germany. The railways of India, South America, Africa and Asia were and, in some cases, are operated by imports from these countries, and in recent years indigenous new construction has developed the old imported designs well beyond their original capacity. This has happened most notably in India, South Africa and China.

A simple solution of the conflict between locomotive size and the maximum permissible axle weight might appear to be the adoption of designs with an exceptional number of driving wheels. This is what Mallet and Garratt types offered, but these had a flexible wheelbase. This 4-14-4 prototype built for Soviet Railways in the 1930s, however, had a rigid wheelbase and, as might have been expected, was virtually unusable because on curves it either derailed itself or broke the rails.

Some special locomotives

There have been some notable heavy goods locomotives. In America, a most successful early type was Ross Winans' 'Camel' 0-8-0 of the 1850s, with large overhanging firebox and the large driver's cab on top of the boiler. This position for the cab lasted long in American practice, there being 'Camel-back' Atlantics and 4-6-0s as well as small-wheeled goods locos. In the same period James Milholland, another great American innovator, produced a twelve-coupled engine on similar lines—a very early precursor of the Union Pacific 4-12-2 type of 1926—which was not only remarkable for having twelve-coupled wheels but also most unusual among modern American classes in

having three cylinders. In France, in 1867, Forquenot of the Paris–Orléans produced some 0-10-0 tank locomotives, the boiler dimensions of which were not exceeded in France until the end of the century. They were for banking purposes, but not long before Jules Petiet of the Nord had built some line freight locomotives for working coal trains from the north of France to Paris, which were also tanks. They had twelve-coupled wheels in two groups of six, in a rigid frame, with four cylinders. They proved more powerful and economical than six-coupled locos in pairs.

Lastly, there have been some special locomotives built for high speeds. Francis Trevithick of the London & North Western built a locomotive with driving wheels nearly 2,743 mm (9 ft) in diameter, and put the boiler beneath the axle. It was later rebuilt in a more normal style, still with the big wheels, and is preserved after long service. This engine is the well-known *Cornwall*. The largest coupled wheels in Britain were those of two 4-4-0s, North Eastern Nos 1869 and 1870, built after the races to Aberdeen in 1895, but never used for racing. They were 2,311 mm (7 ft 7 in) in diameter. J. A. Maffei built a compound 4-4-4 for the Bavarian State Railway, which reached nearly 160 km/h (100 mph) with a 150 tonne train in 1906. This was a special version of the Bavarian Pacific. Thirty years later, Deutsche Reichsbahn built a large wheeled 4-6-4 specially for record breaking. Its speed was at least equalled by the standard LNER streamlined Pacific *Mallard* in 1938.

Surviving
Steam Traction

by John Westwood Why and where steam locomotives
still operate in different parts of the world.

Although steam traction has disappeared from the railways of North America, Australasia and most of Europe it seems unlikely that this form of motive power will have entirely vanished by the beginning of the 21st century. Two of the world's largest railway systems, the Indian and Chinese, make great use of steam locomotives and still manufacture new boilers. Indeed, in China new steam locomotives were being built in the mid 1970s and this may be continuing. Outside these two great systems, South Africa and Indonesia still use hundreds of steamers, and there are sizable pockets of survivors also in Poland, Turkey, Germany and South America.

There are various reasons for this survival of what is regarded as an outmoded form of motive power. One reason is that some railway managements do not accept that the steam locomotive is either outmoded or uneconomic; everything depends on the circumstances. It is a machine which has certain characteristics and these may or may not be suited to a given country at a given time. In any case, say protagonists of the steam locomotive, the dieselization programmes of many railways in the developed world were far too rapid, resembling more a Gadarene rush than a properly considered policy. On several railways the top management decided on dieselization and only then called on the railway economists to make out a case for such a change, the economists obliging with a set of assumptions which could only favour the diesel. On Canadian National Railways, cost comparisons of diesel and steam traction were based on the assumption that both types of locomotive would have a life of twenty years; this was at a time when the Railway's fast passenger services were hauled by machines already thirty years old. On Soviet Railways, when steam costs were compared with diesel it was not the most modern steam design which was chosen as an example.

The present-day distribution of steam traction does tend to reflect the pattern of economic development; it is the countries which have little capital for investment that seem to retain steam. However, this is not an entirely unvarying picture. Until recently West Germany, not the poorest of countries, had a sizable steam-locomotive stock because its management had resisted the urge for all-out dieselization. Main lines were still being electrified, so until the steam units were worn out it was considered better to use them on the non-electrified lines rather than build diesels which, on electrification, would be redundant. Diesel locomotives were built but only in such numbers as were required for a gradual replacement of steam on non-electrified lines. The last steam locomotives in West Germany were withdrawn only in 1977; their survival had meant a considerable saving of capital which was utilized elsewhere. French policy was very similar to that of Germany although steam disappeared a decade earlier. On several American railroads and in Britain the process was different and was characterized by a rush to end steam traction which meant that, in Britain at least, reliable and inexpensive steam locomotives were replaced by expensive and unreliable diesels.

In North America the need to appear progressive and to keep up with competing railroads was a factor encouraging over-rapid dieselization. Just as airlines were hurrying to get into a position where they could proclaim that they were all-jet, so the railroads invested wildly so as to announce that they were all-diesel. A similar process took place in a few other countries, but did not always go according to plan. The Queensland Government Railways, for example, were operating a few steam locomotives a year after proclaiming that they were dieselized. In Malaysia the railways in the mid 1970s had to resurrect some steamers to help the 'all-diesel' fleet to handle the traffic.

Previous pages: Although the steam locomotive no longer hauls regular trains on Japanese National Railways, public demand has been met with occasional steam excursions. The most-favoured type among Japanese railway enthusiasts is the class C62 4-6-4. In this picture two of these locomotives are shown with a Sapporo–Hakodate train towards the end of the steam era.

Asia

In countries like Indonesia, China and India there are several factors favouring steam. The steam locomotive is a relatively simple piece of machinery, well suited to a labour force which is relatively poorly educated. Such a labour force is not likely to provide specialists in diesel and electric technology in the numbers needed for a wholesale shift from steam traction. In these countries economic development means that the best trained workers cannot be spared for the railways; the railways can perform their essential tasks in the traditional way, saving capital and labour for newer enterprises. In South Africa the situation is slightly different although it is changing. The more skilled kinds of job have been reserved for the relatively small white population with the result that there is a labour shortage in all except the labouring grades. This again favours the steam locomotive although in recent years there has been a great effort to dieselize. This dieselization drive, however, is not without its critics for not only does it demand skilled labour but also implies a demand for fuel oil, a commodity lacking in South Africa and one whose import is vulnerable to politically-inspired blockade.

India and China now contain a majority of the world's steam locomotives; they together possess some 12,000 units or more. Both are countries which have good coal resources, small oil production and little hydroelectricity. They are also countries which, from a fairly low level of industrialization, have since the early 1950s entered a stage of rapid industrialization. This has meant great increases of railway traffic, so that despite some electrification and dieselization all but the oldest steam locomotives are kept in operation simply in order to cope with constantly increasing traffic.

In India, steam-locomotive construction ceased only in 1972 and boilers are still manufactured. Although a large number of modern locomotives were received from foreign builders, in the later years two Indian works supplied the railways. Chittaranjan Works was one of the early successes of the Indian five-year plans. Built and equipped with British assistance it turned out hundreds of steam locomotives before transferring to electric-locomotive production. Most of these were standard broad-gauge machines; the metre-gauge lines were supplied by a private locomotive-building company, Tata. Chittaranjan's output was concentrated on the type WG 2-8-2, which by now must be a contender for the title of world's most numerous locomotive type. Externally it has some resemblance to the British-style locomotives used by Indian railways before World War II, and it does in fact incorporate many British features. Some of the first examples were built in Britain, one being exhibited at the Festival of Britain in 1951. 2,450 units of this type have been built and although it is often seen on passenger trains it is primarily used as a heavy freight locomotive. It could well be described as the basic tool of transportation in the first two decades of Indian industrialization. For passenger services on the broad gauge a semi-streamlined 4-6-2 was introduced. This, class WP, was designed with the assistance of the American Baldwin Works and, unlike the WG, has bar frames. But it has many components, including the boiler, standard with the WG. 755 engines of this class were supplied to Indian Railways; a few early units were built in the USA and others came from Canada, Britain, Poland, Austria, France, Germany, Italy and Japan, as well as from Chittaranjan. The WP has driving wheels of diameter 1,700 mm (5 ft 7 in) which might be regarded as somewhat small for a streamlined locomotive. However, the streamlining, which in effect consists simply of a rounded smokebox front, is more for show than practical effect. High speeds were not attempted in the 1950s and 1960s and the WP was perfectly adequate for the heavy but moderately paced long-distance trains. Other postwar types built for the broad gauge have included the WL light 4-6-2, of which about 100 units were built, and a suburban 2-8-4 tank locomotive, class WT, which carries the same boiler.

On the Indian metre gauge, which accounts for about half the Indian mileage, the postwar equivalents to the broad-gauge WG and WP are the YG 2-8-2 and YP 4-6-2. These are of German aspect although the prototypes were built by Baldwin in the USA. The two types are really identical, except for the wheel arrangement, and have been very successful; 1,704 YG and 871 YP units were built. For work on lightly-laid track the YL type of 2-6-2 was designed. The first appeared from Britain in 1953, after which others came from Germany, Hungary and Japan. For narrow-gauge lines postwar production was mainly of the ZB 2-6-2 and ZE 2-8-2 designs, both derived from pre-war types.

On both the metre gauge and the broad gauge there are still many of the US wartime 2-8-2 type at work, received from the USA and Canada in the 1940s. These are classified AWD and CWD on the broad gauge and MAWD on the metre gauge. American locomotives were otherwise rare in India, that subcontinent being almost (but never quite) a monopoly of the British locomotive builders. Many of the pre-war British-built locomotives survive. Among these are the very common 0-6-0 machines, virtually replicas with Indian trimmings of the 0-6-0 locomotives once so common on British railways. Also still in service are the so-called 'mail engines'. These are typically British 4-6-0 engines built, with very slight variations, for Indian railways since before 1914. The newest batch, class HPS, was delivered after World War II to ease a motive power shortage. Similar engines built for the metre gauge also survive in small numbers. Also quite numerous are the standard inter-war Pacifics and Mikados. On the broad gauge the 4-6-2s are classified XB and XA and are used in secondary service; they were never very successful because of a tendency to derail in certain combinations of poor track and high speed. The 2-8-2s are of class XD and are still encountered on secondary freight duties. Also dating from those years are the XT type 0-4-2 tank locomotives designed for light passenger services. On the metre-gauge, inter-war 4-6-2s of class YB and 2-8-2s of class YD are still common.

Tucked away in odd corners of India are other older and non-standard types. It is the latter that are being scrapped, together with some of the inter-war designs. Postwar locomotives seemed destined for many more years of service and there are well over 5,000 units of these classes in existence. Electrification and a steady programme of diesel construction has meant that a number of heavy freight routes, and some of the best long-distance passenger services, are no longer entrusted to steam traction, but the sheer number of trains operated on Indian railways ensures that there are still many prime services behind steam. In Bangladesh and Pakistan, whose railways were once part of the Indian system, other steam locomotives are still at work; in Pakistan these include some broad gauge 4-4-0 engines operating around Wazirabad.

Information about Chinese railways is less plentiful, although it is known that in that country the steam locomotive is not considered old-fashioned merely because diesel and electric locomotives are available. With its abund-

The classic British 4-6-0 may still be seen working on the broad-gauge lines in India, where it is known as the 'Mail Engine'. This locomotive was built in the 1900s for the East India Railway, but units of virtually the same design were exported to Indian Railways from Britain in the 1950s. The Indian market was very important for British locomotive-building companies because a home market hardly existed, with the major British railways designing and building their own rolling stock. The locomotives sent to India were very British in design, even though certain Indian characteristics like powerful headlights, 'cowcatchers', and cab side-shutters were usually fitted.

ance of coal, its thousands of personnel used to steam operation, and workshops equipped for steam-locomotive maintenance, as well as constantly increasing traffic, China does not intend to eliminate steam for many years to come. Whether steam-locomotive construction continues is uncertain but probable. In 1976 visitors to the Tangshan Locomotive Works could see 2-8-2 light-duty locomotives being built. Soon afterwards this works was wrecked by earthquake, but there are other locomotive works in China and it is highly unlikely that they are all completely devoted to electric and diesel construction. Electrification is still at a very early stage, while most diesels are sent to help overcome bottlenecks on the most intensively used sections of line.

Before the communist victory of 1949, followed by its policy of self-sufficiency and rapid industrialization, the Chinese railways obtained their equipment from a variety of sources. The tradition of 'spheres of influence'—in which the country was informally partitioned so that, for example, one region would have British-owned railways and another French or American—lingered on long after that nineteenth-century concept had been discredited. Thus in some regions workshop equipment may still be of British origin and in another American or Japanese. Older locomotive types still include British, American and Japanese designs. However, the main influence is Russian, for during the 1950s the Soviet government offered the Chinese railways extensive technical and material help. Thus one locomotive type in China is the old Soviet 2-10-2 of class FD; with electrification many of these locomotives became surplus in the USSR so they were regauged to standard gauge, reclassified and sent to, among others, the Shanghai–Nanking line, where they haul 3,000-ton freight trains. Russian assistance also included the presentation of the constructional drawings of the Soviet L type 2-10-0 and the LV 2-10-2, both postwar types. The Chinese QJ 2-10-2 is clearly a copy of the LV. Other Chinese locomotives are Soviet in inspiration, including some types whose wheel-arrangements do not match any Soviet type but which have a definite family resemblance to the modern Russian school of locomotive design. These include the standard RM passenger 4-6-2. Other common types are the JS, JF and SY classes of 2-8-2, of which the SY is the most modern. There is also the KD 2-8-0, an American-built machine which was delivered to China in the 1940s; most of these are used for yard work and light freight services.

In Indonesia, the former Dutch East Indies, most of the railway mileage is in Java although there are some short lines in Sumatra. In colonial days the locomotive market was by no means reserved for Dutch builders. What usually happened was that a given design was built by several builders, usually German or Swiss, but including the Dutch Werkspoor and, very occasionally, other builders. The rare British-built machines are old, but the antique 2-4-0 tender locomotives built by Sharp Stewart in the 1880s still survive. Steam tram locomotives supplied by Beyer, Peacock are in service; they work not only the celebrated passenger train from Surabaya docks but also the infrequent roadside mixed trains in the interior.

On the Indonesian main lines diesel locomotives from Germany, the USA and Japan haul the most important passenger trains and much of the freight. They are supplemented by Indonesia's only modern steam locomotives, one hundred 2-8-2s of class D52 supplied by Krupp in the early 1950s. In addition there are several classes introduced before World War II. These include a number of Mallet types, 2-6-6-0s built in Holland and Switzerland, and 2-8-8-2s built by Alco in the USA and by two German works. Older Mallet types are some 2-6-6-0 tank units, used on heavily graded branch lines, built before World War I. Even older Mallets, of the 0-4-4-2 tank type, were in service at least until recently. Because Java is mostly mountainous terrain the Mallet type was once much favoured. For the same reason locomotives with many coupled axles were built and some of these survive, including the class F10 2-12-2 tank locomotives built between 1912 and 1920 in Holland and Germany.

Other old types include 2-6-0 tanks, now used for yard work, 4-6-4 tanks and a variety of 0-4-0 tank locomotives. Many of the latter are tram-type machines used in the countryside. Another light-duty type is the very rare 0-4-0 tender locomotive. However, at any given time it is difficult to describe the locomotive situation in Indonesia, because train services fluctuate. At times of crisis lines may close down with their engines put into store (or sometimes merely abandoned to the weather). At other times, when perhaps the active diesel fleet is reduced through lack of spare parts, antique steam engines may be returned to service. What seems certain is that Indonesia, although it has fewer steam locomotives than India or China, has a great variety of types and a better representation of the older, smaller types. For students of the nineteenth-century German locomotive in particular, this nation is especially rewarding for it is still operating machines which elsewhere would be displayed on pedestals.

Africa

In recent years lovers of the steam locomotive have been visiting the Republic of South Africa in increasing numbers. A hospitable population, exceptionally photogenic landscapes, a sunny climate and over 1,500 steam locomotives compensate for the high cost of travel from Europe and America. The diesel locomotive is a relative newcomer to South Africa, although main-line electrification has a long history. In recent years there has, however, been an acceleration in the building of new diesel locomotives and the SAR plans do envisage the eventual replacement of steam traction. However, dieselization has been criticised inside South Africa, partly on strategic grounds, and the promise of economically producing fuel oil from the country's rich coal resources is not yet a reality. At present, what is anticipated is a withdrawal of all but a handful of steam locomotive types over the next five years; however, nothing is certain and sometimes it seems that the railway administration is itself hazy about its own intentions.

The steam locomotive in South Africa belongs to the British tradition and with a very few exceptions all steam locomotives were built in Britain—the North British Locomotive Company being a favoured supplier, with Beyer, Peacock building Garratt-type machines. Despite this, the more modern locomotives have a somewhat Germanic aspect, thanks perhaps to their large-diameter boilers, squat chimneys and smoke deflectors. Locomotive development has generally consisted of the steady improvement and enlargement of a few basic types. Thus the most common of the main-line general-purpose types, the 4-8-2, has several varieties. The large 4-8-2, however, was finally surpassed by the postwar 4-8-4 of the 25 class. The first example of these, gigantic machines for the 1,067 mm (3 ft 6 in) gauge, was built by Henschel in Germany because that company had experience in the design and building of condensing locomotives but the other 89 units were built in Britain. These heavy-duty locomotives were intended for the main line across the Karoo, a desert region where there are acute water-supply problems. Their tenders are bigger than the locomotive itself, as they accommodate condensing elements and fans for converting the exhaust steam back into boiler water. As such locomotives do not exhaust steam through the chimney, their approach is heralded not by the sound of puffing, but by the whine of their fans, so that they sound like jet aircraft. However, the maintenance costs of such locomotives are high; cases are known of the fans being blown high into the air and of other misadventures. Most of them have therefore been converted to non-condenser locomotives.

The South African Railways also bought numerous Garratt-type machines that are especially suitable for the light, winding track and modest bridge-work. However, it is the various classes of Garratt which are being withdrawn first, presumably because of their somewhat higher maintenance costs. But the Garratts on the narrow-gauge lines probably have a more secure future.

For branch-line service the SAR for many decades built successive variations of its lightweight 19 series of 4-8-2. The final version of this was type 19D, introduced in 1947, and suitable for lines permitting an axle-load of only 14 tons. These engines are fitted with tenders as large as themselves, holding 28,400 litres (6,250 gallons) of water. But these are not the lightest of the light-weight types for there is also class 24, a 2-8-4 with an axle-load as little as 11 tons. A smaller engine is the 0-8-0 tender locomotive designed for yard and dock work. In general, yard engines as such have been rare in South Africa, the work being performed by old main-line locomotives; it is still possible to see Garratt engines employed in such work. This is one of those uneconomic practices which, presumably, dieselization will eliminate.

In the early 1980s it seems likely that the locomotive types remaining in service will comprise the type 15F heavy 4-8-2, the 19D lightweight 4-8-2, the type 24 2-8-4 (which will still be used on the picturesque coast line between George and Knysna, among others) and the non-condensing type 25 4-8-4 which will be centred on Bloemfontein. Doubtless for some years other types will survive longer than planned and even after that it may be expected that some older engines will be working on private lines, typically at collieries, as they do already.

In neighbouring Rhodesia, although diesels began to replace main-line steam units in 1956, steam locomotives are still in service. The imposition of economic sanctions after the unilateral declaration of independence in 1965 meant that completion of the dieselization programme was postponed until better times. Moreover, in 1978 it appeared that special efforts would be made to maintain steam locomotives in service after they became due for normal retirement. So although diesel traction is used on the main trains, steam operations are quite extensive, especially around Bulawayo. The oil embargo was never real enough to deter Rhodesian Railways from scrapping its oldest classes of locomotives, but large numbers of Garratt-type engines are still in use. The oldest class is the most numerous: the 15th Class 4-6-4 + 4-6-4 built in 1947 and later. Other types of Garratt were built up to the mid 1950s, including the very large 20th Class, a 4-8-2 + 2-8-4 design. Bulawayo, with 85 Garratts allocated to its locomotive depot in 1975, was the world's biggest centre for this make of locomotive, and may remain so because Garratts are being withdrawn from its only possible competitors in South Africa. Some Rhodesian Garratts were sold to the Mozambique Railways and are probably still in existence along with the varied assortment of other locomotives used by that system. Across Rhodesia's other border, in Zambia, the same types of locomotive can be seen because Zambian Railways were once part of the Rhodesian system. Further west, in Angola, conditions are difficult for any kind of economic activity, but the wood-burning Garratts of the Benguela Railway are reported to be still in existence along the line leading from Zambia to the Atlantic at Lobito.

Connecting with the Mozambique Railways is the line of the Swaziland Railway, remarkable in that it was built only in the early 1960s and uses steam traction on its western section. Swaziland is an independent state lying between South Africa and Mozambique, and the line, Swaziland's first railway, was built to export local iron-ore through the Mozambique port of Lourenço Marques. Operations were entrusted to the Mozambique Railways, by contract, and this corporation owns the locomotives. The latter include some second-hand types bought from Rhodesia, as well as some large 4-8-2 machines built by the Montreal Locomotive Works. Recently, following political developments in Mozambique, South African steam locomotives have begun to work in Swaziland. The East African Railways, now split between Uganda, Kenya and Tanzania, were once great users of Garratt locomotives, and the big maroon 59 Class are still in existence. In 1978 new diesels were expected to bring steam operation to an end in Tanzania and Kenya, but past experience suggests that steam units will be needed to fill the gaps caused by the diesels' maintenance problems and in particular by the difficulty of ensuring prompt supplies of spare parts.

South America

South America still sees steam operations. These are not so intensive as a few years ago because train services themselves have tended to disappear, and in conditions of diminishing traffic it is the steam locomotives which are withdrawn from active service. On the other hand, diesel locomotives often have low reliability and availability factors and when a diesel breaks down most locomotive depots have a spare steamer which can be pressed into service. But this is not inevitable. In recent years there has been a growing tendency, when a locomotive fails to appear or to move, to cancel the train rather than search for substitute motive power.

Traditional-style British locomotives are to be found in Argentina whose railways, until the Peron regime, were British owned. The 1,676 mm (5 ft 6 in) gauge lines of the former Buenos Aires Great Southern are still served by the 4-8-0 mixed traffic locomotives supplied by British builders between the wars.

One of these designs has been rebuilt on Chapelon principles, resulting, it is said, in greatly increased efficiency and power output. Of the other steamers used by the company the 4-6-0 and 2-6-4T types have been replaced by diesels on their original duties but a few may linger on secondary services. On the standard-gauge lines of the former Central Railway another design of 4-8-0 was recently reported to be still in service. In the north, some old 0-6-0 and 4-6-0 locomotives are probably used in light duties. On the metre gauge the concentration of steam power around Buenos Aires has dissolved away, and it is probably the north-west, on the lines of the former Central Norte Railway, that metre-gauge steam is most evident. This state-owned railway bought its locomotives not only from Britain but also from the USA and Germany. Baldwin supplied most of its later, heavier locomotives and these 4-6-2s, 4-8-2s and 2-10-2s were, at least until recently, the mainstay of operations from Córdoba northwards through mountainous country to and beyond Salta and Tucumán. In the far south, on the southernmost railway of the world in Patagonia, there is a remarkable narrow-gauge main line built in the 1950s for moving coal through Río Gallegos. Traffic on this line was originally handled by 2-8-2 locomotives, but 86-ton 2-10-2s were then ordered from Japan, surely the heaviest locomotives ever to work on the 750 mm (2 ft 6 in) gauge.

Another coal-hauling operation can be seen in Brazil where the Dona Teresa Cristina Railway, now an isolated part of the Brazil state railway organization, hauls coal from scattered mines down to the wharves at Imbituba. Modern US-built 2-10-4 locomotives were acquired for this work, supplementing Baldwin Mallets and Alco 2-8-2s of an earlier generation.

Paraguay, adjoining Brazil, still has one of the world's most decrepit railways. This is the standard-gauge Presidente Carlos Antonio Lopez Railway, once British owned but now nationalized. It is the only main-line railway in the country, and runs 376 kms (234 miles) from the capital Asunción to Encarnación, where a train ferry across the Paraná provides a connection with the Argentinian railways. The backbone of the service is a class of 2-6-0 locomotive built by North British for the Railway in 1910 and 1911. These graceful machines have been supplemented since World War II by a couple of more modern British 2-6-0s and also by two or three Baldwin 2-8-0s.

In Chile the state railways have long been carrying out an electrification and dieselization plan. The northern lines (metre gauge) were the first to witness the disappearance of steam traction. On the 1,676 mm (5 ft 6 in) gauge lines in the south, diesel traction has been progressively extended southwards so that now it is only the southern extremity of the system which is served by steam. Here 2-6-0 and 4-6-0 locomotives of British and German manufacture help 2-8-2s of American design to handle the traffic.

In Bolivia Japanese diesel locomotives have reduced steam operation to a handful of locomotives in the south of the country, although there has been a period when the maintenance problems of the new locomotives resulted in a comeback for steam traction, and this could happen again. The once independent Guaqui Railway, now part of the Bolivian national system, still uses 2-8-0 locomotives of the 'Andes' design. This is a typical American 2-8-0 of the pre-1914 era, once also used in Peru. The units now in Bolivian service were actually built to the old design at Leeds in 1948; they are unusual in that they are named locomotives carrying brass nameplates. Peru's two main lines have long been dieselized but at the extremity of each is a 3 ft gauge railway. The Huancayo–Huancavelica Railway has some British 2-8-0s and Baldwin 2-6-0s while the Cuzco–Santa Ana uses a Baldwin 4-6-0 and some 2-8-2s.

Europe

Since the end of steam in 1977 on the Deutsche Bundesbahn, working steam in western Europe has almost disappeared. In Portugal there are still several metre-gauge branch lines with steam traction, often in the form of Mallet tank locomotives. In Spain a number of collieries use locomotives handed down by national railways, RENFE. Exceptional is the metre-gauge Ponferrada to Villablino Railway, which uses only steam locomotives on its 64 km (40 miles) of route. These are of two classes: Baldwin 2-6-2 tank locomotives and 2-6-0s built in Germany and Spain. It is one of the latter which hauls the daily passenger train. A broad-gauge line which has bought its own locomotives is that owned by the state electricity company and running for 45 km (28 miles) from Andorra to Escatrón. This line has three specially-built 4-8-4 tank locomotives plus a handful of engines received second-hand from RENFE. In Italy a number of locomotives are still in service; mainly 2-6-0s, they are scattered over the network and are used occasionally, but hardly regularly, on light traffic lines.

In central and eastern Europe steam traction still survives. Poland has the largest number of locomotives; its PKP handles the largest volume of traffic in Europe outside the USSR and the need for more and more motive power has meant that despite electrification and dieselization there is still a place for steam traction. With good coal supplies, and a balance of payments problem which does not encourage oil imports, the limiting factor on steam motive power is the effective life of the locomotives. No steamers have been built since the 1950s, and past a certain age the maintenance of locomotives, and especially the provision of new boilers, makes it expensive to retain a steamer in service. On passenger services the Pt47 class 2-8-2 is still encountered, together with the postwar 0149 class 2-6-2. The latter, it is said, was built with Soviet advice and was intended to replace the former Prussian P8 type 4-6-0 although a few of these are still in service. In general, Prussian influence is still strong; after all, much of the PKP serves territory which was formerly Prussian and Polish home-built locomotives were strongly influenced by German practice. Moreover, the German *Kriegslok* 2-10-0, itself built in the Prussian tradition, is still widely used. However, there are still some American engines at work: the US Army 2-8-0 is beginning to disappear but some large Ty246 class 2-10-0s built in America after World War II are still in use.

In East Germany also, steam traction is used in main-line service. The regular use of Pacifics on the Berlin–Dresden service has now ceased. A Pacific locomotive recently made history on the Berlin–Leipzig line, when it blew up with fatal results; apparently its crew were unfamiliar with the class and allowed the firebox top sheet to boil dry. Pacifics of both the 01 and 03 types are in service and some are used on the Berlin–Stralsund line. *Kriegslok* 2-10-0s, and a handful of 2-8-2s and 2-8-4 tanks, are in regular use and there is also a Prussian design of 2-10-2 tank still surviving. As in Poland, narrow-gauge steam locomotives are expected to outlive the standard-gauge types.

Elsewhere in eastern Europe, the Hungarian railways use many units of the class 424 4-8-0 on secondary services as well as a few tank locomotives on branches. The life of the latter, however, is likely to be short with the current (1978) Hungarian policy of closing light-traffic lines. In Yugoslavia there are still several Hungarian types in service, some acquired when the country became independent of Hungary, and some through later purchases. Thus the

424 4-8-0 can still be seen although, unlike the Hungarian railways' examples, it does not have a double chimney. There are former Hungarian tank locomotives and also several survivors of what was once the common mixed traffic locomotive of Hungary, the class 324 2-6-2. In Romania the Prussian tradition lives on. Romania did build some engines of home design, but most of its surviving steam stock is of Prussian origin. The Prussian P8 4-6-0, some units of which were acquired as war reparations and some as the products of domestic locomotive works, is in use on secondary passenger trains. A corresponding freight locomotive, the Prussian 0-10-0, has also survived. However, the level of steam activity in Romania is lower than that in Germany and Poland. Bulgaria and Czechoslovakia are even further along the road to dieselization and will probably run their last steam trains in 1978 or 1979. In the USSR, 0-10-0 locomotives may still be seen in a few locations performing yard duties and a few 2-10-0 locomotives of class L, and 2-6-2 passenger units of class Su, are employed on widely scattered lines still awaiting dieselization. But the end of Russian steam traction must be imminent.

Turkey has a wide variety of steam classes. These include 2-8-0s built in the USA, France and Sweden and 2-8-2s built in Britain and the USA. However, the 2-10-0 is most in evidence. Some of these were built by Vulcan in the USA, although they are somewhat Germanic in design, and the German *Kriegslok* is in evidence too.

The *Kriegslok* is a reminder that certain types can still be regarded as international. This German 2-10-0, built in large numbers during World War II, was used in most of the German-occupied countries and hundreds of units were acquired by different railway systems after the war. The large numbers taken by the Russians are probably now all extinct, as are those of France, Austria and West Germany. But Hungary, Romania, Poland and Turkey still use them. The Prussian P8 4-6-0, probably the most numerous passenger locomotive ever built, may also be regarded as an international type which is still in use, although no longer in Germany. Other examples of the Prussian school of locomotive design are the 0-10-0 and 0-8-0 freight designs. The US locomotive industry has also contributed widely-used designs. Although the war-standard 2-8-0 is now almost extinct, at one time it was widespread mainly in eastern Europe and south Asia. The MacArthur 2-8-2, also widespread after the war, survives in India and Pakistan. The high-boilered Hungarian 4-8-0 had a foreign clientele, being exported to Korea and Yugoslavia and taken also to the USSR. As for the British contribution, there is hardly a specific British type remaining, but the Garratt family is still working in Africa.

One of the range of standard designs built for the German State Railways (DR) in the 1920s. This is the class D3 two-cylinder Pacific, a type still in service in the German Democratic Republic. Like other standard types of that period, it is a late example of the Prussian school of locomotive design. The detachable chimney-top is a result of the Franco–Prussian War of 1870, when Prussian locomotives operating in France damaged their chimneys on the lower French bridges. After that war, as the cynics observed, 'Prussian locomotives were designed to run on other countries' railways'.

Electric Traction

by John Westwood **The principles of electric locomotion and its development up to the present day.**

Characteristics of electric locomotion

Strictly speaking, the electric locomotive is not a locomotive at all because it is not self-propelled; its electric motors draw their power from generating stations miles away. This feature is a great strength of electric traction, but it can also be a source of weakness. It is its strength because the electric locomotive can draw on as much power as it needs without 'running out of steam'. Its output is not limited by the availability of power but by the amount of current which can be utilized by its traction motors without overheating. It can make a special effort for short periods as when hauling a heavy train up a long gradient and this is why electric units have two maximum power ratings: the hourly rating is the output permissible for up to one hour, while the somewhat lower continuous rating can be maintained indefinitely. The weakness of electric traction is the complexity of power supply: this comprises the generating stations, sub-stations, transmission lines and conductor wires. At times this has been regarded not only as an economic weakness but also as a strategic disadvantage; in Russia in the 1930s and in India in the 1960s the alleged vulnerability to bombing of overhead conductor wires was one of the arguments used against railway electrification.

The simplest electric locomotive need only consist of four wheels, an electric motor driving at least two of the wheels, a device to pick up current, and a control system. However, this basic simplicity has been overlaid by increasing sophistication as designers have striven to produce a locomotive which not only does its work but does it as economically as possible. Different kinds of motors, motor suspensions, transmissions, running gear and control systems have been introduced over the decades. More important, different types of current have been tried in a continuing attempt to compromise between the respective advantages and disadvantages of direct current and alternating current, and of high voltage and low voltage.

To the outside observer, the most striking change has been the universal adoption of the double-bogie chassis. Although this chassis was used in the early days of electrification, by the Baltimore & Ohio Railroad in the USA and the North Eastern Railway in Britain among others, most of the early electric locomotives had wheel arrangements similar to steam locomotives, with large driving wheels and small carrying wheels. The drive was transmitted from the electric motors to a jackshaft running athwartships, and cranks on the ends of the jackshaft were connected by rods to the driving wheels. With the modern double-bogie arrangement all the axles are driven, through gearing, so that every wheel is a driving wheel. Moreover, the bogie arrangement, together with modern methods of mounting the motors so that they are fully or partially spring-borne, enables high speeds to be safely and smoothly achieved.

One feature of electrification which has seemed very attractive to managements and governments is the possibility of converting the energy released during braking into electricity which can be fed into the catenary, thereby enabling, for example, a downhill train to supply much of the electricity needed by an uphill train. Put simply, regenerative braking is achieved by using the traction motors in reverse so that they become dynamos. In mountainous areas, where descending trains have to be held back over long distances so as not to exceed a safe speed, there is a good opportunity to use this feature. In practice, however, the difficulties are so great that many railways have decided not to profit by the system. There is always the possibility of too much current

Previous pages: The Rheingold at the Hook of Holland. Its locomotive was originally designed for the British Manchester to Sheffield electrification and in due course became surplus to requirements. Working on the same 1,500 volt system as Netherlands Railways, it was purchased by the latter for passenger service, together with others of the same class. The locomotive on the right is a standard, French-built mixed-traffic unit.

The power system of a European 15,000 V electrified railway. Power from a hydro-electric or thermal station, or from the electricity grid, is fed to transmission lines at 110,000 V and then, close to the railway, is transformed to 15,000 V and fed into the overhead catenary.

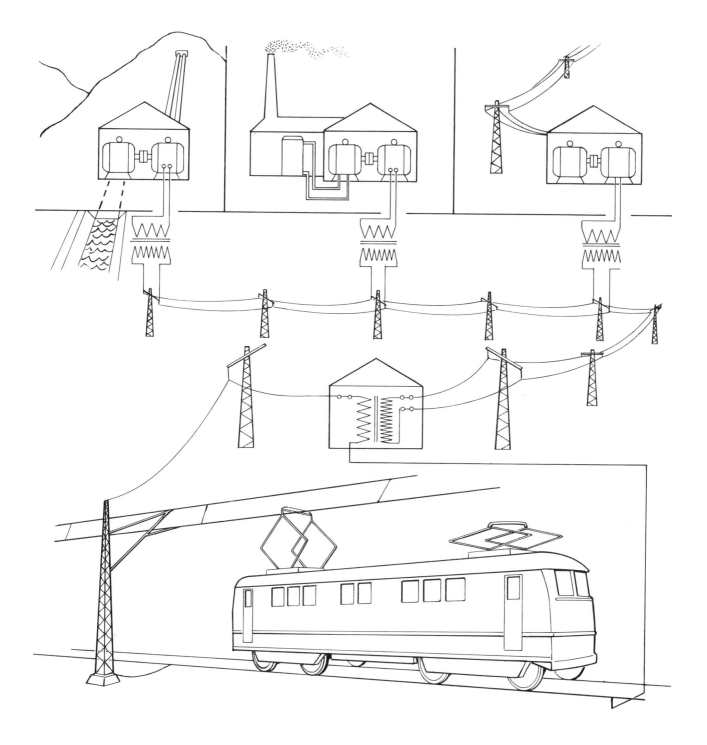

being fed into the catenary with serious consequences. Locomotive crews, therefore, have to match the system voltage with the voltage which the locomotive is generating. This is a technique which is particularly difficult to apply with alternating-current locomotives. In fact, alternating-current loco- motives fitted with regenerative apparatus have since had the equipment removed. In India, for example, it was found that the task of matching the generated current in terms not only of voltage, but also frequency and phase angle, was too demanding. Another kind of electric braking is rheostatic, where the traction motors again act as dynamos activated by the weight of the train turning them against their inherent resistance. But the current thereby generated is not returned to the system but is passed to rheostats in the locomotive which convert the energy to heat, which is then blown into the atmosphere. This rheostatic braking may not produce usable power but it reduces wear on brake-blocks and wheel rims.

One factor which deterred many countries from an early start to electrification was the constantly changing technical situation. Electrification technology has been improving decade by decade. This has meant that an electrification system which is very advanced at the time it is chosen may be obsolescent by the time it is completed. And since railways, above all, need standardization so that trains may run freely all over a given system, it was never very satisfactory to start electrifying with one system and finish with another, more advanced. Since the 1950s, especially in Europe, this problem has been alleviated at quite a high price by building a certain number of locomotives equipped to work on more than one system.

Systems of electrification

Several countries—notably France, Russia, Britain, India and the USA—have more than one system in wide use. Other countries may soon be in the same situation. The first sign of a divergence in Australia has recently appeared, where the new Brisbane suburban electrification is to employ the 25,000V ac system, whereas the existing electrifications around Sydney and Melbourne, dating from 1926 and 1919, use 1,500V dc. On the other hand some countries—like Holland, Belgium and Italy—have felt that the trouble caused by the coexistence of two systems outweighs the advantages of the newer high-voltage technology. In Europe several railway administrations have introduced multi-current locomotives which can haul through trains across frontiers. A quadricurrent locomotive can, for example, work a train through Holland (1,500V dc), Belgium (3,000V dc), France (1,500V dc and 25,000V ac) and Germany (15,000V ac).

Of the several systems, third-rail conductors carrying a low voltage direct current remain the best for commuter services. The trains need carry little auxiliary equipment because the dc traction motors can be fed more or less directly from the third rail which can carry a powerful current, enabling close-running trains to draw enough power to make the rapid starts so important for an efficient commuter service. One disadvantage of this system is that with a low voltage the sub-stations which feed electricity into the third rail need to be quite close, and sub-stations are expensive to build.

The advantage of using ac current, especially at a high voltage and at a frequency identical with, or easily converted from, the so-called industrial frequency supplied by power stations, has always been recognized but until recently was difficult to exploit. It required either an ac motor, which had its own problems, or some means of rectifying the current (changing it to dc). The Hungarian Kando successfully applied three-phase ac current in Italy and Hungary. In Italy the Simplon Tunnel line was one of many sections electrified on his system which, however, because of the inflexibility of the three-phase motor, could offer only four fixed speeds. For Hungary, Kando introduced his phase-convertor locomotive which could use 50 cycles current direct from the national electricity network. However, these solutions were later overtaken by new innovation and no longer survive.

Early railway electrification schemes typically involved short lengths of line which for one reason or another were difficult to operate with steam traction. This picture shows one such line, the 13km (8 mile) heavily graded line of the New Zealand Government Railways from Otira to Arthur's Pass. The three locomotives returning light after handling a heavy freight train resemble most electric locomotives of that time, being box-like in form and of rather heavy construction. The electrification dates from 1924, and uses the then-popular 1,500V system. Later systems of higher voltage can be distinguished by overhead conductor wires visibly lighter than the wires seen in this picture.

Top left: *A modern, but quite conventional, electric locomotive (class 122) of Belgian National Railways.*
Top right: *A pioneer of electric traction was the Volk's Railway at Brighton in England. This is a recent picture, although the line opened in 1883.*
Above: *An elderly electric locomotive of the New York Central Railroad hauls a passenger train towards Grand Central Terminus. A short third-rail system was adopted here to reduce the smoke nuisance of steam locomotives operating within New York City boundaries.*
Right: *The* Brighton Belle, *an all-Pullman train introduced by the Southern Railway for service on the third-rail electrified line from London to Brighton.*

Left: *Austrian State Railways multiple-unit electric trains. The train on the right is one of the latest sets, used in inter-city service.*

Above: *Electric traction in Turkey. The French influence is clearly evident, especially in the locomotive which is virtually an export model of a French National Railways type.*

Below: The Blue Train *of South African Railways. This, one of the world's great luxury trains, is hauled by electric locomotives for much of its 1,540 km (956 mile) passage between Cape Town and Johannesburg. South African electrification dates from 1926, and uses the 3,000 V system.*

Sectioned drawing of Swedish State Railways 2,580 hp, 1,500V, $16\frac{2}{3}$ Hz ac electric locomotive, 1942

1 driving cab
2 transformer oil cooler
3 traction motor blowers
4 traction motors
5 transformer compartment and switchgear
6 transformer cooling oil pump
7 air compressor
8 pantograph
9 high tension busbars connecting pantographs

10 high tension busbar carrying current to transformer
11 main circuit breaker
12 pantograph operating cylinder and springs
13 relay cabinet
14 carrying wheels
15 driving wheels with elastic drive
16 main gear face
17 hollow axle
18 driving axle

19 sandboxes
20 sand delivery pipes
21 axle boxes
22 springs
23 compressed air reservoirs
24 brake shoes and hangers
25 buffers
26 drawgear
27 jumper cables
28 mainframes

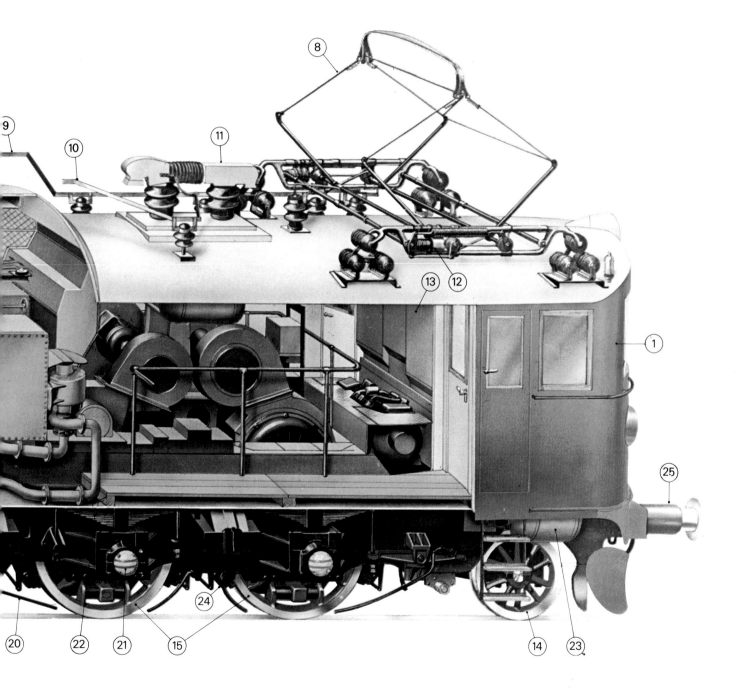

Far left: *The SNCF* Mistral *at Marseilles, behind a class BB9200 electric locomotive.*
Left: *Electrification in Norway. With high voltages, wires and structures can be lightweight.*
Below: *The Trans Siberian Railway at Chelyabinsk, with a Czech-built electric locomotive (3,000 V) in foreground.*

Far left: *A modern high-voltage electric locomotive of the SNCF 15000 class at Strasbourg.*
Above: *One of a series of high-speed electric locomotives built for the German DB in the 1960s.*
Left: *Electric traction on the metre-gauge Rhaetian Railway in Switzerland.*

Above: *A New Haven Railroad locomotive, equipped to take power both from a third rail and from overhead catenary, crosses the Harlem River in New York. The New Haven RR is now part of Conrail.*
Right: *An older type of French electric locomotive, class 2D2 9100, on passenger work at Dijon.*
Below: *One of the Pennsylvania Railroad's class GG1 electric locomotives at work in the New York–Washington service.*

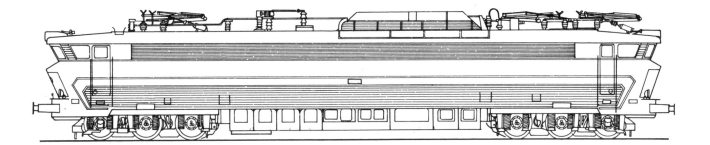

Above: *A highly sophisticated electric locomotive built by the Alsthom company of France for Belgian National Railways. Introduced in 1973, this class 18 type can operate on four different electrical systems: The Belgian 3,000 V dc, the Dutch 1,500 V dc, the French 15,000 V ac and the German 15,000 V ac. The class 40100 of the SNCF is almost identical. Multicurrent locomotives like these, which, for example, can haul trains between Paris, Brussels and Amsterdam, are convenient to operate but rather expensive to build.*

Between the wars most main-line electrifications were undertaken at 1,500 V dc with overhead-wire conductors. Some countries, notably Russia, changed to a similar system at 3,000 V and later converted their existing 1,500 V lines to the new standard. In Britain, the 750 V dc of the Southern Railway, with third-rail conductors, spread until it was no longer just a commuter operation. In Scandinavia, Germany, Austria and Switzerland 15,000 V ac at $16\frac{2}{3}$ cycles was used with overhead conductor wires. In these countries, the locomotives needed to carry very heavy transformers to lower the voltage to a level suitable for the traction motors. However, this disadvantage was considered worth while in view of the economies to be gained by using high-voltage ac: sub-stations were further apart, catenary could be lighter and there were fewer losses in transmission.

The use of high-voltage alternating current at industrial frequency became easier in the 1950s with the development, among other things, of simple light-weight rectifiers for converting the current to dc. The French were the leaders of this new technology and established yet another world standard for electrification, that of 25,000 V 50 cycles ac. The economy in sub-stations, the ease of drawing electricity supplies from national electric grids, the smaller cross-section required for conductor wires (thereby reducing the demand for expensive copper), and the high-power but lightweight locomotives which the system permitted were attractive to all railway systems but especially to those which were just embarking on their first electrification projects. The system has therefore been adopted not only in countries such as France, Britain and Russia but especially in the poorer countries, notably India but including several underdeveloped or developing nations. In some ways the current is difficult to handle: the high voltage means that conductor wires must have wide clearances to avoid flash-overs to stationary or passing objects, and the electrical disturbances set up by the passage of the current tend to affect the more sophisticated electric signalling systems. However, these problems are not insoluble even though they may be expensive. When British Rail electrified its West Coast route from London to Scotland it had to reconstruct its line so as to create virtually a new railway. Signalling had to be reorganized and bridges raised to provide the clearances needed by the high-voltage wires. But the return for all this effort was substantial in terms of convenience of operation, of attraction to clients and, it was said, of return on capital.

Railway electronics

Both the operational and economic virtues of electric traction have been enhanced in recent years by the progress of railway electronics. What might well be termed the electronic locomotive will surely dominate the motive-power stock to be ordered in the 1980s. The so-called 'chopper' locomotive, the thyristor and the current invertor have all reached a stage of development when they can be used in series production locomotives. The chopper is an electronic device for regulating the amount of current passing to the traction motors; that is, it controls the acceleration and deceleration of the loco-motive. Traditionally this has been achieved by switching resistances in or out, with corresponding notches on the driver's controller, but transition from one notch to another is inevitably accompanied by a slight jerk which, among other things, makes wheel slippage more likely. With the chopper, electronic switches admit current to the motors in very short bursts, or pulses, and it is the length of the pulse which determines the voltage supplied. Thus there are no notches but a smooth change in the length of pulse. The result is smoother acceleration, less slipping (which means a greater effective power output) and a reduction of maintenance costs because the chopper is immune to mechanical faults and because with smoother running other parts of the locomotive undergo less stress. The Dutch and Belgian railways were the first to use this device successfully, having chopper railcars running in 1967. Other countries soon followed, applying the technique to multiple unit trains. Chopper locomotive units were subsequently introduced in Italy, Belgium and France and in 1973 French Railways ordered a series of 200 chopper units (classes BB7200 and BB22200).

The thyristor is a new and successful solution to the problem of alternating current electrification. The advantages of high-voltage alternating current in transmission and of low-voltage direct current in the traction motors have always led to imperfect compromises. An advance in the 1950s was the intro-duction of solid-state rectifiers, much lighter and simpler than the old rectifiers. The thyristor both rectifies and regulates the current, thereby simpli-fying and lightening the locomotive still further. In this new technology it was Sweden which set the pace, the Swedish Railways having an experimental thyristor prototype motor coach in operation by 1964. Later a four-axle

Thyristor control was successfully introduced by the Swedish ASEA Company in 1967, with this class Rc2 electric locomotive built for the Swedish State Railways. Five years later the Austrian State Railways imported a batch of similar locomotives. After trials in the USA between New York and Washington, the type was chosen by Amtrak and is to be built under licence by General Motors.

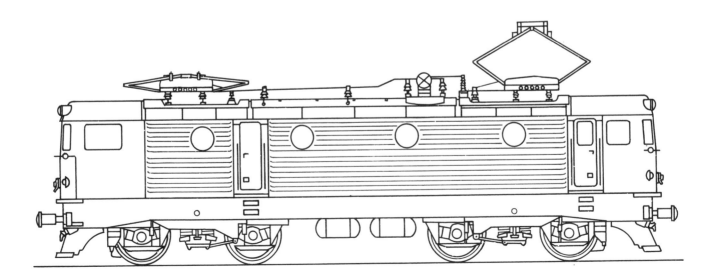

thyristor locomotive was built by ASEA for the Swedish Railways and this prototype was followed by a large order for the similar Rc series and for thyristor motor coaches. In 1967 the same firm supplied a six-axle thyristor locomotive to Romania and then additional Rc units to Austria. These export successes culminated in the trial of an ASEA thyristor locomotive by Amtrak between New York and Washington, which led to an order being placed for this type from the American licensee, General Motors. Meanwhile in Germany the DB introduced its ET420 thyristor electric train which was successful and was built in large numbers. In France the SNCF introduced its BB15000 thyristor electric locomotive series which also performed well. The smooth acceleration achieved by thyristor locomotives, just as with chopper loco-motives, enables heavier loads to be hauled. However, both the chopper and thyristor technologies have the disadvantage that, using powerful electric pulses, they are especially liable to disturb neighbouring electric circuits and in many cases the introduction of such units requires a change in the existing signalling and train control systems, a change which can be very expensive and also rather intricate.

The current invertor, another electronic innovation, promises to overcome the deficiencies of the alternating-current traction motor. Its electronic switches are in triplicate so its pulses create a synthetic three-phase current. The old disadvantage of the three-phase motor, the fact that it can work only at constant speed irrespective of the train's resistance, is overcome because the three-phase motor does respond to frequency changes, and it is a characteris-tic of the new electronic control systems that the frequency of the pulses which they emit can be varied simply by changing the speed of the electronic switch-ing operation. Thus the lightness and ease of maintenance associated with the three-phase ac motor need no longer be outweighed by the old inability to regulate its speed.

Locomotive weight

Overcoming the weight problem hitherto inevitable with ac electrification systems will be a great step forward. With contemporary systems a high-horsepower train like the British HST-125 would need engines and control apparatus weighing only about 50 tonnes if it worked on direct current. If it were designed for the ultra-modern 50 cycles ac system it would need over 80 tonnes. With the American systems using 11,000–12,000 V ac at $16\frac{2}{3}$ cycles, the situation is even less attractive, for about 100 tonnes of tractive equipment would be required. All the same, it should be noted that the HST as it actually is, with diesel-electric traction, requires no less than 137 tonnes of motive-power equipment to speed it on its way.

The advantage of high power output

Although advocates of electric traction have usually been able, with some statistical dexterity, to show that the electric locomotive is cheaper to operate than the steamer, the real advantage of electrification has little connection with costs. Electrification was first adopted by railways to solve operational problems with which the steam locomotive coped only with difficulty. Most main-line railways tried electrification initially with their commuter services, because the fast acceleration which the electric motor offers was the best way to keep the trains moving in these intensively-operated services. Again, on lines with heavy freight traffic, especially where gradients were severe, the high power output promised by electric traction seemed to make the cost of electrification worth while. Among such lines are the Manchester to Sheffield trans-Pennine route in Britain, the Suram Pass route in the Caucasus, the Sydney–Lithgow line through the Blue Mountains in New South Wales, the Breslau to Königszelt line in Prussia, various transalpine lines, and the Great Northern and Milwaukee railroads' transcontinental lines through the Rockies. All these were among the first routes to be electrified in their respective countries. It was after early successes in these services that the railways decided that electrification of other, less critical, lines might be advantageous in terms of convenient operation and appeal to the client; passengers liked smooth, smokeless and swift travel and freight shippers liked the faster services made possible by electrification. But the common determining factor was always the density of traffic; although electric locomotives were not expensive, the cost of providing electricity supply, of distribution networks, sub-stations and the conductor rails or overhead conductor wires was prohibitive unless the cost could be spread over a large number of trains.

Early electrification

The first real public electric railway was Volk's Railway, which still exists at Brighton in England. This was a narrow-gauge passenger line, built in 1883, which ran along the sea front. It used cars similar to streetcars, which picked up their current from a third rail at a low voltage. In 1890 one of the London underground railways received a batch of 100 hp four-wheel electric locomotives which it operated very successfully over a 5.6 km ($3\frac{1}{2}$ mile) length of line. Using 500 V dc, picked up from a third rail, these units could haul passengers at 40 km/h (25 mph) and without filling the tunnel with smoke. Meanwhile in the USA some valuable technical work was being done. Leo Daft in the 1880s built a couple of electric locomotives, van der Poele in 1885 successfully used an overhead wire for conducting the current, and Frank Sprague developed the idea of a multiple-unit electric train in which several motor coaches in a train could be controlled from one driving cab. Despite all this enterprise, neither Britain nor America occupy a very prominent place in the first decades of railway electrification. It was not so much inventiveness as the existence of conditions which made conversion worth while that determined the speed with which different countries electrified their railways. A shortage of coal for steam locomotives, or abundant hydroelectric generating potential, as well as fairly intensive traffic were the important prerequisites. It is hardly surprising, then, that countries like Sweden and Switzerland, where the fuel situation coincided with high technological capacity, played a leading part in early electrification.

Networks in Europe

Switzerland and Austria

Switzerland and Austria, adjoining West Germany, use the same ac system which, now that continuous electrified main lines pass over their frontiers, is a great advantage. Switzerland occupies an honoured place in the history of railway electrification, both because Swiss technology has made so many contributions to the field and because the Swiss Federal Railways are now the most electrified of all. Indeed, the Swiss Railways in the mid 1970s possessed barely a hundred diesel locomotives, and these were of low power. Before World War I there was a chance that the Swiss railways would be electrified on the three-phase system which had already had a limited success in the country. However, the 15,000 V ac system was standardized between the wars. One of several notable Swiss contributions to locomotive technology was the building for the private Berne–Lötschberg–Simplon Railway of the Ac 4/4 class. This had a new type of transmission between the motors and the wheels. The latter were mounted in two bogies and the arrangement was not only compact and light but, for the first time, resulted in an electric locomotive which could run safely at very high speeds. With such a notable electrical engineering companies as Oerlikon and Brown Boveri, it is not surprising that the Swiss railways have, right from the beginning of electrification, operated advanced types of locomotive. It is only now that the earlier types are beginning to be withdrawn. The so-called Crocodiles, for example, which were built from 1920 have lasted into the 1970s. These distinctive machines used steam locomotive type wheels, arranged as 1-6-0 + 0-6-2, and owed their name to their long, low and sinuous aspect. They weighed 130 tonnes and could produce 2,460 hp. Similar locomotives were supplied to Austria. The heavy loads and difficult gradients of the St Gotthard route have been one determining factor in Swiss locomotive design. A recent class of electric locomotives for this line, the Re6/6 class, is designed to haul 800-tonne trains at 80 km/h

Below: *The 'Crocodile' electric locomotive of the Swiss Federal Railways, an early example of the high-power traction needed in Alpine territory.*
Bottom: *Present-day power on the St Gotthard line. These class Re 6/6 locomotives can exert 10,600 hp. They were built from 1972.*

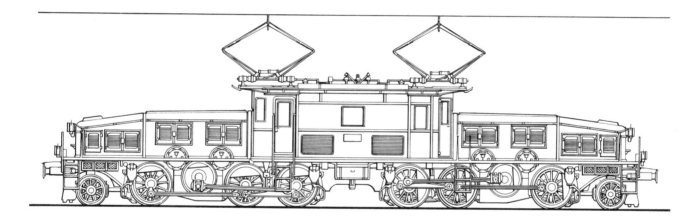

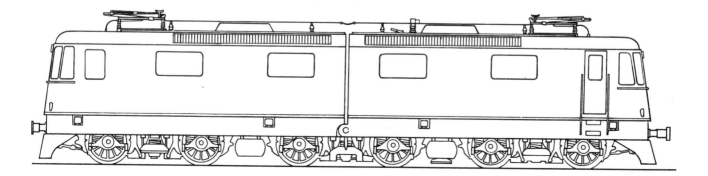

(50 mph) up grades of 1 in 37 (2.7 per cent). Running on two six-wheel bogies, these units weigh 120 tonnes and can exert 10,600 hp on hourly rating. They have regenerative braking.

In Austria, where the terrain is often similar to that of Switzerland and where there are similarly a few routes of high traffic density, electrification was somewhat slower than in Switzerland. This was partly because coal supply was better, partly because of a strong steam-locomotive tradition, and partly because of Austria's peculiar political circumstances. The first electrification was of a narrow-gauge line, the 760 mm (2 ft 6 in) gauge line once known as the Austrian Alpine Railway and now part of the Austrian State Railways. Based on St Polten, this line climbs steeply into the mountains and has many tunnels. It was, therefore, an ideal candidate for electrification which was achieved in 1911. Single-phase 25 cycle ac was used, at a voltage of 5,000 (now 6,500), and the system has remained virtually untouched since then with no attempt to substitute the Austrian State Railway's standard 15,000 V system. The loco-motives were early examples of the double-bogie arrangement, there being three axles in each bogie and each axle being powered. Truly main-line electrification began with the east to west route through Innsbruck and Salzburg, begun in 1925. Before World War I, however, there had been three shorter stretches of line converted at 15,000 V. Although a surprising number of different locomotive types operate on the electrified sections, the OBB has in recent years been distinguished by the excellence of its electric train-sets. The *Transalpin* sets, originally acquired in 1964 for the Basle–Vienna service, are six-car push-and-pull sets in which one of the end vehicles includes driving cab, electrical gear and baggage compartment, while the other has a driving cab, baggage section and passenger compartment. Thus the set is virtually a locomotive-hauled or locomotive-propelled train of fixed formation, the locomotive vehicle exerting 3,400 hp. Twenty-four first-class and 172 second-class seats are provided in both open and compartment-style seating. The high horsepower of these trains enabled 1½ hours to be cut from the Basle–Vienna schedule.

West and East Germany

Good coal supply and a steam-locomotive tradition ensured that the German railways electrified only slowly. Despite this, Germany was the source of many advances in electrification technology. Indeed, a small electric train built by von Siemens for the Berlin Trade Exhibition carried many thousands of passengers over a 274 metre (300 yard) line as early as 1879 and was one of several developments which brought the possibility of electric railways before the public eye. The Siemens and AEG companies, around the turn of the century, built electric test tracks powered by 10,000 V current. A railcar, carrying its heavy transformer, reached 216 km/h (134 mph) in one of these trials. However, the German railway administrations preferred to stay with the well-tried steam traction. But the biggest and most innovative of the German systems, the Prussian State Railways, in 1911 embarked on the first German main-line electrification. This was over the heavily-graded Silesian mountain route and was finished only in 1928. 15,000 V 16⅔ cycles ac was chosen for this conversion which had a successful but rather short life. In 1945 the Russians carried it, lock, stock, and barrel, to the USSR. Other pre-1914 German electrifications included certain commuter lines in Berlin and Hamburg, and a 48 km (30 mile) length of the Bavarian system around Zell. The latter was also at 15,000 V. In the Isar Valley there was a low-voltage system of about 18 km (11 miles) using 1,000 V. In the inter-war years electrification proceeded sporadically, so that by 1945 there were about 1,460 route miles (2,350 km) of electrified line. Half of this was in Bavaria and neighbouring Württemburg, where not only suburban lines in Munich but also long hilly stretches of main line were converted. Another important conversion was that of the north–south main line from Magdeburg to Halle and Leipzig. In the postwar years, and especially in the past two decades, electrification in West Germany has proceeded more rapidly and now includes all the main lines and many secondary routes too. In East Germany progress has been slower but the key east to west route through Karl Marx Stadt and Dresden has been converted. Both Germanies still use the 15,000 V $16\frac{2}{3}$ cycles system, although a start has been made in East Germany with 25,000 V ac. The DB in Western Germany has introduced many notable locomotive types: the 103 class, introduced in 1970, was intended for speeds up to 250 km/h (155 mph) and had an output of 7,200 kW (about 10,000 hp).

Scandinavia

Scandinavia also opted for the 15,000 v system. Indeed, it could almost be styled the Nordic system. With Switzerland, Sweden was the leading country in terms of proportion of mileage electrified by 1945. The electrification of the Lapland Railway, which has a heavy iron-ore traffic through difficult terrain, began before World War I and was finished in 1923 making an electrified route of 450 km (280 miles). The main Stockholm–Göteborg line was converted two years later. As in Switzerland, many private and narrow-gauge lines are also electrified. In Norway, electrification has been slower. Although there was a short conversion of 24 km (15 miles) as early as 1908, by World War II only 605 km (376 miles) of route were electrified. Since then there has been further conversion, so that about one third of the total extent is now under catenary, including the lines from Oslo to Stavanger, Bergen and Trondheim. In neighbouring Denmark electrification has made little progress, since there are no lines which have the heavy traffic or steep grades or tunnels which make conversion desirable. However, the electrification of the Copenhagen commuter system began in 1935 and has continued decade by decade so that in the mid 1970s it totalled 97 km (60 miles) of 1,500 V dc system. Finland, a latecomer to electrification, adopted the 25,000 V 50 cycles ac system, and had 393 km (244 miles) of route electrified by 1975. The main line from Helsinki was the first conversion and was noteworthy in that it made use of Russian-built equipment including locomotives.

Great Britain

In Britain, as elsewhere, it was during the so-called golden age of steam that electrification first began to be seriously considered. Indeed, if World War I had not interrupted progress, British electrification might well have advanced as fast as in other countries. Certainly there were many railway companies before 1914 which were willing to risk trial schemes. In 1904 the Lancashire & Yorkshire Railway began its Liverpool–Southport (59 km or 37 mile) conversion and the North Eastern Railway its 51 km (32 mile) Newcastle scheme. These were both third-rail 600 V schemes but the Midland Railway's Lancaster–Heysham (16 km or 10 miles) and the London Brighton & South Coast Railway's 8-mile (13 km) South London schemes both used 6,600 V 25 cycles ac. During World War I several other schemes came to fruition: the London & North Western Railway's London suburban scheme (630 V with third and fourth rails), the L & Y's Manchester–Bury scheme (1,200 V dc with third rail) and the London & South Western Railway's Waterloo–Wimbledon line (650 V with third rail). Apart from these suburban lines, the enterprising North Eastern Railway completed an experimental freight-line electrification between Newport and Shildon in 1915. However, the NER scheme, for which a promising locomotive had been built, was not proceeded with, partly because the Railway was merged in 1923 into the new London & North Eastern Railway. The NER had been contemplating the electrification of its busy York to Newcastle line and had actually built a fast passenger-locomotive for it. But with the merger of the Railway into a larger company the scheme was abandoned.

In inter-war Britain the main electrification work was that of the new Southern Railway which extended the London & South Western system to cover much of south-east England. By 1939 Brighton and Portsmouth, among others, had been reached and the total route mileage of this third-rail system was 1,126 km (700 miles). In recent decades the Southern Electric has been extended still further, and now includes main lines to Southampton, Bournemouth and Dover. The low-voltage system is well suited to the mainly commuter-type services of this region.

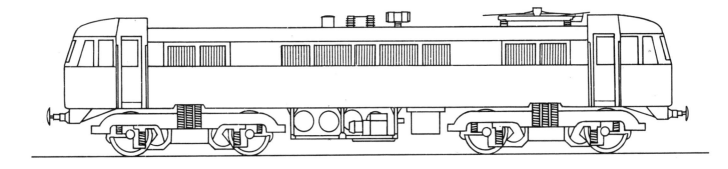

Of the three other British companies, only the London & North Eastern Railway showed real interest in electrification. But its schemes for a suburban conversion from London to Sheffield and for the main-line electrification through the Woodhead Tunnel from Manchester to Sheffield were interrupted by World War II. However, these two projects were completed after the war, both being at 1,500 V dc with overhead transmission. Other British schemes have been at 25 kV ac which has been standardized for future conversions outside the south. The London–Birmingham–Manchester–Liverpool scheme, later extended to Scotland, was a great success even though the conversion was long and expensive, being virtually a rebuilding of one of the world's oldest railway lines. How far it reduced costs is uncertain but it certainly increased revenue from passengers. The fast, frequent and clean services which electrification permitted not only brought passengers back to the

A thyristor-controlled electric locomotive of British Rail. Built with the co-operation of General Electric (GEC) in 1975, it is based on the type 87, introduced earlier for BR's West Coast electrification from London to Glasgow.

railway from competing forms of transport but also attracted travellers who formerly would not have made their journey at all. An extensive electrification of the Glasgow suburban and outer-suburban lines has also been undertaken. The Great Northern electrification scheme was completed in 1977 between Kings Cross (London) and Royston (Hertfordshire). While this is also on the 25 kV system with overhead transmission, the trains are capable of picking up low-voltage direct current from third rails enabling them to terminate at Moorgate, in the centre of London, by running over a line of the Underground system. The next big scheme is for the conversion of the former Midland Railway's main line out of London as far as Bedford, scheduled for completion in 1982.

France

Although it was in the 1950s that France became recognized as the leader in railway electrification, thanks to the SNCF's successful venture into large-scale conversion at 25 kV ac, French railways have a very long tradition of electrification. In 1903 a 30 km (19 mile) metre-gauge line between St-George de Commiers and La Mure was converted at the then high voltage of 2,400 V. The Midi Railway electrified two lines and on one of these, from Perpignan to Villefranche converted at 12,000 V $16\frac{2}{3}$ cycles ac, it tried six prototype locomotives from six manufacturers. However, it was the Paris–Orléans Railway which introduced the biggest scheme. Beginning in 1900, this company progressively electrified at 1,500 V with overhead transmission its line out of Paris to the south-west. The conversion reached Orléans in 1926 and by 1939 comprised two main lines as far as Toulouse, Bordeaux and the Pyrenees. During World War II France almost lost this conversion, for highly-placed Nazis urged that the equipment should be taken to Germany. However, German railway engineers persuaded state officials that the French system was quite incompatible with the German and therefore useless. Another important pre-war electrification was that of the Western Region of the SNCF, from Paris to Le Mans. By 1939 there were about 3,540 km (2,200 route miles) of electrified railway in France.

After the war the first big scheme was the conversion of the old PLM main line south from Paris to Lyon and then to Marseille. This was achieved in stages, enabling the celebrated *Mistral* passenger train to run on progressively shorter timings between Paris and the Mediterranean. By 1952 it was covering the 511 km ($317\frac{1}{2}$ mile) section from Paris to Lyons in $4\frac{1}{4}$ hours. In 1954, during high-speed experiments, a 7100 class six-axled electric locomotive, hauling three passenger cars, achieved a world record of 243 km/h (151 mph). A year later, this was surpassed on the Paris–Bordeaux line, where 431 km/h (205 mph) was reached. Meanwhile, beginning with heavy-traffic lines on the Eastern Region around Metz and Thionville, the SNCF was introducing the 25 kV ac system. The results achieved persuaded management to adopt this system for all future schemes which were not continuations of existing electrification. Since then conversion has proceeded steadily, the main line of the former Nord Railway from Paris to Lille and into Belgium being one of the first and most successful high-voltage conversions. Locomotive technology kept pace with these advances so that in the 1960s and 1970s French consultants and French industry were widely employed by foreign railways undertaking new projects. Performance and reliability of French locomotives remains high even though it was a Swedish locomotive which was chosen in preference to a French design by the American Amtrak organization. Units of

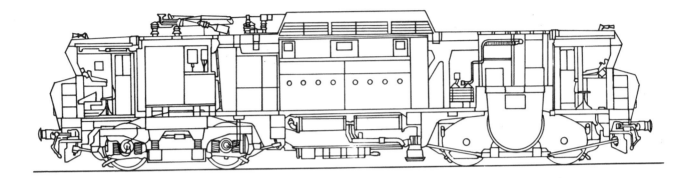

the 15000 type locomotive have been averaging 27,000 km (16,800 miles) per month, and have also shown themselves capable of running 2 million km (1.2 million miles) between overhauls.

A side elevation of the SNCF class 15000 electric locomotive, as illustrated on page 158. This is a 25,000 V ac machine with thyristor control. Intended for passenger service, its maximum speed is 180 kph (110 mph).

Italy

In the inter-war period Italy was the leader in electrification, at least from the point of view of mileage converted. Proponents of electrification in other countries, notably the USSR, took Italy as an example of what could be achieved. There were several reasons for this pre-eminence. Italians were prominent in the early study of electricity and this had established a traditional interest in all forms of electrification. Then there was the lack of coal and the progressively exploited hydroelectricity potential. Then, too, there was Mussolini, anxious to demonstrate how his party had the power and imagination to grasp the opportunities presented by new technologies.

The first Italian electrification was of a short suburban line out of Milan in 1899; this used battery railcars and was electrified less for economic and operational reasons than for the sake of competing with a parallel horse tramway which was about to electrify. In 1901 there was a third-rail electrification of another Milan line. More interesting, technically, was the adoption of the three-phase system for main-line electrification in Piedmont. Three-phase traction was developed by the Hungarian Kando, who was given the opportunity to convert an Italian line in 1901. This was successful and the system spread until by the mid 1930s more than 1,930 km (1,200 miles) had been converted. In the early days of the system it represented the best way to make use of alternating current, which was the easiest current to transmit but was not normally suitable for traction motors. However, the three-phase system had its disadvantages. Its traction motors worked at constant speed, which meant that only one speed was available for the locomotive (in practice, by varying the electrical connections, it was fairly easy to provide two, three or four speeds, but even then the locomotive was somewhat inflexible). Then the overhead catenary was expensive, because two double conductor wires had to be provided. After World War I, what was once regarded as a technical triumph was seen to be obsolete, given the new possibilities that became

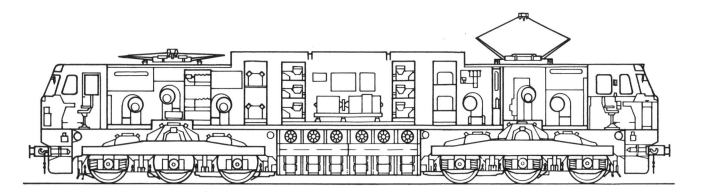

The class E666 passenger locomotive, supplied to the Italian State Railways since 1975. Designed especially for the fast passenger trains of the Rome–Florence route, it is capable of hauling trains of 570 tonnes at speeds up to 200 kph (125 mph).

available with the advent of higher-voltage dc electrification.

Beginning with an experimental line in southern Italy, the 3,000 V dc system was the new Italian standard. Most of the equipment was supplied by domestic firms although these were often subsidiaries of more experienced foreign companies. With 3,000 V, sub-stations could be up to 40 km (25 miles) apart. The Italian State Railway began to build its own hydroelectric stations and, in line with the regime's policy of self-sufficiency, electrification proceeded very rapidly. Fast electric multiple units were the pride of the Italian railways. One of them covered the key Florence–Milan route at an average of 164 km/h (102 mph) on a trial trip in 1939. By the same year the passenger on the 844 km (525 mile) trunk route from Milan to Naples could travel at an average speed of around 112 km/h (70 mph). In World War II the 3,000 V system was considerably damaged although the three-phase system in the north was fairly intact. However, in the late 1940s new electrification was undertaken, a process which has continued ever since. Meanwhile the three-phase system was finally replaced in 1976; at first it had been intended that three-phase lines would be dieselized but because of rising oil prices most were converted to the 3,000 V system.

Networks in North America

North America is one of the few developed regions of the world where electrification has made little headway. In both the USA and Canada the electrified mileage, small as it is, is actually less than it was in the inter-war period. Nevertheless, the electrification which did occur was technically advanced for its time and made use of a variety of systems. With the electrified lines belonging to widely scattered private companies it was inevitable that standardization would not be achieved or even attempted.

The very first electrification, that of the Baltimore & Ohio in 1895, made use of 600 V dc power. Later, the two dominant electrical suppliers (Westinghouse and General Electric) differed in their approach to railway electrification. Westinghouse, which collaborated with the Baldwin Locomotive Works in the locomotive-building field, preferred alternating current, which was more suited to transmission over the longer distances required for main line electrification. General Electric, in league with the American Locomotive Company (Alco), favoured dc systems, because dc was much more suited for use in traction motors; the poorer transmission qualities of dc could be partially alleviated by using voltages as high as 3,000. The 11,000 V, 25-cycle, single-phase alternating-current system which Westinghouse introduced in 1907 on the New Haven Railroad was very successful and was adopted by other lines including the influential Pennsylvania Railroad. If any one system could be called the American standard, this was it.

Most electrification projects were undertaken for so-called social reasons (the elimination of smoke in cities) or to ease the passing of heavy trains through long tunnels; here again it was the smokelessness of the electric locomotive rather than its economics which was the deciding factor. The Baltimore & Ohio adopted electrification as early as 1888, bringing its scheme to fruition seven years later. The B & O had a problem in Baltimore because its western and northern lines had no connection through the city. The local government banned a proposed elevated connecting line so the railroad decided to build a mile-long tunnel beneath the city. Because of the smoke problem and to placate the city fathers, electrification was decided upon. Through trains were hauled through the tunnel by one of three General Electric electric locomotives coupled on ahead of the steam locomotive. The latter, not being required to work through the tunnel, emitted little smoke and no steam.

It was not long before the authorities in New York decided that the smoke of the New York Central trains using Grand Central Station in Manhattan was an intolerable nuisance. The station was approached by the 3 km (2 mile) Park Avenue tunnel and, with 700 trains using the line each day, there was not only a smoke-and-cinder nuisance outside the tunnel but also a dangerously polluted atmosphere inside. The pall was sometimes so thick that accidents were caused by signals being obscured. Therefore in 1903 the local legislature passed an act forbidding the use of steam traction south of the Harlem River after 1908. This more or less forced the company to electrify. The locomotives were built by General Electric with Alco producing the running gear and body. They were fed with 600 V dc current from a third rail; in this they were distinct from the B & O locomotives which had overhead pick-up. However, where the New York Central third rail was interrupted at switches, an overhead catenary was provided which made contact with a tiny pantograph mounted on the locomotive. Thirty-five locomotives were ordered and they were very successful right from the start. Of 1,700 hp, they could easily reach 96 km/h (60 mph) on the level with nine-car trains. Like most electric locomotives they never wore out but merely became obsolete as the years passed. Some were still at work in the 1970s.

The New Haven Railroad shared the New York Central's track and terminus in New York and was similarly required to eliminate steam in Manhattan. As its traffic was already very dense it decided to electrify its main line northwards for 116 km (72 miles), as far as New Haven. This it achieved by 1914. This was not only the biggest American electrification project of the time but also the first real test of the Westinghouse 11,000 V ac system. Moreover, the locomotives which Westinghouse and Baldwin built had not only to perform at 11,000 volts but also needed to collect and use the 600 V dc current from the third rail of the shared NYC track. This dual-track-system capability remained a characteristic of New Haven locomotives in subsequent years. The locomotives were, again, very successful. They could reach 128 km/h (80 mph) and could work in pairs as multiple units controlled from one cab. Many of them lasted in main-line service until the 1940s.

Another notable tunnel electrification was that of the Canadian Northern (later Canadian National) Railway through Mount Royal at Montreal. As part of a scheme to provide an outlet to the north of the city, and to found a new suburb at the Town of Mount Royal, the 4.5 km (3 mile) tunnel was opened in 1918. Electric traction was needed and the General Electric system was chosen using dc at 2,400 volts. The first route was of 13 km (8 miles) to a suburban terminus at Cartierville, but extensions in 1925 and 1947 raised the operated mileage to 29 km (18 miles). Until the dieselization of the CNR the electric locomotives were also used to haul main-line trains out to the suburbs where the steam engines took over.

Electrification of tunnel sections outside cities was sometimes undertaken for both anti-pollution and operating reasons. Where gradients were unfavourable, and the loads heavy, steam locomotives would work so hard that tunnels would be filled with steam and noxious gases. Locomotive crews of the time were prepared to endure much but there was a point at which they could no longer carry on. In West Virginia before World War I the Norfolk & Western had just such a problem with its Elkhorn Tunnel. This was a single-track section interposed in a double-track main line and situated at the top of a steep grade (2.4 per cent, or 1 in 42). Loads were limited to 3,300 tonnes but even so three Mallet-type steam locomotives were needed to move trains at little more than 8 km/h (5 mph). The solution was ready by 1915—electrification on the Westinghouse 11,000 V ac system. The locomotives were very novel. The Westinghouse designers at this time were enamoured of the three-phase motor, which was steady-running and made it easier to employ regenerative braking. The single-phase current picked up by the locomotive pantographs was therefore passed through a phase-converter to emerge as three-phase current ready for the traction motors. A drawback of the three-phase system was that motors ran at the same speed automatically, irrespective of the load. But it was fairly easy to arrange for the single speed to produce a choice of two operating speeds, in this case 22 km/h and 45 km/h (14 and 28 mph) and for slow drag work this was not a serious limitation. But the three-phase system found little favour with other American railroads although the N & W expanded it to cover 112 km (70 miles) of route. When ever-expanding coal traffic after World War II persuaded the company to widen the Elkhorn Tunnel and to ease its gradient, the electrification was abandoned in favour of steam traction. Another coal-hauling line of the region, the Virginian Railroad, electrified 216 km (134 miles) of its densely-trafficked main line in 1925 from Mullens to Roanoke, where 6,000-tonne trains moved over 2 per cent (1 in 50) grades. But after this company was absorbed by the Norfolk & Western its 11,000 V electric system was soon replaced by diesel traction.

The first big company to opt for electrification for reasons which had little to do with the smoke nuisance was the Milwaukee Railroad. When it built America's last transcontinental line in 1909 it crossed five mountain ranges and found that even its powerful Mallet-type steam locomotives were not really good enough for this arduous line. Beginning in 1914, and ending in 1927, the Milwaukee progressively electrified 1,055 km (656 miles) of its route from Montana to the Pacific. At its peak this project involved 116 locomotives,

22 sub-stations and about 4,800 km (3,000 miles) of transmission and conductor wiring. The catenary was supported on wooden poles but despite this the Milwaukee's electrification seemed a foretaste of the new technology which, it was believed, was just round the corner for American railroads. The Railroad's publicity department thoroughly exploited this feeling with new advertising slogans about 'making nature drive the wheels' and by staging a tug-of-war between a new electric locomotive and a Mallet steamer. This latter was, more accurately, a push-of-war, with the competing locomotives nose to nose, and the result went according to plan: as the movie cameras whirred the electric slowly but surely pushed its furiously steaming rival back down the line. Quite apart from attracting passengers who were glad to be spared smoke and cinders, the electrification was estimated to have saved enough in operating costs to pay for itself within nine years.

Hydroelectricity, transmitted at as much as 100,000 V and then transformed to 3,000 V dc, was the power source. The first passenger locomotives, built by General Electric, were unique 264-tonne machines with bipolar motors which could produce 3,500 hp on hourly rating. They were displaced only after the dieselization of the 1950s.

Competing with the Milwaukee Railroad, the parallel Great Northern also had its mountain and tunnel problems. In 1909 it electrified its Cascade Tunnel section on the three-phase ac system. However, in the 1920s the Railroad reconstructed and extended this electrification, choosing the 11,000 V system which it installed over 119 km (74 miles) of route. In 1947 the company bought from General Electric two enormous locomotives which were, at the time, the world's most powerful single-unit electric locomotives. Each weighed 360 tonnes and could exert 5,000 hp on continuous rating. These machines were capable of hauling heavy passenger trains at 105 km/h (65 mph) up fearsome gradients but they had a short life; when diesels were introduced the Great Northern management deemed its electrification superfluous and in 1956 the Railroad was de-electrified.

The most successful of the American main-line electrifications was, and remains, that of the Pennsylvania Railroad. The Railroad had been contemplating electrification since as early as 1908 although the line originally thought suitable for conversion was not the route which, twenty years later, was finally chosen. Originally electrification had seemed a suitable solution for the Railroad's problem of excessive traffic density. In terms of tonne-kilometres per kilometre of track per year, the Pittsburg division of the Railroad was America's busiest length of railway. Moreover, the heavily graded Horseshoe Pass was nearby, on which heavy trains laboured in the care of two or more engines and managed to achieve average speeds of around 16 km/h (10 mph). However, the still-uncertain prospects of long electrified routes, and the acquisition by the Railroad of a fleet of very capable 2-10-0 steam locomotives, led to the shelving of these plans. Then, in 1928, the Pennsylvania Railroad decided to electrify its easily graded main line from New York to Washington.

The reason for this change of thinking was the rapidly increasing traffic, both passenger and freight, of this trunk route and the fact that the Railroad had already begun to electrify the northern end in order to operate a commuter service southwards from New York. In economic terms, as distinct from operating terms, electrification here was the most promising. So during the 1930s the line was electrified not only to Washington but also beyond as far as Harrisburg. The system chosen was 11,000 V ac and Westinghouse provided most of the electrical equipment. In 1934 appeared what has since become recognized as the classic American electric locomotive, the GG1, built jointly by Westinghouse and the Railroad's own Altoona Workshops. 139 of these 230-ton units were built. They were of 4,600 hp on continuous rating and could reach speeds of 185 km/h (115 mph). Their outward form—rounded, streamlined, tall and lean—was the result of co-operation between their designers and an industrial artist. Some are still in service. In the late 1950s, impressed with its new diesel locomotives, this Railroad, like the New Haven Railroad, did contemplate de-electrification, but studies showed that the most economic decision was to replace the oldest of the electric freight machines with new units and to regard the electrification as permanent. Since electrification in the previous decades had enabled the Railroad to handle its traffic very efficiently, and to provide an excellent passenger service on the New York–Washington route (a very sensitive route from the publicity point of view), the decision seems wise. At the present time, with the Pennsylvania merged into the Conrail system and the passenger service handled by Amtrak trains, the value of the electrification is still evident. The question of electrifying the western sections to Pittsburg remains open; Congress, in 1976, when legislating the establishment of Conrail, specifically provided for a loan guarantee to enable the new organization to electrify from Harrisburg to Pittsburg if it wished. One problem of such an electrification would be that a difficult choice would need to be made between continuing the old-established 11,000 V system or introducing a more modern system, which would be cheaper but would involve a change of current at Harrisburg.

In general, the US electric locomotive was threatened after World War II by dieselization, just as the steam locomotive was threatened. US electrified mileage, which had once totalled 4,990 km (3,100 miles) was down to less than 3,200 km (2,000 miles) by 1975 and most of that was commuter line. However, in the 1970s a number of American railroads began to show new signs of interest in electrification. This happened even before the steep rise of fuel-oil prices; locomotive fuel costs were rising because more fuel was being used. For years diesel fuel cost only ten cents per $4\frac{1}{2}$ litres (1 gallon), but because the railroads for competitive reasons were speeding up their freight trains they were consuming more and more oil. The traditional motive power provision of one horsepower of capacity for every tonne of train soon rose to more than two horsepower and fuel costs began to exceed labour costs on the fastest trains. At the same time the first generation of diesel locomotives was ageing, maintenance costs were rising and European railways were showing what could be achieved with the latest technologies. In particular, the silicon rectifier was a cheap and easy way of combining the advantages of high-voltage transmission of ac power with the advantages of low-voltage dc traction motors. When the Pennsylvania Railroad bought new freight electric locomotives in the 1960s the mercury rectifiers of the original design were soon replaced by silicon.

The Canadian Pacific, facing a heavy traffic problem with export grain and coal, has been considering the electrification of its line through the Rockies and has carried out trials of various items of equipment. But American railroads are still reluctant to take the final plunge. One reason for this reluctance is the failure to reach suitable agreements with electric-supply companies about the rates which would be charged for electric power. The companies stipulate a so-called demand charge. This is a device which they levy on industrial customers and in effect is an extra rate for electricity supplied during peak hours. The railroads, perhaps realizing that this would mean extra costs for their commuter services, are reluctant to concede this or to acknowledge that the demand-charge concept is, in principle, favourable for the railroads since so much of their heavy freight traffic moves at night in the off-peak period. Another quite reasonable demand of the power companies, that the railways should consume an agreed minimum of electricity and thereby make worth while the extra investment which they would have to undertake, is also an obstacle.

The question of minimum demand for power is linked with the question of the minimum traffic level needed to make electrification worth while for a railroad which has no gradient problems. For a double-track line, about 60 million gross tonnes per kilometre was regarded as the minimum. The subsequent rise in fuel prices reduced this, but not as much as might be expected, because the cost of generating electricity rose in the same period. Very few US railroads could approach this traffic density, or even 30 million gross tonnes on single-track routes. The Pennsylvania Railroad's Pittsburg division was one obvious candidate, and the transcontinental lines of the Union Pacific, Southern Pacific and Santa Fe railroads were others. Elsewhere, the multiplicity of competing railroads meant that traffic was spread thinly over a number of lines and it was not practicable, as in Europe, to electrify with the intention of diverting traffic from parallel lines to the electrified route. The merging of several companies into new larger undertakings, a trend which in the past two decades has characterized American railroading, might have been expected to reduce the number of main lines and at the same time increase the intensity of traffic using the surviving lines. However, this has been slow to happen so far but it may occur in the future. For the time being the merger movement is an obstacle to electrification because it is an ongoing process and until it is finished it will not be clear which lines will in fact survive as high-density routes.

Moreover, it is only a few railroads which can be confident of a long, prosperous future. When losses are as common as profits no railroad management which has the interests of its shareholders at heart can envisage making investments which will need decades to pay for themselves. Electrification really needs a thirty-year recoupment period and not many railroads, especially in the eastern states, can be confident that they will survive that long.

One very concrete electrification plan held up because of the possibility of a merger which would undermine all the assumptions on which it had been based was that of the Illinois Central Gulf Railroad. This company, which already operated a 1,500 V commuter service out of Chicago, drew up a plan in 1973 for the electrification of its main line from Chicago southwards to the Gulf of Mexico. A 30-year life for the installations was assumed and it was also assumed that the Railroad's operating pattern would be unchanged: that is, like most American main lines, its trains would be few but long, weighing up to 13,000 tonnes. The local power companies were expected to levy a heavy demand charge amounting to one half or more of the total electricity cost. The 50,000 V 60 cycles system was chosen and it was calculated that conversion of the northern half of the route, from Chicago to Memphis, would bring a rate of return of at least 30 per cent. With the high voltage, sub-stations would be needed only at intervals of 56 km (35 miles). Because electric locomotives are more powerful, and make much better use of their adhesion than do diesels, in the first stage only 88 electrics would be needed to replace 195 diesels. Moreover, maintenance costs of electrics would be considerably lower, since an electric locomotive only costs 40 per cent of the maintenance costs of an average diesel (and less than 40 per cent of a high-power diesel). The electric locomotive was also reckoned to have 95 per cent availability as against the diesel's 85 per cent. However, attributing a life of 15 years to a diesel locomotive was perhaps pessimistic, although proponents of electrification could also argue that the 35 years taken to be the life of an electric locomotive was also an underestimate. After all, the GG1 electrics of the Pennsylvania Railroad are well into their fifth decade.

The locomotive manufacturers have not been conspicuously enthusiastic about electrification. Electric locomotives would be built by companies which are at present happy enough to build diesel locomotives. The diesel locomotive is a more complex machine than the electric and the latter therefore should be cheaper. Yet electric locomotives cost much more than comparable diesel locomotives built by the same company. The explanation given is that the diesel units have much bigger production runs and therefore are cheaper to build, but not everyone accepts this as a full answer.

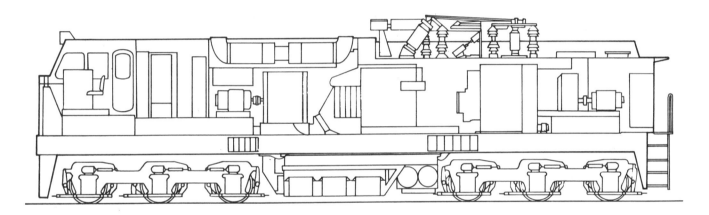

For the Black Mesa and Lake Powell Railroad in the USA, General Electric designed and built this locomotive type in 1974. It uses current at 50,000 V and is rated at 5,600 hp. Although a man rides on the locomotive to supervise its operation, it is fully automated and could be driverless.

If American railroads are on the brink of electrification, which is quite possible because most of the difficulties outlined above are not insoluble, then the first manifestation of the new technology is probably the Muskingum Electric Railroad, opened in 1968. This was built by an electric-power company and had the dual purpose of transporting coal 24 km (15 miles) to the power station and of demonstrating the new potentialities of modern electrification. The power was supplied as 25,000 V ac; it was also 60 cycle, instead of the 25-cycle current hitherto supplied to ac railroads. The advantage of 60 cycles was that it corresponds to the current of the commercial public grid and did not require conversion to 25 cycles for supply to the railroad. Two rectifier locomotives were built by General Electric for this line and gave excellent results. The general success of this railroad, although it has not yet resulted in converting the larger railroad managements to the electrification cause, was at least followed by the construction of another electrified railroad for the use of a power company. This was the Black Mesa and Lake Powell Railroad in Arizona where 6,000 hp electric locomotives haul coal 125 km (78 miles) from pit to power station.

One result of these demonstrations has been a move to change the current of the existing electrification of the former New Haven and Pennsylvania railroads from 25 cycle to 60 cycle, although it is the reluctance of the power-supply companies to continue providing 25-cycle current that is probably the determining factor. This change would mean that some electric locomotives, like the famous GG1 type, would be made obsolete, for conversion to the new system is not economic for older locomotives. The General Electric type E60CP locomotives ordered by Amtrak primarily for passenger services on the former Pennsylvania Railroad's New York to Washington route are designed as tri-current locomotives. Amtrak, however, has not been completely satisfied with home-designed electric locomotives and in the mid-1970s decided to borrow a French CC21000 and a Swedish ASEA electric locomotive for trials between New York and Washington. The French locomotive performed well but was handicapped by its sensitivity to the somewhat rough track. The Swedish locomotive, of the well-tried Rc4 type, gave very good results and Amtrak has decided to order more of this type, which are being built under licence by General Motors. The inability of American designers to produce designs comparable with European locomotives is, probably, a consequence of the lack of orders from US railroads over the past decades; no industry is likely to remain in the first rank if it has few orders to fill.

New electrification

Elsewhere in the world many railways are electrifying. Not only the less intensively used systems of Europe, like those of Spain and Portugal and south-eastern Europe, but also in many formerly colonial territories. Japanese electrification has proceeded fast. In 1939 it comprised barely 650 km (400 miles), mainly in the Tokyo suburban area, but since then the main lines have been converted and with the wider-gauge Shinkansen section, with its 'bullet trains', Japanese industry and engineers have begun to offer severe competition to the French in the export business. However, these two countries are not alone in overseas markets: Sweden, Germany and Britain are also leading contractors, consultants and suppliers. British participation has been particularly strong in projects in former British territories and at present this tendency is demonstrated in Pakistan, where the main line from Karachi to Rawalpindi and beyond is being electrified with British equipment. The British General Electric Company is also building the locomotives for the new Sishen-Saldanha ore-carrying line in southern Africa. This 864 km (537 mile) route is electrified at 50,000 V, like the Black Mesa and Lake Powell Railroad. This ultra-high ac system is believed by some engineers to set a new standard for future electrifications.

British advice and equipment also played a large part in the early Indian electrifications although India is now almost self-sufficient in this field. The first electrification in the sub-continent was undertaken in the Imperial period, with the conversion of the lines from Bombay to Poona and Igatpuri on the 1,500 V dc system. Since Independence conversion has continued. With its abundant but somewhat low-grade coal reserves India is a natural candidate for electrification, especially as the country lacks adequate oil resources. Trunk lines such as those from Delhi to Calcutta and Bombay to Ahmedabad have been the first of the major postwar conversions. India, too,

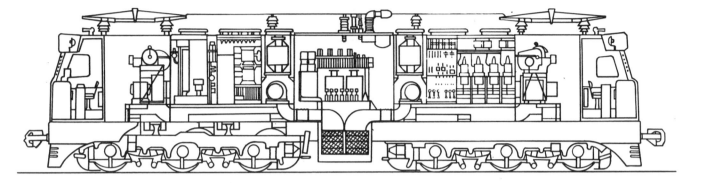

The first mass-production locomotive built for the Soviet Railways 25,000 V electrification was this type VL60. It appeared in the late 1950s, being sent to the central section of the Trans Siberian Railway. The design was not altogether satisfactory, and many modifications were required before the performance of these locomotives could be regarded as acceptable. The type has since been superseded by more powerful designs.

has opted for the 25,000 V system even though the earlier projects were executed with 1,500 V dc.

To some extent India is following the Russian example, being a formerly backward country in the process of rapid industrialization. Rather than build new lines to haul the rapidly increased traffic, the USSR found it preferable to electrify thereby enabling existing lines to carry heavier, faster and more numerous trains. Although electrification in the 1930s was well behind schedule, some difficult heavy-traffic lines in the Urals and Caucasus, as well as a climatically difficult section of the Murmansk Railway, were successfully converted. Since the mid 1950s, with extra funds granted for railway modernization, conversion has been rapid. The main lines are now finished, and it is possible to travel from Leningrad to the Caucasus and from Moscow to eastern Siberia by electric train. The more recent conversions have been on the 25,000 V system except in areas where the existing 3,000 V dc system already predominates.

The oil crisis of the mid 1970s was not, as might have been expected, followed by a burst of railway electrification. This was because the prices of all fuels rose so that electricity became more expensive too. But in the long term the prospects for electrification have been enhanced by the expected shortage of fossil fuels after the 1980s. Electricity can be generated by whichever fuels are available at a given time, including nuclear fuel, whereas the production of synthetic diesel oil is likely to be expensive. Because railway electrification is a long process, governments are now looking more kindly on the electrification projects put forward by railway managements. This change of heart is especially notable in Britain and it is likely that the recently approved London–Bedford electrification will be followed by other projects. In that other laggard in railway electrification, North America, a similar situation may be expected, with Amtrak's projected extension of electrification from New Haven to Boston encouraging the private railroads to take the plunge.

Diesel Traction

by John Westwood The principles, history
and development of diesel locomotion.

Most of the world's railways, on their non-electrified lines, have replaced the steam locomotive with the diesel. In main-line service they have usually chosen the diesel-electric, which may be regarded as an electric locomotive that carries its own power-station. In a sense, therefore, the diesel locomotive provides some of the benefits of electrification without the cost and complication of sub-stations, wiring and conductors. Being virtually two machines in one, the locomotive is heavier and more expensive than the electric locomotive, so railway managements tend to electrify lines on which many locomotives are needed and to dieselize those where only a few are required.

The heart of a diesel locomotive is its engine. Indeed, the major reason why railways chose diesel traction is this engine, for in terms of converting fuel into energy, that is, of thermal efficiency, it is superior to the steam locomotive; a diesel converts about 20–28 per cent of the fuel's potential energy into useful work, whereas a steam locomotive in good condition converts only about 10 per cent. Moreover, when dieselization got under way, in the 1940s, 1950s and 1960s, diesel fuel was very cheap and even now it is one of the cheapest of fuels.

The workings of a diesel locomotive

The diesel engine works by compression-ignition; there are no spark-plugs because the piston compresses air in the cylinder so powerfully that its temperature rises enough to ignite the fuel which is then injected into the cylinder. The maximum power of the combustion is limited by the amount of air which can be trapped inside the cylinder, for it is fairly easy to inject as much fuel as is needed. In order to increase the available air, supercharging may be used to push the air into the cylinder in an already partially compressed form. Many diesels have turbosuperchargers which, driven from the diesel's own shaft, act like a windmill in pushing the air into the cylinder. The speed of the engine (revolutions per minute, or rpm) is regulated by the amount of fuel which is admitted for each power stroke. In the past, fairly slow moving engines were preferred, of around 500 rpm, for they suffered less wear and tear. However, since by increasing the rpm an engine becomes more powerful with little weight increase, high-speed engines are now more popular, typically of 1,000 to 1,500 rpm. There are limits to the numbers of revolutions; in the days before maximum rpm were limited automatically, there was always a danger that an engine would speed up until it literally shook itself to pieces.

Engines may be two-stroke or four-stroke; some designers prefer the former and others the latter, and there really seems to be little difference between them. The power of an engine is largely determined by the cubic capacity of its cylinders. This means that, as one would expect, the biggest engines are the most powerful. However, over the years all kinds of ingenious arrangements have been devised to cram the highest possible cubic capacity into the smallest possible space. Indeed, one of the most important factors holding back dieselization in the inter-war period was the lack of a diesel engine of suitably high-power and low-weight characteristics. In recent years the 'Deltic' engine, in which the cylinders are arranged in a triangle, has been a notable success in reducing weight and size. V-form engines and opposed-piston engines have also been quite successful. A good example of a postwar locomotive diesel is the Sulzer engine of the French 68000-class locomotive. This has 12 cylinders arranged in two banks inclined towards each other at 50 degrees, thus forming a V-form engine in which all pistons drive a common

Previous pages: One of the most successful concepts in diesel locomotive design was the road-switcher general-purpose unit, which originated in America on the eve of World War II. This picture shows a modern example of the type, working on one of the world's most arduous railways, the Central Railway of Peru. It is hauling a Lima to Huancayo train in the Andes at Meiggs, 4,270 metres (14,000 ft) above sea level.

crankshaft. The cylinders are 240mm × 280mm (9.4in × 11in) and maximum speed is 1,050rpm. All this produces up to 3,000hp for an engine weight of 15 tonnes. However, the engine horsepower is not quite the same as the locomotive's horsepower available for moving a train. In the 68000 class the locomotive exerts about 2,700hp.

The diesel engine is coupled to an electric generator whose current is used to drive the traction motors. The latter are of the same type as electric locomotive motors; indeed they may be identical. General Electric in the USA, for example, uses the same motors for its electric and diesel locomotives. Traction motors use direct current, as dc motors produce more turning power (torque) for the same current. However, the ac motor, which does not have brushes or commutator, is far easier to maintain and many engineers would prefer it to the traditional dc motor. In the past, to match the motors, a dc generator was used but there has been a recent break with this tradition. An alternating-current generator (alternator) is much smaller for the same capacity and now that solid-state rectifiers are available to convert ac into dc it has become possible to generate alternating current which is immediately rectified into dc for the motors.

Although the engine/generator/traction-motors sequence is basically simple, in practice it is intricate because each process has to be exactly matched with the others. The diesel locomotive is a machine of varying horsepower and varying speed, and this produces complications. Hauling a heavy load at high speed means that the traction motors demand as much current as the generator can provide, but simply increasing the revolutions of the diesel engine is not practical; the magnetic field of the generator has to be strengthened to provide the energy-inducing drag against the revolutions of the engine shaft. On the other hand, when current requirements are low, generation cannot be reduced by slowing down the revolutions because below a certain but quite high critical speed the engine will stall. In such a case the magnetic field of the generator has to be reduced so that with reduced drag it can rotate quite fast without producing a dangerous excess of current. This was a serious problem in the pioneer days of the diesel locomotive because a mismatching of the three elements could result in a stalled engine or burnt-out electrical gear. It was Hermann Lemp, a Swiss engineer working for the US General Electric Company, who solved this. In his self-regulating system the excitation current (the current which passes through the generator field coils to create the magnetic field) is generated from an exciter, or from windings, worked by the generator itself so that the amount of excitation current produced is directly dependent on the speed of the generator. From this advance, the control of a diesel locomotive through a single control handle in the cab became possible; it was no longer necessary for the operator to match up the field-control settings manually.

The motors of a diesel locomotive can usually be connected in parallel and in series-parallel, according to need. The change is usually, though not always, effected automatically. This is necessary because as traction motors turn they produce a counter-rotation force, as in a generator, and this increases as rotation speed increases. This means that at higher speeds an increasing proportion of the available current is consumed in overcoming this force. However, by varying the connections between the motors this drag can be minimized.

At slow speeds, where traction motors may be exerting great tractive power but not moving very fast, heat may build up to such a degree that the insulation is charred away thereby necessitating expensive repair. The gearing which connects the traction motors with the driving axles is therefore different for fast locomotives and those intended for freight service. Since some over-heating can be tolerated, locomotives can be operated for very brief periods at slow speeds and full throttle; an ammeter in the cab is marked to show how long certain amperages can be tolerated at given speeds. Thus, like an electric locomotive, a diesel has a short-term rating. However, this does not mean that the diesel can call upon almost unlimited power, as can the electric, for its maximum output can never exceed the capacity of its diesel engine.

Having a generator, the diesel-electric locomotive can be equipped for rheostatic braking just like an electric locomotive. Obviously, since there is no third rail or overhead wire it cannot utilize regenerative braking. Not all railways favour rheostatic brakes; they are most valuable when speed has to be controlled for long distances over falling gradients. Locomotives which are so equipped can be recognized by their extra air vents through which the hot air is exhausted to atmosphere. On an American-style road-switcher, for example, there are typically three circular exhaust fans in the forward part of the roof for cooling the engine radiator, with another pair in the central roof for the braking resistances.

The history of diesel locomotion in Europe

Diesel-locomotive development dates from the end of the past century and the idea took longer than the steam locomotive to become accepted. The first stage was to design and build a locomotive which actually worked, and after-wards to refine it to create a locomotive so efficient that railway adminis-trations would want to buy it. It was this second stage which took so long. For decades protagonists of the diesel locomotive were in the tantalizing situation of promoting a form of motive power which was three or four times more efficient than the steam locomotive yet which remained unattractive to railway managements. This unattractiveness derived from several factors, quite apart from the inherent conservatism of most railways. There was the high capital cost—three or four times that of a corresponding steam locomotive—and there was the heavy weight of diesel locomotives. Also, the diesel protagonists had to fight on two fronts: there were those who believed that the steam locomotive, despite its low thermal efficiency, had sufficient other virtues to justify its continued use, and there were those who said that the 'straight' electric locomotive could do everything the diesel could do and more. The dieselizers replied that electrification was costly and that the steam loco-motive had had its day, and quietly sought roles for the diesel locomotive where it would be unrivalled: service in waterless areas; yard work where continuous availability was a great advantage, and branch-line passenger services where a diesel-engined railcar would be much cheaper to operate than a steam train.

The diesel engine is merely a version of what was once called the oil engine, so the first 'diesel' locomotives actually preceded the successful development of Rudolf Diesel's engine. The Yorkshireman Priestman's 12 hp four-wheel dockyard locomotive of 1894 is generally regarded as the first oil-engined locomotive. Another Yorkshireman, Stuart, developed a type of engine which was used by the English firm of Richard Hornsby to power six locomotives built between 1894 and 1903. These were sold to the government for special duties; arsenals were an early target of diesel-locomotive salesman because steam locomotives, with their sparks, were regarded as hazardous. However, later British yard locomotives used gasoline (petrol) rather than oil engines. But for the outbreak of World War I, a very advanced gasoline-electric locomotive would have been built by the English firm of Hawthorn Leslie for the Trans-Australian Railway, which had a water-supply problem. Inspired by an engineer who had worked with the steam-electric locomotives of France's Western Railway and who had also succeeded in evolving an advanced control system, this locomotive was designed to produce 800 hp from its 1,000 hp engine.

The steam-electric locomotives of France's Western Railway can be regarded as true precursors of the diesel-electric for they introduced the idea of electric generators on board the locomotive itself. They were also 'total-adhesion' locomotives, running on bogies, or trucks, in which each axle was a driving axle thereby enabling a high tractive power to be exerted without wheel-slip. But these *locomotives thermo-électriques système Heilmann* were not a commercial success because they were heavier and more expensive than corresponding steam locomotives. In pre-1914 France, as in Britain, the gasoline-engined locomotive for yard work was developed rather than the diesel locomotive. The French were also interested in gasoline-engined railcars, beginning a tradition of railcar operation which has continued until this day. The railcars supplied by Dion Bouton to the Hungarian Railways in 1904 were remarkable in that their benzine engines transmitted power through generator and traction motors. Also, in 1911, a local railway operated by Les Mines de Carvin bought a gasoline-engined railcar with electric transmission. Two years later the same line bought a 150 hp railcar with a Leroux diesel and mechanical transmission; both were destroyed during the fighting of World War I. More fortunate were the pre-war Swedish railcars built by ASEA. Bought by a short line in 1912, these were the first diesel-electric railcars and worked well for many years.

Meanwhile in Germany Rudolf Diesel was trying to interest industrialists in the possibility of high-powered diesel locomotives. He had handed over the final version of his oil engine to the MAN company which made several fundamental changes to the concept before a really useful engine emerged. MAN licensed other companies to make these engines and it was one of these, Sulzer, that joined with the locomotive-builder Borsig to construct the world's first main-line diesel locomotive. This was built in 1912 and was tried on the Prussian State Railways. It had a 1,200 hp Sulzer V-form engine of four cylinders. As would be the case with subsequent pioneer diesel locomotives the transmission was the great problem. In this machine the crankshaft was transverse, lying across the centre of the locomotive, and it drove the axles through a jackshaft and rods. For starting and for speeds up to 10 km/h (6 mph) compressed air was used to drive the pistons. This air was stored in cylinders charged by an auxiliary compressor. However, expansion of compressed air in the cylinders was accompanied by a drastic fall of temperature so that starting the diesel ignition when sufficient speed was reached was by no means easy. Frequently the cylinder was flooded with unignited fuel or there was a misfire; the locomotive evidently could not be rostered to haul regular trains. However, it provided experience and after World War I German industry would again attempt to produce a viable diesel locomotive. But this would be without Dr Diesel who mysteriously disappeared overboard from a cross-channel ferry in 1913.

The development of the internal-combustion locomotive in the USA

On the USA railways internal-combustion engines before World War I were widely employed in railcars for light passenger services. As early as 1880 a gasoline-electric railcar was demonstrated at Chicago. This was technically interesting in that during acceleration the generator was supplemented by current from a battery, itself charged by the generator during the journey. A larger (but still rather small) unit was built in 1897. This had a 25 hp engine and could pull a trailer. Neither of these cars was a commercial success but it is probable that they inspired French companies in their railcar ventures of the same period.

The McKeen railcar became quite popular in the USA. William McKeen had been motive-power superintendent of the Union Pacific Railroad at a time when that company was seeking ways to reduce train costs on its branch lines. The McKeen railcar which resulted from this quest had a powerful six-cylinder gasoline engine for driving its forward truck. Transmission was by gear and chain offering two speeds. McKeen resigned from the Railroad to start his own company and sold well over one hundred units by 1914. Recognizable by their solid build and pointed noses, they were good enough to deter competitors but not quite good enough to attract more than a handful of the bigger railroads. The branch lines for which they were intended were too roughly laid, and the engine and transmission, heavy though they were, were affected by the shocks of loose rail joints.

It needed a big company, able to provide capital and inventive engineers over a number of years, to develop the railcar concept. Such a company was General Electric which, with Westinghouse, already dominated the American market for electrical equipment and was always on the lookout for new outlets. The General Electric management, apparently, had been attracted by a British railcar design, a wooden-bodied vehicle powered by an 85 hp Wolseley engine connected to a generator powering two traction motors. Other technical features of this design were a battery starting arrangement and electrical braking (the traction motors were used as generators, not only providing rolling resistance but also power to magnetize track brakes which lowered a shoe on to the rail surface). In 1904 General Electric entered this field, partly to win a potentially vast market and partly to deter any competitor from following and thereby threatening General Electric's existing business in railway electrification.

The first GE venture was a railcar powered by a Wolseley engine and GE traction motors. This was reconstructed from a heavy wooden passenger car provided by the Delaware & Hudson Railroad. It was on this Railroad that trials were held; the car worked in regular service satisfactorily but it was rather too heavy for the engine. The engine was started by replacing the spark-plugs in three cylinders with explosive plugs, containing cordite, which were triggered in turn to get the engine moving. GE then designed its own engine and two more trial railcars were built. These were somewhat lighter than the first and the third unit was started not by explosive plugs but compressed air. This third car, with its 125 hp 550 rpm gasoline engine, weighing 36 tonnes and providing 45 seats, ran for thousands of kilometres on demonstration trips over various interested railroads in 1909. The Southern Railway was the first to place an order and was followed by several others. About ninety units of this and improved designs were sold before World War I.

While it was busily building gas-electric railcars General Electric had been exploring related fields. It was inevitable that sooner or later a railroad which had made a success of the railcar would ask whether a locomotive could be built on the same principles. The first railroad to make this request was the Minneapolis, St Paul, Rochester & Dubuque Electric Traction Company (usually and more conveniently known as the Dan Patch Lines). For this company, GE built a 400 hp gas-electric locomotive. This new design took the forward part of two railcars—each with their engine, generator and traction truck—and placed them back to back, with a control system which enabled one or both engines to be controlled from either the front or rear cab. The Dan Patch Lines liked this vehicle and ordered two more in 1915 which enabled it to dispense with steam traction for passenger services.

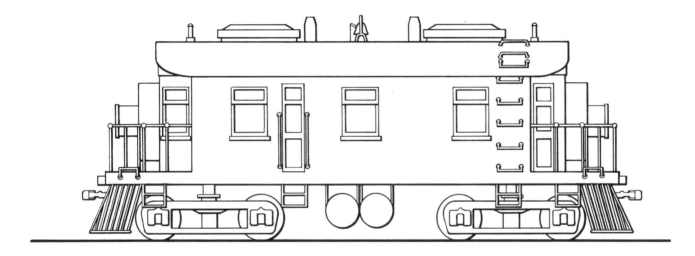

An early and successful internal-combustion locomotive, the Dan Patch Railroad's gas-electric. A forerunner of the diesel-electric locomotive, this American improvisation was built by General Electric.

In 1910 Rudolf Diesel visited the USA to promote his version of the oil engine. Among those he met was Hermann Lemp, who was working for GE and already experimenting with his automatic-control system. Lemp and his colleagues were impressed with the diesel engine and visited Europe in order to pick up useful ideas. They bought the patent for the German Junkers opposed-piston diesel engine, and in the following years improved on this design to produce GE's own diesel engine. This, however, was not a complete success and its problems were among the reasons why the company's management temporarily lost interest in the internal-combustion engine. However, in 1922 the small Electro-Motive Corporation, impressed by Lemp's work on control systems for diesel-electric systems, asked GE to co-operate in producing a new diesel-engine control system. This resulted in the final version of Lemp's system, a big step forward towards acceptance of the diesel-locomotive concept. With this system, control of a diesel-electric locomotive through a single driving handle was finally achieved.

The Russian development of diesel locomotion

It was in the inter-war years that the protagonists of the diesel made their greatest design and research effort to evolve a locomotive which railway administrations would actually want to buy as standard equipment. This effort was notable in the USA, Russia and Germany, although other countries, including Britain and France, made their own contribution.

The work of Lomonosov, Meinecke and Shelest

In Russia, a new revolutionary regime was ready to consider anything which seemed technically revolutionary. In 1921 a conference of engineers unanimously rejected a proposal to build trial diesel locomotives but was overruled by Lenin. Russia's dieselizers could therefore for many years use Lenin's approval as a lever to extract more funds from the government for their work. There was at that time a Russian Railway Mission in Germany, ostensibly arranging for the importation of several hundred steam locomotives for the war-torn Soviet Railways, and the head of this mission, Lomonosov, had an interest in diesel locomotives. Together with his colleague Lipets, he had designed two diesel locomotives for the Tashkent Railway and obtained government funds for their construction in 1914. Only the outbreak of war had prevented their completion. Also in Germany, and co-operating with the Russian Railway Mission, was Felix Meinecke, one of the greatest of German locomotive engineers. Meinecke had been chief draughtsman at the Kolomna Locomotive Works in tsarist Russia. This works also built diesel engines for industry and Meinecke had designed a locomotive (never built) to use similar engines. A third member of the Mission was the young engineer Shelest, who had written as his student's dissertation a critique of the pre-war Sulzer diesel locomotive. Shelest was a great upholder of the idea of a diesel gas-generator locomotive to solve the transmission problem.

The Soviet Council of Ministers granted funds for the construction of three main-line diesel locomotives in Germany. One of these was to be diesel-electric, one diesel-mechanical and the other a Shelest-type locomotive. The latter was never built although part of the gas generator, built by Armstrongs in Newcastle, was shipped later from England to the basement of a technical school in Moscow where Shelest tinkered with it for the rest of his life. His idea, modified over the years, was that a diesel engine should power a compressor which would force air and exhaust gas at high pressure into a reservoir

The least successful of the pioneer Russian diesel locomotives was this diesel-mechanical 1,200 hp unit built in Germany in 1926. On trial runs south of Moscow, it demonstrated that a non-electric transmission would pose many problems for main-line operation. Changing gear sometimes took twenty seconds and was so jerky that there were frequent breakages of train couplings.

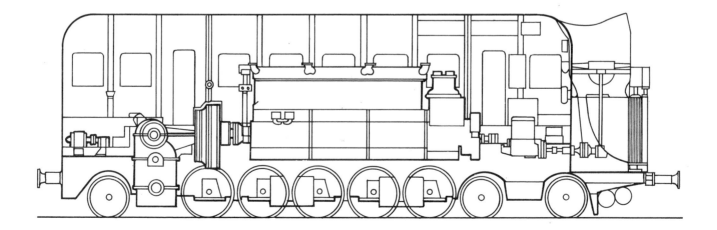

from where it would be drawn off to power normal steam-locomotive-type cylinders. This was an attractive idea which never quite seemed to work out in practice. Other Russian researchers pursued another promising solution to what they called the 'diesel-locomotive problem'. This was to use a diesel engine to pump highly compressed air into a locomotive boiler where it would simply take the place of steam. The beauty of this system was that it would enable existing steam locomotives to be cheaply converted into diesels. Unfortunately the sharp fall in temperature when the compressed air expanded in the cylinders and steam pipes aroused such difficulties of condensation and freezing that the project, after many years, had to be abandoned.

Meanwhile in Germany, Lomonosov, Meinecke and their team worked out the design of a diesel-electric locomotive and the order was given to the Hohenzollern Locomotive Works. Lomonosov was also a specialist in locomotive testing and he designed a testing plant which could be taken apart and sent to Russia when the Germans had finished with it (some sources say that the Germans never returned it, others that they built an identical plant to replace it). A diesel engine built by MAN was used. This was an engine successfully used in U-boats. The electrical equipment came from Brown Boveri, and Hohenzollern built the frame, chassis and body (this split between diesel, electrical and locomotive works would become a typical arrangement for diesel-locomotive construction in most countries). The result was a 1,200 hp locomotive of 2-10-2 wheel arrangement; the chassis with its large driving wheels and smaller carrying wheels, all carried in a rigid frame, was of steam-locomotive type.

The work of the Gakkel team

In Russia, funds had been granted almost simultaneously for the building of another diesel locomotive by another, entirely Russian, consortium of designers. This was based in Leningrad and the design team was led by Professor Gakkel. Using a Vickers diesel engine, intended for submarine use, that Gakkel had discovered and using streetcar-type traction motors, a locomotive was constructed of similar power to the Lomonosov unit but rather different in principle. It was of the 2-6-0 + 0-8-0 + 0-6-2 wheel arrangement and the wheels were placed in trucks; this was a step towards the double-bogie diesel locomotive of the present day although the carrying wheels meant that it would not be a total-adhesion locomotive. Although rivalry between Lomonosov and Gakkel was denied, there seems little reason to doubt that there was some kind of competition between them to be the builder of the world's first 'successful' main-line diesel locomotive. Both projects suffered unexpected setbacks. Lomonosov's locomotive had to be transferred hurriedly to another builder when the French occupied the Ruhr, and Gakkel's was delayed by the Leningrad floods of 1924 in which it was partially immersed for several days. Then, when the Lomonosov locomotive was finished and had passed its first trials, Lomonosov staged a ceremony in Germany to which high railway officials of Germany and Holland were invited. The locomotive was demonstrated and the visitors signed a protocol declaring that they had just witnessed the beginning of a new era. This was on 6 November 1924. Lomonosov presumably knew that Gakkel's team would try to hand over their locomotive on the anniversary of the Russian Revolution, which was 7 November. In this he was correct, but the Gakkel locomotive made a short run on Soviet Railways track the day before. Since the Lomonosov locomotive did not arrive in Russia until some weeks later, and the Gakkel locomotive was never really successful, the question of which was first depends on how 'first' is defined. The present Soviet view is that Gakkel's locomotive was the world's first successful main-line diesel locomotive.

Inter-war developments and failures

Lomonosov's locomotive worked for many years and may even have survived World War II. It was the basis of other diesel locomotives built for Soviet Railways between the wars. After two years it was joined by the diesel-mechanical locomotive, in which Krupp had played a leading role in the transmission system. This system replaced the electric transmission system with a gearbox and provision to change gear for different speeds. Since it took 17 seconds for an experienced operator to change from one gear to another, during which period the train would lose speed or bunch up, this unit was a failure although Soviet engineers persevered many years with it.

The attraction of a mechanical transmission was that it eliminated the heavy and expensive generator required by diesel-electric locomotives. But it is almost impossible, in the space available, to design gears which can withstand the heavy stresses imposed both by a locomotive riding on rough track and by a 1,000 hp engine. This is why mechanical transmissions are still confined to small yard locomotives and a few railcars. Hydro-mechanical transmission is somewhat more practical. This interested the inter-war Russian and German designers, and in the postwar years German builders sold many main-line diesel-hydraulic locomotives with Voith and Mekydro transmissions which had been developed before the war. However, the simplicity and lightness of such locomotives were balanced by the extra maintenance expenses demanded by these transmissions.

Although Lomonosov left the USSR in the late 1920s, never to return, the locomotives he inspired continued to attract the Soviet authorities. Or rather, perhaps, it was the Communist Party which was most interested in them, for the Ministry of Railways showed no great enthusiasm. Some more, improved, units were built in Germany and then production began at the Kolomna Locomotive Works at first using German-built components.

Meanwhile, Gakkel's locomotive had been abandoned. This was a pity because the design was more promising than that of the Lomonosov machine. It was the individual components which failed rather than the overall concept. Gakkel had, after all, moved away from the conventional steam-locomotive chassis and he realized the advantage of a locomotive which could be driven from either end. He was probably one of the most competent of Soviet engineers but only one of his many subsequent diesel-locomotive designs was ever built. This was a six-wheeled yard locomotive whose diesel engine was so abysmal in construction that the locomotive failed on almost every trial run and was soon abandoned.

When the USSR had assembled a dozen or so diesel locomotives they were transferred from their experimental base near Moscow to the heart of central Asia. The dieselizers had always argued that the diesel was especially suited to waterless lines like the Ashkhabad Railway, where the steam locomotives consumed water which had to be delivered in tankers. They had also argued, again correctly, that to make a realistic comparison between diesel and steam costs it would be necessary entirely to dieselize a section of railway, since joint operation of steam and diesel units was certain to be expensive. So a section of the Ashkhabad Railway was dieselized and as Kolomna Works built new units they were sent to join the rest of the fleet in central Asia. No doubt there were those in the Ministry of Railways who welcomed the transfer of the diesels to a suitably remote part of the Union; the Ministry had many more important questions to think about.

Although glowing reports of the work by Soviet diesel units were periodically published, in retrospect it would seem that in the early years at least the locomotives were a disaster for the railway transport of that region. One trouble was that it was not until 1938 that proper maintenance facilities were provided. But the design itself was faulty. When the units had been working close to Moscow it had been possible to give them the daily care which they needed and to obtain spare parts promptly. In central Asia this was not so, and there were problems with dust and heat in addition. Cooling the diesel engines, generators and motors had been a problem which had troubled Lomonosov in his first design (and which he had finally solved, inelegantly, by mounting radiators on a separate vehicle attached like a tender to the locomotive). In central Asia, cooling air entered at a far higher initial temperature, so locomotives overheated readily unless their loads were limited. Furthermore, there were manufacturing faults, so that cylinder covers tended to fracture, essential pumps to stop working and motors to burn out. On several occasions the crews had to run for their lives when their locomotives burst into flame. In 1937 it was decided to cease the construction of diesel locomotives for a few years. Ironically, it was in the following year that diesel performance began to improve as lessons were learnt and the new maintenance facilities came into operation.

Evidently the bold Soviet enterprise, persevered with for almost two decades, was premature. Too much had been attempted too quickly. Partly this was due to the Communist Party's predilection for quick results and new technologies but often the Party tended to restrain rather than encourage the dieselizers. The latter were enthusiasts who had been given a chance and thought that only by moving fast and producing rapid results could they continue to enjoy that chance. Their ambitions were much greater than what the Party and the planners could allow. In the early 1930s a production of 200 diesel locomotives a year was envisaged in some quarters, something which Soviet industry was in no position to achieve. In reality, production was usually at the rate of 4–5 units per year although 13 were turned out in 1936. The standard unit was obsolete even at the time it was adopted for series production. The steam-locomotive-type chassis, too rigid for fast running, was one old-fashioned feature. Another was the failure to employ the Lemp system of control. The reason for this is mysterious, unless it was simply a reluctance to pay the licensing fee. Soviet diesel locomotives, moreover, were very difficult to drive. There was no partition between the driver and the machinery because it was thought that he should be able to see and hear the engine; consequently he worked in conditions of heat, noise and smell which affected his competence and vigilance. There was a three-man crew (driver, dieselman and electrician) and control duties were shared between them. On a big experimental diesel locomotive built in the mid 1930s the driver was separated from the machinery and control operations were performed by a crew member who received his instructions through a code of lights and bells, rather like a ship's engineroom telegraph.

All the same, despite the apparent but unadmitted failure of the dieselization programme, it was not an entire waste of time. The Russian and German diesel locomotive industry had gained much experience, attention had been attracted in Russia to the idea of diesel traction, and Russian engineers had been trained. And after all, for the first time experience had been gained of operating a railway with diesel traction alone. Thus a tradition had been established which seemed to promise that once a successful diesel locomotive appeared on the scene, dieselization could go rapidly ahead. A successful diesel locomotive would appear in the USSR in 1945; it would be quite unlike the pre-war machines, however, and would be built by the American Locomotive Company.

Inter-war developments in Europe

Profiting from their experience with Russian locomotives, and meantime developing some of their own ideas, German locomotive builders began to turn their attention to diesel traction. Few main-line locomotives were built in the inter-war period but several companies, notably Deutz, built diesel yard locomotives in large numbers. This was the kind of service for which steam traction was highly uneconomic, and many industries decided to replace their steam works locomotives with diesels. The diesel railcar was an early success in Germany. It was built for many services, and in such large numbers that the oil shortages of World War II had a serious effect on passenger services. The best known of these railcar designs was the twin-unit *Flying Hamburger*, a streamlined high-speed train introduced on the Berlin–Hamburg run in 1933 with an average speed of 125 km/h (78 mph). It was equipped with Mayback high-speed engines and transmission was by a hydraulic system. Another diesel-hydraulic machine was a main-line 1,500 hp locomotive built in 1935 by Krauss-Maffei. This used a Voith transmission, destined to become very popular in Germany after the war. German exports included 600 hp diesel-electrics for the Japanese Government Railways and, in 1938, a massive twin-unit 4,400 hp locomotive supplied by Henschel to Romania. This locomotive, equipped with Sulzer engines, weighed 230 tonnes, demonstrating that diesel locomotives, though they might be practicable, were not yet as powerful as steam locomotives of the same size.

France was also an early adherent of the diesel railcar. Many companies built these vehicles, which took over an increasing share of rail passenger traffic; in 1938 the SNCF was using no fewer than 650 railcars. The Paris–Lyon–Méditerranée Railway organized a competition for railcar designs in 1932 and several of the successful entries became standard types in France. They used German or French diesel engines of about 200 hp but soon developed 600 hp or more by using two somewhat enlarged engines. The Renault Company was one enterprise which made a success of railcars. Another was the Michelin rubber company, which went into the railcar business to show (not altogether successfully) that rubber tyres could be used in railway service. In their efforts to demonstrate this point, the Michelin designers introduced many useful innovations such as the use of lightweight materials, shock-absorbers and vibration dampeners. But probably the best-known railcars were the high-speed, streamlined units introduced by the Bugatti firm in 1933. Not without resemblance to the famous racing cars of the same company, they covered the Paris–Deauville run (221 km or 137 miles) in two hours. In general, the characteristic of French railcars was, apart from their large number, the wide variety of designs which were not only built but actually accepted for regular service. So far as diesel locomotives were concerned, the French moved slowly. The PLM Railway organized a competition for diesel

The standard SNCF diesel-electric locomotive for main-line service on non-electrified lines is the 6800 class. In this photograph No. 68026 is arriving at Angers, in western France, with a train from Tours.

Sectioned drawing of General Motors 3,600hp
Co-Co diesel electric 'hood unit' locomotive, 1967

1 horns
2 control desk
3 control cabinet
4 air intakes for engine room
5 traction motor blower
6 generator blower
7 exhaust stack
8 auxiliary generator
9 fans for dynamic brakes
10 engine water tank
11 radiator fans

12 radiator air intakes
13 sand pipes
14 air compressor
15 driving wheels
16 axle boxes
17 lubricating oil filter
18 brake cylinder
19 sand pipes
20 diesel engine
21 air reservoir
22 fuel tanks

23 air duct to rear traction motors
24 main generator and alternator
25 warning bell
26 traction motor
27 batteries
28 pilot (cow catcher)
29 buck-eye coupler
30 socket for multiple-unit control
   jumpers

Left: *A West German diesel-hydraulic locomotive of the 220 class with a Stuttgart–Milan international train.*
Right: *A British Rail High Speed Train near Reading.*
Below right: *The Canadian Pacific's* Canadian *threading through the Rockies. The General Motors diesel locomotive works from Montreal to Vancouver without change.*

Above left: *One of the latest diesel locomotives of the Danish State Railways, a class M2 unit with a freight train.*
Above right: *A British Rail class 45 diesel-electric unit at work on the bleak Settle and Carlisle line.*
Below left: *A British Rail Deltic type diesel-electric with the* Flying Scotsman *near Selby.*
Below right: *A Union Pacific RR train in Wyoming, with two 6,600 hp Centennial diesel units in the lead.*

yard locomotives and built four of the designs submitted. These gave satisfactory results but were not built as standard types. In 1937 there appeared two large diesel-electrics, designed with a view to replacing 4-8-2 steam locomotives on the Paris–Menton run (1,111 km or 690 miles) without a change of engine. They were twin-unit machines, with a 4-6-4 + 4-6-4 wheel arrangement and of 4,000 hp. One had Sulzer engines, the other MAN. They worked well on trial but the war put a stop to their further development, although they remained in service until 1950. By that year they were undoubtedly obsolete for they weighed 230 tonnes compared to the 160 tonnes of comparable steam locomotives.

In Britain the internal-combustion locomotive in the 1920s was almost entirely confined to petrol-engined yard and light-duty units. As in France and Germany, much experience had been gained with this type of locomotive during World War I when it was used for the trench railways. In the 1930s several steam-locomotive builders added small diesel locomotives to their catalogues, and many were exported. When the firm of Beardmore developed a promising diesel engine of quite light weight the possibility of building main-line locomotives became real. However this opportunity was only partially exploited. Only the firm of Armstrong Whitworth made any kind of a success of this business. This firm, like others, concentrated on low-power units but did build a few large machines for export. Among these were some successful units for Argentina. Some of these were in the form of so-called 'power houses'; in these the locomotive contained a diesel engine and generator but only a reduced complement of traction motors, the surplus current being fed to traction motors driving the axles of the train. The resultant diesel-electric train set was evidently very successful in commuter service out of Buenos Aires, for further units were soon ordered and they remained in service for many years, as did similar, smaller, units supplied earlier to Brazil. The company also built an orthodox diesel-electric for the same railway (the Buenos Aires Great Southern). This was a 1,700 hp twin-unit and weighed 147 tonnes. This too, was an operating success, being used in regular passenger service for many years.

Meanwhile in inter-war Britain a start was being made with diesel-electric yard locomotives for the home railways. It was the LMS Railway which was the pioneer, ordering different locomotives from various builders. The most successful was a type built by Hawthorn Leslie, using English Electric motors and an English Electric diesel engine with six in-line cylinders producing 300 hp at 650 rpm. More of these were ordered, and the type was used overseas by the army during the war and by the Netherlands Railways after the war. Furthermore, it was the basis of the present generation of diesel yard locomotives (Type 08) used by British Rail.

As a generalization, it might be said that between the wars it was the builders rather than the railways who were more enthusiastic about main-line diesel traction. True, the railways offered to hold trials of the new locomotives, but they did not expect to place large orders for them. A notable and surprising exception was the Royal State Railways of Thailand which in the early 1930s imported small, but nevertheless 'main-line', diesel-electric locomotives from Sulzer and Frichs. The latter was a Danish company, which made a steady, if unspectacular, success of the diesel-electric locomotive. Its 1,000 hp and 1,500 hp locomotives for Thailand ran for two decades at least, and were welcomed in a country whose steam locomotives traditionally burned the diminishing local supply of high-quality teak.

Not all American passenger trains in the 1950s and 1960s were powered by General Motors locomotives. The Alco PA diesel-electric, introduced in 1946, was preferred by some railways. In this picture a Delaware & Hudson Railroad train skirts Lake Champlain, on the line between New York and Montreal, with an international train, the Laurentian. *Two Alco units provide the power.*

The rise of diesel locomotion in the USA

While the Europeans were developing their own types of diesel locomotive, Americans were building on their past experience to produce a range of locomotives which, in retrospect, can be regarded as the beginning of the end for the steam locomotive. General Electric had regained its old interest in internal-combustion locomotives by 1924, in which year it combined with Ingersoll-Rand, makers of a suitable diesel engine, to build a demonstration diesel-electric yard locomotive. This had a 300 hp engine and the traction motors were based on standard GE designs for electric streetcars. Although this locomotive was never sold, its performance was such that GE and Ingersoll-Rand built five more units to sell to the first customers who might make offers. For these five units the American Locomotive Company (Alco) built the bodies and chassis. The first customer was the Central of New Jersey Railroad which placed one into switching service at its Bronx yards in 1925. This locomotive, No 1000, is regarded as the first commercially successful diesel-electric locomotive in the USA, and after a long working life is now in the railway museum at Baltimore.

Subsequent locomotives by this consortium were of the same design. Known as 'box-cabs', like similar-looking electric locomotives, they had a square body mounted on two four-wheel trucks, and had a cab at each end. A few units with two engines were built, weighing 100 tonnes instead of the standard 60 tonnes, and delivering 600 hp. However, 600 hp was not the most powerful rating for an American diesel. The president of the Baldwin Locomotive Works visited Russia and rode on one of Lomonosov's locomotives. On his return he said that the diesel locomotive did not seem very promising, but nevertheless in 1925 and 1929 his works built 1,000 hp units, neither of which found a buyer.

In 1928 GE ceased using Alco as supplier of bodies. However, by this time Alco was interested in diesel traction on its own account. Being one of the American big three steam-locomotive builders, Alco viewed the diesel with mixed feelings, preferring to continue with steam construction while at the same time preparing to enter the diesel market. One of Alco's leading consultants, and the man regarded as representing the diesel interest, was an emigré Russian, Lipets, who had worked with Lomonosov in tsarist Russia on the design of the Tashkent Railway's diesel locomotives. Alco's first order came from the New York Central which took three experimental units for use on light-traffic lines. This was a duty somewhat more imposing than yard service and in some quarters the locomotives were described as main-line units. Of the three, the freight unit was the most successful, working regularly in local freight service on the Putnam Division for about ten years. Although of only 750 hp, it convinced observers that the diesel locomotive had a future which included more than yard switching.

Even though after 1937 new work rules made it impossible to use one-man crews on yard diesel locomotives, the switching unit was the first type to be bought in numbers. Because the diesel locomotive could work almost 24 hours daily, one diesel could often replace two steamers, and it did not require auxiliary staff to light its fire, empty its ashes and wash out its boiler. In isolated yards it had sometimes been necessary to employ steam-locomotive workers simply to look after one or two engines; with diesel switchers such men could be dispensed with. Alco continued to build switchers, usually of

300 or 600 hp, throughout the 1930s. It was also notable as the first US builder to use the turbocharger, with which it raised its standard diesel engine from 600 hp to 900 hp.

Diesel traction really entered the American public consciousness with the arrival of the streamline era. When the Burlington Railroad introduced its lightweight three-car stainless-steel *Zephyr*, the publicity material pointed out that this was not a steam train, but a diesel-electric. Because of its light weight a 600 hp engine was sufficient for this train, which made a demonstration run from Denver to Chicago (1,640 km or 1,015 miles) at an average speed of 120 km/h (78 mph). The Union Pacific, also in 1934, introduced its own Chicago–Portland streamliner and this was followed by streamliners of other railroads. Alco had its share in these enterprises but it still regarded the steam locomotive as the major passenger locomotive; after all, the diesel trains were still short and flimsy.

In the late 1930s the market for diesel yard locomotives expanded, despite the difficult economic circumstances of the time. Alco shared in this expansion but after 1937 sold fewer units than did a relative newcomer to the market, General Motors. Henceforth it would be General Motors which would dominate diesel-locomotive sales. Nevertheless, Alco was always willing to innovate and in 1940 turned out the first dual-service locomotive. This had two engines, totalling 2,000 hp, and rode on two six-wheel trucks. When these locomotives were introduced on the New Haven Railroad they were an immediate success, for they could haul heavy passenger trains during the daytime and freights at night. In 1941 Alco went even further, introducing the first 'road-switcher'. This combined features of the yard locomotive with those of a main-line diesel; many such units were exported to Iran during World War II to work on the Trans Iranian Railway. It was these Iranian units which went to Russia in 1945 and formed the basis for the USSR's postwar diesel-locomotive design.

A twin-unit diesel-electric locomotive of Soviet Railways, the class TE2 owed much to American practice. Each unit produced 1,000 hp and its internal layout was little different from Alco units received by the USSR in 1945. The body style, however, was new.

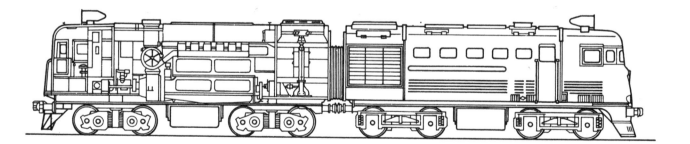

General Motors, the newcomer

General Motors, hitherto an automobile company, entered the diesel locomotive field in 1930. It bought up a small but quite remarkable company, the Electro-Motive Corporation which consisted of little more than an office that designed and marketed a fairly successful gas-electric railcar, built by sub-contractors. One of Electro-Motive's main sub-contractors, Winton Engine, was bought at the same time. This company was building a new lightweight diesel engine especially suitable for railway use. Having acquired these two companies, with their valuable accumulated experience, GM built a new diesel-locomotive plant near Chicago and laid down its new range of locomotives. It was a Winton/GM engine which powered the Burlington's *Zephyr*, and GM yard locomotives began to rival those of Alco. By 1938 GM was building entire locomotives, having ceased to purchase traction motors from General Electric. Among its output were streamline 1,800 hp passenger locomotives which were being ordered by an increasing number of railroads. Unlike the steam-locomotive builders, GM built only standard designs, making no changes to suit individual customers. It was thereby enabled to build its locomotives like automobiles in long series, with a resultant lowering of cost. The diesel locomotive never cost less than a comparable steamer, but it began to be a good bargain for the railroads, given its higher availability for service and its lower operating costs.

The event which marked the final acceptance of diesel traction was the demonstration over many railroads of the GM freight locomotive of 1939. This four-unit streamlined machine produced 5,400 hp and amazed railroad managers with its reliability and its hauling power. After running 133,500 km (83,000 miles) as a demonstrator it was bought by the Southern Railway and GM waited for more orders to come in. Such orders were not slow to arrive and GM was helped by wartime regulations which named the company as the only producer of main-line diesel locomotives (Alco was allocated orders for yard locomotives). Santa Fe Railroad bought the first of the GM production models and used them over long sections; locomotive changes were not practised, only crew changes. Thus when the Santa Fe locomotives began to make 2,833 km (1,761 mile) trips from Kansas to California they replaced seven steam locomotives. They could, moreover, haul trains of 3,000 tonnes over this difficult route at average speeds in excess of 48 km/h (30 mph) and on the long downhill sections they could hold back the trains' speed with their rheostatic brakes. The Santa Fe eventually bought no fewer than 320 units of this design, known as the FT series.

The changeover from steam to diesel construction—and the keen competition between builders, as well as the combination of luck, good judgment and enormous technical and financial resources enjoyed by General Motors—brought great changes in the structure of the American locomotive industry. General Motors' government-imposed monopoly of main-line diesel-locomotive construction in the war years placed it in an excellent situation after 1945. More and more railroads decided to place no further orders for steam locomotives, and they favoured GM as supplier because it was more

The well-known General Motors F series diesel-electric for two post-war decades dominated the American market for passenger locomotives. This drawing shows the F3A type, of which about one thousand examples were built in the late 1940s. It was of 1,500 hp, but two or three units were assigned to most trains. By the end of the 1970s this type had almost disappeared, partly because the trains it was designed to haul had, to a large extent, also disappeared and partly because diesel locomotives, although they can be re-engined and rebuilt, have a short life compared to steam locomotives.

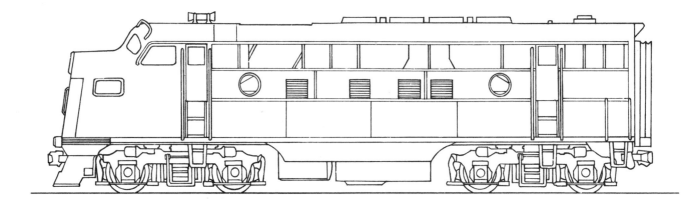

experienced and had a good reputation. This reputation was certainly deserved, for GM locomotives were the world's best by that time. The closest competitor was Alco, which had fallen behind GM in total sales before the war and was now additionally handicapped because its new diesel engine, due to the delays of wartime, was still imperfect. Alco soon combined with GE to market a range of diesel locomotives, while other entrants to the business included Fairbanks Morse, makers of an excellent opposed-piston diesel for the US Navy that was adapted for railway use. The steam locomotive builders Lima and Baldwin also built the new locomotives but did not achieve great success. These two makers soon merged into Baldwin-Lima-Hamilton but then abandoned the locomotive business.

Fairbanks Morse also left the field. It was the first to market a high-horse-power locomotive, the 2,400 hp Trainmaster, but only 127 units were sold. Essentially it was ahead of its time, for subsequently the railroads did decide that they needed more powerful locomotives. But the industry was so dominated by GM that no innovation seemed likely to win a market unless it was imitated or introduced by General Motors. But when General Electric entered the home market for main-line locomotives on its own account, GM faced a substantial competitor.

General Electric in the home market
GE had a long history in the locomotive business. It had pioneered the diesel-electric before 1920 and had built yard locomotives in the 1930s. It had decided not to enter the main-line locomotive market in the 1930s; it was already supplying nine-tenths of the generators and traction motors as sub-contractor for Alco and GM, so was quite satisfied with its share of the business. But when in 1938 GM decided to make its own electrical gear (copying GE designs insofar as GE's patents permitted), General Electric's position was less happy. In the postwar years GE shared Alco's successes and failures and meantime built its own locomotives for export, as well as yard switchers for the home market. Its speciality was the 44-tonne diesel-electric branch and switch locomotive, built in large numbers for American short lines because work rules permitted one-man crews for locomotives weighing less than 45 tonnes. Then, perhaps sensing that Alco was fighting a losing battle, GE left the partnership with that company in 1953. In 1960—after years of research, innovation and testing—GE offered its own main-line locomotive to the American railroads. This was the U25B, a 2,500 hp road-switcher with several novel features: pressurized engine and control compartments, bodies which were largely maintenance-free, and electronic control systems. This locomotive was so successful that it enabled GE to grasp a sizable share of the market, no small achievement in the face of GM's dominant position. GM still remains the biggest supplier, and Alco has withdrawn from the locomotive business. However, Alco's subsidiary, Montreal Locomotive, has continued to build Alco locomotives for Canadian railways and for export. Thus there are now three American builders—GM, GE and Montreal—offering between them about 20 different off-the-shelf models.

The need for high-power diesel locomotives
The last major US railroad to abandon steam was the Norfolk & Western, which, being a coal-hauling line, remained hostile to oil-burning motive power until the mid 1950s. Its final effort to preserve coal as its source of energy came with *Jawn Henry*, a steam-turbine/electric locomotive that was an updated

version of the steam-electrics of 19th-century France. However, *Jawn Henry* did not defeat the diesel, and the dieselization of the Norfolk & Western brought to a close the first stage of the motive-power revolution. Henceforth the diesel salesmen had to think of new reasons why the railroads should buy their latest products. Luckily, managements soon began to look for more powerful locomotives. Competition from highway transport forced the railroads to offer ever-faster services and, in order to keep down costs so that competitive tariffs could be offered, long heavy trains were operated. What the railroads required was more power at high speeds and they achieved this at first by simply adding more units at the head of their trains. With multiple-unit control one crew could operate six diesel units as easily as one or two. It became common to have six, seven or eight units; these were not to provide extra tractive power at starting, for a pair of units would have sufficed for that (indeed, six diesel units starting a train at full power would merely have broken the couplings). The problem was that the horsepower delivered by diesel locomotives tends to fall at the higher speeds, so that increasing average speeds meant more than a proportional increase in locomotive power. After successfully operating multi-unit locomotives in these services the railroads realized that their costs would be reduced if they operated a smaller number of more powerful units. Hence the demand for new locomotives of higher horsepower. Since the railroads were in a weak financial situation, the locomotive builders offered to take older diesel units from the railroads, recondition them, and fit them with more powerful engines and equipment. This seemed good business both for the railroads and for the builders, and also for the several banks that helped impecunious companies by buying diesel locomotives and then leasing them to the railroads. The remanufacturing concept was somewhat confusing for the accountants, for it became even more difficult than before to decide how many years should be taken as the life of a diesel locomotive. It also meant that, for example, locomotives which were outwardly Alco, riding on Alco trucks, might be reconditioned with GM equipment and sent back to the owning railroad as new GM locomotives.

The road-switcher type has come to dominate production in the USA. The 'cab' locomotive seems likely to disappear, at least in its classical form as exemplified by the first GM freight and passenger units. In these the body extended the full width of the locomotive, forming an enclosed engine room, and the front was streamlined in 'A' units (as opposed to 'B' units, which had no cab and were designed for attachment behind 'A' units). The road-switcher was of 'hood' form, with the engine and generator under a narrow hood, and inspected from walkways extending along the side of the locomotive.

US diesels today

The diesel locomotives being built now are very different from those of the early postwar years. In particular, horsepower has grown. Most US railroads dieselized with units which were of 1,200 to 1,500 hp although some 1,800 hp units were also sold. Then came the 2,000 to 3,000 hp units, while railroads operating fast freights sometimes went as high as 3,600 hp. Most units were carried on two four-wheel trucks, with two traction motors per truck, but six-wheel trucks, making a six-motor locomotive, were increasingly used; increasing the number of axles, and hence of traction motors, was a convenient way of increasing power output. In the 1960s the transcontinental Union Pacific Railroad, which operated fast heavy trains over its main line to the Rockies, decided it needed very powerful locomotives, and the locomotive

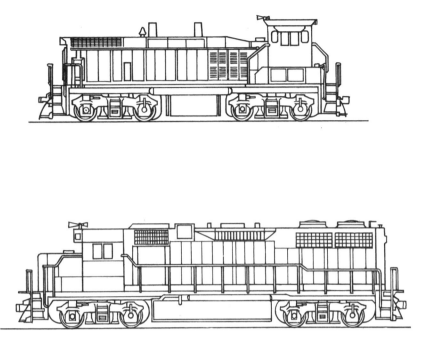

builders produced freight designs of 5,000 hp. These were virtually two locomotives in one. The GM DD35A type, for example, had two standard diesel engines inside its long body and was mounted on two eight-wheel trucks, each with four motors. But not many of these high-power units were sold.

Passenger locomotives have been built in rather small numbers, for no railroad wished to buy new motive power for services that might be soon withdrawn. However Amtrak still remains a sporadic customer for passenger units, but hardly a satisfied customer. This organization ordered large passenger units from GM in the 1970s. These, class SDP40f, were of 3,000 hp and of the cab type. In service, they demonstrated a tendency to derail at the higher speeds; several railroads whose tracks were used by Amtrak trains imposed speed limits and eventually it was decided to modify these locomotives, at a rather high price. Apparently the 6-wheel trucks on which they rode were unsuited to the somewhat rough and poorly maintained tracks of some railroads.

The application of new technology, such as ac generators with dc motors, has maintained a demand for new locomotives, and in any case the older units are steadily being replaced with new or rebuilt ones. Meanwhile, all the North-American builders have a substantial export business. They also have overseas subsidiaries or licensees which build their own versions of the diesel locomotive using the main company's designs or components. In Canada there is General Motors of Canada. In Sweden Nohab uses GM components for its range of diesel locomotives which it has sold to Scandinavian and other railways. In New South Wales the Clyde Engineering Company built several interesting versions of GM designs. Its cab-type six-axle units have a streamlined nose identical with GM's US cab units, but a flat-nosed cab is provided at the other end of the locomotive so that it does not need to be turned. Alco designs are also used in New South Wales, built mainly by Goodwins. Some of these, too, are cab units with a flat cab at the rear.

Dieselization in Europe

The success of the diesel locomotive in the USA, where already by the mid 1950s several major railways had entirely eliminated the steam locomotive, encouraged railway administrations in other countries to take dieselization much more seriously than they had before the war. For some war-ravaged railways, like those of the Netherlands, total elimination of steam traction was achieved early although in that country electrification was more significant than dieselization. Some countries, notably Germany and Britain, where coal and labour were relatively abundant, approached dieselization more slowly. Germany and France are two examples of a rational approach to dieselization; steam locomotives of the types with lowest maintenance costs were kept in service until they had served their natural lives, or at least their depreciation lives. Retention of this declining stock of steam locomotives enabled electrification to go ahead steadily, and for diesel locomotives to be introduced gradually, allowing time for the best diesel types to be developed and tested in operation. In Germany there was a trend towards diesel-hydraulic locomotives. By dispensing with the heavy electrical equipment locomotives could be made less complex, less heavy and less expensive. However, since the 1950s, when the Voith and Mekydro transmissions were at the peak of their popularity, the diesel-electric locomotive has been considerably improved and most German engineers feel that the higher maintenance costs of hydraulic transmission outweigh their advantages. France is notable for the small number of diesel-locomotive types that were chosen for series production. So far as main-line service is concerned, five types do all the work on services which are not electrified or provided by railcars. The 1,000 hp 64000 class and the 2,000 hp 65000 class of the mid 1950s were supplemented in the mid 1960s by the 2,400 hp 67000 series and the 3,000 hp 68000. For lighter work a road-switcher type, the 1,400 hp 66000 class, was introduced.

Whereas French motive-power policy was distinguished by a cool rationality which derived the most benefit from existing steam locomotives, British policy at the same period was noticeably irrational. The pre-nationalization companies had experimented with dieselization before the war, notably the LMS with its diesel-electric shunters and the GWR with its railcars. In the immediate postwar years both the Southern Railway and the LMS designed and built main-line diesel units after a study of American practice. After nationalization in 1948 British Railways opted for a new range of steam locomotives that were little better than existing steam locomotives and that, not only in retrospect but in the opinion of outside observers at the time, were quite an unnecessary expenditure of the taxpayer's money. Yet in the mid 1950s total dieselization of non-electrified lines was decided upon. By this time some British locomotive builders had experience of building diesel locomotives for export, but the British Railways management decided on a policy of let-all-flowers-bloom and gave orders to almost all the locomotive builders, experienced or not, competent or not. The result was an enormous expenditure on a stock of locomotives which included far too many different types, and far too many no-hope designs. Moreover, in this bonanza of orders the US builders were carefully excluded, even though they were then producing locomotives that were technically superior to any in the world. Of the multitude of designs received by British Railways, only those based on export experience or, via the LMS and SR prototypes, on US experience, proved viable in the long term. The others had high maintenance costs, or high failure rates or were too heavy; it was only natural that steam-locomotive builders confronted with diesel-locomotive orders should build machines in the steam-locomotive tradition: solid but excessively heavy. The one, perhaps only, exception to this generalization was the Deltic locomotive, in which a high-power D-form marine engine was successfully adapted for railway use and powered what was then the most powerful single-unit diesel locomotive in the world: a 3,300 hp type of which British Railways bought 22 units to transform its East Coast Route passenger service.

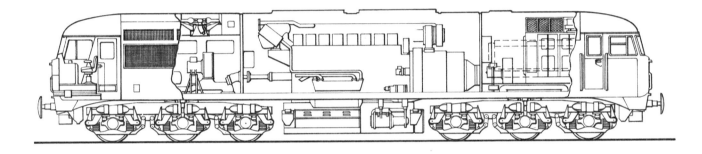

British Rail's latest type of diesel-electric locomotive, class 56, is designed to haul the heaviest freight trains, the type being somewhat similar to the older class 47. Part of the order was built in Romania, and the locomotive runs on standard Romanian Railways three-axle trucks. The mechanical design, however, is mainly the work of Brush, the British company that also built the class 47.

So great was the waste of capital during Britain's dieselization drive—a drive which resulted in recently-built steam locomotives being sold for scrap well before the end of their natural lives, and even more recently-built diesel locomotives being sold for scrap because they were defective—that even in the late 1970s British dieselization had still not recouped the investment. In other words, in honest accounting terms, the money spent on dieselization might have brought more benefit, in financial terms, if it had been spent on modernizing the steam-traction establishment. However, in operational terms, in convenience and appeal to clients, and in environmental terms too, the diesel locomotive brought undoubted gains. This distinction between the real gains of dieselization and the potential gains which were claimed by railways and builders in the course of dieselization is not unique to Britain. Almost everywhere, the virtues of dieselization were expressed in the amount of money which it would save but the elaborate costings produced by railway economists had a distinctly fictitious element about them. By a careful choice of assumptions, for example that both a diesel locomotive and a steamer had an identical twenty-year life or that a steam locomotive wore out track twice as fast as a diesel, economists were able to justify what their managements had already decided. And yet, despite the window-dressing, despite the fact that in many countries, especially Britain, dieselization cannot be shown to have justified itself financially, in practical ways, ways which cannot easily be expressed in figures, the diesel locomotive has made a vital contribution to the survival of railways in this very competitive age.

Passenger Travel

by David Jenkinson   The history and development of passenger trains, the improvements in the design and amenities of coaches.

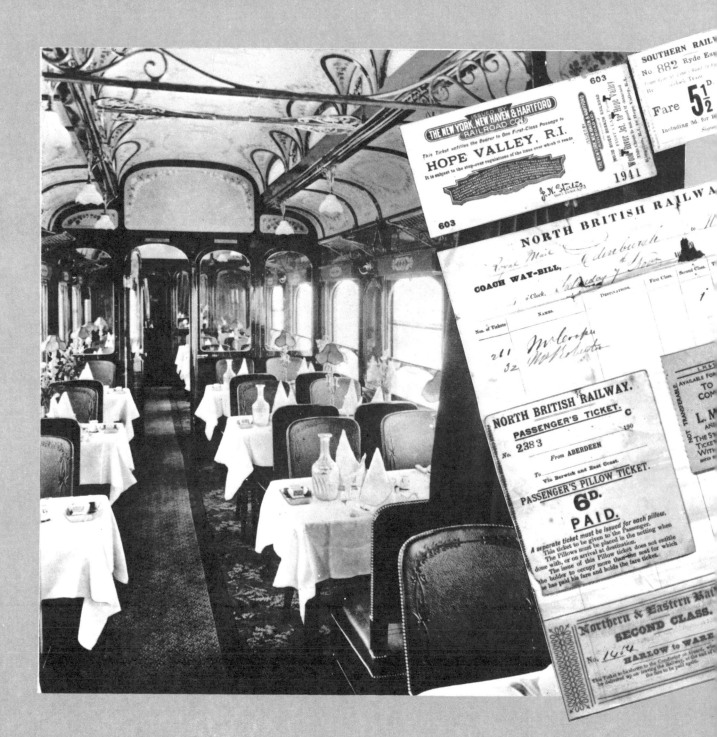

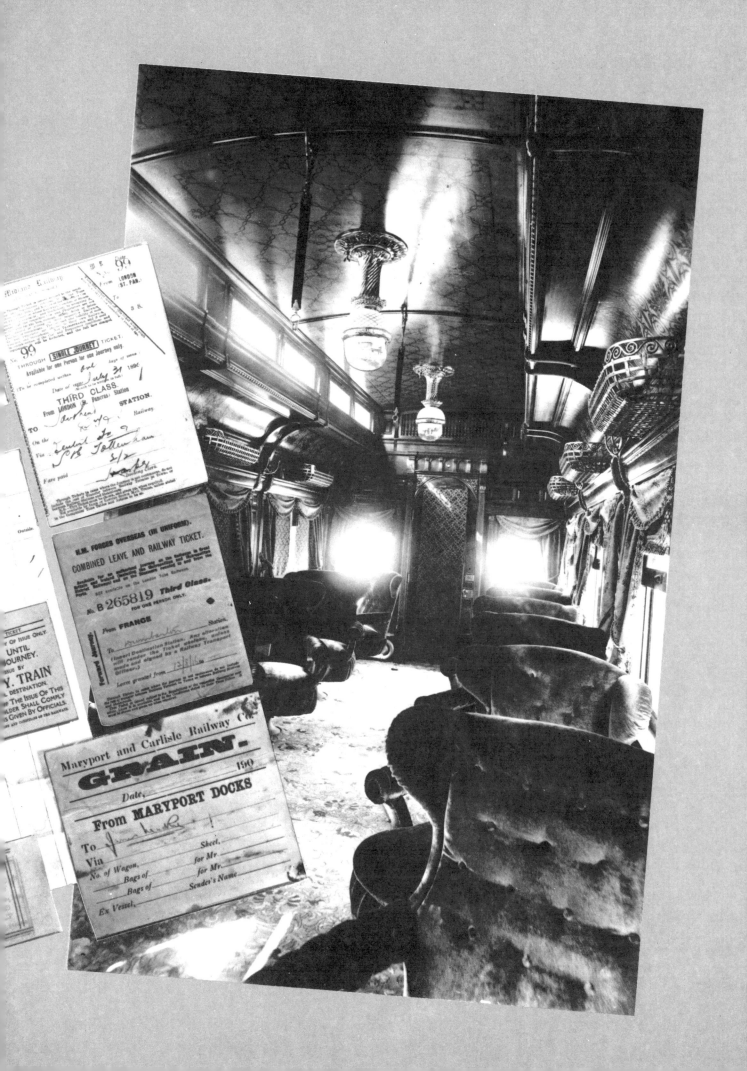

Most people who have encountered railways at all probably made their first direct contact with the iron road at the door to a railway carriage. Indeed, for many, rail transport is synonymous with passenger travel and they probably give little thought to the fact that, at first, railways were never seen as a means for improving communication between members of the human race. Yet such was the case. The builders of the medieval mining railways in Central Europe or the 18th-century mineral tramways and waggonways of Britain were most certainly not thinking of carrying *people* in their new-fangled vehicles.

It is not known when the first passenger journeyed on the railway—it was probably an illicit ride anyway—but history does record that the first public passenger railway (horse-drawn) was opened between Swansea and Mumbles in south Wales in 1807 and that Richard Trevithick carried the world's first steam-hauled fare-paying passengers by way of a private demonstration railway at Euston Square, London, in 1809. Both seem to have been a little ahead of their time and arguably the new order did not really become established for almost another generation. Controversy rages over the first true passenger railway in the accepted modern sense of the word. There are three prime contenders, two English and one American.

In September 1825, the Stockton & Darlington Railway opened for business with a steam-hauled train carrying passengers. This was the first occasion on which passengers had ridden behind steam on a public railway. However, after opening day, passenger haulage reverted to the horse-drawn mode until 1833, the new steam engines being far too precious to haul people rather than the really valuable cargo—coal. The two other rivals were the Baltimore & Ohio and the Liverpool & Manchester railways. Of these two, the Americans were first in the field in 1827 but they, like the S & D, favoured horses. It was a few years before steam came into its own. The Liverpool & Manchester on the other hand was designed from the outset as an inter-city route using mechanical means of propulsion and when it was opened in 1830 the modern concept of a true main-line railway was realized for the first time.

Another essential difference was that the L & M owned its own carriages as well as the right-of-way. Some early companies, including the S & D, regarded the railway, like the canals and roads of earlier years, simply as a right-of-way along which private hauliers could ply for hire. The L & M realized that the technological nature of a railway would pose problems for such an approach and from the outset held that the railway should be a complete transport system within itself—so was born the modern railway idea.

Early days

The first locomotives were small and not very powerful and the potential ability of the steam locomotive to haul heavy loads was not fully realized, if even anticipated. There was little realization that vehicles of a size vastly bigger than road transport could be hauled on rails. Early trains drew heavily from earlier technology.

Most early railway development took place in Europe and North America. On both sides of the Atlantic, the original carriage-builders drew their inspiration from other contemporary forms of land transport. What might be termed the 'stage-coach' style rapidly became dominant. Interestingly, this type of vehicle became a familiar sight in many parts of the world and most were recognizably of the same species. However, an early clue to the later

Previous pages, left: *Interior of a restaurant car built in Italy for the Wagons-Lits Company in the heyday of the great international trains.*
Centre: *Assorted railway tickets of the past, showing just a few of the different forms such tickets took.*
Right: *The last word in passenger comfort in America in 1889; a Pullman parlor car for a Chicago–Cincinnatti service.*

dominance of rail can probably be traced to the very first horse-drawn vehicle on rails. By fitting a stage coach with railway wheels it was discovered that one horse could pull on rail a weight which would demand four or six animals by road. Before long, someone in the railway business realized that this ability to pull heavier loads per unit of power made possible the building of bigger vehicles. The favourite solution was the building of carriages which, effectively, consisted of several stage-coach bodies fastened together on one rigid railway chassis.

Problems, however, were encountered. On the old road coaches, passengers had been allowed to ride at lower fares outside the coach on bench seats fitted to the roof and to the front and rear of the coach. This, risky and dangerous enough on a 16 km/h (10 mph) horse-drawn stage-coach over a bad road was a potentially lethal recipe on a 48 km/h (30 mph) steam-hauled train with limited bridge and structure clearances. The attempt was, of course, made but was soon abandoned. Yet demand for economic travel, which the cheaper 'outside' coach seats had created, could not be ignored. Some form of economy railway vehicle was urgently needed. Regrettably, most European railways responded grudgingly with a variety of open-top four-wheelers scarcely better than coal wagons. Perhaps the one redeeming feature was the difficulty of falling out; often no seats were provided at all and protection against bad weather was frequently confined to provision of holes in the floor for the escape of rainwater. All this contrasted starkly with the often elaborately furnished covered coaches provided for the wealthier passengers—yet people in increasing numbers travelled in these harsh economy conditions.

Between these two extremes of comfort, an intermediate standard also developed which essentially married the roofed-in quality of the upholstered coach with the accommodation of the open-top vehicles. This development established the beginnings of a three-class system of travel which remained the standard in Britain and Europe for many years. Nevertheless, there were many regional variations as well as considerable differences in quality between different railway systems.

The stage-coach type of vehicle remained the most dominant form of carriage for many generations throughout Britain and Europe and in those parts of the world where European nations were responsible for railway development. However, in North America a distinctive and new approach was rapidly established.

The first railways in North America were constructed when the USA was barely fifty years old and when large tracts of land were still under separate and often colonial administrations; a contrast to the situation in Europe where most countries (with the notable exception of Germany) were already well-established political units. In Europe, the early railways were built to reinforce existing economic patterns in an already partially industrialized region. The railways were well engineered, built at considerable expense and exhibited remarkable feats of civil engineering to maintain good alignment. In a phrase, European railways were built tolerably straight and level. Thus the rigid four-wheel vehicle, and its later derivative with six wheels, gave no problems on the well-engineered and well-drained lines characteristic of most early routes in West and Central Europe.

This was not the case in North America. Some of the early lines on the eastern seaboard did clearly show their European ancestry. Very soon, however, the railway was seen as a major instrument for 'opening up' the new lands across the Appalachian mountains. The sheer speed of railway travel made the railroads a vital, unifying factor in the rapidly developing USA and, later, in Canada. Lines were needed quickly over what, by European standards, were vast distances. Compromise with the rigid civil-engineering standards established by European builders offered the only possible way. Lines of a more contorted nature were laid down—with heavier gradients and sharper curves to minimize construction costs. Many of these lines were later upgraded to carry heavier modern traffic but, in the fledgling years, this very different approach had a profound effect upon vehicle design.

The characteristic rigid-frame European-style coach performed badly on the sharply curving and unconsolidated early American railroads. In consequence, from the 1830s, the Americans had developed what became the global standard for a railway coach—a long vehicle running on two independent bogies, or trucks. The bogies permitted the building of a much larger coach since each bogie could pivot and move independently of its partner.

Allied to this mechanical difference was the equally rapid adoption of a totally different concept of interior layout. The traditional compartment-style coach found limited acceptance in North America. The open 'saloon' with centre gangway rapidly became standard. The 'saloon' was more neighbourly and, across the great distances, afforded an opportunity for passengers to stretch their legs from time to time—an impossibility in the contemporary European train. Early American trains, moreover, did not generally provide as many different classes or categories of accommodation as those in Europe.

From a very early stage, these separate lines of development emerged and continued their own independent evolution for over a century. There was a certain amount of cross-fertilization to and fro across the Atlantic but, even in the second half of the 20th century, coaches can still be regarded as either American or European in basic inspiration for this distinction is not confined to these two areas of the world.

Railways spread rapidly throughout the globe from the mid-19th century onwards. The newly-developing systems in Latin America, Africa, Asia and Australasia not unnaturally drew on the experience (and mistakes) of the early European and American pioneers. Naturally enough—for in many cases the new systems were financed and built by capital from the older industrial nations—railways in the developing continents tended to exhibit many of the characteristics of the parent country. This was as true of passenger vehicles as of any other aspect. Throughout the Americas, North American concepts gained the ascendancy, despite a considerable infusion of European capital, ideas and equipment. In India, railways tended to be British in style of operation but, in response to the particular nature of that sub-continent, the coaches quickly developed their own characteristics; in Australia and New Zealand, although coaches frequently exhibited both American and European features, they were usually recognizably one or the other.

In Africa and in many parts of Asia, the railway was often built to narrow gauge (for economy), but with vehicles scarcely distinguishable from their standard-gauge contemporaries in terms of physical size.

So much for the origins of the passenger train—what of its later ramifications? Early trains were all very similar and the majority stopped at almost every station. In time, different categories of traveller emerged, each category with individual needs. Railway designers were but a short step from the realization that coach design ought to reflect changing circumstances and needs. The era of specialization began in this way and it is still with us. Over the years,

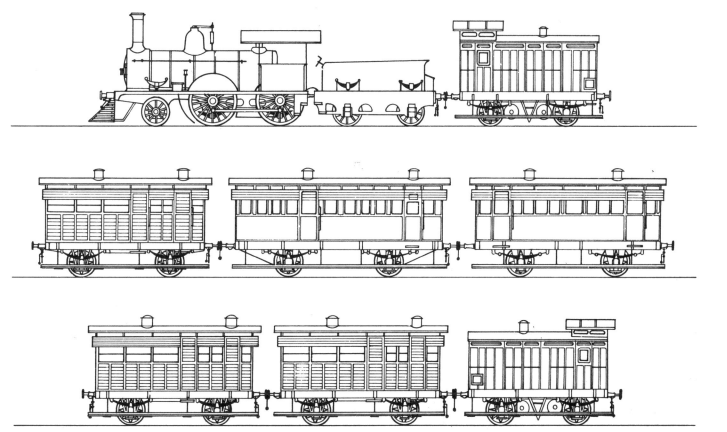

The Indian railway system was virtually an export version of British home railways. Although the rolling stock had superficial differences, in fundamentals it clearly belonged to the British school of design. This is the Bombay–Poona Mail of the Great Indian Peninsular Railway, shown as it was in the 1860s. The 2-4-0 locomotive is clearly British, although the cab design has been adapted to Indian circumstances. The passenger cars, too, have been modified to fit them for the high temperatures and burning sun of the locality: they have double roofs and window shades. The first and last vehicles have brake drums, part of an early continuous chain-operated brake system.

this has presented an astonishingly variable, yet historically accurate, reflection of changing ideas and social customs. At the top of the list, inevitably, comes the long-distance inter-city express.

The inter-city train

The phrase 'inter-city' is relatively modern, a part of the contemporary jargon seemingly indispensable to our modern civilization—yet the reality behind the expression is rooted in railway history. The Liverpool & Manchester Railway pioneered easier communications between large centres of population and the long-distance main-line train has been at the heart of passenger operation since that time.

At first, all passenger trains stopped frequently, wherever and whenever travellers might be expected to board. As railways expanded and the distances involved increased, so did the number of stops. Before long, management realized that division of its basic service was a possibility. A large number and wide distribution of stations offered a greater passenger potential. Gradually, certain trains were able to omit some intermediate stops (at the smaller settlements) yet still retain adequate fare-paying passenger loads from the larger centres. This was the beginning of the concept of the express train for long and medium distances and of the stopping train to cater for smaller stations over shorter stretches of line. The omission of certain stops on some journeys had the advantage of reducing end-to-end times of the journey—from time immemorial a certain way of increasing the attractiveness of the service.

Nevertheless, journey times were lengthy and, even in the small countries of Europe, it became necessary to consider what might most delicately be described as the 'bodily needs' of the passenger. This sensitive matter was almost an unmentionable subject in Victorian Britain and certain worthy citizens probably recoiled in horror at the thought of a lavatory in a train. Progress was, however, inevitable and lavatory-equipped coaches gradually made their appearance. Some companies went to extraordinary lengths to disguise the presence of such essential conveniences.

Lavatories, of course, occupied floor space and this space was not, in the strictest sense, revenue earning. The railways were consequently reluctant to provide more than minimum facilities and often these were for first-class passengers only. Even when lavatory facilities were available for all classes of travel, not all compartments could gain access to lavatories. It became for the passengers a test of their knowledge of carriage construction in selecting an adequately equipped compartment. The obvious solution was some form of continuous passageway throughout the length of the coach, but despite the American example of the centre-gangway open saloon, European railways were slow to follow suit. After all, corridors implied even more non-revenue space, larger and heavier coaches and larger locomotives to pull the trains—and this would demand new capital investment. Shareholders would, naturally, expect to see a healthy return on their investment.

Early improvements in amenities

It is hard to pin-point accurately the precise moment when improved passenger amenities began to create the forerunner of today's inter-city express. Neither is it possible to pin down with certainty the reasons which impelled the railways to begin to mend their ways. What is certain is that, by the 1870s, railway administrations throughout the world were responding to pressures for improvement. Whatever the precise reasons, the last quarter of the 19th century saw rapid improvements. These tended to appear first in the countries of origin of the early railway systems. This was distinctly fortunate for later-developing countries (in the railway sense). Latecomers to railways were spared many of the miseries which had beset early travellers in Europe and North America.

As was common in the Victorian period, improvement was a combination of private entrepreneurial activity and corporate shrewdness. Space precludes mention of all the activities which took place, but three noteworthy personalities merit special mention.

Chronologically, the first was the American George Mortimer Pullman who, during the recovery from the American Civil War in the 1860s, had quarried a rich vein of 'railway gold' by the introduction of a fleet of luxurious parlor cars and sleeping cars. He persuaded the companies of the USA to operate these luxury cars across their various railway 'frontiers'. Built on the American pattern, large, spacious and more agreeable than their railway-owned contemporaries, the Pullman 'Palace' cars became the symbols of the best in American railroading. The very early Pullman cars were not always comfortable and some were distinctly basic. They were marketed with considerable vigour, however, and, as the 19th century progressed, their amenities and comfort improved in giant steps forward. The companies reacted to Pullman competition by providing comparable stock of their own—often purchasing the coaches from Pullman's own works.

Pullman himself was neither innovator nor inventor. Many others were operating sleeping and parlor cars long before he seriously entered the trade. Although Pullman eventually dominated the North American scene, other operators, such as Woodruff and Wagner, should not be forgotten. They too operated some very agreeable vehicles, some even better than Pullman's own cars, but the Pullman organization proved to have the better staying power.

In continental Europe, the frontiers were not only international borders but often boundaries between railway companies as well. It was just as difficult for the various national railway companies to agree as it was for their political masters. The prospect of international through-services, desirable as they were to the traveller, seemed increasingly remote. One visionary—a Belgian entrepreneur called Georges Nagelmackers of Liège—refused to be discouraged. He had visited North America in the 1860s and was highly impressed with Pullman's activities. He was less impressed with the quality of the early Pullman cars than he was with the service the Pullman cars provided. Consequently, in 1869, Nagelmackers began a similar development in Europe. At first, his cars were small but, from the beginning, were designed to give greater comfort and privacy than the Pullman cars of his original inspiration. His were, initially, all sleeping cars (convertible for day use) and available only by payment of a supplementary charge.

Unlike Pullman, Nagelmackers had more than railways with which to contend. Customs barriers, politicians and the chaos of the Franco-Prussian war must have complicated matters hugely. Nagelmackers had his rivals including those who wished ill of his endeavours. His main rival was the American William D'Alton Mann. Mann was also trying to establish a similar European service. Mann was arguably less of a visionary than Nagelmackers and in 1876 the two effectively resolved their differences by amalgamation. Nagelmackers took full control of a newly-constituted International Sleeping Car Company, better known as the 'Compagnie Internationale des Wagons-Lits et des Grands Express Européens' or just 'Wagons-Lits' as the public knew them.

To the names of Pullman and Nagelmackers must be added a third—James Allport of England. If his name is internationally less well known than the other two, his influence was no less significant. Although he served only one British company, the Midland Railway—one of the three or four major British systems—his influence was to spread throughout Britain and eventually the world. Allport had also visited North America and had travelled many thousands of miles in some of Pullman's more splendid cars. He even persuaded Pullman to visit Britain and describe his coaches. In 1874, the first Pullman sleeping car in Britain was introduced by the Midland Railway. The car was made in America, dismantled and re-erected in England. Its size, comparatively modest by American standards, positively dwarfed the home product. As a result of this importation Midland adopted bogie coaches as standard well before most other British companies.

Allport was quick to capitalize on his lead and, very significantly for the ordinary passenger, resolved that everyone should share in the higher standards established by Pullman and Wagons-Lits. In two short years the Midland, as well as introducing Pullman cars on the best services, in quick succession admitted third-class passengers to all trains, abolished second class completely (but destroyed the third-class coaches, thus providing the third-class passenger with the former second-class coaches at no increase in fare), and reduced first-class fares to second-class levels. In the staid boardrooms of the other British companies, this reform was tantamount to revolution and the British

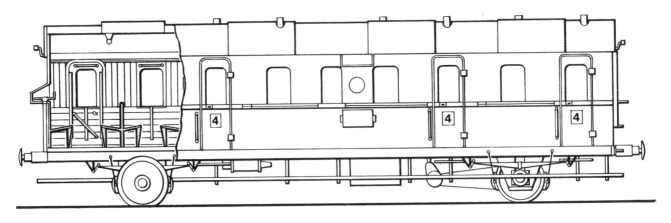

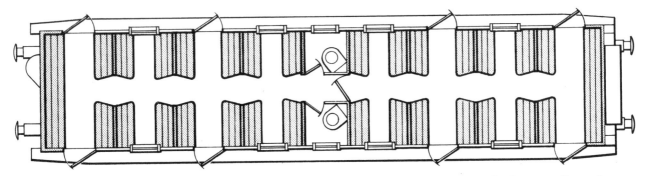

rivals were not at all pleased with this competitor's innovations.

If Pullman and Nagelmackers made a reality of the long-distance luxury train, Allport showed that a railway system could provide comfort for all passengers. The Midland was now a two-class railway and, by World War I, most British companies had fallen into line. In America, two-class travel had virtually always existed. In Europe, the anachronism of multi-class travel finally succumbed in recent years to the basic and almost universal international standard—regardless of the specific labels on the coaches.

These events of the 1870s mark the start of real carriage evolution. Access to a lavatory was absolutely essential in the newly-introduced sleeping cars and the day coaches were not long to follow suit. In America, where the centre gangway was universal, such access was readily available, but in Europe the individual compartment with its limited seating capacity and its pair of facing sets of seats (entirely in the stage-coach tradition) was still the preferred mode. Thus the only suitable method was the side-corridor arrangement.

Side corridors inevitably caused an increase in coach weight per passenger and the European railways gradually realized the virtue of the American bogie-coach concept for long distance trains. Four- and six-wheelers were cheap to build and economical to operate. They were perfectly adequate for short-distance trains and remained commonplace. Thus the real inter-city express gradually became identifiable outside the American sphere of influence by its larger bogie coaches and gangway access to the essential lavatories. Evolution to a continuous connection between adjacent coaches was a slow process, but had become fairly widespread by the latter part of the 19th century. Pioneer work was carried out by Waterbury and Atkins in the United States during the 1850s, while history suggests that the first real connection between adjacent coaches in Europe was seen in Queen Victoria's twin, six-wheel saloons. These were built by the London & North Western Railway in 1869 and are

The German railways for many decades provided fourth-class passenger accommodation. The vehicle illustrated is relatively modern, having been built after the formation of the Deutsche Reichsbahn at the close of World War I. The four-wheel passenger car was long favoured in continental Europe. Indeed, in present-day Germany, although fourth class has now disappeared, the four-wheeler is still used.

happily preserved, now united on a single bogie underframe, at Britain's National Railway Museum in York.

The real spur to widespread development was the introduction of dining-car services. Allied to the need for lavatories and sleeping accommodation on long-distance trains was the need for refreshments. Commonly in early practice the train stopped at some suitable station for a short period to allow passengers to have a meal at the refreshment room. This solution was fraught with problems for the passenger. There was the inevitable rush for the refreshment room and unscrupulous proprietors were not above serving inferior food to this captive market—composed mainly of travellers unlikely to pass that way again for some time. Not infrequently the soup course would be so hot that passengers could not complete the meal before departure time—a splendid opportunity for profiteering by the restaurant proprietor who had (naturally) collected the cost of the full meal!

Passengers objected vehemently and some refreshment rooms gained real notoriety. The railways responded with the introduction of luncheon baskets —often of real splendour—which could be taken on to the train and by the first tentative attempts at dining cars. Refreshment-room proprietors were unhappy and for many years, especially in Britain, insisted on trains continuing to make meal stops. A combination of the elimination of meal stops to speed journey times, expiry of refreshment-room contracts and gradual improvement of dining cars led to the permanent establishment of the train catering services as we know them today.

At the same time the provision of a dining car produced its own problems. A simple passage-way within an individual coach provided adequate access to the lavatory but access to the dining car involved movement between coaches, hence the spur to develop corridor connections. At first, some railways took the view that not all passengers would wish to eat on the train—a perfectly valid assumption—and that those who wished to eat could join the dining car at the start of the journey, and remain with it throughout. Before long the more enterprising companies realized that though some passengers would not want to eat, there might be more hungry people than could be accommodated at one sitting in the dining car. It became more sensible to have the diner integrated with the rest of the train—the alternative being an undignified scramble between carriages at a station stop. Even so, the tradition of riding all the way in the dining car died hard and, in Britain at least, the Pullman car concept, renowned in America more for sleeping than for day coaches, became synonymous with a luxury 'meal at every seat' facility. Today the word 'Pullman' in British railway usage now merely refers to this version of meal service.

With dining cars and continuous corridors added to the established sleeping cars and gangwayed day coaches, all the ingredients of the inter-city train had finally arrived. The 20th century has been more noteworthy for adaptation of these basic concepts than for any significantly new evolutionary moves. In essence, the inter-city train was evolved in the late 19th century and has matured in the 20th.

Early inter-city travel

At the end of the Victorian period the most effective and agreeable way of travel by land was by train. Whether one was rich or poor, the railway had a virtual monopoly, especially in long-distance travel. In this situation, one might have expected that service to the public would suffer—in most cases it did not. Even where no directly-competing rival company spurred development, most of the better railways of the world took their monopoly status seriously and responsibly. Furthermore, they frequently provided trains of a quality over and above their minimum duty. The Wagons-Lits company provided superb services throughout Europe. Pullman cars in all their glory spanned the length and breadth of America, while in India and Asia fine trains were steadily increasing in number. Probably it was in Britain that the late 19th- and early 20th-century express train reached its high point of perfection —at least for the ordinary passenger.

Untroubled by political disturbances and unworried by the pressures of developing unexplored hinterlands (at least in the United Kingdom), Great Britain was basking in that Indian summer of the Empire, the late Victorian and the Edwardian era—and the trains exuded the same confidence. Because of the limited British loading gauge, the trains were physically smaller than many of those found elsewhere in the world, and the distances covered were in no way comparable with the vast hauls of the major global transcontinental lines, particularly in America and Asia. Nevertheless, in terms of their general average speed they were immeasurably superior to all save the better trains in the USA. So far as comfort was concerned, only the various supplementary-fee luxury coaches elsewhere could compete with the best British coaches— generally available to any passenger without additional charge. At that time, nothing in the railway world matched the upholstered third class. This was a well-nigh universal feature of most reputable British railways at the turn of the century—even on less-prestigious trains. Furthermore, third-class passengers were commonly admitted to the vast majority of British inter-city trains. In many parts of the world no such provision was made.

This pre-eminent position was held by Great Britain for about 25 years prior to World War I. In the late 1880s and early 1890s, the best British expresses, led by those of the Great Northern and Midland Railways, were generally averaging 64 km/h (40 mph) or more, where the rest of the world outside the USA and Australia was hard pressed to realize 48 km/h (30 mph). By the Edwardian period, the speed differentials had been eroded but the standard of train still gave Britain the edge, possibly reaching an all-time high when the London & North Western Railway in 1908 provided a superb set of 12-wheel

In 1925 the newly-formed Southern Railway began to re-equip its London–Bournemouth trains. This is a composite coach (that is, composed of both first- and third-class compartments). The provision of doors for all compartments, the use of wood for bodywork, and destination boards attached above the roof eaves were typical British features of this period.

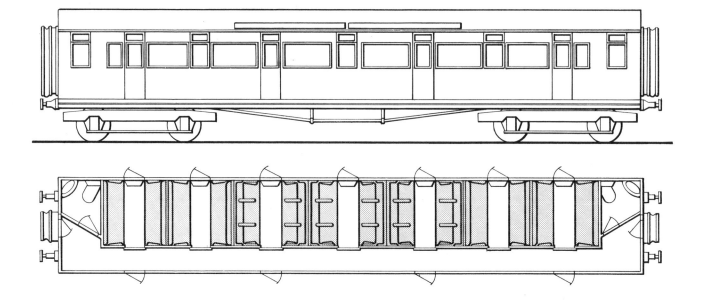

coaches (at no extra charge) for its celebrated '2 p.m. all corridor' train from Euston to Glasgow and Edinburgh—first and third class only, it should be noted.

If the modern inter-city service underwent an adolescent phase before World War I in which British influence was probably predominant, then its full adult maturity began during the 1920s, when the pacemaker was unquestionably the United States of America. As will be seen, the best American coaches had been without peer from a much earlier date but, until the 1920s, these superb coaches had carried a limited range of passengers. The inter-war years were to change all that. With the advent of the Pullman Standard company, the emphasis changed to the complete train, a movement rapidly consolidated during the ensuing streamline era of the 1930s and 1940s.

The sudden improvement was in part a response to the growing use of the motor car—especially among ordinary people. The USA was the cradle of the modern mass-produced automobile and, during the 1920s, these vehicles were produced at an astonishingly low unit cost. The ordinary (or 'coach' class) rail passenger of North America—equivalent to the British and European second- or third-class traveller—had not received much attention during the 'wood and varnish' era of the Pullman 'Palace' car and was still being offered a rudimentary ride. He proved a willing disciple at the shrine of Henry Ford and his fellow high priests. As a result, North American railways made strenuous efforts to win back favour and this time they no longer had a monopoly.

It had long been common US practice for railways to buy equipment, whether locomotives or freight and passenger stock, from outside suppliers. During World War I the United States Railroad Administration (USRA), formed to administer the railways during the national emergency, had standardized a limited number of vehicle designs. The advantages of standardization remained desirable when the companies had resumed full control of their affairs after the war, and provided Pullman (and others) with a splendid springboard from which to launch a re-equipment programme to provide North America with a vast fleet of new coaches.

From the outside, these massive 24 m (80 ft) cars looked much the same, whether Pullman owned and operated (in the traditional way) or Pullman built and company owned. Furthermore, Pullman was required to paint its own cars in the colours of the leasing railroad. But inside the vehicles every opportunity was taken to exhibit individuality according to the trends and fashions of the day and the particular idiosyncracies of the owners. Throughout the length and breadth of North America, the steel-built, Pullman Standard car became the very epitome of rail passenger travel; the era of the 'Limited' had dawned.

The name 'Limited' derived from the concept of a limited number of stops—thus a shortened journey time—but in some cases it was also legitimately applied to the limited number of people allowed to travel on the train. These trains were very popular and demand frequently outstripped supply. Though the motor car was not exactly routed, its competition over long and medium distances was certainly opposed determinedly. Speed was the essence of the 'Limited', and speedy trains were built. *Broadway Limited, Twentieth Century Limited, Blue Comet, Empire State Express, Yankee Clipper, Columbine*—the names read like a catalogue, made even more familiar by the tremendous influence of the Hollywood film industry.

When, in due course, the streamline fashion emerged in the 1930s and 1940s the railways were not slow to take advantage of it. More exotic names were added to the list and some supremely beautiful trains were built. Who but a man with no soul could fail to be moved by the 160 km/h (100 mph) flights of the Milwaukee Road's *Hiawatha*, the majestic sight of the Santa Fe's *Super Chief*, the *California Zephyr* as it traversed the unbelievable scenery of Colorado, or the progress through California of Southern Pacific's *Daylight* trains—acclaimed by many as the most beautiful in the world.

Sadly the great trains of North America were to enjoy something of a butterfly-like existence. Great trains emerged in all their magnificence, but within barely more than a generation had succumbed to the aeroplane. If the motorized era after World War I caused their birth, then the development of air traffic after the second great conflict just as surely killed them off.

This great era of North American railroading lasted long enough, however, to inspire not only imitators in the rest of the world but also to affect profoundly the development of inter-city travel in general. In continental Europe, superb trains like *Rheingold* and the Wagons-Lits' *Blue Train* were just as impressive as the North American 'Limited'. This same period produced in Britain not only magnificent trains like the streamlined LNER *Silver Jubilee* and the LMS *Coronation Scot* but also stimulated considerable improvements in locomotive design. Sadly the war in Europe brought a stop to development along these lines earlier than in the USA.

Outside Europe and North America, the development of high-speed inter-city travel was a slower process. This was mainly because many areas were less highly industrialized or urbanized than the older (by railway standards) countries. Railways in Latin America and Africa were used more in the 19th-century American 'colonial' fashion and, often of a narrow gauge, could not match the USA and Europe for speed. But by any standards, South African Railways' *Blue Train* was as magnificent a concept as any North American 'Limited', even though its average speed on the 1,067 mm (3 ft 6 in) gauge was slower.

In continental Asia, the Trans Siberian Express, although not a 'flier' by global standards, indicated more than any other single service the ability of the railway to shrink distance and unify a large land mass during the pre-airline phase. The various trans-Indian trains of the pre-independence period were something of a unique institution. The railways of India were largely British in concept and operation and, in their later 19th-century days, were not renowned for high speed. In view of the number of large towns, considerable areas of tolerably flat country and the ample supply of highly qualified engineers, both locally trained and expatriate, it is surprising that the fast inter-city concept did not make greater headway. However, long-distance services were developed and made a considerable contribution to unifying this diverse sub-continent before independence.

Elsewhere in Asia, much development took place for economic reasons and utilized sub-standard-gauge systems. This inhibited growth of rapid inter-city services. At the same time, as in Africa, the choice of a narrower gauge did not prevent the long-distance train from making its mark. For example, the Malayan State Railway, though modest in terms of network complexity, operated some fine trains from Singapore northwards to Kuala Lumpur and across the frontier into Thailand. At the other end of the scale, the Japanese achieved a remarkable degree of complexity on the 1,067 mm (3 ft 6 in) gauge.

The nearest approach to the classic European/American train occurred in Australasia, particularly in Australia itself. Australia was, and is still to some extent, bedevilled by its multiple-gauge problem, the origins of which recede into railway history. Within each state, distances between cities are considerable—more on the American scale than the European. Fortunately, the more densely populated states adopted standard- or broader-than-standard gauges, which permitted higher speeds. Although the first steam trains did not run in Australia until 1854, by the 1880s the Australians were operating the fastest trains outside Britain and North America.

The trains displayed a curious mixture of British and American influence which, oddly yet accurately, reflected the various periods of history. During the late 19th and early 20th centuries, British influence was predominant, especially in outward appearance; during the inter-war years and afterwards, trains exhibited increasingly American characteristics. If the pre-World War I *Sydney Express* looked as if it had escaped by magic from some London terminus, then the *Spirit of Progress* some two generations later would not have looked out of place at Grand Central station, New York!

New Zealand's ability to develop a true inter-city service was, like that of many of the developing countries, inhibited in speed terms by the use of the narrower 1,067 mm (3 ft 6 in) gauge. Construction did not begin in earnest until the 1870s and New Zealand was able to take advantage of the lessons and mistakes of earlier pioneers in other countries. Although much earlier equipment was British, American technology in the event proved more suited to New Zealand operations. By the 1920s, New Zealanders boasted some splendid 'Limiteds' built and operated on very similar lines to their larger American contemporaries. Furthermore, track had been upgraded to permit higher running speeds than were often possible on the narrow gauge.

By the 1940s, the long-distance train was the accepted norm for overland travel throughout the world. The motor car was well established and was already dominant over shorter-distance operations, but the inter-city express seemed secure. The express could out-match the car in both speed and comfort over most distances above 160 km (100 miles) and, for those without cars, was a far superior alternative to the motor coach for anything but short hauls. This situation did not last long. Stimulated by vast orders for military equipment during World War II, manufacturers had revolutionized aircraft construction. During the 20 years after 1945, a major revolution in long-distance passenger haulage took place. The airliner was no longer a somewhat temperamental plaything for the wealthy but afforded a means of mass high-speed communication for all and especially over distances above 480 km (300 miles); so the inter-city train came under greater threat. Not only that—much-improved motor cars and the construction of motorways produced even more competition on the medium-distance journeys.

The longer-haul operators were the first to feel the effects. In spite of increasing efforts to modernize trains and devise more ingenious methods of entertaining travellers *en route*, the railways rediscovered that transit time between departure and arrival was the prime factor in many passengers' choice of transport mode. The railways should not have been surprised—after all, railways had used the very same argument in staving off early road competition. The great era of the 'Limiteds' and streamliners came to an end. Some sort of eleventh-hour reprieve was at hand, however, stimulated this time by events far from the North American scene—back, in the original heartland of railways, in Western Europe, where road and air competition grew more or less simultaneously.

The motor car was invented in Europe but did not achieve mass ownership in this region until later than in North America—not until after World War II. However, Western Europe faced the post-1945 world with a war-ravaged countryside and the urgent priority to rebuild shattered economies. The universal language was that of priorities. No place existed, at least initially, for the self-indulgence of private motor cars and intensive airline services. The railways had suffered huge war damage and were high on the list of priorities for rebuilding in order to restore commerce and industry. The dramatic effect of mass car-ownership and the newer threat of the airliner were delayed. The traditional express train had a chance to re-establish itself before facing the full competition of air and road. This delay gave European railways a chance to think out their attitude to the new order of things. The railways could not afford to be sanguine. To many millions of travellers mindful of the misery of wartime rail journeys, the chance to own a car or to sample the new glamour of air travel could not come too quickly.

As in many parts of the world, the most vulnerable area of rail travel was the longer-distance train and reductions took place in the face of air competition. In one respect Europe had a real advantage. Although many trains covered long enough distances to make the airliner a more attractive proposition in terms of total journey time, many passengers were not travelling the whole distance. The continent as a whole is compact enough for many services to remain competitive over these intermediate stages and this stems largely from delays to the air traveller going to and from the out-of-town airports. The railways were city-centre to city-centre routes and, provided that speed and frequency of service was maintained, could remain highly competitive on journeys up to 400 km (250 miles) and reasonably attractive over journeys of twice that distance.

At the close of World War II the London & North Eastern Railway introduced new designs of passenger car. This is a first-class vehicle seating 36 passengers in six compartments. A new arrangement of doors has been adopted, windows have been enlarged, and there is a greater use of steel in the bodywork. The left-hand half of the illustration below shows the compartment side of the car and the right-hand half shows the corridor side.

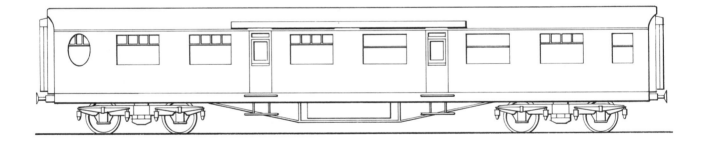

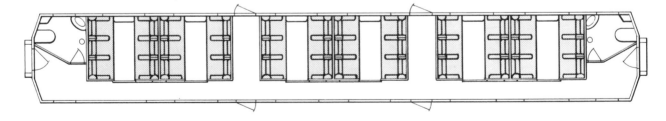

Developments after World War II

In response after the war, a fine network of high-speed inter-city services was developed in Europe. This was usually scheduled with the businessman in mind and captured not only the public imagination but also heavy traffic. Aided by a complete change in attitude towards European unity, these services, spearheaded by the *Trans-Europ Express* (TEE) trains, cross Western European frontiers with a frequency which Georges Nagelmackers would have envied. The trains, moreover, are running over systems which, except for route alignment, have been totally rebuilt and re-equipped since 1945. They are thoroughly modern in concept. The modern *Rheingold, Mistral* and *Settebello* are totally in keeping with the last quarter of the 20th century.

Equally impressive are the giant strides made by the ordinary express trains of Britain and Western Europe. TEE trains still keep to the traditional 'Limited' plan—in this case, first class only (plus supplement) allied with limited stops—but, throughout Europe during the 1960s and 1970s, their success has stimulated similar improvements on non-supplementary-fare trains. The 160 km/h (100 mph) train is now commonplace whereas, in the streamline era, it was the prerogative of a few specially-equipped prestige services.

The British railway system, brought under public ownership in 1948, faced the postwar world in a run-down state. Unlike the continental systems, the British system was still recognizably intact and usable and did not receive the same degree of priority in re-equipment and new investment. Intensive modernization did not begin until the late 1950s and early 1960s. Under these circumstances, rail travel was not always attractive and large parts of the network—generally marginal routes—were closed in the face of road competition. The inter-city network, however, survived. During the 1960s the inter-city service began to win back traffic in a spectacular way. Electrification of the London–Manchester/Liverpool line with consequent faster services all but eliminated effective competition from the domestic airlines while a similar transformation took place on the East Coast route made possible by the high-power Deltic diesels.

Spurred by these successes, European railways began in the late 1960s to rethink the whole question of the trains themselves. They were undoubtedly influenced by events in Japan. The Japanese economic recovery since 1945 is one of the most remarkable features of the modern world and the railways played a major part. Japan, like much of Europe, is a compact industrial area and the Japanese were quick to realize the value of a growing network of high-speed inter-city trains, predominantly patronized by businessmen. However, Japanese railways run on 1,067 mm (3 ft 6 in) gauge and could not be developed to the high-speed category. Great steps were made—up to 120 km/h (75 mph)—but the demand for speed continued to grow. In 1964, the Japanese opened the New Tokaido Line—a totally new 1,435 mm (4 ft 8½ in) gauge railway designed from the outset for really high speeds and along which enormous trains run at 210 km/h (130 mph) at frequent intervals. Its success was instantaneous.

The New Tokaido-style lines in Europe (and elsewhere) have stimulated development of a new generation of trains built for speed. Construction has begun on two new lines on the Japanese fashion, Mannheim–Stuttgart in West Germany and Paris–Lyons in France, but many other routes are already capable of considerable upgrading without major rebuilding. Elimination of sharper than desirable curves, removal of 'bottlenecks' and the rationalization of track layouts have done much to improve matters and have permitted considerably increased speeds. Already in service, typifying the new order of things, are the 200 km/h (125 mph) high-speed diesel trains introduced in Britain in 1976, the futuristic West German inter-city multiple-unit ET 403, and the French turbo trains. Within a few years, if all goes well, the new British advanced passenger train (APT) will make London to Glasgow (640 km or 400 miles) in four hours.

The modern inter-city train on the Japanese/European pattern owes much of its success to patronage by business travellers. Railways have been far less successful at retaining the recreational traveller. The airlines—aided by the package-tour industry—have developed a virtual monopoly in longer-distance holiday travel, while the motor car, with its convenience and flexibility, is still the first choice for the traditional family holidaymaker.

Modern airline travel is a time-saving people-processing exercise rather than a worthwhile experience in itself. This factor, plus the general improvement of trains since the early 1960s and the boost to rail travel from the fuel crisis of the early 1970s, has caused many people to think again about the 'old fashioned' train. The environmentalist lobby has helped, by making clear that the railway is neither as prodigal of space nor as environmentally polluting as the motor vehicle, motorway and airline. The railway is not as flexible as the car but makes more economic use of expensive fuel, and is infinitely more economical of fuel than the jet plane.

A most significant pointer to the rebirth of interest in the traditional long-distance train can be found in Australia—probably the first large country in which domestic airliners made impact. The completion of a standard-gauge link across Western Australia in 1970 made possible through-train communication, without change of coach, over the 3,960 km (2,461 miles) between Sydney and Perth for the first time ever. This had obvious economic advantages for freight haulage but a courageous decision indeed led to the establishment of a new passenger service over such a distance—particularly in the light of American experience during the 1950s and 1960s. A three-day rail journey seemed unlikely to offer real competition to an eight-hour air schedule. Yet the *Indian Pacific*—as the new train was called—was an instant success. The *Indian Pacific* is a deluxe train of the old-fashioned type. Not only has accommodation on the train been increased since the service's inauguration but service frequency has been doubled.

It is too soon to predict whether all these post-1945 developments will cause a major rebirth of rail travel in those countries most affected by alternative modes of transport. The signs are quite encouraging, even in North America where all seemed lost in the late 1960s. It is no exaggeration that, with the exception of commuter services and a few shorter-distance hauls mainly on the Eastern seaboard, most US railroads had little time for the passenger train in the mid 1960s. A few noteworthy exceptions existed, like the Southern Railway and a few of the western lines, but in general the passenger was not welcomed. However, in 1971, prompted by pressure to maintain, for social reasons, a basic inter-city network of passenger trains, the Nixon administration was responsible for introducing the most revolutionary change that had

The power unit of the British High Speed Train, introduced in 1976. One such unit is at each end of the train, the combined power being sufficient to maintain speeds up to 200 kph (125 mph). Used at first between London, Bristol and Cardiff, these trains have also, since 1978, provided services between London, the north-east and Edinburgh. The rear compartments of the power units accommodate baggage, as well as a somewhat noisy compartment for the train's guard.

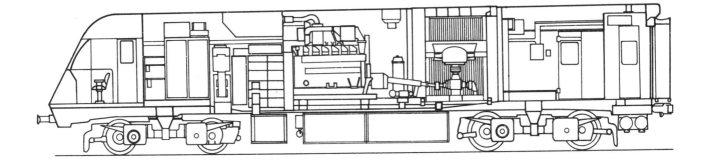

ever been seen in American railroading—Amtrak.

This was a new corporation responsible for maintaining a basic inter-city passenger network throughout the USA and redeveloping some of the routes. Amtrak is effectively a quasi-nationalization of rail passenger travel and, with few exceptions, the railroads were happy to hand to Amtrak the remains of their once fabulous fleets of 'Limiteds'. But painting old equipment in new standard colours and providing a new name did not, of itself, suddenly revitalize passenger travel.

The first years of Amtrak were touch-and-go. Motley collections of coaches, still at first decked in all the variety of their old company colours and not always in the best condition, bore no comparison with the superb trains of previous generations. Selective weeding out of the poorer coaches, gradual re-equipment with new stock and locomotives, and the unexpected bonus of the 1973 oil crisis together enabled Amtrak to survive its first five years. It seems that the worst may now be over. Interestingly enough, the USA is for the first time seriously examining the European concept of inter-city trains and has introduced European equipment on some services.

So much for the older traditional railway regions; but what of the rest of the world? Inter-city travel in the modern meaning of the phrase is essentially a feature of the developed industrial nations—hence the emphasis on Europe, North America and, to a lesser degree, Japan and Australia in this survey. Outside these areas, the long-distance train, although it exists, has never been developed as extensively. This is explained in part by the stage reached in the economic evolution of the countries concerned. Curiously, this may be advantageous to the railways in the long term. As mentioned earlier, passenger railways in the developed world have reflected changes in social and economic conditions over the years. The prerogative of the pioneer has always been to make the first mistakes as well as the first really progressive improvements—in this, railways were no exception. The British pioneers of the mechanized railway built their bridges and fixed structures too small and consequently restricted development of the railway vehicle in a technological sense. The Americans were perhaps too ready to abandon the passenger train. Throughout much of the developed world, some lines may prove to have been abandoned over-hastily.

The developing world will, hopefully, profit from these mistakes and the signs are tolerably encouraging. In areas such as Latin America and the Indian sub-continent, where universal car ownership is still some time away, trains serve the same purpose that they did in Europe and America a generation or two ago. As only a small proportion of the population can afford long-distance air travel, the long-haul express is still viable though its overall speed

The French TGV prototype. Long trials of this gas-turbine high-speed five-car train have now ceased. Weighing less than 200 tonnes, and with electric traction motors developing 4,920 hp, this train could run at speeds of up to 300 kph (187 mph). It was therefore a very suitable vehicle for testing suspension design, and it may be regarded as a prototype of the electric trains which are to be built for the new Paris–Sudest high-speed railway.

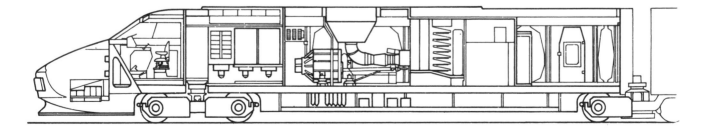

is limited. New lines are still being built in many parts of the world. Unfortunately, we know comparatively little about activities in Russia and China where railways are still a prime means of moving both people and goods.

All told, therefore, the inter-city train does not appear quite as much of an obsolete institution as some of its detractors would have had us believe only a few years ago. The inter-city train can still, along with the ocean liner, be the most agreeable form of mass transport where time-saving is not crucial and can compete even in terms of the time factor over intermediate distances.

The rural train

More books have probably been devoted to the rural train than to any other aspect of railways except the locomotive; it forms part of the folk-lore of many nations. Perhaps deep down we regard rural train travel as somehow more human than most sections of the railway.

The first train ever to traverse open country and stop at an intermediate location was a rural train, but the real rural train, as the term is generally understood, evolved as a special category.

The main-line services developed along the two lines of evolution already discussed. A third type of passenger and train began to emerge. Some of the intermediate stopping places were too distant from the main cities to afford any prospect of selection as residential areas for the new-style commuters. Such centres were too small to attract the patronage of the major expresses. Consequently, fewer trains stopped at these stations and did so mainly to permit passengers to transact business at that station. These stations were not subservient to the demands of a nearby city but centres in their own right. The passengers were usually using the train in the course of their daily life as part of that particular community: the local shopkeeper, perhaps, travelling to town for the day to order supplies for the village store, or a farmer travelling to a nearby market town to inspect livestock. The variations are endless but shared a relevance to the local community which other kinds of journeys lacked. Gradually there developed a direct involvement between community and railway—for these were the days when the railway represented the only form of speedy transport.

In time, the railways provided minor lines to feed their main routes and the era of the branch line began. Many of these grew to some importance and a number, even in the motor-oriented countries, survive today. These routes were more locally relevant than the principal main lines (whose function was essentially to connect larger centres) and they developed distinctive characteristics of their own. Their function, so far as the promoting railway company was concerned, was to provide additional traffic for the main lines. This was a two-way process, particularly in terms of freight traffic. Commodities from other areas were brought in by rail and, in this sense, the minor routes were branches. In originating traffic from the local centre, these lesser lines were the essential roots of the parent system.

From the passenger standpoint, the issues are less clear. Most rural lines were built more to carry freight than people. Rural lines afforded a means of distributing the products of the new manufacturing industries more widely and psychologically helped the rural dwellers feel part of the larger community. But rural communities were (and often are) largely self-sufficient. Why should rural dwellers want to travel on the trains? The railway ensured the all-important commercial contact with the wider world without need for travel on the train—surely that was sufficient? In many instances it was and passenger travel was minimal. To attach the odd passenger coach to the regular freight train often sufficed and produced that characteristic phenomenon of the rural railway, the mixed train.

Development was more rapid in some areas. The growing pace of industrial activity even in the smaller towns attracted the population away from the rural areas to man the growing number of factories and workshops. Industrial working conditions were mixed but at least offered a prospect of regular employment—not always guaranteed in the farming areas—and the wages were often more attractive than in agriculture. Then as now the lure of the town was strong. Rural depopulation became a real threat. The coming of the railways to rural areas enabled some people to remain in the villages and to work in the nearby town. It was a miniature repetition of the commuting pattern already established by the railways around the larger cities—but with one important difference. The growth of city commuting led to the development of suburbs—work-people were encouraged to move out of the city and to live in the countryside. In the rural areas, the growth of the commuting habit enabled some of the isolated settlements to retain a community identity simply because the railway afforded a means of taking surplus manpower to a source of employment without depopulating the settlement. Some evidence exists in the British population statistics that in some parts where a rural railway was present (or a station on a main-line railway), the shift of population to the towns was less.

With the growth of flexible motor traffic, the rural train is, at least in the developed world, no longer seen as a vital factor. It is more sensible to load cattle on to a motor vehicle and take them direct to the destination without the two intermediate transhipment operations which rail haulage would imply. This applies to many other freight operations and, not surprisingly, this aspect of the rural railway has witnessed decline in many parts of the world. Unfortunately, without freight revenue, the passenger services are unable to cover operating costs on their own. The rural passenger services are threatened. Since not everyone possesses or wishes to possess their own mechanized transport, the threat to the passenger service is serious.

This chain of events has often been repeated in the older industrial regions, such as those of Western Europe and North America, and there is no guarantee that it will not spread to other areas of the world in time. With both the commuter train and the rural train social problems are posed.

Possibly some sort of compromise solution will emerge. In addition to the rural branch-line train, which only in exceptional circumstances has a promising future, were services to the intermediate centres from the main lines passing through rural areas. Many of these intermediate centres have been closed to local traffic although the main-line service still exists. Perhaps there is more hope in these cases. In north-west England, on the main line between Leeds and Carlisle, a limited restoration of local passenger services has been experimentally promoted by the Yorkshire Dales National Park in collaboration with British Rail. Essentially this affords a monthly opportunity for the citizens of the surrounding industrial areas to enjoy a day in a strikingly beautiful and remote rural region, while the balancing workings of the trains allow local inhabitants of the National Park to make a day excursion for shopping and so on to the nearby cities. This has been extremely successful and has managed to cover its direct operating costs.

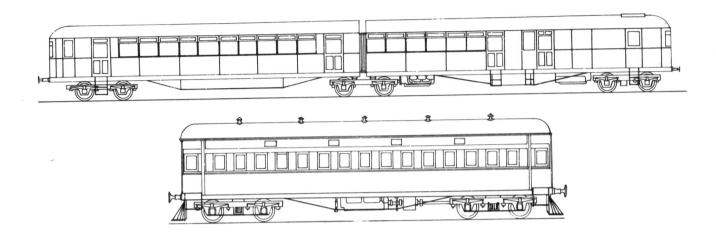

One principal exception to this general picture ought to be mentioned, namely, the intermediate train. Over the years, many countries have developed a type of passenger train not easily categorized. It was not an inter-city express nor did it cover vast distances. Neither was it rural or commuter-like in its operation. Covering distances in the 50 to 200 km (30 to 125 mile) range, this train carried various names depending on the country of operation. In the English-speaking world, it was named 'semi-fast', 'cross-country' or 'inter-district', for example. Since it offered connectional intermediate services on reasonably busy lines its survival rate has been good, even in the most motor-conscious regions. Indistinguishable in its early days from more celebrated trains (save to the expert) it has latterly been monopolized world wide by the multiple-unit train, propelled by an internal-combustion engine—usually diesel.

Despite the question mark over the future of the rural train, where it still survives, its past is unquestionably a significant part of railway history. Yet its long-term contribution to the evolution of passenger travel was probably minimal. Unlike the inter-city train which has constantly changed to suit the circumstances of the day, unlike the commuter train which inevitably has had to respond to increasing passenger traffic, the rural train changed little. For the most part, the rural train has made do with 'cast-off' rolling stock from the rest of the system.

Some noteworthy exceptions to this trend can be identified. During the early phase of road competition, many railways experimented with small self-propelled railcars. The idea was basically sound. In theory the operating cost from self-propelled railcars, whether steam-propelled or driven by some form of internal-combustion engine, was cheaper than that of the conventional locomotive and separate coaches. Unfortunately the early railcars lacked flexibility. At times of peak loading the railcars were too small, yet lacked sufficient power to haul additional coaches, although some valiant attempts were made. Neither could railcars collect the odd freight wagon with the same facility as the locomotive-hauled train. Nevertheless, they provided a vital service for many years and their lineal descendants, in the form of the various diesel multiple-unit trains, can be seen throughout the world on intermediate services.

Before the internal-combustion engine proved itself for railway traction, several companies operated steam railcars for their lightly-loaded passenger services. Top: A late example of the steam railcar was Phenomena *of the London & North Eastern Railway. Built in 1930, it was an articulated twin-car unit powered by the 'Sentinel-Cammell' system, with chain drive and high-pressure boiler (21 kg/cm² or 300 p.s.i.). Above: Seven years earlier, the New South Wales Government Railways took the plunge with an internal-combustion-powered railcar. This was a standard passenger car modified to accommodate a petrol engine. Although not really reliable in service, such a vehicle did have low running costs, and subsequently the NSWGR was a great user of diesel railcars.*

Another and predominantly British innovation, which was partly a response to the needs and problems of the rural railway, was the so-called 'push-pull' train. In this type of train, a conventional locomotive is semi-permanently coupled to a small number of carriages (generally one or two) and, with the minimum of modification, altered for driving remotely from a small compartment at the opposite end of the train from the engine. This avoided the job of uncoupling the locomotive at the end of the journey. The 'push-pull' train was successful and lasted well into the 1960s. First, it solved the problem of augmenting the train at busy times, since the locomotive was capable of hauling several additional coaches. Second, the modification was reasonably inexpensive to install. And third, the locomotive could be detached from the train to perform additional revenue work of an unrelated kind.

In passing, note that the push-pull principle has been successfully employed on a grander scale in recent years as a partial solution to the commuter-train problem. In Germany, France, Britain and the USA, to mention but four countries, many suburban trains are operated in the push-pull mode. This saves turnround time and, as with its rural ancestor, releases a valuable locomotive at off-peak periods for other duties.

Finally, we must not forget the multiplicity of rural railways which were built to narrow gauge. Again the aim was provision of an essential and economic rural service. These lines should not be confused with those widespread main-line systems on the metre and 1,067 mm (3 ft 6 in) gauges such as those found in Africa, Asia and New Zealand, or even the 914 mm (3 ft) gauge lines built in many parts and particularly the southwest of the USA. In concept and operation, these systems rank with standard-gauge railways.

The rural narrow-gauge systems were self-contained small units and, in respect of passenger stock, they differed from standard-gauge branch lines. Gauge difference prevented operation with older main-line stock. Consequently they used purpose-built stock—often miniature versions of contemporary main-line coaches.

Special trains

A large variety of trains and services do not fit the broad and simple classification of rail passenger service discussed so far. The mechanized railway has carried passengers throughout the world for a century and a half. Inevitably, over this period, a wide variety of specialized uses has emerged.

More than any other invention, before or since, railways revolutionized attitudes to travel. Before the coming of the railways, society (save for the wealthy) was predominantly static. A visit of even a few kilometres was planned with great care and not undertaken lightly. The railway made possible travel over distances formerly considered beyond the reach of the ordinary man. At first the expense of such a venture was an inhibiting factor but before long countries realized, sometimes reluctantly, the railway could not be confined to the wealthy. As early as 1844, the British parliament passed a law obliging all railways in Britain to carry third-class passengers at no more than a penny a mile on at least one train a day (the so-called 'Parliamentary Train'). From this seed grew the universally accepted principle that economically-priced railway passenger travel should apply to everyone.

Inevitably, the first regular services were directed to the daily needs and requirements of the local population. Stimulated by the growing acceptance of rail communication the railways (and the public) were soon to develop more specialized uses of the new mode. It is uncertain when specialized trains could first be identified, but the earliest recognizable class of specialization was the excursion train. We do not know whether the first excursions were designed to use equipment otherwise lying idle or whether the railways were seeking methods of encouraging people to sample rail travel for the first time.

Excursion and holiday trains

The earliest excursion journeys were those which could be completed within a day and were confined to areas where specific towns and cities lay within a few hours' travelling time one from the other. Fare levels were kept low because a full load for the whole distance was a virtual certainty—a basic principle utilized later by modern package air-tour operators. The excursion idea was not wholeheartedly approved. One particular contentious aspect was the Sunday excursion. A six-day working week was normal and annual holidays were hardly common. Sunday was the only day for an excursion for many folk despite the objections of the clergy and the more privileged.

Things were changing in a way which can only be understood with hindsight. In spite of constant objections and fulminations, the excursion train survived. Any excuse justified an excursion. Trains were run to the seaside for benefit of the children. Trains were operated in connection with race meetings, football matches or any other sporting occasion. As railways penetrated more rural regions, the attractions of the countryside received attention and scenic excursions were arranged—with specially-designed observation coaches to attract more customers. Nor were the rural dwellers forgotten. Excursions took them to the nearby cities and towns.

More than anything else, the railway excursion helped to promote the holiday habit. The realization that seaside towns and rural beauty spots lay within a few hours' travelling time stimulated an appetite in the growing industrial regions for an annual break from the work routine and the 'day at the seaside' gradually turned into the 'holiday week'. For reasons connected with economic operation of the railway system, it made sense to carry as many holidaymakers as possible on one day. If all the employers in one town could be persuaded to cease operations during the same week, the railway could gain some very profitable business and yet keep fares to an absurdly low level. The trains which took holidaymakers from town X during one week could be moved to town Y the following week if town Y could be persuaded to close its business premises at a different time from town X.

The resorts approved of this. Properly organized, this kind of holiday traffic could guarantee fully-booked hotels and guest houses during the holiday season, promising highly competitive accommodation charges. Small seaside villages were transformed almost overnight into thriving holiday centres, as the popularity of holiday travel grew. It needed only a stretch of beach, close to centres of high population density and a railway willing to build a connecting line and to provide a station with a multiplicity of tracks to cater for the procession of weekend holiday excursions. The entrepreneurs made sure that hotels, shops and the like were built apace with growing traffic; a whole new life-style became possible for the ordinary family. That this life-style persists and thrives under the greater flexibility of the motor coach or the package-tour airliner should not blur the fact that the railway made possible that life-style in the first place.

As society was at last liberated by the train from the more objectionable

The steam-hauled passenger train can still be encountered in many parts of the world. Here a British-built 4-8-2 (class 15A) of South African Railways struggles upgrade through parched landscape near Groenbult. The black smoke suggests the unsuitability for railway use of much of the local coal output, one of the factors which has led the South African government to favour dieselization, despite dependence on the import of oil.

For fast 'IC' (inter-city) services of the future the Federal German Railways built the E403 high-speed multiple-unit prototype. Designed for use on the new high-speed rail links, on which 300 kph (187 mph) speeds will be possible, it had an air-piercing nose configuration.

The French TGV prototype on a trial high-speed run.

In pre-Amtrak days, a Santa Fe RR passenger train en route to Los Angeles tops the summit of Raton Pass in New Mexico. Two General Motors F-series diesel units are in charge.

characteristics of 19th-century life, the railways were developing sophisticated methods of attracting other categories of specialist travel. The realization that travel itself was pleasurable prompted the idea of the rail tour. Pullman and Wagons-Lits had shown the enjoyment possible in a railway journey in the right conditions, but this type of travel was a means of making a necessary journey more agreeable. Gradually the notion of spending a whole holiday on a train became viable. The 'holiday cruise train' had arrived. Sometimes it was a mobile hotel and was equipped with sleeping and dining cars. At other times, its journeys were co-ordinated with night stops at suitable locations where the railway had thoughtfully located one of its own hotels.

One cannot separate the growth of railway hotels from the ever-increasing elaboration of railway travel. Though the hotels were not part of the train, the reality of their existence was very much part of the transport 'package' which the more ambitious railways felt obliged to provide. Whether located in cities, principally for the benefit of business travellers, or at holiday centres, railway hotels blossomed wherever there seemed likely custom—and though many have been maligned, many more were very impressive. Though it is invidious to single out particular instances if one of the later examples can serve for the whole, then a prime contender is the Gleneagles hotel in Scotland, opened by the London, Midland & Scottish Railway in 1924. This edifice (no other word will do) was a latecomer, arriving almost at the close of the great railway age. The Gleneagles hotel had (and has) almost everything. Brand new and set amid incomparable scenery, it was matched by incomparable service and a fine provision of trains. In addition, as it was situated in Scotland it was naturally given a stupendous golf course by way of bonus. One wonders if any of today's golf addicts on the pilgrimage to Gleneagles to watch their modern demi-gods compete realize that they are walking over a part of transport history.

Varied and sophisticated modes of modern transport together with the tendency to stagger annual holidays has removed a considerable portion of the railway's dominance in this field of travel. But the railway remains important in the leisure field and the railways have been valiant in attempts to fight the competition of road and air.

Of all the threats to rail passenger travel, the private automobile has proved the most serious. Once across the Rubicon of car ownership, the average traveller is not convinced of the economic advantages of rail travel. The financial disadvantages of car ownership, such as loss of interest on capital, depreciation, garaging and maintenance costs, taxes and insurance, are all overwhelmed by the sheer convenience of personal door-to-door transport. 'Freedom of the road' seemed a tempting concept to which railways at first offered no alternative; and nowhere has the private car had greater impact than in leisure travel.

Obviously, the more developed nations were first to experience the problem and at first were unsure of the best solution. Excursion and holiday trains were reduced in number and scope as traffic dwindled. Once-busy excursion platforms at holiday centres became less and less used until many were abandoned altogether (often becoming car- or motor-coach parks in the process). The whole raison d'être of the marginal 'holiday' railway was often destroyed and the lines closed completely. But the success of the private car carried the seeds of a major problem. The railways fought back, making their appeal to the pleasure and comfort of the rail excursion as an alternative rather than substitute for the car.

A more spectacular development of the rail service has been designed with

Top left: *A compartment in a Wagons-Lit sleeping car, arranged for day use.* Centre left: *The same compartment made up for night occupancy.* Top right: *The dome car was not quite an exclusively North American attraction. This picture shows the interior of such a car once used in the Trans-Europe Express* Rheingold *service.*
Centre right: *An example of Amtrak's more modern equipment: the* Saint Clair *at Detroit, awaiting departure for Chicago.*
Left: *The West Coast Route from London to Glasgow is now electrified, which eases the problems posed by long gradients like the Shap Incline, where this photograph was taken. In the early morning a night train from London is pulled by a grimy class 5 mixed-traffic locomotive helped by a second engine banking at the rear.*

the motorist in mind. The prime innovation has been the growing network of car-carrier trains over the past 20 years. From the start of the motor age, railways have been willing to carry motor vehicles as freight and have designed a whole variety of special wagons. Attachment of genuine passenger coaches to the car-transporter wagons enabled the motorist to drive his car—a container for his bulky luggage—on to the train, and transfer with his family to the comfort of the coach. The railway takes care of the tedious first few hundred kilometres of the holiday journey. The addition of sleeping cars provided an overnight option and there is now a well established network of this new form of inter-city travel in Britain and Europe.

Water is no particular obstacle. From an early stage, railways developed shipping services to connect with and extend their train services. These were originally passenger services. The passengers would leave the trains and embark in the conventional way. In time came the introduction of the rail ferry which carried trains across the water barriers. The only Wagons-Lits operation which penetrates into Great Britain (the Paris–London *Night Ferry*) crosses the English Channel by rail ferry. Ferry boats which carry railway coaches can also carry car-transporters, and this facility has been developed. For the motorist without need of the train, the railway-owned 'roll-on/roll-off' car ferries, and hovercraft, are doing splendidly.

Competition with the airlines has been less easy; much of the long-haul trade has been abandoned to air. Occasionally, the railway has been able to co-operate with the airlines to provide integrated services. These services usually take the form of a high-speed rail link to newly-built stations at out-of-town airports. In favourable conditions an integrated rail/air/rail service can prove extremely attractive. A good example is the *Silver Arrow* operation between Paris and London.

Holiday and excursion traffic has, over the years, been a noteworthy example of socially-significant railway-passenger specialization.

Mail trains

Pride of place goes to the mail train. This seems an unlikely candidate for passenger patronage but such an assumption ignores the facts. From the beginning postal authorities throughout the world realized that the railway offered the speediest and most efficient method of carrying mail over long distances. The small volume of passenger traffic in the early days meant that mail could be loaded easily into a small portion of the passenger train. Postal authorities, predominantly interested in swift and reliable transit, negotiated terms dependent on the railway's ability to keep schedules. In consequence, mail trains became the fastest on the system and passengers appreciated the fact. The nature of the services was largely indistinguishable from orthodox inter-city operations though travelling by 'The Mail' was always something special. Reliability and timekeeping was of a higher order since mail trains received absolute priority over other traffic. Penalty clauses were written into mail contracts obliging railways to make financial compensation in the event of delay to the post.

The early mail operations were so successful that many intermediate towns and cities wished to be included in the service. To do so would have increased the transit time and displeased the postal authority. The railway's solution was to develop the travelling post office. Mail was not only collected and delivered to the lineside without stopping the train but also sorted *en route*. The first example emerged in Great Britain as early as 1837. Though trackside pick-up and dropping of mail ceased in Britain a few years ago, the system is still used in operations elsewhere and the *en-route* sorting of mail is universal wherever mail trains operate.

As the volume of mail increased it became necessary to provide additional mail coaches. Only some were equipped for pick-up and dropping of mail and for postal sorting, since the volume of 'end-to-end' traffic was increasing. Over the years certain mail trains became almost exclusively utilized for mail with little of the train available to passengers. In accordance with what became a universal custom mail coaches travelled at the front, or 'head' of the train and, especially in North America, a whole train (save for one or two coaches at the rear) composed of so-called 'head-end' cars was a familiar sight. Mail trains without passenger facilities appeared in due course. These 'Solid Mails' were operated at speeds comparable to or even faster than orthodox passenger-carrying expresses.

'Special-interest' and special-purpose trains

The railway's unique and early ability to transport both people and goods with equal facility originally produced the 'special-interest' train. It is impossible to describe all the variations of 'special-interest' trains and it is sometimes difficult to decide whether or not the train is properly defined as a passenger service. If the broad definition that a *bona fide* passenger operation exists if people are legitimately and purposefully conveyed is an acceptable one then some very odd cases deserve a mention. The most unusual were those trains provided by the railways in pursuit of railway expansion. This sort of operation enjoys more scope where distances are greater. The special-purpose train probably achieved its greatest variety in North America, though such trains were used over a much wider area of operation.

During the expansion into undeveloped territory, it was impossible to relate railway expansion to existing settlements—there were none. The workmen needed temporary housing and this took the form of a mobile settlement which moved forward to keep pace with the railhead advance. Not content merely to provide a normal coach where men ate, slept and lived, the expanding railways took whole trainloads of portable buildings as well as an army of camp followers. At the end of the line, the whole infrastructure of a small town was offloaded from the flat cars. Within hours saloons, bars, shops, hotels and other less salubrious establishments sprang up. After a few weeks (or a few days), the whole township was dismantled, reloaded and moved to the next 'head' of the advancing line. Nicknamed 'Hell-on-Wheels' in the USA, they established a legend.

The special-purpose train was a step away from the concept of 'promotional' train, in all its variety. The mobile-exhibition train, aimed at commercial promotion, became an effective means of publicizing products over a wide territory. It carried a greater variety of goods, displayed in semi-permanent form, and were more effective than the lone salesman. Such trains are still with us, generally converted from old passenger coaches. Their passengers, limited to company staff and potential customers, are a specialized charter category.

Such an enterprise is only marginally included in the category 'passenger train'. Other special-interest activities are almost indistinguishable from orthodox operations. If a local charity group charters a train to take deprived children on holiday, the end-product is scarcely distinguishable from the conventional excursion. Train charter of this type has been widespread and is not insignificant. Nor is the interest in the actual railway by enthusiast groups who often charter trains to cover interesting sections of railway line, organize trips behind especially significant locomotives, arrange for the provision of particular carriages and so on. The most glamorous of all special-purpose trains is the provision made for Very Important Persons.

The essentials of VIP rail travel have always been luxury and privacy. Throughout railway history leaders have normally been provided with the most luxurious carriages available—insulated from the ordinary traveller. This provision ranges from exclusive use of one of the best coaches owned by the railway to the other extreme—provision and operation of a complete train of sumptuous coaches. The travelling entourage can then share some of the luxury.

Naturally the most impressive coaches have been reserved for heads of state. Since many railways developed under monarchical systems, the greatest variety is witnessed in the various royal trains down the ages. The longest continuous story is that of the British Royal Family, whose first saloons were provided in the 1840s and for whom two new coaches are being built at the time of writing. Interestingly these coaches, from a variety of railway companies, faithfully reflected contemporary railway fashions; fortunately, some have survived at the British National Railway Museum for posterity to examine. Some of these services in their own way were rather innovative. Queen Adelaide's saloon of 1842 was one of the first coaches to include sleeping facilities in the form of a bed compartment; Queen Victoria's saloon of 1869 was, when built, two six-wheelers connected by a bellows gangway—the first European example of such a feature. Other royal coaches, such as those built for King Edward VII's superb train of 1903, tended to utilize the finest traditions of craftsmanship rather than introduce revolutionary new features; Queen Elizabeth II's saloon, built in 1941 and now ending its service, embodies the fashions of the period of its construction, just as the air-conditioned 160 km/h (100 mph) successor reflects the ideas and fashions of the 1970s.

Outside Britain, royal saloons tended to lack continuity of evolution as many countries abandoned monarchy during the railway age. Nevertheless provision of coaches for heads of state continued to be important. Sometimes the ideas and requirements of the new order differed remarkably from those of royalty. The coaches often reflected the differences. Nowhere can this be seen more strikingly than at the Transport Museum in Nuremberg where the astonishing baroque splendour of the Bavarian royal saloons (from the 1860s) stands in complete contrast to the severe austerity of the simple four-wheeler built over ten years later for Bismarck.

It is not generally known that most of the ultra-special saloons were actually owned by the railway itself and that the VIP travellers paid to ride in them like anyone else. Clearly the possession of a luxury coach was regarded as a status symbol by the railway. Most systems with pretensions to respectability felt obliged to have one or two in stock. Such coaches brought prestige to the owning company and an opportunity to display their best coach-building technique.

In these instances it was not uncommon to provide what might be termed a general-purpose state saloon, equally appropriate to kings or presidents. In these cases, the precise title of the head of state mattered less and many of the vehicles survived in use after the original monarch had, perhaps, been replaced by a non-royal head of state. A venerable example of this type of carriage, dating from 1897 but much modernized later, is the state saloon of Coras Iompair Eireann (Irish Railways), originally built for royal patronage but afterwards utilized as a state coach; while the austerely grand presidential saloon of French Railways, now preserved at Mulhouse, represents a later version of a similar concept.

Acceptance from a very early date of railway travel by royalty and other influential people undoubtedly placed a seal of respectability on the railway which the companies were not slow to take up, and there developed a form of super-first-class accommodation for the benefit of what might be termed 'other' VIPs. The coaches provided, whether they were called private saloons, special saloons, family saloons or whatever, generally had in common a degree of luxury and privacy which payment for their use entitled the traveller to enjoy. They were usually completely self-contained, incorporating day and night accommodation, cooking and toilet facilities, and were either available for private hire or reserved for the semi-exclusive use of senior railway officials on their tours of inspection.

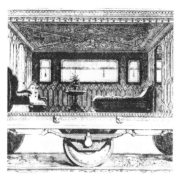

Part of the Great Eastern Railway saloon built for the Prince and Princess of Wales for their journeys to and from Sandringham Castle, Norfolk, in the 1860s.

Arising from these vehicles came the idea of the genuine privately-owned saloon which, for a fee, the railway would agree to convey attached to one of its own service trains for the benefit of the owner. This was not a particularly common feature of the European scene, where travelling distances were generally quite modest and the railways could usually themselves provide a suitable vehicle from their own stock. But there were one or two noteworthy exceptions such as the Duke of Sutherland's private saloons in Scotland. At least three coaches were built for this wealthy Scottish landowner, of which two still survive, one in Canada and the other in the British National Railway Museum.

It was, however, in North America where the private saloon achieved its most magnificent expression. The distances covered by the railways of this continent, coupled with the prosperity which built them, made it a perfectly practical proposition for wealthy businessmen, railway officials, or private families to embark on a trans-continental journey surrounded by every convenience which the ingenuity of the carriage builder could devise. Just as in Europe, once the train became respectable as a result of patronage by the wealthy and influential, the idea took strong root. In this, as in many other aspects of passenger travel in North America, the influence of Pullman was considerable. He was not alone in this field of private-saloon construction and other companies also built to order. However his company was, of course, only too happy to build the coaches if so requested.

Externally, the American private coach kept pace with and differed but little from the normal coaches of the day, but inside the builders frequently ran riot. No specific interior layout was evolved, the customer being left to specify his requirements within a basically standardized bodyshell; but over the years most tended to incorporate open-plan day, dining and observation saloons, lavishly equipped private suites of sitting and sleeping compartments and, of course, the inevitable open-platform observation verandah. One could live in such a coach for weeks if desired and so popular did they become that they were not only built for private ownership but some were built as speculative ventures for hire. It was even possible to hire a complete train of them. Their interior appointments undoubtedly set many precedents for the great public trains of the Pullman Standard era. Their influence spread abroad and some were exported.

The special saloon, be it for an Indian Maharajah, an American railway president, a well-to-do family or the King of England was, without doubt, a highly privileged form of rail travel enjoyed by but a minute fraction of the world's population. Yet, like so many other aspects of the passenger scene, it was an accurate reflection of society. Furthermore, although limited in numbers compared with common-user vehicles, their influence on the evolution of general service carriage design was out of all proportion to their numerical strength. Fortunately, because of their generally low annual mileage, many of them lasted well beyond the lifespan of their more mundane contemporaries and are available for us to examine in museums throughout the world.

Carriage design and evolution

So far in this survey, attention has been concentrated on the passenger services provided by the railways with the coaches themselves being given but brief mention. However, the railway is an example of applied technology and development of the coach is an important aspect of the story. The human cargo is the only form of revenue traffic which can voice its feelings and needs to management and it is not too surprising, therefore, that the evolution of railway carriages has been more strongly influenced by social attitudes than almost any other aspect of the railway scene. Bearing in mind the dangers implicit in generalization, development of coaches can be divided into two main categories: the vehicle itself (its riding quality and safety), and the interior appointments provided to meet the differing requirements of the customers. To meet the requirements of one category would often influence the other.

The first railway vehicles were, literally, open boxes on wheels for the conveyance of coal, minerals and the like. Simply made and totally unsprung, they sufficed for the cargo they carried. However, with the evolution of passenger travel, an unsprung and uncovered vehicle was no adequate substitute even for the road coach which, for all its slowness, was often quite elaborately sprung and appointed. Consequently, provision of cover and springing on carriages was an early point of departure from freight wagons. The early coaches were, of course, four-wheeled and although some attempts were made to provide wheel springs on the road-coach pattern, a much more acceptable method quickly achieved dominance. This took the form of a movable box, housing the bearings for the end of the axle, which was free to move vertically between two restraining guides fixed to the chassis. The axle-box itself was in turn attached (most commonly) to a simple leaf spring also fixed to the chassis, which absorbed vertical shocks.

However, vertical springing was not enough since the essence of railway operation was the use of a series of vehicles coupled together to form a train. The most common form of coupling was at first a chain link attached to a hook at the vehicle end but, since at first only the locomotive had brakes, whenever trains came to a halt the coaches inevitably came to rest by bumping into the vehicle ahead. It was thus necessary to provide some form of device to absorb end-shocks. At first these were simply projections padded with leather but in time they evolved into projecting, spring-loaded buffers, one at each of the four corners of the coach. This went some way to improve matters but the absence of carriage brakes, together with the loose chain connections, still caused jerking at the start of a journey and bumping and banging when the train halted.

Although some early carriages had brakes, most did not, but it was not long before the situation changed. Essentially, brakes took the form of blocks which rubbed against the wheel, thus slowing its rate of progress and they were operated by mechanical levers controlled by a guard or brakeman, who not infrequently rode on the carriage roof. It became quite an art to co-ordinate the braking on a series of loose-coupled vehicles and accidents were not un-known. Matters were improved somewhat, at least in Europe, by the evolution of the screw coupling in place of the loose chain. In this device, invented by Henry Booth in the 1830s, the centre link of the chain was replaced by an adjustable screw link which enabled the couplings between vehicles to be tight-ened so that there was little or no slack between adjacent vehicles, thus reducing the end-shocks. In these circumstances, some means of applying all the brakes in the train simultaneously became desirable and, after many and various experimental devices were tried and rejected, there evolved in time automatic brakes controlled by the engine driver.

It took some considerable time for all these processes to evolve in carriage coupling and braking, during which period other significant changes were taking place. The American coach quickly departed from its European counterpart in many respects, particularly size, and this too had its effect. The early European carriage builders were extremely conservative in their assess-ment of the potential size of a coach. Influenced strongly by the long tradition of road-coach practice and often constructed by the same coach-building concerns, early coaches were distinctly modest in size and it was many years before there was much change from the original four-wheel concept. The broad-gauge trains of the British Great Western Railway had, however, shown that larger and wider coaches were possible and it was not long before other railways began to copy. In most cases the limit of width and height (deter-mined by the size of fixed structures like bridges and tunnels) was fairly quickly reached and the only potentially expandable dimension was coach length. Mechanically, this necessitated more wheels to carry the extra weight and, because of this increased weight, not to mention the growing speed of trains, much-improved brakes and couplings were also essential. In conse-quence, there evolved in Europe the six-wheel coach, which is still common.

To enable rigid six-wheel vehicles to negotiate curves, some form of side-ways wheel movement is essential on all but the most gentle of curves if the vehicle is not to derail. Furthermore, vertical changes in track alignment must also be kept strictly limited so as not to exceed the limit of tolerance of the vertical springing of each axle. In Europe, because of the substantial mileage of well-engineered line, this was not unduly difficult to achieve, but in North America, as has been previously stated, the pioneering nature of many early railways made an alternative solution necessary and stimulated development of the independently pivoting bogie or truck.

The carriage bogie is an extremely ingenious yet basically simple device. It consists of four or, less commonly, six wheels, set quite close together and fixed to a rigid frame in which the wheels are sprung in the conventional manner. It is in the means of attachment of the vehicle itself to the bogie that the significance lies. Within the rigid frame of the bogie there is set a second structure or 'bolster' which is hung from the frame in such a way that it is free to move, vertically and laterally, quite independently of the main frame carry-ing the wheels. This, too, can be given its own springing for additional cushioning and restraint, and it is to this bolster that the carriage body is attached via a pivoting device. Thus the weight of the body actually hangs from the frame of the bogie on an independently movable frame. In turn this permits each bogie to adjust itself separately to track irregularities (both vertical and horizontal) and, because of the centre pivot, also allows the bogie to swivel at an angle to the coach body.

Development of this device in North America quickly freed the coach from most of the size constraints hitherto experienced. Furthermore, the double-springing effect occasioned by the use of an independently-sprung bolster gave a very much more comfortable ride. Not surprisingly, the bogie coach became adopted world-wide by most railways, especially for longer-distance services.

Allied with development of the large American bogie coach was a very different approach to the question of coupling between vehicles. The simple chain link and side buffer was quite incapable of controlling the more massive structure of the American coach and there developed a central rigid coupling (or bar) between the vehicles. At first these were held in place by a simple pin dropped through a hole at the end of the bar into a 'pocket' at the end of the adjacent vehicle into which the bar coupling fitted. This acted both as a coupler and a longitudinal restraint, and the side buffer vanished from the American scene. It did not altogether eliminate the 'snatch' effect when starting from rest, but it did materially improve matters. In time, this method of coupling evolved into an automatic hook which engaged a similar hook on the adjacent vehicle which, on modern coaches, not only makes a physical connection but has been further developed to incorporate brake, lighting and other electrical connections.

In Europe, the centre screw coupling and side buffer, which became progressively improved throughout the four- and six-wheel phase remained the norm long after introduction of bogie coaches, largely to ensure compatability between old and new vehicles, but the American-inspired 'buckeye' hook coupling was introduced on a progressively wider scale and is now widespread throughout Europe, and indeed the world, on modern coaches where it is often found combined with side buffers. It is often incorporated in such a fashion as to hinge out of the way to reveal the older pattern of screw coupler hook, in order that vehicles with the older coupling can still be incorporated in the train.

Much credit for the adoption outside America of this form of coupling, sometimes also referred to as the 'Pullman' type, can be attributed to Nigel Gresley, much more famous during the 1920s and 1930s as a British steam-locomotive designer. What is less well known is that prior to his involvement with locomotives, he was carriage and wagon superintendent of the British Great Northern Railway where, during the Edwardian period, he introduced a variety of modern innovations into carriage building. Apart from the adoption of American-inspired couplings, he was also responsible for perfecting a double-bolster bogie design, incorporating two sets of moving structures within the frame, and the idea of articulation whereby the adjacent ends of two vehicles were carried on one bogie mounted between them. This method saved valuable train weight and has been widely copied and adapted, notably on the British advanced passenger train and, at an early stage and in an applied form, on the Spanish *Talgo* trains. In these ultra-lightweight formations, each coach is carried essentially on a single axle only at one end, to which the non-axle end of the adjacent coach is attached by means of a flexible joint.

Allied to the questions of ride quality, coupling and braking is the general matter of safety. Much could be done by improved signalling methods, which are covered elsewhere, but correct designs of coach bodies could play a considerable part in minimizing damage if, unfortunately, an accident took place. In this, as in other areas, American experience was to prove important.

The Americans, thanks to the use of the bogie, quickly developed a characteristic form of body construction which incorporated heavy longitudinal timber sections as integral strengtheners forming part of the body structure. In effect, the typical American coach of the 19th century was a semi-rigid box girder heavily constructed in timber with all the ancillary equipment fixed, as it were, on the outside. When such coaches were imported into other parts of the world, notably Europe, their rigidity was seen to give considerably better shock-absorbing qualities when involved in accidents. The traditional European coach, more lightly constructed and fixed to a separate chassis, tended to break up completely when involved in a collision, whereas the body of an American-type coach, though not immune from danger, would often remain structurally intact after an accident even though all the wheels, brakes and other gear had become detached from the structure.

Unfortunately, marshalling heavy American-style coaches alongside their much more flimsy European contemporaries merely made the problem worse, since the American coaches could act rather like battering rams against the lighter vehicles. Consequently, although there was much agitation for safer coaches, European railways and those predominantly influenced by European thinking were rather slow to adopt heavier coaches. In time, however, it was discovered that whether on the American integral principle or the more traditional body-plus-chassis principle, a heavier and more massive coach was intrinsically safer than a small lightweight coach.

Another serious risk was fire, to which the timber coach, regardless of its type, was particularly vulnerable. Most of the fire risk, at least in Europe, was caused by interior coach lighting. Early carriages were lit by oil pot lamps and candles, both extremely dangerous unless adequately safeguarded, and even when towards the end of the 19th century they were generally superseded by compressed oil gas, the incendiary risk was still high. It was only the invention of a reliable form of electric carriage lighting that caused a real improvement to the safety factor. However, in North America, the greatest fire risk was the solid-fuel heating stove.

Safety improvements did not take place simultaneously on all railways, some of which were distinctly sluggish in altering their ways; and some quite horrendous accidents took place long after the development of safer types of coach. Much the same story was true of the change from all-timber to steel construction.

The use of steel in carriage building made a very marked contribution to both the rigidity of the vehicle and its fire-resistant properties. Basically, the evolution started with the increasing use of steel in the vehicle chassis, at first in combination with heavy timber sections, but later entirely on its own. This imparted considerable extra rigidity to the train and, in those areas where separate chassis were favoured, enabled the timber body to enjoy a new lease of life. In these instances, well exemplified by most of British practice, there was only a gradual change-over to steel bodies as well as chassis. A favourite compromise was to use steel panelling on teak framing, but all-wood bodies were still being constructed as late as 1940.

Where, as in America, the concept of the integral body had already become well established, transformation to the all-steel coach was more rapid, starting just after the turn of the century and reaching its famous high point during the Standard steel era, already discussed. The major disincentive to widespread adoption of steel vehicles was train weight. It was not just that steel coaches weighed more in themselves, 70 or 80 tonnes per vehicle being a quite common North American figure, but the demands of the passenger were simultaneously reducing the revenue load per coach as the number of ancillary fittings (lavatories, corridors, heating systems, air conditioning and so forth) took up ever increasing amounts of space. Extra weight implied larger units of motive power to pull the trains, which in turn involved yet more capital expenditure. There was, therefore, every commercial incentive on the part of the railways to keep train weight down, made even more desirable by growing competition from road and air.

This problem is still relevant to carriage construction today, but the continuing improvement in metallurgy and development of alternative high-strength lightweight materials has enabled most railways to make substantial improvements, sometimes of a spectacular nature. Even in countries like Britain, where heavyweight vehicles were rather rare, a modern 72-seat open second-class coach with full air conditioning weighs little more than some turn-of-the-century corridor firsts with maybe only 24 seats, and is immeasurably safer and stronger.

As a result of these gradually improving techniques, the modern railway coach is probably the strongest and safest vehicle generally available for regular travel. Taking all factors into account, the railway passenger has always been at considerably less risk than in most alternative contemporary forms of public transport and the present day is no exception.

However, as speeds increased, even these improvements had their limitations. No matter how good the suspension and couplings may be, the intrinsic nature of a railway coach will cause the periodic vibration to reach an unacceptable degree of discomfort as speed increases. To some extent this is mitigated by a heavier coach whose periodic vibration is slower, and which, therefore, can attain a higher speed before reaching the threshold of discomfort. Consequently, so long as the faster trains were also increasing in weight, the onset of the problem was delayed and had little influence on the

From 1925 the Paris–Orléans Railway used all-metal passenger cars for its electric commuter services out of Paris. The roofs were of aluminium alloy, with steel being used elsewhere, although the steel flooring was covered with a layer of cement compound, reputed to be very wear-resistant. In later versions aluminium or duralmin was used for other parts of the body. The trucks were of American inspiration, being similar to those of the Pennsylvania Railroad. The three compartments seated 100 passengers, and there was standing room for another 78. The Nord and Etat companies adopted the design for their own suburban services.

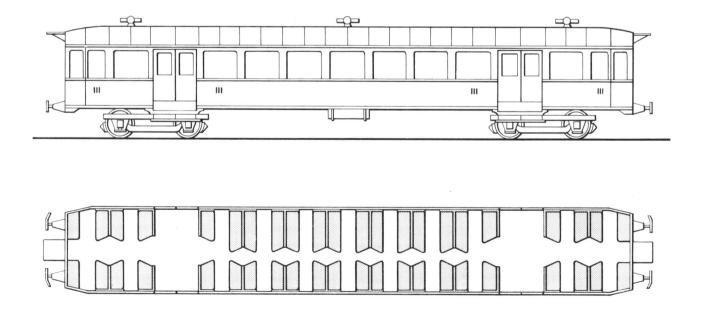

development of coaches up to the time of World War II. All the same, onset of the streamline era began to make railways look again at the problem. The Americans, in general, managed to run their fliers of the 1930s at high speed largely because of their heavy weight, but those observers who were honest about the British streamliners of the late 1930s will confirm that the 160 km/h (100 mph) or more speeds achieved by the LMS and LNER trains often caused an extreme degree of discomfort and unease to the passenger.

Fortunately, the discomfort threshold is reached well before the normal limits of safety of the flanged wheel on steel rail. However, there is a world of difference in comfort terms between running a train at an average speed of 96 km/h (60 mph) with occasional short stretches at 145 to 160 km/h (90 to 100 mph) and trying to achieve the consistent high-speed performance which railways see as essential today. Coupled with their wish to reduce coach weight, railways therefore realized that the whole question of vehicle suspension had to be re-examined.

To a considerable extent they were assisted by the great improvements made in track technology. Deeper ballasting of permanent way and long stretches of continuously welded rail both served to reduce markedly the track-to-wheel shocks experienced by the train itself. However, improvements also took place in the vehicles. The whole question of wheel springing was critically examined. New forms of primary and secondary suspension, embodying increasing use of coil springs, torsion bars and shock absorbers have all come into widespread use. Rather surprisingly, given these improvements, the old-fashioned bogie with its movable bolster has still proved to be the most effective means of connecting the coach body with the rail. Even the traditional wheel profile has been re-examined and it has been found that, by slight modification, the tendency of the wheel tread to oscillate slightly at high speed from side to side of the rail (until restrained by the flange) can be almost eliminated. On a modern wheelset, the flange hardly, if ever, comes into contact with the side of the rail except at points and crossings.

All these improvements have made it possible for modern trains to progress safely at steady speeds of up to 200 km/h (125 mph), even on curves; but at this point their success tends to pose a new generation of problems. As is well known, negotiating a curve in a vehicle brings into play a familiar set of cornering forces. In its simplest form this is best illustrated by the need for a cyclist to lean inwards as he negotiates a bend. At its most uncomfortable it can be experienced by trying to negotiate a bend in the road too quickly in a motor car, when one experiences a sensation of being forced to the outside of the bend. Actually what is felt is the vehicle side pushing the occupant towards the centre of the curve.

In the railway context this problem is generally solved in two ways. First, as with modern roads, the track itself can be raised (or super-elevated) at the outside of the curve, thus causing the vehicle to lean inwards and, by its own weight, generate a force acting towards the centre of the curve which helps the vehicle negotiate the corner. The second is a by-product of the use of the bogie itself. Being free to move, via the bolster, within the bogie frame, the carriage body tends to move towards the outside of the curve it is negotiating. Because of the arrangement of swinging links by which the carriage hangs from the bogie, this has the effect of causing the outside link to adopt a near-vertical position while the link on the inside of the curve adopts a position at an angle to the vertical. Since both links are the same length and fixed to the coach, the automatic effect is to lower the height of the coach on the inside of the curve, thus causing it to tilt inwards, which is precisely what the passenger wants.

The combined effect of these two factors can make it possible for a conventional coach to negotiate even quite severe curves with little reduction in speed. However, as speed increases, even though it would be perfectly safe to traverse sharp corners, the comfort threshold would be reached. To effect an improvement one must either increase the amount of super-elevation or alter the vehicle characteristics. To adopt the former approach might well produce a degree of super-elevation which is too great for comfort on slower-moving trains so most modern research has concentrated on the vehicle itself, culminating in the so-called 'pendulum' suspension which has now reached an advanced state of development.

In this system, electronic sensors detect when a coach is rounding a curve and actuate mechanisms that tilt the body into the curve even more than would naturally take place. This, in turn, enables higher speed to be attempted without the need to rebuild whole stretches of line (or even build new railways) and thus has considerable appeal.

Increased speed and comfort of ride will in turn cause fresh developments in the brake, coupling and structural fields. The process is, as it has always been, essentially cyclic and is likely to remain so as long as there are railways responsive to the wishes of their passengers.

Change in interior amenities has continued. Upholstery fabrics, compartment and saloon finishing materials, and detail trimmings have faithfully reflected changing fashions, from the heavy and dark button-down fabrics of the Victorian period with extensive use of wood-veneer decoration, to the modern coach which makes increasing use of man-made materials in lighter and brighter colours. Lamps have changed from elaborately embellished pseudo-chandeliers glittering with polished brass to the modern flush-mounted electric arrangements, and heating has progressed from the non-existent via the footwarmer to the modern electrically heated coach with individually adjustable controls for the passenger to operate.

Allied to heating has been the change in carriage ventilation methods over the years. In early days, ventilation was achieved solely by opening a window, which often allowed more than fresh air to enter the coach. Even in the great days of American Pullman operations, one of the more common problems of travel was the unpleasant choice between open windows which let in the dust from the prairies or the soot from the engine, or closed windows which rendered the interior hot and unbearable. The problem was not confined to America, and most railways developed a variety of systems to cope with the difficulty. In general this took two forms. One was the roof-top ventilator which, while admitting air, could be so shaped as to deflect the air into the carriage while trapping most of the unwanted matter. The second method was to provide ventilators over the tops of doors and windows which could perform similar functions. Both were under passenger control. Combined with opening windows they could at least provide some variation in fresh-air supply.

The real saviour was air-conditioning. Introduced in North America to cope with the climatic extremes encountered over the vast distances involved, the air-conditioned coach is now a feature of better trains throughout the world. Above all it makes them cleaner inside.

It is not difficult to see why, in spite of detail improvements, the basic design of a coach has remained so consistent. Its fundamental object is to carry people and, setting all other considerations aside, the greater the number of people that can be carried per vehicle, the fewer vehicles the railway has to provide. This has obvious advantages in strictly economic terms and undoubtedly explains why coach sizes have continually increased. Railways quickly discovered that to carry 100 people in one large coach cost them less, both in capital expenditure and running costs, than to convey the same number in two smaller coaches.

However, life is not as simple as all that. The passenger who will tolerate high-density seating for a short trip to the office will not accept similar accommodation for a longer journey. He will probably want more space within the vehicle and almost certainly wish to cater for his bodily needs on any trip lasting more than an hour or two. Hence, as has already been mentioned, the necessity for the railway to provide additional amenities on the longer-distance trains made itself felt at an early stage.

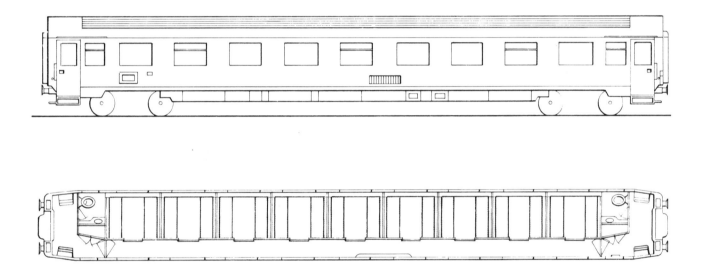

Auxiliary facilities

The trouble with providing auxiliary facilities is that, even at the level of the humble lavatory, they do not add to the revenue-earning capacity of the train. In fact, they actually reduce it in most cases. Consequently, provision of additional features inevitably raises the question of costs; it is not too surprising, therefore, that they have been most often provided in those countries where *per capita* income is high enough to meet this extra cost without the passenger feeling obliged to desert the railway. For the railway, this has always led to a very delicate balancing operation between improved amenities on the one hand and reduced accommodation on the other. Nowhere has this problem made itself more manifest than in sleeping and dining cars.

The necessity to provide sleeping and dining facilities on long-distance trains has taxed the ingenuity of carriage builders since the time they first appeared. The sleeping car, in particular, causes a fundamental problem, for it has to come to terms with the inescapable anatomical fact that when we lie down to sleep we occupy more floor space than when we sit on a seat. The ratio is approximately 3:1 and there is no way in which a train can suddenly treble its size without provision of a large number of additional vehicles. Furthermore, the problem is compounded by the distance over which the train is travelling. If the journey is of several days' duration, the train must provide both day and night accommodation, whereas if the trip can be completed in, say, 12 hours or so, then the vehicles can be provided to meet but one of the two prime considerations. This has led over the years to the development of two basic types of coach: the sleeping car which is convertible for day use and the pure sleeping car which generally only operates at night.

The convertible sleeping car, inevitably, made its first appearance in North America with the development of long-distance and transcontinental routes. Not surprisingly, Pullman and his contemporaries were the prime movers. In this they were aided by the ever increasing size which the American style of open saloon was assuming. During the mid-Victorian period, the normal seating arrangement was in pairs on either side of a central gangway. Often these all faced the direction of travel, with seat backs which were reversible at the end of the journey, but Woodruff devised the idea of adopting an arrangement of facing pairs of seats in which half the passengers rode with their backs to the direction of travel. He built coaches in which facing pairs of seats could be drawn together at night to form a bed—which would accommodate two of the four passengers. Utilizing the great height of American coaches, he then arranged for a second bed to be let down from the roof above the top of the window for the second pair of passengers, thus accommodating four sleeping passengers in no more floor space than four sitting passengers.

It had one particular advantage which none of the alternatives has totally managed to achieve. It was universally applicable to all degrees of luxury. At its most basic it could be applied to fairly rudimentary wooden or hard leather twin or triple seats, arranged in opposing pairs, while at its most opulent it could apply to facing pairs of luxurious single seats which would produce space for two large single beds for the wealthy traveller. At night, the sections could be screened off by longitudinal curtains suspended from the sides of the elevated centre section of the roof (the clerestory).

When the American concept of sleeping cars was first brought to Europe, it was not altogether well received. The greater comfort of the massive American-style bogie coaches was much appreciated, but the open saloon arrangement and the lack of privacy were not always in accord with Victorian ideas of rectitude in the old world. There, the travellers much preferred their individual compartments. Furthermore, there was less need, particularly in Britain, for a dual-purpose sleeping-cum-day coach. In consequence, although some Pullman-type sleeping cars were operated, particularly by the Midland Railway in Britain, the general European trend was to try to adapt the familiar compartment to the sleeping mode. In Britain this led to the almost universal development of the pure sleeping car where no real provision was made for daytime riding.

Most commonly, therefore, the British sleeping car took the form of a conventional side-corridor compartment coach in which beds, arranged transversely, were located in the place normally occupied by the seats. This, with the corridor door closed, provided a private twin bedroom, much more to the liking of the British—moreover it could be fitted with a washbasin between the beds and did give space to disrobe. For the single traveller, a half compartment with but one bed was provided and in time became the standard form, still in use today. A double room could be contrived by unlocking a connecting door between two adjacent single berths.

In this type of sleeping car, the passenger had all the privacy he needed but the number which could be accommodated was, and still is, strictly limited, rarely exceeding 12 per vehicle. Not surprisingly, therefore, the cost of providing such a facility could only be met by the first-class passenger and it was not until 1928 that the lower orders were given sleeping accommodation in British trains in the form of compartments with upper and lower berths.

This problem was not, perhaps, very significant in Britain. Distances were short, overnight travel was not common and never involved more than one night on the train. Throughout the rest of Europe, however, things were different. The distances were not of American proportions but, since trains could take between 24 and 48 hours to make a journey, some form of convertible coach was essential; the Europeans, however, did not like the open-coach solution. Neither did Georges Nagelmackers. When he returned from North America, impressed by Pullman's ideas but not quite so enamoured of the standard Pullman sleeping section, he endeavoured with his Wagons-Lits vehicles to produce a compromise.

Many ideas, including Pullman-style coaches, were tried but the most typical solution was to provide coaches with a series of half-compartments, connected by a side corridor. Within these compartments a conventional day seat was provided along one side, but at night a second bed could be hinged out from the partition above the seat to form a twin-bunk arrangement. Sometimes, if the height of the vehicle allowed it, a third berth could be thus provided and on other occasions the high-level berth folded out from above the window at right angles to the day seat. To make room for more compartments, it was common practice for the partitions between compartments which did not carry the seats/bunks to be set at an angle, thus giving a variable-width compartment whose average dimension was rather less than a purely rectangular arrangement. Washing facilities were provided in each compartment and, of course, space was available for undressing purposes. The Wagons-Lits, therefore, combined the privacy of the British sleeper with a greater passenger capacity and an ability to use the compartment during the daytime.

Elsewhere in the world, high supplementary charges were a distinct disincentive to rail travel. They could only be sustained by the wealthy and yet in many developing areas widespread use of trains over long distances was absolutely essential if the general level of prosperity was to increase. The basic Pullman section did give relatively low-cost sleeping accommodation but it was only widely used where American influence was strong. In such vast countries as Russia, China and India, early development of railways was considerably influenced by European ideas and the fixation with the compartment took some time to change. Imperial Russia and China were strongly class-conscious societies; separation of the various classes of traveller was normal and the compartment concept proved ideally suitable. Nowhere was this more apparent than in pre-independence India where there were at least four classes of travel in places, and problems were not made any easier to solve by the various religious differences.

There thus grew up a sort of basic overnight accommodation which took the form of triple tiers of bunks arranged within the confines of a normal compartment. Their furnishings were very simple and the bunks themselves were often no more than frames made from wood slats. They were no more austere in themselves than the basic Pullman section provided in the North American 'colonial' trains.

Sleeping accommodation provided in modern trains shows the influence of all these historical developments, overlaid with ideas borrowed from current

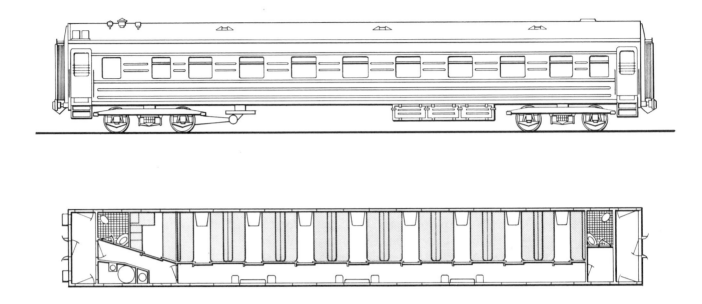

hotel and airline practice, not to mention considerable cross-fertilization which has taken place between the various countries of the world. The European liking for privacy was taken back to North America where the traditional Pullman section was installed in private compartments to form small state-rooms, bedrooms or roomettes, depending on precise size and accommodation offered. The reclining seat idea, dating back to the 1840s, has been updated in open coaches to offer an alternative form of night travel. The high-density double- or triple-deck compartment berth arrangement has been introduced widely in Europe in the form of the *couchette* for low-cost sleeping accommodation, while the permutations within the super-luxury category seem to be determined only by the willingness of the traveller to pay for them or the inventiveness of the designer in thinking up new ideas.

The design and evolution of the sleeping car were basically governed by the need to balance the spatial requirements of a sleeping person and the need to keep within economic limits on the part of the railway and within the passengers' ability to pay; but at least it did provide revenue traffic. The dining car on the other hand is literally dead weight added to the train. In this case, the railway is in something of a dilemma and it has always been a moot point whether or not the dining car is a genuine revenue earner. On the one hand, the presence of catering facilities may well cause passengers to be attracted to the train; alternatively the absence of a dining car could cause the passenger to desert the railway. On balance, railways have tended to regard provision of meals as an essential part of their operations, if only as a 'loss-leader', ever since the unsatisfactory days of refreshment stops.

The classic dining car is a coach comprising a kitchen and pantry at one end with an open saloon equipped with tables at the other. It was, of course, derived from the pioneer open-saloon coaches of North America. In order to tempt people to use it, the railways were obliged to enable passengers to gain access and then make the provision of meals a pleasurable experience. As a result, the vestibule connection between coaches was developed to meet the one consideration, and the appointments inside the coach were often made as elaborate as possible to meet the other.

After World War II thousands of new all-steel passenger cars were built for Soviet Railways, replacing the wooden-bodied pre-war stock. Of a standard basic pattern, there were several different internal configurations, to suit the different standards of accommodation demanded by the fine passenger-class distinctions prevalent in the USSR. This is the 'hard' compartmented category of vehicle, with 4-berth compartments. Among its facilities is the traditional hot-water boiler for making tea, located at the end of the corridor opposite the attendants' compartment. The car was built in the German Democratic Republic.

There was, and still is, a real sense of occasion in partaking of a meal in a well-equipped dining car. It probably appeals to some basic human need over and above the mere necessity of taking in regular supplies of food and, once the idea was introduced, railways were not slow to appreciate the possibilities. Here was a genuine shop-window for their service which eventually came to be enjoyed by all, not just the wealthy. In fact it was not unknown for passengers to opt deliberately for a lower standard of accommodation in order that they could save enough on the fare to fully participate in the delights of the dining car *en route*. Properly planned, one could spend much of one's journey in these sumptuous vehicles and several railways positively encouraged the practice, particularly in Great Britain. Elsewhere in the world, the dining car was usually rather more of a travelling restaurant and the temptation to linger after the meal could well depend on the comfort of the vehicle itself.

As with most railway vehicles, the original dining-car interior layout has stood the test of time and proved itself surprisingly adaptable to changing eating habits whether they be historic changes within one nation or contemporary regional differences between different nations. In fact on the international Wagons-Lits operations it is a feature of the service that, on crossing frontiers, the food and drink provided in the dining car can be changed to suit the country being traversed.

Not infrequently, the dining car evolved into what might be called the social focus of the train. Areas were provided for pre-meal drinks and, sometimes, a whole coach devoted to recreational activities (equipped with bar, piano and the necessary staff) would be connected to the dining car proper.

From the public dining car evolved in time such related features as the dining sections of private saloons or the exclusive club car. The latter were provided for, say, a group of regular users of the train who could guarantee to purchase enough meals and drinks to justify provision of semi-exclusive facilities. It was, in some areas, developed into a high-class commuter service —providing a very pleasant way to start and finish work. Even some normal service dining cars developed a sort of club atmosphere.

In more recent years, the dining car has undergone something of a transformation. The one-time universal 'full-meal' service has been augmented and in many cases replaced by a whole range of alternative facilities masquerading under a variety of pseudonyms, but generally embodying the buffet principle of self-service, tray meals or, at best, counter service. Some of these are very good, offering substantial fare at competitive prices while others are, frankly, squalid. Among the better offerings can be mentioned the recent re-introduction (1970 onwards) of rail catering on a modest scale but of a very high standard in New Zealand; British Rail's griddle cars operating in Scotland, which contain a pleasant saloon bar and a small dining saloon flanking a centre kitchen which can produce very tempting food; the modern cars operated by Amtrak which are generally commendably clean, and a particularly civilized Wagons-Lits operation in France where a bar counter offering substantial food in addition to some excellent claret is placed in the same car as a supremely comfortable dining saloon. Vehicle design, too, has changed to take account of these altered eating habits.

Some of these changes have been occasioned by the need to reduce staffing levels in dining cars and others to take account, particularly in Europe, of the much reduced journey times which often no longer embrace a conventional meal time. Sadly, this has gone hand-in-glove with a tendency towards 'instant packaging' of almost anything from French mustard to toothpicks.

However, it is still possible to have excellent ham and eggs cooked to order in the old solid-fuel heated wood-panelled blue Wagons-Lits cars after an overnight ferry passage to the Hook of Holland or, by contrast, dine in great splendour after a pre-meal aperitif in the beautiful modern refreshment cars of the *Rheingold*. Traditional afternoon tea with toasted teacake, real cups and proper teapots can still be obtained on British railways while the cooked breakfasts are justly famous. In India traditional catering for the various religious persuasions continues at its customary excellence.

Outside the sleeping- and dining-car field, the change in emphasis from the original concepts of vehicle interior design, other than the obvious changes of upholstery material and interior trimmings, were more subtle. The traditional compartments changed hardly at all. They became more spacious between partitions on long-distance trains and, if possible, even more cramped for suburban and commuter service. For this purpose coaches were made as wide as possible with intermediate partitions close together to maximize seating. To help distribute passengers within the coach, interior passageways were sometimes provided along one or both sides, but they were not really proper corridors, while, to save expense, the intermediate partitions in some designs were not taken to full height. In this form, there was precious little difference between them and a conventional open coach, save for the full array of outside doors. Wooden or hardwearing leather seats were provided to reduce maintenance and many minor variations could be seen in different parts of the world.

The open saloon developed into such widely disparate vehicles as the special coaches already described, not forgetting observation and dome cars with glass areas at the ends or in the roof and, at the other extreme, high-density suburban coaches, both double and single deck. In more recent years these have often appeared with intermediate side doors, increasingly of the sliding variety, to speed up loading and unloading, while in some areas there has been a tendency to reduce the number of seats and increase the standing accommodation where it is impossible to provide a seat for every passenger at peak periods.

The external appearance

One final aspect of carriage design remains to be considered and that is perhaps the most obvious of all—its external appearance.

The external style of coaches has, for the most part, been a reasonably honest expression of functional form, but within the parameters imposed by the fundamental shape and size of the vehicles there has always been ample opportunity to display regional, national and even purely idiosyncratic differences. Coaches need doors and windows but the precise nature of either feature permits infinite variety in detail. A roof must be provided but the choice available is considerable. The vehicle needs side walls but the materials used and the favoured construction method can have considerable influence on the final style of vehicle. For this reason, perhaps, although carriage interiors may have displayed reasonably similar features on a global basis, exteriors tended to have more strongly marked regional or national characteristics.

In Europe, old-fashioned coach-building traditions were strong and the wooden-body coach evolved fairly harmoniously from earlier road-vehicle practice. Bodies were made of timber frames covered with wooden sheets, whose joins were capped with raised strips (or beading) to prevent moisture from entering. These raised strips gave considerable scope for decorative treatment, especially at the painting stage where they were often embellished with gilding and coloured lining to contrast with the main colour of the vehicle. Colour choices themselves were highly variable, often being copied from the old stage-coaches; but fairly early in the development of railways it was realized that a standard colour scheme for all the coaches of one railway could have considerable publicity value. This led to some very attractive company liveries being developed, particularly in Britain and Ireland, many of which lasted right through until the 1940s, albeit with some reduction in variety after the various amalgamations of 1923 and later.

The British liking for colourful coaches did not apply to quite the same extent to the rest of Europe, where sombre and austere-looking coaches were the order of the day, usually finished in plain varnished wood or very subdued colours with a minimum of lining or decoration. There were eventually a few noteworthy exceptions such as the famous Wagons-Lits blue with gold trimmings (still to be seen today) and the rather brighter colours adopted for some special services, for example the purple and cream of the *Rheingold*.

Reverting to vehicle design, the traditional European style of coach building was only slowly modified, except for size. Eventually, however, steel outer panelling replaced the traditional wood finishes, and coaches gradually evolved into their modern form with an all-metal structure and smooth-sided exteriors.

The American-style coach was very different in appearance from its European counterpart. The favourite method of covering wooden trussed framework adopted in North America was with a series of close-boarded vertical planks between and below the windows with a wider horizontal board running above. Furthermore, American railways rarely adopted the common European technique of curving the sides in below the waist-line; their coaches were almost universally flat-sided. Another point of difference was that, being of integral construction, American coaches had no separate chassis as such and this characteristically visible feature of European-style coaches was absent from American vehicles.

Although there were eventually exceptions, especially from the 1920s onwards, such as the Milwaukee Road, which painted its coaches in orange and red, the characteristic colour schemes adopted by most American railroads during the bulk of both the wooden and Pullman Standard steel eras were rather sombre, partly because of the widespread standardization on Pullman-owned or Pullman-built equipment. Pullman green (a sort of olive green with brown overtones) was commonly adopted by railways to produce a matching ensemble and even where this was not chosen, dark reds and greens were normal. However, the earlier wooden coaches were almost always lavishly decorated with a considerable degree of gilt ornamentation; they were frequently elaborately lettered and named, they displayed considerable variety and artistry in window, door and verandah ornamentation, and they were, almost without exception, highly varnished. They looked, and indeed were, both dignified and opulent.

Perhaps the most characteristic feature of the American coach during its heyday was the roof shape. Most European coach builders of the mid-19th century adopted a fairly flat roof form, probably inspired more by stage-coach practice than by any critical need to keep the height down to clear fixed structures on the railway. In America, however, the even larger structure gauge and the need for improved ventilation saw early widespread adoption of a high roof form with a conspicuously elevated centre section or clerestory. Fitted with ornately decorated side windows and, usually, terminated at the end of the coach by smoothly flowing downward curves, the American clerestory, sometimes also called a 'monitor' roof, was instantly recognizable. It was used throughout the wooden-body era and was retained during the all-steel Pullman Standard period. Even during the move to air-conditioning, the structure remained a feature although often disguised from outside view. The lower side sections of the roof afforded a suitable location for air-conditioning equipment and many all-steel clerestory cars were thus modified with new sheeting over the whole roof structure giving the superficial appearance of a full-width high roof.

The other railways of the world were not slow to appreciate the virtues of the clerestory roof. It added light and air to the interior and could be made an outstanding decorative feature in its own right. Although some railways did have structure clearance problems, many did not and they introduced the clerestory without serious difficulty. In Europe it even began to take on a character of its own. In Britain it was married to the traditional style of coach and was more commonly extended to the full length of the body, without the down-curved ends. Railways like the Great Western and the Midland found it so much to their liking that the feature became almost a company trademark, particularly on the Midland where the clerestory was so designed as to seem an integral part of the whole carriage, rather than an appendage on top. Other British systems favoured limited use of the clerestory for more important trains and for dining and sleeping cars.

However, it was on the mainland of Europe that the marriage of European and American coach-building styles probably achieved its finest expression and, as might be expected, Wagons-Lits played a major part. In the early part of the 20th century, there were built for this company some very elegant coaches which combined the American style of body with vertical boarding and varnish with a European-type chassis and a distinctive roof arrangement in which the clerestory was terminated slightly before the extreme end of the coach. Large windows were combined with recessed and angled end doors to produce a style which eventually became the hallmark of the great deluxe trains of Europe. Many countries adopted them and they were built throughout Europe.

Inevitably over the years, further cross-fertilization of carriage-building ideas took place world-wide. Australia, with its American-scale distances, tended to adopt American ideas for long-distance services, although remaining faithful to British concepts for its local trains. South Africa, too, followed quasi-American practice but in other areas of British influence quite different styles evolved. This was particularly the case in tropical regions where carriage design had to cater for quite different climatic conditions. In East Africa and India, elaborate screens, often extending from the roof nearly halfway down the body side, were fitted to the sides of basically European-style coaches to shield passengers from the sun. Coaches were often given a double roof for the same purpose and pale colour schemes were commonly adopted for similar reasons.

The use of brighter colours on railway carriages is, apart from some early examples already mentioned, something of a latter-day phenomenon. In part, widespread adoption of dark colours in the early days was to offset the dirt created by the steam locomotive but this is not the whole story. With the gradual erosion of the railway monopoly as a result of road and air competition, the railways had to rethink their publicity and it is not entirely without significance that the introduction of bright, eye-catching colour schemes together with stainless steel, dates in general from the streamline era. Led by the American examples but imitated world-wide with greater or lesser degrees of success, the train gradually took upon itself a less and less sombre hue until, today, almost any colour scheme can be witnessed.

Today, too, there are less obvious external differences between the trains of the world. Railways are not unique in this respect. With improved communications, all countries of the world are increasingly aware of developments elsewhere in all fields of human activity. The modern motor car, be it Italian, Japanese, German, British or American, is tending to become less regionally differentiated as the years go by. Interior design, furnishing ideas, town-planning methods and so on are tending to become increasingly similar and it would be surprising indeed if railways did not reflect this trend. Thus it is that as the world enters the closing decades of the 20th century, the train, as it has always done since it first came onto the scene, still represents a faithful barometer of the society it serves. Fortunately, however, it takes some time for ideas to spread globally, by which time there are new innovations to be seen, so there is still plenty of variety.

Conclusion

What of the future of the train? Honesty compels one to admit that, however pro-rail one might be, the passenger train can never again achieve the total dominance of inland transport which it once possessed. The railway itself was a product of change and, in its turn, it brought fresh changes. The railway all but exterminated its passenger-carrying competitors during the 19th century, so we should not be too surprised if, in its turn, the train itself is threatened by more modern modes of travel.

However, the train has shown far more resilience in meeting competition than did its 19th-century forebears and this fact alone can permit a cautious degree of optimism. The infinite variety of uses to which the passenger train has been put during its long lifetime cannot be matched by any other transport alternative. Whether it be moving thousands of people to work in a crowded metropolitan area, conveying businessmen at high speed in great comfort, acting as an essential lifeline both in remote districts and developing countries, or providing a more relaxed alternative to the motor car, the train still has its place. The use of a fixed track has disadvantages in terms of total flexibility but it is now widely accepted that the railway causes less environmental disturbance and uses proportionally less energy than most of its competitors—possibly important points in its favour in the future.

On balance it seems likely that, as has already happened in the industrial world, so too eventually in the developing world, the passenger railway will tend to concentrate on those tasks which it can best fulfil. When there is no alternative, the train has to serve all purposes, some of which it is manifestly less able to perform than its competitors. However, the experience of the North Americans tends to suggest that the process of rationalization can go too far. One must hope therefore that those countries which still have passenger railways will assess the problem rather more carefully than has been the case with some of the older-established systems. The indications are that they probably will.

Great Trains

by John Westwood The stories of ten trains that have become famous throughout the world.

The *Irish Mail*

The *Irish Mail*, like most of the named mail trains, acquired its name not as a publicity gesture but as a factual description. The carriage of mails was one of the most important tasks of the first railways, and still is, even though road and air transport have taken over some of the business. In some countries, governments considered the fast carriage of mail to be the most important service offered by the railways and, in granting concessions for lines, often insisted that the railway should carry the mail free or at reduced rates. Despite the low rate of return railways made great efforts to co-operate with the post offices. In some countries, Britain especially, not only did mail trains include sorting cars where post-office workers got to grips with late, unsorted mail but apparatus was put into service with which trains at full speed could pick up and set down mailbags. In America, the mail contracts were often sufficiently lucrative to enable passenger trains to run which would otherwise have been impossibly uneconomic; the progressive loss of these mail contracts was one major reason for the American passenger-train crisis of the 1960s.

The first *Irish Mail* left Euston Station of the London & North Western Railway on 1 August 1848. It may well have been the first train in the world to have an official title, although it was not until 1927 that the name was carried on the train itself. Departure time was 20.45 and this has hardly varied since. At Chester the Chester & Holyhead Railway took over the train, hauling it over its north Wales coast line as far as the Menai Straits where the bags were transferred to a road coach for the water crossing; Robert Stephenson's tubular railway bridge was completed only two years later. On the other side of the Straits, the mail was taken by an isolated railway for the final few miles to Holyhead Quay and the steamship for Dublin.

Dublin then being a vital British city, the government insisted on the best possible service in its successive mail contracts. It was for the *Irish Mail* that pick-up and set-down apparatus for mailbags was developed. With this, the train could deal with Irish mail to and from intermediate points without losing time starting and stopping. In 1860 the Post Office demanded an average speed of 68 km/h (42 mph) between London and the Quay. The LNWR, which had taken over the Chester & Holyhead Railway, responded by the first-ever water troughs, enabling the locomotive to take water without stopping near Conway in north Wales. By this time, too, there was only one change of engine, at Stafford.

But the hard winter of 1860–61 was almost catastrophic for the service. Not only did the water troughs freeze up but also vital metal parts of the rolling stock fractured, being unable to withstand normal stresses at abnormally low temperatures. Even without the big freeze, the LNWR would have been unhappy, for the effort to achieve high average speed was very costly, especially in terms of locomotive working expenses.

But in 1863 it all seemed worth while when the LNWR and its Irish service won great acclaim in the Trent Affair. This diplomatic crisis between London and Washington was settled after the arrival of a long-awaited despatch from the US government, which was sent as usual by steamer to Queenstown, rail to Dublin, steamer to Holyhead and thence by the Irish Mail route to London. For a week the LNWR kept an engine in steam at Holyhead awaiting the arrival of the special ship which would bring the despatch. When this eventually berthed, the LNWR whisked the despatch to London in under five hours,

Previous pages, above left: *The* Sunset Limited *in its modern guise, operated by the Amtrak Corporation over the tracks of the Southern Pacific Railroad. It is seen here setting down passengers at El Paso, Texas.*
Below left: *The* Orange Express, *bound for Cape Town. The photograph was taken in the early morning, as the train left Virginia.*
Right: *For three decades the* Cornish Riviera Limited *was entrusted to the King class 4-6-0 locomotives of the Great Western Railway. One of these powerful four-cylinder machines is shown leaving Paddington Station, London, with the train in 1953. The large white number of the smokebox door was part of a system used by the Great Western Railway to enable signalmen en route instantly to identify an approaching train.*

The route of the Irish Mail.

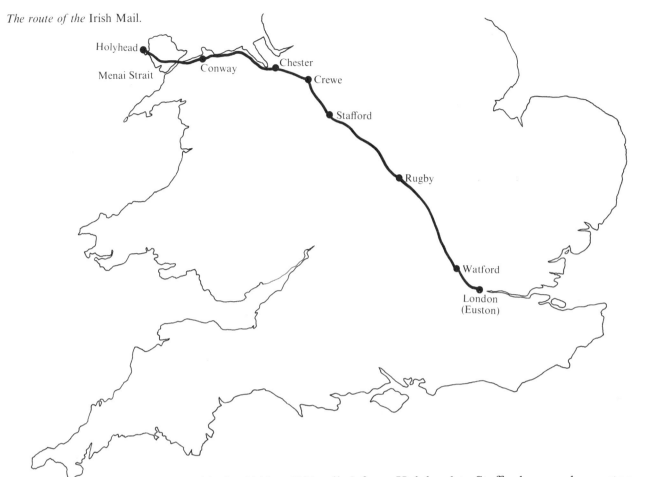

with the 211 km (131 miles) from Holyhead to Stafford covered non-stop.

In 1880 the Prince of Wales opened the new LNWR dock at Holyhead, carefully planned to secure full co-ordination between the railway, the ships and the LNWR hotel. Trains stopped alongside the steamers so that the bleary-eyed passengers had only a short distance to walk. Nevertheless, passengers were hardly well served by schedules which meant that they had to transfer from train to ship at around 02.00; the *Irish Mail* ran to suit the Post Office, and passengers took second place. The postal-distribution service of Ireland was largely keyed to the arrival of the mail steamer from Holyhead. Main-line trains from Dublin were scheduled so as to carry the mail and passengers from this steamer—and it was possible for a letter sent from Britain to be delivered the next day in Ireland, and a prompt reply could reach the correspondent the day after that, again by the *Irish Mail*.

In the early 1920s, in the early days of the Irish Free State, traffic dropped so that not more than nine cars were needed. By the 1930s, 'Royal Scot' type locomotives of the LMS Railway were in charge of the trains, which were becoming heavier. The locomotives worked through without change. Nowadays, though, it is a blue electric locomotive which leads the train as it leaves the new Euston station, although a diesel locomotive takes over at Crewe for the non-electrified part of the route in north Wales. Departure from Euston is at 21.30 and arrival at Holyhead Quay at 02.25; so passengers still have to leave their seats or sleeping berths at an uncomfortable time. Over the 424 km (263 miles) this represents an average speed of only 86 km/h (53 mph), but 13 minutes are allowed at Crewe and there are three other intermediate stops.

The *Cornish Riviera Limited*

The Great Western was hardly Britain's best railway in the 1880s; for some reason the company had lost its earlier zest. Perhaps the coexistence of two gauges was one reason for this. Certainly, the final abolition of the broad gauge in 1892 was followed by a corporate renaissance. Trains were speeded up and new, often novel, rolling stock introduced. Moreover, the GWR, once known as the Great Way Round, began to build cut-off routes to shorten the distance between main centres. The Severn Tunnel project had been one of these, considerably reducing the journey from London to south Wales. In the early twentieth century a shortened route to Birmingham was opened, and also the Berks and Hants line that enabled trains from London to reach the west of England without meandering over the old line through Swindon and Bristol. In 1904 what was perhaps the GWR's best-known train began to run. This was the *Cornish Riviera Limited* from London (Paddington) to Plymouth and Cornwall.

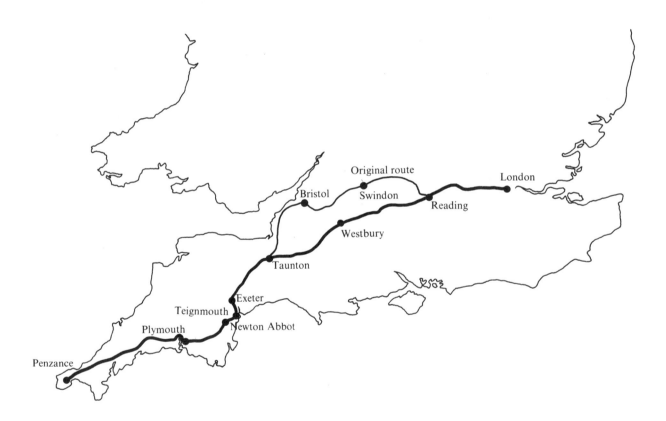

For two years the train was routed through Bristol but in 1906 the Berks and Hants line was opened and over the shortened route a schedule of three hours was attained for the non-stop London–Exeter sector. This train became the great test of GWR locomotive design with its fairly heavy load, its fast passage over the relatively level road to Taunton, and the challenging gradients of Devon. Great Western locomotive engineers designed successively bigger locomotives with this train in mind; what was good for the *Cornish Riviera Limited* was regarded as good for the other main trains too. Outside framed 4-4-0 engines soon gave place to Churchward's 4-6-0 machines; first came the

The route of the Cornish Riviera Limited *showing the old route through Bristol as well as the later direct route.*

two-cylinder Saints class, then the four-cylinder Stars. From the Stars Churchward's successor developed the famous Castles and then the even larger King 4-6-0. The passenger cars were also the company's best. Because the train was so popular it was decided to build a new kind of vehicle which would seat the greatest number of passengers in comfort without an excessive increase of train weight. The result was the first 21.3 metre (70 ft) coaches. These had white-painted roofs, a side corridor and, in the third class, ten compartments each accommodating eight passengers (although, as usual in British compartmented stock, six was more comfortable).

Locomotives of the King class, which took over the service in the late 1920s, often hauled thirteen or fourteen of these coaches in the peak period implying a load of 1,000 or more passengers, which is considerably more than the present-day *Cornish Riviera Limited*; however, the modern diesel-hauled train is somewhat faster, taking 2½ hours to the first stop at Exeter (278 km or 173 miles). But it was in the inter-war period that the train was at its peak. With its chocolate and cream rolling stock and a spotless King-class locomotive at the front in its green paintwork and brass fittings speeding through the Vale of the White Horse at over 129 km/h (80 mph), the train must have been a stirring sight, especially to the Great Western employees who regarded it with pride as the flagship of their line.

The Great Western was a strong protagonist of the slip coach. The first slip was at Westbury, then an important junction. As the train skirted the Wiltshire hills the guard made sure that all Westbury passengers were out of the dining car and back in the Westbury section at the rear of the train. This section was then closed off and at the right moment the section's guard pulled a lever and the train parted. The main train continued at speed over the Westbury avoiding line while the Westbury section followed behind, gradually losing momentum. The rapidly widening gap between the two sections enabled the signalmen to re-set the road, so the slip coaches could be diverted into the platforms of the station and be brought to a halt by the guard's manipulation of the vacuum brake. In summer another slip coach was detached as the train passed Taunton.

After leaving Exeter the train passed along the sea wall through Dawlish and Teignmouth where, when the wind and tides were right, it would be bathed in salt spray. After Newton Abbot the severest gradients began as the train skirted the southern edge of Dartmoor. Dainton Bank with its 1 in 40 (2.5 per cent) grades was the big test of the Kings, and speed would be brought down below 48 km/h (30 mph). Plymouth, 361 km (226 miles) from Paddington, was reached in exactly four hours. Here the King was taken off as it was too heavy for the line in Cornwall. A smaller 4-6-0 would be substituted and the train would leave Plymouth, cross Brunel's Royal Albert Bridge into Cornwall and reach Penzance 2 hr 20 min later; this was not a great speed for just 127 km (79 miles) but high speeds were never expected in Cornwall because of the winding track and the frequency of stops.

The present-day *Cornish Riviera* leaves London at 11.30 instead of the traditional 10.30, stops briefly at Exeter, and then reaches Plymouth at 15.04 and Penzance at 17.05. Thus the passenger from London to Penzance saves 80 minutes compared with the Great Western's steam service. But he probably arrives at his destination with less sense of occasion than he did in the heyday of this train. When the HST is introduced on this run the schedule will no doubt be cut further, but the individuality of the old train can hardly be recaptured.

The *Night Ferry*

Since its inauguration in 1936, and apart from interruption during the war, the *Night Ferry* has been providing an overnight sleeping-car service between London and Paris. It is a train unique in many ways: it is the only operation in England of the International Sleeping Car Company (Wagons-Lits); it is the only international through train to run in Britain, and it is the only train to provide life-jackets in its sleeping cars. For the British and French railway administrations, it is also something of a problem. They provide that part of the train which is not a Wagons-Lits enterprise, and in the late 1970s it became evident that the rolling stock specially designed for this service would

The route of the Night Ferry.

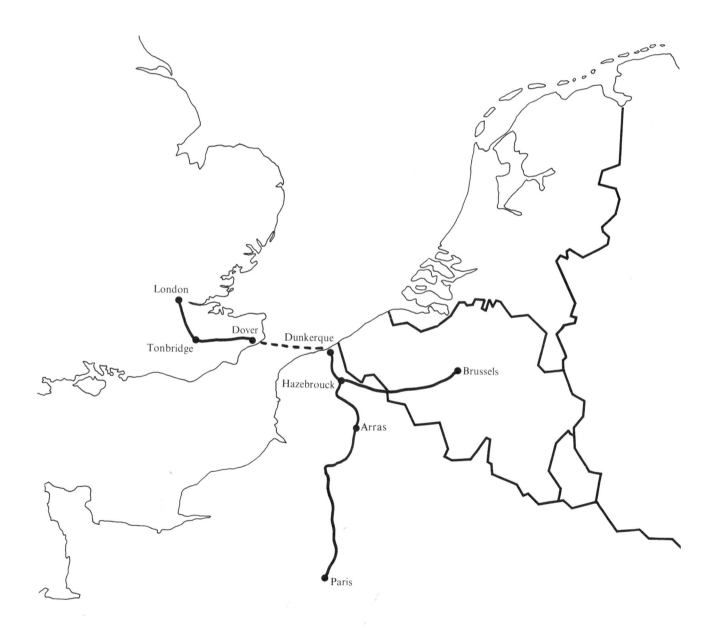

soon need replacement. Such a replacement would be expensive and hardly justified by any likelihood of future profits. Patronage of the train is not great, although there is a hard core of devoted and influential passengers who would raise loud objections to the train's withdrawal. The Channel Tunnel project was once expected to solve this problem, but since the project was shelved by the British government the future of the *Night Ferry* has still to be decided. It seems likely, however, that British Rail standard rolling stock will be allocated to this service.

Since the train runs on both sides of the Channel, special rolling stock is used. Thus the Wagons-Lits vehicles, mostly dating from the 1950s, are considerably narrower than that company's cars, operating on the Continent only. Since these cars cannot otherwise provide all the amenities expected from Wagons-Lits, they have one compartment fewer than the standard vehicles in order to provide space for the water-heating boiler. Having doors at only one end of the cars also releases extra space.

At peak periods ten sleeping cars may be provided, and the train also includes ordinary coaches for passengers who are prepared to change from train to ship and then from ship to train at the two ports. Thus there may be a load of 500 tonnes behind the locomotive when it pulls out of Victoria Station and begins the climb to Grosvenor Bridge. In the steam days a pair of locomotives were used, with a third, the engine which had brought in the empty stock, pushing for a few minutes at the rear. For years it was a pair of 4-4-0s which were used, but from 1947 a 'Merchant Navy' Pacific was made available. But even this was not enough and until 1959, when electric traction was introduced, a 4-4-0 piloting a light Pacific was the usual motive power. Nowadays the train is one of the few hauled over a significant distance by an electric locomotive drawing its power from a third rail. This is because the Southern Region of British Rail, primarily a commuter network, uses the third-rail low-voltage system.

At Dover the sleeping cars are detached and a diesel yard locomotive pushes them gently over a ramp on to the train deck of the stern-loading train ferry. Here, jacks between the deck and the underframes take the weight off the springs, and the cars' special tie-down rings are attached by chains to the deck. Passengers are allowed to leave their vehicles to explore the ship if they wish but, since the object of this service is to provide an unbroken night for its clients, few do so.

On arrival at Dunkerque, an SNCF locomotive comes aboard and draws out the sections of the train from the four sets of rails. When the train is re-assembled, it is taken to the main line where an electric locomotive is coupled on to take it forward. The route is via the main station at Dunkerque where early passengers for Paris board the SNCF cars which, together with a dining car, have been attached. At Hazebrouck one or two through sleeping cars from London to Brussels are detached. The Brussels section of the *Night Ferry* was introduced in 1957. It had long been desired by passengers and its delayed introduction was attributed by many to the Belgian State Railways' reluctance to inaugurate a service which would attract passengers from its own Calais–Ostend service.

Leaving London Victoria at 22.00, the London–Paris journey is accomplished in $9\frac{3}{4}$ hours. In this time the passenger can, if he is fortunate, get a good night's sleep. If he is a light sleeper, or if the sea is rough, he may not enjoy his night but the Wagons-Lits organization is considerate enough to provide him with a portable basin, which can be fixed to the bed just beneath his head.

The *Nord Express*

The founder of the Wagons-Lits Company, Nagelmackers, at the time of his death in 1905 was hoping to run his *Nord Express* from Lisbon to St Petersburg (now Leningrad), thereby serving seven capitals and running over lines of three different gauges. The gauge problem was to be overcome with interchangeable axles. However, this dream was never realized; although the *Nord Express* now serves five capitals these are not quite the same capitals which Nagelmackers had in mind. Through vehicles over the standard gauge and the Russian 1,524 mm (5 ft) and Iberian 1,676 mm (5 ft 6 in) are operated nowadays, but not by Wagons-Lits; cars from Russia, which have their wheel-sets changed at the frontiers, are provided by Soviet Railways, while the Barcelona–Geneva 'Catalan–Talgo', whose axles are adjusted from the Spanish to the standard gauge at Cerbère, is very much a Spanish enterprise.

The original *Nord Express* began running in May 1896, following years of resistance by the Prussian State Railways, which disliked the idea of a non-German train running over Prussian tracks. It ran once a week from Paris and

The present-day route of the Nord Express *from Paris to Copenhagen.*

Ostend, the two sections uniting at Liège. On arrival at Eydtkuhen, then the Russo-Prussian frontier station, passengers had to change trains, stepping into Wagons-Lits broad-gauge cars for the journey onwards to St Petersburg. The same year the company introduced its first sleeping cars on internal Russian services from Moscow to Sevastopol; by 1914 there were 48 such services in Russia.

The war left the company in a difficult position. In 1915 the Prussian Railways had broken all contracts and set up their own international sleeping-car company, using sequestered Wagons-Lits rolling stock. It was not until 1921 that the *Nord Express* was restored. It ran to the new Russo-Polish frontier station at Negoreloye, where the usually meagre complement of passengers detrained in order to take a Soviet Railways train to Moscow. However, a through car was soon provided to serve Riga, the capital of newly-independent Latvia. Thus, although the pre-1914 clientele of Russian nobility had disappeared, the train could still make a useful income from the traffic originated at the capitals of Riga, Warsaw and Berlin.

After the interruption of World War II the *Nord Express* was reinaugurated in 1946. Before the war it had included through cars to Copenhagen, and it was as a Paris/Ostend to Scandinavia train that it was resurrected. By 1947 it included a Paris–Stockholm car which was sent forward beyond Copenhagen by the train ferry. It was one of three international trains which awaited the arrival of the day Channel Ferry at Ostend and was the first of the trio to leave. From Ostend to Brussels it consisted of four vehicles for Copenhagen: one for Vienna, a dining car, one or two vehicles for Brussels, and, thrice weekly, two cars for Prague. The rolling stock was provided by the Wagons-Lits Company, with the German, Danish, Austrian and Czech administrations providing the non-sleeping vehicles. At this period the train was hauled to Brussels by an SNCB Atlantic locomotive. At Brussels, where the train was remarshalled, a Flamme Pacific took over for the hilly route to the German frontier. At Cologne the Vienna and Prague cars were detached, and the main train proceeded over the north German plain, hauled by a Pacific or, sometimes, a Prussian P8 4-6-0. Soon after leaving Hamburg the train crossed the Kiel Canal by a high bridge and then entered the frontier station at Flensburg. Here a Danish Atlantic or 4-6-0 took over. On the train ferry across the Great Belt the *Nord Express* was divided into three parts to suit the three tracks on the train deck. In summer, when there were more than 10 vehicles, some passengers had to leave the train and, after travelling in the ferry's lounge, find new accommodation in Danish vehicles attached to the train for the final run to Copenhagen. At that city the Paris–Stockholm sleeper was detached and sent forward. For the majority of passengers, however, the journey was over; from Paris to Copenhagen, about 1,290 km (800 miles), the journey had lasted 27 hours, of which 90 minutes were spent on the train ferry. The highest speeds would have been attained between Ostend and Brussels (121 km or 75 miles) for which 90 minutes were allowed, and between Bremen and Hamburg (116 km or 72 miles) for which 108 minutes were scheduled.

At that period, of course, the European railways were still affected by the deferred maintenance of wartime. Nowadays, with electric traction for almost all the way, the schedule is much reduced. In the summer 1978 timetable the train left the Gare du Nord at Paris at 18.11, joining the Ostend section at Liège 3¾ hours later. Arrival at Copenhagen was at 08.59. Allowing for one hour gained by crossing a time zone, this represented an overall average speed of 80 km/h (50 mph), a vast improvement on the 48 km/h (30 mph) of 1947.

The *Rome Express*

Inaugurated in the 1890s and running ever since, except for wartime interruptions, the *Rome Express* is one of the oldest of the great international trains. At times in its life it has been an exclusive *train de luxe*, conveying only patrons of the sleeping cars of the Wagons-Lits Company; at other times it has been a train of variegated rolling stock which happened to carry a proud name and convey one or two of the blue Wagons-Lits vehicles. Its route, too, has varied and nowadays it does not provide through sleeping cars between Calais and Rome.

The inaugural all-Wagons-Lits train, which connected with the boat from Dover, left Calais as a five-car train conveying only 18 passengers. These were distributed between two Wagons-Lits sleepers, each providing 20 places in two- and four-berth compartments. The other vehicles were a dining car, which also provided a smoking saloon, and two mail/baggage cars. As usual with the company, everything was in the grand style, and dinner on that November day included peas brought to Calais by the Peninsular Express from Brindisi. This new service replaced an earlier *Rome Express*, running since 1890, in which the luxury vehicles were merely attached to a succession of ordinary trains. The new *Rome Express* was, however, at first joined to the *Calais–Mediterranean Express* between Calais and Paris. But soon the company found it worthwhile to run the once-weekly train independently.

At Paris the Calais–Rome vehicles were detached at the Gare du Nord and taken round to the Gare de Lyon over the Paris Belt Railway. At the latter they were attached to the main section of the train, which started from the capital. This was taken forward over the PLM Railway to the Italian frontier. The heavy train, penetrating the French Alps, was one of the hardest jobs entrusted to PLM locomotives but what was arduous for the locomotive crews was enjoyable for passengers, for the climb towards the $13\frac{1}{2}$ km ($8\frac{1}{2}$ mile) Mont Cenis Tunnel was the most spectacular part of a journey that, throughout, was one of the most scenic in Europe. The section was electrified after World War I, not so much because of its difficulty but rather to eliminate the problem of fumes in the tunnel sections.

Breakfast in bed was one of the luxuries offered to the sleeping-car passengers, the car porter spreading a spotless white serviette on the bedside table and then bringing toast, brioches, and tea, coffee or chocolate. But after World War II, according to regular passengers, things were never quite the same; higher speeds are now attained but this can be an unattractive feature to those who patronize the train for its sense of unhurried ease. In the early 1950s the Calais section comprised two or sometimes three vehicles that were attached to a regular Calais–Paris fast train. The *Rome Express* which finally left the Gare de Lyon at 19.55 consisted of the Calais vehicles, which had been attached to the front end; a couple of first/second-class composite cars; two sleepers to Rome and another to Florence; two or three third-class coaches to Genoa, and a dining car. The latter, having served dinner, would be removed at Dijon, but at Modane an Italian diner would be attached to serve breakfast. The ordinary cars were largely supplied by the Italian Railways, so the train would mix the dull brown of the Italian vehicles with the blue of the Wagons-Lits, with here and there a French contribution adding a splash of olive green. Eighty minutes were spent at the Franco-Italian frontier, and at Turin, where the train reversed, passengers waited another 75 minutes while the train was

The route of the Rome Express *as it used to be. Nowadays this train starts its journey at the Gare de Lyon in Paris.*

cleaned and watered. From Turin the Genoa coaches, which had been dropped at Modane, were replaced by four or five Italian State Railways vehicles providing a fast Turin–Rome service. With electric haulage throughout Italy fairly high speeds were reached, even though the after-effects of wartime damage still lingered. The final stretch of the journey, after Spezia, included some flat coastal stretches and the 335 km (208 miles) from Pisa to Rome were covered in 4 hr 11 min with two intermediate stops. The 1,447 km (899 mile) run from Paris to Rome occupied 25 hr 35 min.

Nowadays the PLM steam locomotives of this train have disappeared, and it is electrically hauled in France as well as in Italy. In 1978 it left Paris at 20.39 and arrived in Rome at 13.20 the following day. The Wagons-Lits cars from Calais had disappeared; passengers from England who left London at 11.00 had to be content with through couchette or sitting vehicles which were provided from Boulogne to Rome, or they could transfer to the Wagons-Lits sleepers at Paris. The train, though much faster now, still retains something of its old atmosphere. An interpretation of that atmosphere can still be seen in the inter-war feature film *Rome Express*, one of whose stars is a PLM 4-8-2 locomotive, carefully modelled in plywood.

The *North Coast Limited*

The oldest named train serving the north-western states of the USA, the *North Coast Limited* has, since being taken over by Amtrak, been renamed the *North Coast Hiawatha*. It first ran in 1900 and at the time was regarded as the best train in America, for it not only had the usual sleeping, parlour, and dining cars but also boasted a bath-tub and electric lighting throughout. The schedule from Chicago to the Pacific at Seattle allowed four and a half days, which was good going for that time. And, moreover, the Northern Pacific could claim that this, its entrant in the contest for transcontinental honours, passed through scenery whose grandeur surpassed that of any other line, even that of the Canadian Pacific.

The Northern Pacific Railway took thirteen years to build, partly because of the difficulties of laying a line through mountainous and largely unpopulated terrain, partly because it was difficult to obtain capital for so hardy an enterprise. It ran from St Paul in Minnesota to Seattle in Washington, although at the time it was built the states of the north-west had not been delineated. Indeed, it was the coming of the railway which put those states on the map. When the line was completed in 1883, North and South Dakota, Montana, Idaho and Washington were merely virgin federal territory, but by summer 1890 they had all joined the Union. However, ten years after completion the Railway was forced into bankruptcy, as most investors had forecast, and a new company was formed in 1896. More optimistic, perhaps because settlement and industry were at last beginning to provide hope of profitable traffic, the new management created the *North Coast Limited* as a means of building up the public prestige of the line.

The *North Coast Limited* started from Chicago, running over the metals of the Burlington Railroad as far as St Paul. That Railroad and the NP had financial links at an early stage in their history, and nowadays are united— together with the former Great Northern Railroad—in the extensive Burlington Northern Railroad. From St Paul westwards the NP line passes first over prairies but soon climbs alongside the Yellowstone River to what the Railway's publicity described as its 'thousand miles of mountains'. This description was quite accurate, for the line climbs over, round, or through a succession of ranges before reaching the main spine of the Rockies, which it crosses at an elevation of 1,928 metres (6,328 ft) at Homestake Pass. The Railway made a gallant effort to develop tourist traffic. Indeed, the celebrated Yellowstone National Park owes its creation to the railway, being served by motor coaches from the nearby NP station of Livingston. This country is rich in American folklore, too, for it was the scene of General Custer's battles against Indians who, incidentally, were attacking Northern Pacific surveying parties at the time.

It was to attract tourist traffic that the Railway introduced new trains to the service in 1954. Painted in the NP livery of medium and light leaf-green, and hauled by streamlined diesel units, these trains brought dome cars to the route. Of the train's thirteen cars, four had domes from which passengers could get an unbroken view of the mountain peaks towering above the train. The 3,751 km (2,331 miles) separating Chicago and Seattle were covered in 45 hr 40 min; obviously the train could not compete with the airliner on timings but it could certainly show the passenger more of the real America. Special attractions of the train were the stewardess-nurses, who not only knew how to amuse children but also administered oxygen to any passenger who might need it in the rarefied air around Homestake Pass. In the dining car the traditional NP speciality was the giant Idaho baked potato, served on a separate dish because it weighed at least 1 kg (2 lb). A buffet-lounge was provided for coach passengers, and an observation lounge for Pullman clients.

Despite all these blandishments, traffic fell off over the years. Indeed, it is doubtful whether the train made a profit in any postwar year. Nevertheless, because the train performs a useful social function, especially for those isolated communities which do not have air services, it remains in the timetable. Amtrak, apart from taking over the responsibility for the train, has also rescheduled it. It now runs three times weekly except during the summer, when it is daily. It still has its dome cars and the giant Idaho potato still figures on the menu. It makes 35 intermediate stops, including one of 15 minutes where the locomotive, which runs through without change, is examined and serviced. Its schedule from Chicago to Seattle is now $52\frac{1}{2}$ hours.

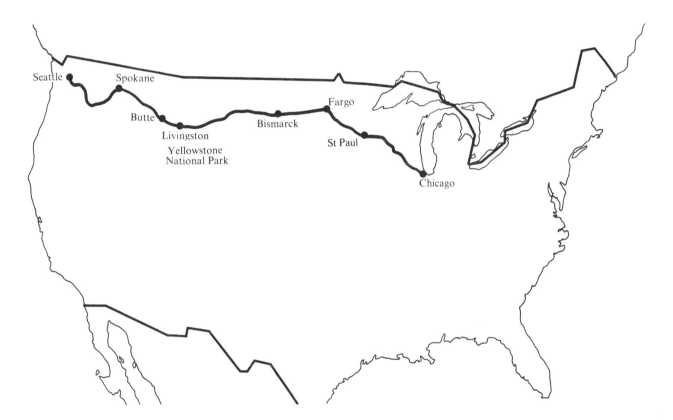

The route of the North Coast Limited.

The crest of the Northern Pacific Railway, operator of the North Coast Limited.

The *Sunset Limited*

The Southern Pacific Railroad, apart from owning the western part of America's first transcontinental railroad, also possesses the second. This is the line from New Orleans westwards through Texas, New Mexico, Arizona and California to the Pacific. Over this line, since the 1890s, the *Sunset Limited* has run from New Orleans to Los Angeles, providing a service which at times has been regarded as one of America's finest. By the 1950s the *Sunset Limited* was already one of the oldest name trains in the USA, and also one of the few remaining extra-fare trains. Five stainless-steel trains were built by Budd for this service in 1950, five being the number required to ensure a daily service in each direction over the 3,329 km (2,069 mile) route. The interiors were expensively styled; the dining room and the *French Quarter* lounge were in New Orleans style while the coffee shop was decorated with cattle brands and Texas longhorn heads. Sleeping accommodation was in the form of roomettes and bedrooms, the latter sometimes connected en suite. The sleeping-car passengers had the use of a full-length lounge which also provided showers

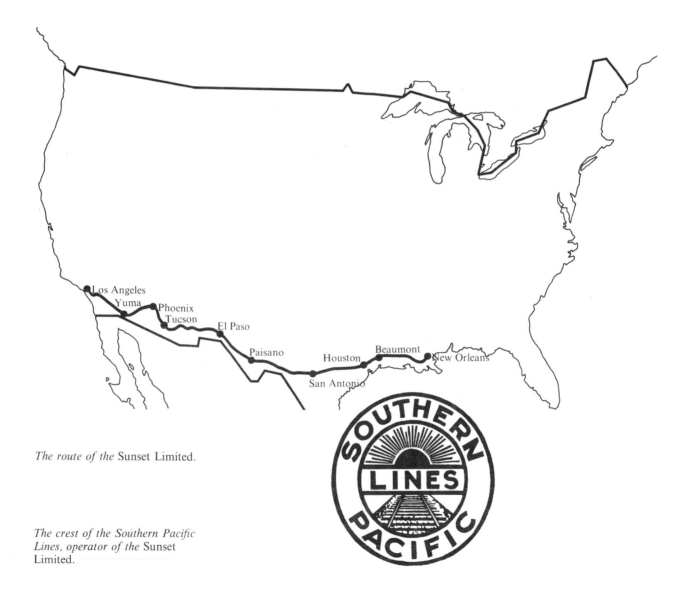

The route of the Sunset Limited.

The crest of the Southern Pacific Lines, operator of the Sunset Limited.

and a valet service. Coaches for sitting passengers had foam-rubber seats and padded leg-rests.

In the mid 1950s the train left New Orleans at 23.30 although passengers could embark after 22.00. A through sleeping car from Washington to Los Angeles was included, this having arrived in New Orleans via the Southern Railway some four and a half hours previously. The two- or three-unit diesel locomotive moved cautiously over the first few kilometres. A stop was made at a suburban station just 3 km (2 miles) from the Union Terminal, and then the *Sunset Limited* passed on to the $7\frac{1}{4}$ km ($4\frac{1}{2}$ mile) Public Belt Bridge. Having thus crossed the Mississippi, the train passed through the bayou country of water hyacinths and Spanish moss. In this part of Louisiana the place names are mainly French but before long Spanish names become more and more prominent. In fact, the Sunset route comes close to the Mexican border at many points and passes over territory which was once part of Mexico. After three more intermediate stops, Beaumont (449 km or 279 miles) was reached at 05.43. This is the centre of the Texas oil industry and small Dutch pumps are scattered for many miles alongside the line. Soon after, at 07.20, the train pulled into Houston (584 km or 363 miles) for a 20-minute stop. And so it went on: San Antonio at noon (Central Time), El Paso at midnight (Mountain Time), Yuma at 10.35 (Pacific Time) and arrival at Los Angeles at 16.15. 42 hr 45 mins was the schedule, during which the train had passed through five states; climbed to 1,546 metres (5,074 ft) at Paisano, Texas, and descended to 70 metres (231 ft) below sea level at Salton Sea, California; crossed the Pecos River in Texas by a bridge 98 metres (321 feet) above water, and made 23 intermediate stops as well as perhaps one or two by-request stops.

By the late 1960s this once-proud train had fallen on bad days. Regarded as an essential service, even though it lost money for the Railroad, it could not be withdrawn. Instead, an economy operation was substituted, devoid of all sleeping accommodation. This train was of five or six coaches, plus an auto-buffet car and a baggage/parcels car, and was hauled by a twin-unit diesel. The coaches provided eau-de-nil plastic-covered reclining seats which, however, had plenty of leg room. The automatic buffet was not automatic, as it required two attendants to provide change for the machines, assist in opening cans, clean up litter and stick 'Out of Order' notices to the machines. But when all the machines were working it was possible to sit down at a table with its own toaster, obtain refrigerated beer, prepare a hamburger in a microwave oven, or draw some gastronomic surprise from the soup-and-stew machine. In all, this economy service was manned by a crew of no fewer than twelve men (a two-man locomotive crew, two conductors, two brakemen, two porters, two buffet attendants, and two men looking after the parcels and baggage).

When the Southern Pacific enthusiastically transferred its long-distance passenger services to the new Amtrak Corporation, the *Sunset Limited* was among them. Since then the train has been rescued from its low status. It runs three times weekly, providing coach, sleeper, lounge and dining facilities. It leaves New Orleans at 13.00 and arrives on the third day at 07.40, making eighteen intermediate stops over a route which is now 3,255 km (2,023 miles) long. The through sleeper off the Southern Railway now starts in New York and arrives in New Orleans the day before departure of the *Sunset Limited*. Its passengers thereby are enabled to spend a night in New Orleans, using the sleeping car as their hotel. However, some doubt hangs over this sleeper operation, because the *Southern Crescent*, the train in which it runs from New York, may be discontinued.

Auto-Train

The car-sleeper train, like the corresponding piggyback freight operation, is a concept which bears a trace of irrationality for essentially it involves the carriage of wheeled vehicles by other wheeled vehicles. Yet in recent years both modes have developed rapidly, often at times when traditional traffic seemed to be falling off. Both enable the railway to provide a service which attracts users of its great competitor, the highway. The car-sleeper train exploits the modern paradox that many people like to have their cars with them but do not enjoy driving them.

Such trains, under various names (*Auto-couchette, Motorail,* etc.) have been a great success in Europe for they enable holidaymakers to take their families and their cars hundreds of miles to the sunshine without the strain and the risk of driving those miles. Paris to Milan, Hamburg to Verona, London to

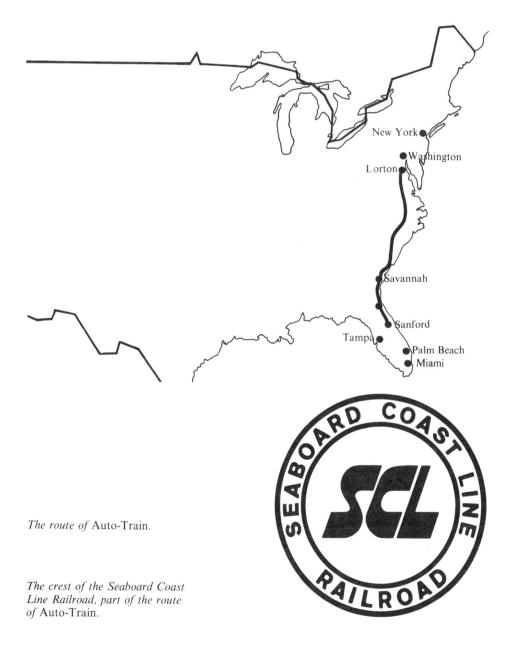

The route of Auto-Train.

The crest of the Seaboard Coast Line Railroad, part of the route of Auto-Train.

Cornwall. North Sea and Channel ports to the Mediterranean are just a few of the routes now offered to motorists. The basic routine is always the same. The motorist presents his car to the loading station where it is put on a car-carrier vehicle while the car's occupants go to sitting or sleeping accommodation in the train. All the car carriers are coupled to the passenger section of the train, which then moves to its destination. The next morning the passengers step out of the train and find their car waiting for them.

The USA was a little late in this field, but when the first *Auto-Train* service began it was rather different from the European services. It was provided not by railroad companies but by a private corporation. The role of the railroads was simply, for a price, to move the train over their tracks between the two terminals; the Auto-Train Corporation would do everything else. The train is intended to serve holidaymakers from the north-eastern states who wish to avoid the long drive to Florida. The starting point is not far from Washington, at Lorton, and the southern terminus is at Sanford, which is within convenient motoring distance of most Florida resorts. The distance is 1,377 km (856 miles) and the train leaves at 1600 to arrive the next day at 0900. Passenger accommodation includes some observation cars, sleepers, reclining seats with free blankets and pillows, buffet-dining facilities, and cinema and night-club attractions. Typically the train consists of nine passenger cars and about thirty car-carriers. The latter are former Canadian National freight cars fitted with passenger-car chassis. The whole train, including the two diesel locomotives (which also belong to the Auto-Train Corporation), is painted white with red and purple stripes.

On arrival at the terminal, passengers are received by Auto-Train personnel in brightly-coloured uniforms. There is a great deal of superficial glamour about these employees but this is in addition to, not a substitute for, genuine service; these are not railroad employees, but Auto-Train employees. This means, among other things, that there are no demarcation rules preventing them from making themselves as useful as possible to their clients. In particular, they change from one job to another in accordance with requirements; thus some of the train hostesses who are so plentiful when they are most required, at embarkation and disembarkation, may work at other tasks in the quiet hours. Train personnel take turns to man the hourly clean-up patrol which goes through the train to clear up litter, empty waste containers and in general keep the passenger cars spick and span.

About 400 passengers are accommodated. Reservations are required and passengers without cars are not carried. Undoubtedly it is a special clientele which is attracted, a clientele which has a higher than average income and which likes trains but does not necessarily like railroads. In fact, the two railroads over which the train operates (the Richmond, Fredericksburg & Potomac RR and the Seaboard Coast Line) do provide the regulation crew to handle the movement (four men in the case of the RF & P, five on the Seaboard). But those railroadmen who need to be inside the train wear plain clothes and talk to Auto-Train personnel, not to the passengers. Auto-Train's management has always insisted on a kind of *cordon sanitaire* between railroaders and passengers. Perhaps this is just one of those vaunted 'attentions to detail' which have made the *Auto-Train* so successful in terms of attracting full loads, perhaps not. But the undeniable fact is that Auto-Train, an independent company, has made a profit by doing something which the railroads themselves could have done, if only they could have assembled the same managerial enterprise, talent, and willing workers.

The *Spirit of Progress*

Although it is no longer the fastest or most luxurious service between Sydney and Melbourne, many interstate passengers still prefer to travel by the *Spirit of Progress*. It was introduced in 1937 and, until the introduction of the *Southern Aurora* in 1962, was the smartest night train in Australia. In those days the command 'All change! Albury!' was said to be the most-hated three words in Australia, for they meant that the Melbourne–Sydney train had arrived at the break-of-gauge station at Albury and passengers had to leave their Victorian Railways 1,600 mm (5 ft 3 in) gauge train and tramp up the long Albury station platform to join the New South Wales Government Railways stand-ard-gauge train for Sydney. At times, too, there has been a fruit inspection at this border crossing, at which passengers are required either to eat or to discard fruit which, just possibly, might otherwise carry fruit pests from one state to the other.

Thus the original *Spirit of Progress* ran only between Melbourne and the New South Wales border at Albury, where it connected with the NSWGR's *Sydney Limited*. The new train was semi-streamlined, with all-metal vehicles incorporating a new lightweight steel alloy. The locomotives were S class streamlined Pacifics, fitted with modified tenders whose 59,100 litre (13,000 gallon) water capacity enabled them to run non-stop over the remaining 306 km (190 miles); this was not only a record non-stop distance in Australia but also in the southern hemisphere. The load varied from seven to thirteen vehicles but the typical weight behind the engine was about 500 tonnes. The average speed northbound was 80 km/h (50 mph), but southbound the schedule was clipped by 25 minutes giving a time of 3 hr 35 min for the trip (85 km/h or 53 mph). The difference was due to the easier grades southbound, especially over the 48 km (30 miles) outside Melbourne where northbound trains had to climb up to the level of the Continental Divide, encountering grades of up to 1 in 50 (2 per cent). Although the first 109 km (68 miles) out of Melbourne were double track, the remainder of the run was single. However, automatic exchange equipment allowed the successive staffs to be picked up at 97 km/h (60 mph) and these permitted the train to pass from one signalling section to the next. Even so, the high average speed was quite an achievement especially as there were permanent speed restrictions to 40 km/h (25 mph) and 32 km/h (20 mph) at Seymour and Wodonga. To ensure that the hard-pressed locomotive crews actually observed these restrictions Flaman speed recorders, as used by French railways, were installed on the locomotives.

In 1962 the standard-gauge link between Albury and Melbourne was opened and it became possible to realize at last the dream of through trains between Sydney and Melbourne. A service of three trains, all diesel-hauled, was established. The old day train, formerly the *Daylight*, became the *Intercapital Daylight*. For this, the NSWGR provided air-conditioned but otherwise comfortless cars; these included a buffet car which served, among other things, Shredded Wheat with water. However, as though to compensate for the mediocrities of the day service, the night service was doubled by the introduction of a splendid new train, the *Southern Aurora*. The two trainsets required by this service were provided jointly by the two state railways. They were of fluted stainless steel, like Budd-built cars in the USA, and air-conditioned. Each train accommodated 198 passengers in twinette or roomette compartments (seated passengers were not carried). There was also a de-luxe bedroom, a dining car and a very relaxing bar and lounge. A feature of the dining car was that it opened for service at Melbourne one hour before the 20.00 departure, so that people who came to see off their friends could have a last meal with them on the train.

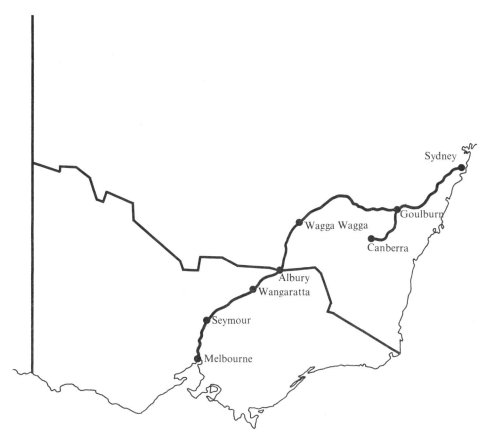

The route of the Spirit of Progress.

As for the *Spirit of Progress*, this was fitted with standard-gauge axles and began to run as a through train between the two capitals. Because the *Southern Aurora*, until recently, made no passenger stops at intermediate stations, the *Spirit of Progress* was the best train serving townships such as Albury, Wagga Wagga and Goulburn. It also conveyed through vehicles for Canberra which were detached at Goulburn. It was, moreover, the only night service providing accommodation for sitting passengers and, for the benefit of the latter, its buffet remained open through the night. It presented a somewhat piebald appearance because it contained both stainless-steel cars and the standard blue-painted vehicles of the Victorian Railways. However, its passengers often claim that it has 'more class' than the glamorous *Southern Aurora*. Its running speeds are in fact little inferior to those of the latter. On the south-bound trip, for example, the *'Spirit'* leaves ten minutes after the *'Rora'* and arrives at Melbourne 55 minutes after, but its schedule includes a 15-minute stop at Goulburn and several others. Nowadays the *Southern Aurora* also calls at Goulburn and Albury, and (in some passengers' opinion) has further declined in comparison with the *Spirit of Progress* by its mutation to a kind of car-sleeper service; it is not quite a full-blooded Auto-Train though, for its passengers are merely advised that they may take their cars on the train with them if they so wish.

The *Orange Express*

Passenger-train services in South Africa reflect the situation of the South African Railways, which is one of the world's biggest transport monopolies. This state corporation not only runs trains but also internal road and air services, to say nothing of its international services. Latterly there have been indications that the corporation would prefer its long-distance passengers to move by air rather than by train and, indeed, it has never made much effort to maximise its railway-ticket sales. The number of places available on its better services has always been restricted, so that these trains run with load factors which are the envy of other railways—railways which, unlike the SAR, provide sufficient places to enable a passenger to present himself at a station to buy a ticket for the next train. In South Africa, reservations for places on trains open three months before the train leaves. The famous *Blue Train*, running between Cape Town and Johannesburg and still one of the world's most luxurious trains, provides barely a hundred places on its weekly run.

The route of the Orange Express.

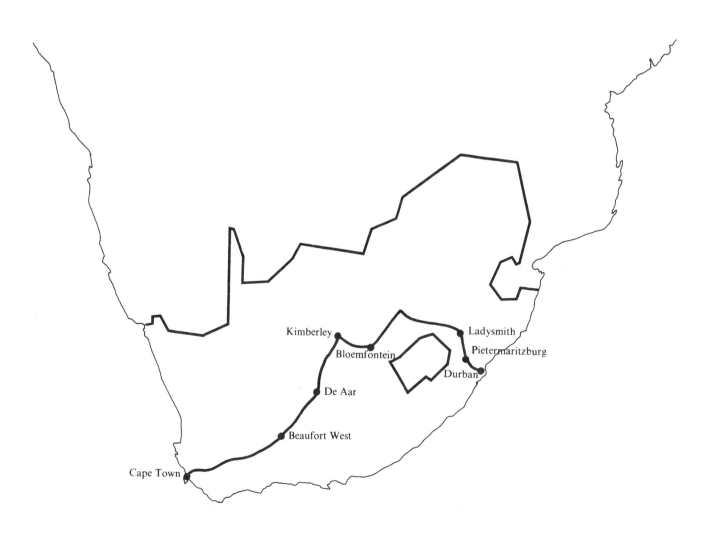

The *Orange Express* is not quite as limited as the *Blue Train* but nevertheless in the busy seasons it is likely to be completely sold out many weeks before departure. And this despite the fact that its Cape Town to Durban route is one of long distance, very suited to air transport. Despite the encouragements offered to the air traveller, many passengers still seem to retain a preference for the train; this may partly be because of the lower fare, but a substantial point in the railway's favour is that the haunting South African landscape is best viewed from a train. This is particularly true of the *Orange Express*, which crosses the Drakensberg Mountains as well as the Karoo.

Although this train was once painted bright orange it derives its name from its route, for it crosses right through the Orange Free State. It is now painted in the standard cream and brownish red, but there is a possibility that a more exciting colour scheme will be readopted now that steam locomotives on the non-electrified sections are being replaced by diesels. At present rather more than half of its 2,091 km (1,299 mile) journey is with electric traction. The central segment, once covered by a succession of 4-8-2 and 4-8-4 steam locomotives, is now becoming diesel territory so far as the best passenger trains are concerned. The condenser locomotives which once hauled the train over the arid Karoo are themselves disappearing; they were interesting locomotives, whining rather than puffing because their exhaust steam was recycled to their tenders rather than expelled through their chimneys.

The *Orange Express* leaves Durban at 1600 on Mondays and returns from Cape Town at 1800 on Fridays. The sleeping cars are divided in the usual South African manner and provide two-, four- and six-berth compartments. One end of the train is reserved for passengers falling outside the official definition of white. Typically the train consists of fifteen or sixteen vehicles and weighs well over 1,000 tonnes. The southbound train is perhaps the most difficult from the traction point of view, for soon after leaving Durban it begins to climb through the Zulu uplands to the first stop at the capital of Natal, Pietermaritzburg. After leaving this city, which is itself 676 metres (2,218 feet) above sea level, the train climbs into the Drakensbergs and reaches almost 1,463 metres (4,800 feet) before dropping down towards Ladysmith. Soon after leaving Ladysmith the train enters the Orange Free State, and also enters non-electrified territory. Bloemfontein is reached at 0930; this is still one of the biggest centres for steam traction in the Republic, if not in the world, despite the influx of diesel units, and its locomotive depot is still regarded as something of a Mecca by railway enthusiasts. The station, too, has escaped modernization; like the Durban station it resembles a British nineteenth-century station gone to seed.

From Bloemfontein the Kimberley line is taken. From Kimberley, the main line to Cape Town goes through De Aar Junction, the intersection of South Africa's great trunk routes. It is on this line that the highest speeds are likely to be reached. With its 1,067 mm (3 ft 6 in) gauge, the SAR has never really attempted to impress its clientele with high speeds. Nor are its stops very brief. Nevertheless, in steam days speeds of 115 km/h (70 mph) were regularly reached on this section.

The last part of the journey, from Beaufort West to Cape Town, is once more with electric traction and the 544 km (338 miles) are covered in just under 14 hours. At Cape Town, white and yellow passengers leave the train and enter the wide, spotless concourse of the modern terminal, a concourse which among its other offerings has a preserved locomotive of the old Cape Government Railway. Passengers of other hues make a less grand exit.

Narrow Gauge Railways

by John Westwood   The history and development of narrow gauge in different parts of the world.

It is not so easy as it might seem to define a narrow-gauge railway, for one country's narrow gauge may be another's standard gauge. In Europe, the 1,067 mm (3 ft 6 in) gauge is regarded as narrow but in South Africa it is the standard gauge and carries heavy traffic. In India the 750 mm (2 ft 6 in) gauge is regarded as narrow, but the entire network of Sierra Leone was of this gauge. In Japan 1,067 mm (3 ft 6 in) was the normal gauge until 1964 when, with the construction of a new 1,435 mm (4 ft 8½ in) line the normal gauge became narrow gauge almost overnight. Perhaps it is safest to describe a narrow-gauge railway as a railway whose gauge is smaller than other lines in the same area.

Advantages and disadvantages of narrow gauge

Narrow-gauge lines became popular not at the beginning of the Railway Age but halfway through it when the cost of the normal gauge was looming larger in the minds of those who still wanted to expand the networks. When major cities and traffic centres had been linked, smaller and less prosperous communities realized that without a railway they would fall even further behind. But since conventional railways were too expensive for such communities, cheaper ways of achieving the same object had to be sought. The narrow gauge seemed an admirable solution to this problem as it was so much cheaper. Railway companies liked it for another more subtle reason: whereas clients of standard-gauge branch lines ceaselessly agitated for costly improvements of services, for some psychological reason patrons of the narrow gauge were much more tolerant of slow and infrequent services.

The big economy of the narrow gauge was its ability to follow a very curved alignment, enabling it to clasp the contours of the landscape. This was especially advantageous in mountainous areas, because ranges could be crossed simply by clinging to successive hillsides. Expensive earthworks and tunnelling could be largely eliminated. Since everything was on a small scale, rails, locomotives and cars cost less. The less sophisticated safety and train-working regulations meant that fewer men were required and little, if any, signalling equipment. The cost difference between the gauges varied according to local circumstances, but at the turn of the century the Queensland Government Railways reckoned that adoption of the 1,067 mm (3 ft 6 in) gauge had saved two thirds of the cost which a standard-gauge line would have entailed. About the same time, it was reckoned that an Indian 750 mm (2 ft 6 in) gauge line cost almost one third less to build than a broad-gauge railway. The rather noticeable difference between Queensland and India is explained by the fact that the Indian lines were in flat country, whereas the Queensland examples were in hilly terrain where the narrow gauge is exceptionally advantageous.

The big disadvantage of the narrow gauge is that it is non-standard. In particular, through vehicles cannot run on to it from the main lines. For passengers this is not too serious, because they usually change trains at branch-line junctions in any case. But for freight, transhipment is required. At the time when narrow-gauge railways were most in favour, labour costs were low so transhipment was not expensive. Indeed it had the advantage that a main-line freight car, instead of passing down a branch line from where it might be returned weeks later, could be freed for other work as soon as its load had been transhipped. In later years labour costs did make transhipment expensive, but it was also found that transhipment depots were rich hunting grounds for pilferers for whose depredations the railways were, of course, obliged to pay compensation.

Previous pages: *On the 915 mm (3 ft) gauge in Peru, a British-built 2-8-2 of the Ferrocarril Huancayo–Huancavelica in Huancayo station. The line used by the locomotive is dual gauge, giving the narrow gauge access to the mainly standard-gauge station. After assembling its train No. 108 will haul it to Huancavelica.*

British influence and British engineers

Much of the force behind the narrow-gauge movement came from Britain, even though Britain never had many narrow-gauge lines. There was a strong preference among British railwaymen for the light railway—a concept enshrined in various acts of parliament. A light railway could be of any gauge, but in Britain was usually of standard gauge to secure that free interchange of rolling stock which was so valued in Britain. What made a light railway cheap was its freedom from many of the government regulations imposed on mainline railways. Since its trains were infrequent and did not need to move fast, parliament was willing, provided speed limits were observed, to relax the safety regulations. So signalling and signalmen were not required, nor were level-crossing gates and gatekeepers. Track could be light and earthworks elementary. Thus in general, apart from Ireland where narrow-gauge railways were very extensive, the narrow-gauge lines in Britain were to be found in the mountainous areas, especially in Wales.

It was one of the Welsh narrow-gauge lines, the Festiniog Railway, which was the inspiration of many other small lines, especially outside Britain. Built primarily to bring down slate from Festiniog, this 600 mm (2 ft) gauge line carried a very heavy traffic, despite its curves and gradients. In the 1870s it began to operate double-boiler, double-bogie. Fairlie-type engines, which were ideally suited to this kind of line because they provided high power and plenty of adhesion weight together with the low axle-weight and flexibility demanded by the light rails and sharp curves. As an example of the traffic capacity of narrow-gauge lines, the Festiniog was advertised by proponents of the narrow gauge everywhere; even railway officials from tsarist Russia appeared in Portmadoc to inspect operations.

British influence was also important overseas because so many colonial railways were engineered by British expatriates and planned by British officials. There were, too, several well-known British practitioners of the art of narrow-gauge engineering. Perhaps the most important of these was E.R. Calthrop, who not only developed his own theories of the narrow-gauge railway but also had the opportunity to apply them. He believed that the 750 mm (2 ft 6 in) gauge was by far the best for undeveloped country although he was prepared to accept the 600 mm (2 ft) gauge, with its disproportionately smaller capacity, where traffic was very low or the terrain exceptionally difficult. He also held that a standard maximum axle-loading should be imposed, preferably of five tonnes where his recommended rail weight of 15 kg/m (30 lbs/yd) was adopted. Together with a standard maximum speed of 24 km/h (15 mph) this would enable cheap rail to be used without excessive track maintenance expense. He was also an advocate of high-capacity bogie rolling stock, preferably of stressed-steel construction. A fifteen-tonne capacity was especially recommended for colonial lines which were usually quite long and carried a heavy bulk traffic. Stressed steel had the great advantage that it was much lighter than wood and thereby enabled more payload to be hauled. Calthrop's shop window was the Barsi railway in India. Owned (until 1954) by a London company, this Railway had appointed Calthrop to be its engineer and he made it so that it could, he claimed, carry nearly one million passengers annually as well as 600,000 tonnes of freight. This railway, 185 km (115 miles) long, still survives and the locomotives and the rails, as Calthrop had promised, did last a long time. One of the big 4-8-4 tank locomotives, built in 1907, served for at least sixty years; true to Calthrop principles it had an axle weight of only 5 tonnes yet an adhesion weight of 20 tonnes, all on a wheelbase of only 5.56 m (18 ft 3 in). Calthrop's reputation grew over the years. It was on his advice that the government of Victoria in Australia adopted the 750 mm (2 ft 6 in) standard for its narrow-gauge network in preference to 600 mm (2 ft). Later he became engineer of a British narrow-gauge line, the Leek & Manifold in Staffordshire, a line which delighted many tourists but which was short-lived.

Another prominent Englishman was Sir Arthur Heywood. More a gifted amateur than a professional engineer, he was a great advocate of the ultra-narrow gauge. The 380 mm (15 in) gauge was his favourite and he built a demonstration line in his own grounds. Among the advantages which he claimed were the obvious economies resulting from smaller equipment, the ability of such railways to enter buildings—and thus provide something even better than a door-to-door service—and the avoidance of the unsightliness associated with larger-size railways. Heywood was by no means a crank; he realized that the 380 mm (15 in) gauge was unsuitable where significant connections were made with main-line railways. Several lines built to his gauge still flourish in England; they owe their survival to tourist traffic but nevertheless prove that the gauge can be something more than a toy.

France

The narrow gauge, and especially the metre gauge, became very popular in France in the last quarter of the nineteenth century. Neither the big railway companies nor the government felt able to pay for the extension of the main-line network, yet secondary railways were obviously needed to open up isolated areas. Cheaply-built lines to a narrower gauge seemed the answer. Known as 'departmental lines' when they were controlled by a local *département*, or as either 'economic railways' or 'lines of local significance', they were financed partly by the local government and partly by the central government. Successive legislation tried to develop their virtues and eliminate what appeared to be their faults. At first, rather generous financial incentives were granted to companies willing to build and operate these lines, with the result that many companies worked their lines in such a way as to oblige the local government to disburse crippling sums each year. This generosity enabled several big companies to develop, owning and operating metre-gauge lines in various parts of the country and having the ambition of linking their separate lines to form big networks. The government did legislate to prevent the metre-gauge lines from exceeding a certain length, but this could not stop one short line making an end-on junction with another, thereby creating long lines which could be dangerous competition for the main-line railway companies. In fact, the threat was never realized to any extent. However, the big metre-gauge companies survived and even now are still active, albeit with a reduced mileage and with much of their service worked by motor transport.

After two such companies the CFD (Departmental Railway Company) and SE (Economic Railways Company) had succeeded in building minor empires, the framework was changed. Henceforth a given *département* would build its line and then grant a concession to an operating company or it subsidized a private company to both build and operate the line, taking care to impose conditions which would guarantee an efficient operation.

The mid 1920s witnessed the peak of French narrow-gauge mileage. In 1925 the total extent of departmental and local railways was 13,000 km (8,080 miles) of which almost all was narrow gauge. The last new line to be built was opened in 1928; this was the electrified Toulouse–Castres Railway, belonging to the

The Fairlie double-boiler locomotive, which in the 1870s convinced many engineers that the narrow-gauge railway had a great future, can still be seen working on the very same line on which the original engines of the type made their debut. The Festiniog Railway in Wales, now a tourist line, uses the type for some of its services.

Two 1,800 hp diesel units, built in Australia by English Electric, haul a heavy bauxite train over the 1,067 mm (3 ft 6 in) gauge Western Australian Government Railways' line to Kwinana.

Above: *A special steam train on the narrow-gauge Sardinian Railways.*
Below: *Narrow-gauge steam is still active in Austria. No. 298.53, an 0-6-2 tank locomotive working on the Steyertal line, is pictured at Grunberg.*

Below: 600 mm (2 ft) gauge sugar-cane lines are still active in Queensland, although steam traction is now largely displaced by diesel.
Bottom: On the Denver & Rio Grande RR's narrow-gauge network in Colorado, in the days before it was reduced to a short tourist line.

Below: *Mallet 2-4-6-0 compound tank engines on the Portuguese metre-gauge system at Sernada-de-Vluga. These locomotives have now been displaced from most of their duties by new diesel locomotives.*

Right: *Three 760 mm (2 ft 6 in) locomotives at work on the Western Railway in India. From top to bottom they are an 0-6-2, an 0-6-4T, and another 0-6-2. All are still in service.*

railway system of the Midi *département*. By the 1930s, however, many lines had closed due to road competition. At the same time some lines flourished for a while and bought railcars to handle their traffic; the old steam passenger train, often conducting interminable shunting operations at intermediate stations, could not hold its passengers against the attractions of the country bus. The demise of the narrow-gauge lines was accelerated by government policy which in the interests of co-ordination seemed to put the SNCF first, the road system second and the local railways a poor third. World War II further reduced the mileage, although for a decade after the war a few railways continued to provide a valued service. One of the last to close was the Réseau Breton centred on Carhaix in Brittany. Owned by the SNCF but worked in the interests of economy by the CE, this line had at the time of closure 21 steam locomotives (twelve 4-6-OT and nine Mallet 0-6-0 + 0-6-OT) and 40 passenger cars. It served an extensive area, having developed its network from 1891, when it began as a 49 km (30 mile) connection between Carhaix and Morlaix, to 1926, when it added its last line. One section, Carhaix to Guingamp, survived after 1968 as a standard-gauge line of the SNCF.

Apart from the metre-gauge lines, one or two of which still survive either as dieselized freight lines or as preserved tourist railways, France had many 600 mm (2 ft) gauge railways. The upsurge of this gauge followed the introduction by Paul Décauville of his 'portable railway'. Intended originally for agricultural use, these light and inexpensive railways were soon bought also by the war ministries of several countries as battlefield railways which could be laid and removed rapidly as troops advanced or retreated. Lines of this gauge did much to develop the French sugar-beet industry and it was a sugar-beet line which was the last to survive; this was the Tramway de Pithiviers à Toury, a 31 km (19 mile) line opened in 1890 and closed in 1964. One of several actually built and owned by the Décauville Company, it possessed about twenty locomotives, most of which only worked during the sugar-beet season. Part of it has been resurrected as a tourist line.

Belgium

In Belgium the narrow-gauge railways were as rationally organized as the main lines. This was perhaps due to the readiness with which Belgians accepted government control and co-ordination. Facing the common problem of communities wanting transport while being unable to provide enough traffic to justify normal railways, the government as early as 1875 was legislating for the development of secondary or light railways. In the mid 1880s laws were passed which established a special organization for local railways. This was the Société Nationale des Chemins de Fer Vicinaux (SNCV), which still exists. The SNCV planned the construction and operation of a network of cheaply-built lines, mainly of metre gauge and often built alongside the highways so as to cheapen construction. Care was taken that a minimum of two thirds of the capital should be provided by the state, the province or local communes, thereby guaranteeing that private speculators could not obtain control. Perhaps because of this restriction private investment was negligible. At first the SNCV proposed, studied, and built the new lines. It also provided rolling stock but leased out its lines to private operating companies. It adopted a common, and quite high, standard of construction and imposed a common series of working regulations. For example, there was a speed limit of 10 km/h (6 mph) in towns and 30 km/h (18 mph) elsewhere. Standard locomotives were used, being almost entirely of the six-wheeled

Another view of the now-abandoned freight operations of the narrow-gauge system of the Denver & Rio Grande RR. A 2-8-2, fitted with snowplough, climbs Cumbres Hill in Colorado.

tram type. By the turn of the century the SNCV possessed over 250 loco-motives, 700 passenger cars and about 1,800 freight cars.

By 1914 the system had grown to more than 4,000 km (2,480 miles) and about 400 km (248 miles) of the suburban routes had been electrified. Agri-culture had benefited greatly, sugar-beet production in particular. But World War I was fought largely over Belgium and the system was split between the Allies and the German occupiers. In occupied Belgium, because the Germans had commandeered the State Railway, the SNCV lines were of vital import-ance for society. As it was possible to travel almost everywhere, albeit rather slowly, by these lines, commerce and social intercourse could just continue. But towards the end of the war the Germans began to remove the tracks so postwar restoration was a long process. In the inter-war years the SNCV lines coped with road competition, invested in diesel railcars and continued with electrification. When the Germans came for a second time in 1940 there were 4,800 km (2,980 miles) of SNCV line, of which almost 1,500 km (930 miles) were electrified. Once again the Germans made no use of the network, leaving it for the use of the locals. But damage was great, even though the occupiers never carried out their intention of transferring about 1,000 km (621 miles) of the system to the Ukraine. Over a million passengers were car-ried during the war.

Since 1945 the SNCV lines have been thinned out by the closure of routes hopelessly damaged by road competition. But several hundred kilometres still survive. The steam locomotive has disappeared and so has passenger service on the non-electrified sections. It is no longer possible to travel all over the country by SNCV. On the other hand there are still many routes which seem to prosper. Of the electrified services, that from Ostend along the coast to Knokke is especially popular both for tourists and for light-railway enthusiasts.

Austria

Another country in which narrow-gauge railways were carefully thought out by the state and provincial authorities is Austria. In the 1870s the central government built several light railways and this stimulated a demand for such facilities from several rural districts. In the 1880s laws were passed to en-courage the building of light railways. The state was prepared to give financial help and also arranged that at junctions with the main-line railways the stations would be the financial responsibility of the state, and this included the cost of transhipment of freight from narrow-gauge to standard-gauge vehicles. Moreover, several provinces made their own provisions for financial help. Especially generous was, and remains, the province of Styria.

The narrow gauge was favoured for these light railways, largely because of the success achieved with the state-built 750 mm (2 ft 6 in) lines in the Austrian Empire's mountainous territory of Bosnia and Hercegovina (remnants of these lines are still operated by the Yugoslav State Railways). By 1914 the Empire possessed about 1,300 km (808 miles) of narrow-gauge routes. The dismemberment of the Empire meant that the narrow-gauge mileage was reduced and further reduction was made by the closure of a few lines in the inter-war period. Several lines were taken over by the Austrian State Railways (OBB), while those in Styria were taken over by the local government. World War II was followed by a period of foreign occupation which divided up the country. However, since most of the narrow-gauge lines were isolated routes most often serving mountain settlements, this had little disruptive effect.

Since capital has never been plentiful in postwar Austria, new highways paralleling the narrow-gauge lines have been slow to appear. Moreover, there is a central control over local transport ensuring that buses, trains and postal services work in close co-ordination. For these reasons the narrow-gauge lines have usually survived, and perform their original purpose of serving settlements which would otherwise be without a reliable and regular transport service. When one line was closed (the province-owned Salzkammergut Railway) in connection with highway development, opposition was strong and vocal. The strength of the protest, and the fact that a plausible case can be made for the claim that the closure of this line had a more serious economic effect than anticipated, may be a factor deterring other local governments from similar action. For although neither the provincial nor the OBB narrow-gauge lines are really profitable, they bring great gains to the areas they serve.

For this reason the narrow-gauge lines of Austria do not usually exhibit the sleepy and antiquated atmosphere nowadays associated with most such lines. Their rolling stock is usually modern and the OBB has introduced modern diesel locomotives to haul it. Steam traction does survive on some lines, notably on the Garsten line opened in 1889 and whose remaining mileage is now owned by the state. The narrow-gauge OBB locomotives of this line seem likely to remain in service for some time. Elsewhere the Zillertalbahn maintains steam traction, not because it cannot afford to dieselize completely but because it has found that steam attracts extra tourist traffic. Around Gmund, on the frontier with Czechoslovakia, there is a flourishing OBB narrow-gauge system where in the late 1970s steam 0-8-0 locomotives were still sharing the traffic with diesels.

Switzerland

Even more than in Austria, the narrow-gauge lines of Switzerland are far removed from the popular conception of such lines. Typically built to connect mountain communities with the main lines which followed the major valleys, these lines have been pampered by the central and canton governments. From 1916 they were more or less protected, by legislation, from highway competition. This has certainly preserved them as flourishing concerns. Indeed, most of them are electrified. But with their virtual monopoly they have been able to impose high tariffs, so that they can hardly be described now as lines intended to serve poorer communities.

Outstanding among narrow-gauge railways, even in Switzerland, is the Rhaetian Railway, which operates no fewer than 390 km (293 miles) of electrified route. This metre-gauge line was started in 1889 to serve the Grisons area of Switzerland—a task which it has performed very well. It carries enough traffic to make it the envy of many standard-gauge railways and has done much to aid the development of its territory, especially of its tourist potential. A more traditional narrow-gauge line is the Brienz to Rothorn mountain railway, the only Swiss line to make regular use of steam traction—in this case 800 mm (2 ft 7½ in) gauge rack engines.

West Germany

In Germany, the rise of the narrow gauge towards the end of the last century coincided with a period in which the separate states were edging close together under the leadership of Prussia, but were at the same time jealous of their independence in railway matters. Thus there was a variety of arrangements for the building and operation of these lines. Nevertheless, the narrow gauge was utilized in a rational way, being built to serve outlying districts and to act as a feeder to the main-line system. The metre gauge and the 750 mm (2 ft 6 in) gauge were regarded as standard for small railways. The Imperial government did succeed in introducing two acts in the 1870s which had an all-German significance. One of these helped light railways by relieving them of the obligation to carry mails free, and the other relieved them of other obligations imposed on the main-line railways in return for a speed limit of 30 km/h (18 mph). Such reliefs included relaxed regulations concerning brakes, signals and track, and also the level of manning. In 1892 the biggest state, Prussia, put the light railways under its postal department and arranged for more financial aid from the central and local authorities. This was followed by a spurt of new construction. The other great user of narrow-gauge railways, Saxony, operated them as part of the Saxon State Railways. Meanwhile, the 600 mm (2 ft) gauge made an appearance, being especially favoured for agricultural railways in East Prussia; here again it was the sugar-beet industry which was especially benefited.

It is the former narrow-gauge systems of Prussia and Saxony which have best survived the two wars and the rise of highway competition. In West Germany some narrow-gauge lines still exist, worked by local companies or by the DB. These have been dieselized although in Bavaria there still exists a narrow-gauge tramway operation of the traditional kind. This is the short line from Prien to Stock, connecting the main-line station with a lake steamer quay. Operating in summer only, this 90-year old Chiemseebahn still uses its steam tramway-type locomotive. Elsewhere in West Germany, steam narrow-gauge operations are confined to preserved lines.

Eastern Europe

In East Germany, however, many narrow-gauge branches of the old Saxon and Prussian system still survive under steam traction. Although the government in 1977 announced the imminent closure of some of these, this decision had a silver lining, for it seemed to indicate that the lines to be spared would have a definite future. The picturesque system in the Harz mountains is expected to survive. Based on Wernigerode, this line uses comparatively modern 2-10-2 tank locomotives to overcome the severe gradients. Not far away, and also of metre gauge, another Harz line runs from Gernrode and is operated largely by Mallet tank locomotives. Also once part of the Prussian system is the 900 mm (3 ft) gauge line from Bad Doberan on the Baltic coast. Not far away is the 750 mm (2 ft 6 in) line of the island of Rügen. In Saxony there are two lines in the Dresden area. The 26 km (16 mile) line to the mountain resort of Kurort Kipsdorf is expected to last many years yet, and is operated by 2-10-2 tank locomotives. Other Saxon lines still use the type of locomotive known as the Saxon-Meyer, a variant of the Mallet system. Former narrow-gauge lines of the Prussian system survive in Poland where such railways are still numerous. Some of them are common-carriers while others are industrial, typically serving the sugar-beet and timber industries. Elsewhere in eastern Europe Czechoslovakia and Romania still use narrow-gauge forestry lines, and it is not unusual to find that the original steam locomotives remain in operation.

Southern Europe

In southern Europe Italy has some narrow-gauge short lines, usually electrified and serving suburban communities. Several of these are of the unusual

950 mm (3 ft 1½ in) gauge. In Greece the Hellenic State Railways operate a considerable mileage of narrow-gauge trackage. The first railway in Greece was the 163 km (101 mile) Thessaly Railway from Kalampaka to Volos. This was built to the metre gauge while a subsequent narrow-gauge system, the Peloponnesus Railways, also chose that gauge. 600 mm (2 ft) and 750 mm (2 ft 6 in) railways were also to be found in Greece. Some of this narrow-gauge trackage has now disappeared, some has received the ultimate symbol of success—being converted to standard gauge—but there is still a substantial metre-gauge mileage. However, it is in Portugal that the metre gauge remains at its strongest, for only a few main lines in that country were built to the 1,676 mm (5 ft 6 in) gauge of neighbouring Spain. Being a poor nation, Portugal could afford only a narrow gauge for its secondary lines. Most of these still exist, performing a useful service, and although the intensive metre-gauge suburban service out of Oporto has recently been modernized with diesel traction, steam locomotives still work some of the country branches. In neighbouring Spain the broad gauge is much more dominant but narrower gauges (in this case including the 1,435 mm (4 ft 8½ in) gauge) were adopted for some lines. When the national railway company, RENFE, was formed, it did not embrace the narrow gauges which for the most part were placed under another state department. This has closed some lines but fostered others, sometimes by hiring out modern rolling stock. So although the 600 mm (2 ft) and 750 mm (2 ft 6 in) gauges have not escaped the fate of those gauges in neighbouring countries, there is still a considerable mileage of metre gauge. Most of this is operated by industry, especially mining companies. The best known perhaps is the Ponferrada to Villablino line, still steam operated, which in 1978 was still running a daily passenger train as well as numerous coal trains. Other gauges include the 1,067 mm (3 ft 6 in) used by a British mining company, Rio Tinto, for its extensive industrial system around Bilbao and the 1,219 mm (4 ft) of a copper-ore line near Huelva.

The USSR

Outside Europe, the Asiatic part of the USSR is unique in that it witnessed a considerable growth of narrow-gauge mileage in the late 1950s. At least 650 km (404 miles) of the Russian narrow gauge (750 mm or 2 ft 6 in) was laid in Kazakhstan in connection with the 'Virgin Lands' campaign, proving that the narrow gauge was still capable of fulfilling its classic function, that of developing agricultural areas lacking road transport. Elsewhere in the USSR there is a considerable mileage of 750 mm (2 ft 6 in) trackage in Estonia, with one passenger train, following a roundabout route, covering 245 km (152 miles) on its nightly run. In the Ukraine there is a somewhat less developed system centred on Vinnitsa. In Russia, as elsewhere, interest in the narrow gauge arose in the 1870s following visits by influential Russians to Wales. Both the government's state railway and private companies then built some lines but they never became widely popular because transhipment costs were high. Possibly they were misapplied. Instead of being built in remote regions they tended to be cheap extensions of existing railways. This was the case of the Yaroslavl–Archangel railway, whose narrow gauge was converted to mixed gauge only a few years after construction. Since funds were scarce, for some years narrow-gauge locomotives were used to haul broad-gauge trains on this line. It was only the strategic implications of the line, as demonstrated during the course of World War I, that enabled funds to be found for a proper reconstruction.

India

There are still about 4,830 km (3,000 miles) of narrow-gauge railway in India, and this figure excludes the metre gauge which is regarded as one of the two standard gauges. The metre-gauge system began to develop after 1879 when it was decided that the long Rajputana to Malwa line should be of that gauge in order to lower costs. Only a few years earlier Lord Salisbury (then the Secretary of State for India) had ordered that an earlier metre-gauge line up the Indus Valley should be relaid to the Indian standard broad gauge; the local commander-in-chief had decided that two gauges was one too many if troops and supplies were to be rapidly moved in wartime. However, as soon as the Malwa line was built and showing good results there was a spurt of metre-gauge construction. Whatever its military disadvantages, the consequent extension of the railway into the less prosperous agricultural regions did much to eliminate the local famines which had been the curse of India. As in France, the government of India made great efforts to ensure that the metre-gauge routes should not combine to form long-distance railways which might compete with the main lines. In these endeavours it was not wholly successful. The intention to exclude the metre gauge from the ports was achieved in the cases of Bombay and Calcutta, but not of Madras. The intention of preventing any physical connection between the extensive and dense metre-gauge network of the Ganges Valley and the equally extensive network of southern India was achieved, but only until the British left; soon after Independence in 1947 a 302 km (188 mile) link was built, thereby creating what was almost an all-India network of metre-gauge railways.

The arguments which had been so convincingly proved by the success of most metre-gauge lines could be equally well used in favour of gauges smaller than the metre standard. Once the concept of one gauge for the whole territory had been breached, it was more difficult to prevent the emergence of a third and even a fourth gauge. Indeed, India can still be regarded as a nation of four railway gauges. The first 750 mm (2 ft 6 in) line was built by the Gaekwar of Baroda as a bullock-hauled tramway to connect with the main line. It was later extended to form one of the two big Indian narrow-gauge networks. This network, centred on Dabhoi, near Baroda, is now part of India's Western Railway and operates what may well be the world's most intensive steam narrow-gauge timetable. The other big Indian network is now operated by the South Eastern Railway. Built by the old Bengal Nagpur Railway to serve the district north and east of Nagpur, this 1,006 km (625 mile) system is operated partly by German-built diesel locomotives. Its best passenger train often loads to 14 vehicles, including a Travelling Post Office. The 600 mm (2 ft) gauge was introduced to India by the celebrated Darjeeling Himalaya Railway, and soon afterwards the maharajah of Gwalior laid a line of similar gauge to connect his palace with his favourite fishing spots. Later the Maharajah's toy developed into a very serious and extensive 405 km (252 mile) system around Gwalior; it still exists, with a busy steam-hauled train service.

There developed a miniature Battle of the Gauges between the two narrower gauges and this came to a head in 1897 when the military authorities realized that the narrow-gauge strategic lines being built in the North West Frontier region would, in case of war, need to borrow equipment from other narrow-gauge lines. Such a transfer might well have been hampered if the strategic railways were of a different gauge from their closest neighbours. The military would have preferred to standardize the 600 mm (2 ft) gauge, for this was the recognized gauge for military railways in France (Décauville's

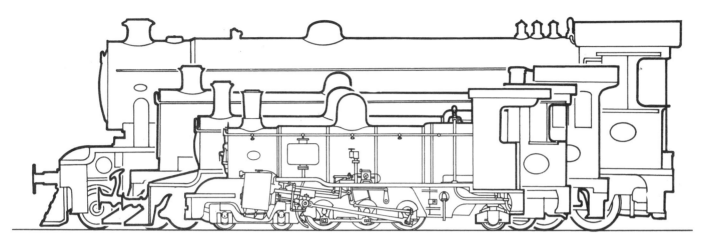

A revealing impression of the Indian gauge differences in practice is given by this drawing, first published in a British railway journal in 1924. It shows four Pacifics of types then being delivered by British builders (and which still exist in the Indian sub-continent). From rear to front they are of the 1,676 mm (5 ft 6 in), metre, 750 mm (2 ft 6 in) and 600 mm (2 ft) gauges. The uselessly small difference between the two narrowest gauges is evident. The 750 mm (2 ft 6 in) gauge would seem to be superfluous, yet in fact it was this gauge which was usually preferred to the 600 mm (2 ft) gauge, because in terms of carrying capacity it was much superior to the latter.

system) and Germany (the Feldbahn regime). However, the 750 mm (2 ft 6 in) gauge was finally chosen, and this became a standard narrow gauge elsewhere in the British Empire. This was perhaps fortunate, because the carrying capacity of the 750 mm (2 ft 6 in) railway is much greater than that of the 600 mm (2 ft). In India, modern freight cars for this gauge can carry 21 tonnes, for an axle load of only eight tonnes. The width of rolling stock is three times the track gauge. That is, 750 mm (2 ft 6 in) gauge vehicles may be 2.28 m (7 ft 6 in) wide, compared to the 3.25 m (10 ft 8 in) of the broad gauge and 2.74 m (9 ft) of the metre gauges.

Australia

In Australia it was Victoria which built most of the narrow-gauge trackage. New South Wales preferred to build its secondary lines as light railways to the standard gauge. Queensland and Western Australia, having adopted the 1,067 mm (3 ft 6 in) gauge as standard, found that their lines were almost as cheap as the true narrow gauge. In Queensland, however, there is a considerable mileage of private 600 mm (2 ft) gauge sugar-cane lines, intensively operated in the cane season. South Australia built considerable 1,067 mm (3 ft 6 in) gauge line to serve parts which could not justify the main-line 1,600 mm (5 ft 3 in) gauge. The line to Alice Springs, built more as a social and political asset than with any hope of carrying profitable traffic, was built to this gauge and some of it still survives. South Australia found itself in severe financial difficulties after overreaching itself in the construction of its broad-gauge railways, so it had little choice except to introduce a narrower gauge; it was a case of either narrow gauge or no more railways at all. In fact, because track materials had to be imported expensively from England, and because there was much extra expenditure on providing water supply for the locomotives, narrow-gauge railways in South Australia often cost more to build than standard-gauge lines elsewhere.

In Victoria, which by the turn of the century had a considerable network of 1,600 mm (5 ft 3 in) gauge lines, it was decided that remote settlements in hilly and not very prosperous areas could only be served by narrow-gauge lines. 750 mm (2 ft 6 in) was the chosen gauge. The Railway Department was not in favour of a new gauge but had to submit to political pressures. Although the lines were well planned, they hardly justified their existence. In one case, the Wangaratta to Whitfield line, the country was very poor but it was expected that the railway would bring prosperity. This did not happen, so for years the line was worked by just a daily inspection car. The other three lines might have been commercially successful but before they had developed much traffic they were overtaken by the onset of highway competition. All four lines, which had totalled 212 km (132 miles), were closed in the 1950s and 1960s although part of one, the Upper Ferntree Gully to Gembrook line, has been restored as a tourist line. This railway in the early 1920s was notable in that it had a considerable commuter traffic, being close to Melbourne.

South Africa

One part of the British Empire that did not adhere to the 750 mm (2 ft 6 in) standard was South Africa, where 600 mm (2 ft) was favoured. The Germans introduced their 600 mm (2 ft) Feldbahn-type railway in German South West Africa, but this was either closed or converted to 1,067 mm (3 ft 6 in) when the South African Railways took over after World War I. In Natal and Cape Colony separate 600 mm (2 ft) gauge lines appeared around the turn of the century, when railway building was slowing down because of lack of capital. Since the 750 mm (2 ft 6 in) gauge was considered too close to the standard 1,067 mm (3 ft 6 in) gauge to make the introduction of a second gauge worthwhile, the 600 mm (2 ft) gauge was chosen instead—a classical example of muddled thinking. However, a great effort was made to ensure that this narrow gauge would have a substantial carrying capacity. Wide clearances were allowed, so that rolling stock could be wide, and the gentle terrain permitted wide radius curves and hence locomotives with quite long wheelbases. By 1914 there were about 1,046 km (650 miles) of 600 mm (2 ft) route and two more lines were built in the 1920s. The Avontuur line, a system running from Port Elizabeth, is the oldest surviving narrow-gauge line and is still in use for freight service. In Natal the so-called Stuartstown Railway, built originally by the Natal Government Railways, has the 151 km (94 mile) main line from Umzinto to Donnybrook that featured in the novel *Cry the Beloved Country*. It carries timber and farm products, as well as sugar beet in season. Several other lines are still in use, some with a passenger service. Steam traction is used including some modern Garratt-type locomotives.

USA

In the USA narrow-gauge lines were less popular than in Europe, except in a few states. The celebrated 'Maine Two-Footers' originated in the 1870s when George Mansfield, a New Englander who had seen narrow-gauge operations in Wales, persuaded the promoters of the Billerica & Bedford Railroad to adopt the 600 mm (2 ft) gauge. This they did but it did not prevent their line from going bankrupt within a few years of completion. The track and equipment were sold to the fledgling Sandy River Railroad nearby, which in 1908 became a basic element of the Sandy River and Rangeley Lakes Railroad, an amalgamation of the various Maine narrow-gauge lines. However, the mainline Maine Central Railroad obtained control in 1911. The following three decades witnessed the familiar story of gradual abandonment, first of passenger service and then of entire lines. The last line was closed in 1941 although some locomotives and rolling stock were salvaged to form the basis of a short line in Massachusetts. This, the Edaville Railroad, is now operated as a tourist line. Another narrow-gauge line which partly survives as a tourist attraction is the 915 mm (3 ft) gauge East Tennesee and Western.

This width was also the chosen gauge of many railroads in Colorado where the Rocky Mountain terrain made narrow gauge especially advantageous. In 1942, of the 2,253 km (1,400 miles) of narrow-gauge route in the USA, 1,448 km (900 miles) were in Colorado. These lines followed a winding course through the mountains, taking out minerals and timber and also running a passenger service. The latter was typically, but by no means always, provided by gasoline-powered railcars. The main-line Denver & Rio Grande Western owned much of the Colorado narrow-gauge mileage, including the last section to survive. Part, in fact, is still functioning as the 72 km (45 mile) Silverton Railway, which operates a summer tourist train hauled by one or other of the original steam locomotives. Another 915 mm (3 ft) line was the Sumpter Valley Railroad in Oregon. Known locally as the Polygamy Central Railroad, because most of its shareholders were Mormons, the line carried lumber and minerals outwards and beer for the miners inwards.

The most successful of the 915 mm (3 ft) gauge railways, surprisingly, ran over some of North America's bleakest territory. The White Pass & Yukon Railway was opened in 1900, three years after the Klondike gold rush had seemed to promise marvellous prosperity for the region. The trek to White Horse, the centre of the Yukon territory, was a dangerous and fearsome adventure; but building a railroad from tidewater at Skagway, Alaska, over the mountains to White Horse was regarded as an impossible enterprise. After all, most of the line would be well above the tree-line, and parts could expect to receive 10 m (30 ft) of snow each winter. Yet it was done by a combination of English financiers and Canadian engineers. It was 178 km (110 miles) long and climbed incessantly almost the whole way, some gradients being as steep as 3.9 per cent (1 in 27) and with curves equally forbidding. Despite the collapse of the gold rush the line continued to operate; indeed, the situation of the Klondike would have been much worse without the Railway. In the inter-war years it made a pathetic although not entirely unpromising effort to develop a tourist traffic. At last, during World War II, it obtained the heavy traffic for which it was suited. It was taken over by the US Army, that sometimes needed to operate more than fifteen trains daily. However, it was worn out by 1945 and with declining traffic seemed likely to meet the fate of narrow-gauge lines facing similar circumstances in Europe. But British finance again came to the rescue and a new company was formed. Mineral traffic from the Yukon has developed rapidly and the railway takes this down to Skagway for shipment. It also owns a very profitable oil pipeline and a regional road-transport enterprise. Its lead and zinc traffic is, unusually, loaded into containers at the mines and transported in that form. The container ship introduced in 1955 was said to be the world's first, and the Railway may well have been the first to provide rail–ship container services. The ore trains are 1,000-tonne loads, hauled by Canadian-built 1,200 hp diesel locomotives that are claimed to be the most powerful locomotives built for the narrow gauge. The tourist traffic is at last developing with, in summer, a regular steamship landing passengers for a trip up the line as far as Bennett where they take lunch in the bleakest imaginable landscape. In addition, the Railway operates a weekday passenger service from Skagway to White Horse.

The White Pass & Yukon is, perhaps, the most successful of the world's narrow-gauge lines. But although the survival rate of such railways has been exceptionally low, there are several parts of the world whose social and economic life still depends on this rare form of transportation.

Suburban and Commuter Railways

by John Westwood The establishment and development of suburban and commuter networks.

The terms 'commuter' and 'suburban' are two of many words which entered the language during the railway age. Railway transport enabled people to work in an old urban area while living in new settlements in the nearby countryside, and such residential areas were soon described as sub-urban. When the railways offered suburban passengers weekly, monthly, quarterly or annual tickets at reduced rates the word 'commuter' was used, at first in America, to describe those who commuted their daily payments into one periodical lump sum. In most countries commuters are by far the most numerous type of passenger but usually they are also the least profitable.

Although most commuters travel on short-distance trains using the tracks of main-line services, some railways have been built especially to attract commuter traffic. In many countries the first railways were what would now be called commuter lines. In Germany the Nürnberg to Fürth line, in France the Paris to St Germain, and in Russia the St Petersburg to Tsarskoye Selo were pioneer lines which nowadays carry a heavy commuter traffic. Later in the nineteenth century—when railway managements believed, rightly or wrongly, that suburban services were a paying proposition—lines were built out of cities in the hope, realized only too successfully, of inducing city workers to buy new houses in the countryside thereby creating new communities dependent on daily rail transport. In the age of the automobile, passengers deserted the railway in favour of the highway but, after a decade or two in which local governments believed that all problems could be solved by expressways, there is now a trend towards reinstating old, and creating new, suburban services, with the railways being compensated for the attendant financial losses.

The growth and needs of suburban traffic

It was in the 1850s and 1860s that European railways began to foster their suburban traffic. Around London, for example, the railways which converged on the capital from all directions found that their wayside stations just outside the city were encouraging builders to erect houses and city workers to buy them. Gradually the traffic from these stations built up so that it was no longer expedient to handle it by ordinary stopping trains. Special rolling stock, and indeed special locomotives, were designed and built. As the new villa belt widened in the outer suburbs, inner suburbs developed too, following the introduction of cheap workmen's fares. It was the otherwise rather discreditable London, Chatham & Dover Railway which first introduced cheap workmen's trains, and in 1883 Parliament passed the Cheap Trains Act which required the running on suburban lines of early morning and early evening trains on which special low fares were charged. The Workmen's Ticket survived in Britain until quite recently and in practice was sold to anyone travelling on a suburban train at a suitably early hour.

Although railways sometimes used old main-line coaches and locomotives to handle their commuters, the bigger companies built special equipment. With passenger cars, the object was to increase the number of passengers carried by each train without lengthening the train beyond the length of station platforms. In continental Europe several companies solved this problem by introducing double-deck coaches, and this expedient is once more becoming common. Railways with sufficient headroom over their tracks can almost double their capacity in this way. New South Wales, with its intensive

Previous pages: *Calcutta-style commuting in London. Travellers crowd round the departure indicator at Waterloo Station during a train drivers' overtime ban. In general, the more intensive a service, the more disruptive are mishaps and labour troubles; the electrified railways to the south of London are complex both in geography and scheduling, and hence highly vulnerable.*

and extensive suburban traffic around Sydney, expects to equip all its commuter trains with double-deck stock, and several US railroads have also invested heavily in such vehicles. In Britain, although the Southern Railway did produce a prototype, clearance difficulties seem likely to bar this solution. Traditionally, the British suburban coach was a compartment vehicle with no aisle or corridor, and no toilet. With compartments seating twelve passengers face-to-face, and the entire length of the vehicle occupied by compartments, very high-capacity, short, and lightweight trains could be formed. Six-a-side seating was, of course, not comfortable, although in practice it was only between the city and the closest stations that the trains were filled to capacity. The arrangement meant that there were doors for each compartment, enabling passengers to leave and enter without delay; reducing station time not only shortened the passengers' journey but also enabled a railway to cram in more trains during the rush-hour.

The problem of peak-hours meant that trains not only had to avoid station delays but also accelerate rapidly in order to clear the line for the next, close-following, train. The need for this acceleration was one reason why electrification was adopted for many suburban railways. Prior to electrification, tank engines of good accelerative qualities were used by many railways. Even in America, where railroads usually preferred to save money by using old main-line passenger engines, or even freight engines, a type of locomotive known as the Forney-tank was bought by many companies for this service. Tank engines were favoured because they were shorter, thereby at terminal stations enabling an extra car to be squeezed into the station platform, and because they did not need to be turned at each terminus. In the most intensive services an arriving locomotive would uncouple, run back along an exit track, and back on to its train to take it on the return trip. A few termini had a traverser at the head of the track; the incoming locomotive would stand on this and be shifted sideways to the adjoining exit track.

An extreme example of the suburban steam tank locomotive was built in Britain in 1902. The chief mechanical engineer of the Great Eastern Railway, which carried a very dense suburban traffic, was faced by a move within the company to electrify. Being a steam man, and having allies in the management, he constructed an 0-10-0 tank locomotive of massive boiler, three large

The Great Eastern Railway's massive 0-10-0 tank locomotive of 1902 was built more for propaganda than operation. Too cumbersome for regular use, its accelerative and haulage power was sufficient to persuade the company's management that the London suburban traffic would be best left in the care of steam locomotives; electrification, it seemed, would only be a second-best alternative. Apart from its unsuitable weight and wheelbase, the locomotive only just fitted the Railway's height limitation; hence the undersized chimney and squat boiler fittings.

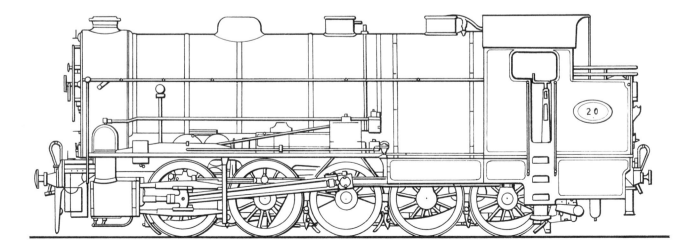

cylinders and rather small wheels. Since the advocates of electrification had been loudly advertising the ability of an electric train to reach 30 mph in 30 seconds from starting, the steam men demonstrated an even faster start with their new locomotive. With a normal load the engine accelerated at a rate of $0.45 \, \text{m/sec}^2$ ($1.46 \, \text{ft/sec}^2$) and electrification was shelved. However, no more locomotives like this were built; as its designer well knew, it was far too heavy for regular service. It was only the grandsons of the Great Eastern commuters who would enjoy accelerated electric services.

The networks of London, Berlin, Paris and New York had begun to electrify by 1914, by which year they were still the most developed of the world's sub-urban systems. However, by 1914 there were few big cities anywhere in the world which did not have at least some rail suburban services. It was not a European or American phenomenon, although it originated in those more developed continents. For example, the suburbanization of Australia was well under way, with the residential suburbs of Sydney and Melbourne extending like fingers along the lines of the railway networks. In India, the Great Indian Peninsular Railway was operating sixty daily trains in its Bombay–Kalyan service. With 19 intermediate stops, these trains, usually of six cars hauled by an 0-6-2 tank locomotive, covered the 55 km (34 miles) in 64 minutes, but electrification was only a decade away. In South America the Buenos Aires Great Southern Railway was operating out of the Argentinian capital one of the most intensive steam-worked services of the world. In Russia the com-muter services were less frequent. On the St Petersburg to Oranienbaum line there were 26 trains each way, the first leaving at 07.00 and the last at 00.40; with five intermediate stops the 35 km (22 miles) were covered in 65 minutes, making an average speed of 32 km/h (20 mph). The Moscow–Klin service was not very different. Its first train left at 07.30 and its last at 00.35; there were 16 trains in each direction, and with twelve intermediate halts the 89 km (55 mile) journey was completed in 2h 25m. As in other countries, concessionary season tickets were issued but whereas in other countries season tickets had nothing to do with the seasons of the year, in Russia they did: since the Russian urban middle class liked to spend the summer in their country cottages or bungalows, a special four-month summer ticket was offered by the suburban railway companies. There were also one-year and monthly tickets, and some railways offered two-month and three-month seasons. For those who did not have much ready money, it was possible to buy these tickets on the instalment plan. Otherwise a passenger could buy one of the ten-ride tickets. On the Russian State Railways, however, a ten-ride ticket cost ten times a single one-ride ticket, the administration claiming that the passenger still gained because he did not need to line up outside the ticket window ten times. The private Russian railways were more generous in this instance, but some-times the state railways offered a better bargain: on the Baltic–Pskov–Riga Railway, for example, a yearly ticket cost eight times more than a monthly.

Competition and financial problems

The financial difficulties which struck the railways of Europe and North America in the inter-war years were occasioned by higher costs, especially of fuel and labour, and by growing competition. Steam commuter services with their frequent stops and short runs were very demanding in terms of fuel per passenger-mile, while they were especially sensitive to competition. Competition from other modes of transport was not new, for around the turn of the century there had been a threat from electric streetcars. This threat, in Europe, had been met partly by electrifying and partly by accepting that the tramway companies should handle the shorter-distance traffic, which was less profitable anyway. In North America there was a different pattern, for the longer-distance streetcar, known as the interurban railway, appeared and this did much of the work which in other countries would have been performed by the conventional suburban railways. In the 1920s it was the private automobile and the bus which began to erode the railways' commuter traffic. At the same time the railways began to look more carefully at their costing methods, and discovered that what had been believed to be profitable operations had probably been making a loss ever since they had been started. Railway costing is a difficult process and can never be certain because in costing each service certain assumptions have to be made: how to divide the cost of the track between different types of train; how to share out the cost of running a terminus when it is clear that cancelling a train would not result in any cost reduction but that each train had to bear a proportion of the cost, and so on. With a convenient choice of assumptions it was always possible for managements to obtain the finding that they wanted, or expected, and this seems to have been the case with suburban services.

In general, however, despite growing doubts about costs and revenues, railways tended to retain their suburban services and often improved them by electrification. Whatever the true cost–revenue situation, managements could at least persuade themselves that electrification would reduce running costs and, by enhancing the attraction of their service, gain more fare-paying passengers. Thus in Britain the inter-war years were marked by the development of the Southern Electric system, which provided a dense network of lines through new residential areas to the south of London. With fast, clean and frequent services between these new outer suburbs and London, a new life-style was created for city office workers. Electrification may or may not have been a long-term financial success for the Southern Railway but it certainly added millions of pounds to property values in the electrified areas.

It began to be realized that the phenomenon of the peak-hour might be responsible for the difficulty of running commuter services at a profit. In order to accommodate three or four hours of intense traffic each day, trains, stations, and often track had to be provided which would hardly be used for the other twenty hours. When old locomotives and rolling stock were used — equipment which had long passed its depreciation life — this situation did not look too bad in the accounts. But since electrification is really only justified if its high capital cost can be spread over a high traffic volume, this problem seemed to grow as the suburban railways were modernized. Attracting a new type of off-peak traffic by offering cheap fares in the middle of the day was one commonly-practised attempt to improve this situation. To some extent it succeeded, especially in creating a shoppers' traffic of housewives going into the nearest town. But this was an alleviation rather than a complete solution. The obvious remedy, for a classical economist, would have been to raise commuter fares until they covered costs; but this was impossible for two reasons. Firstly, railways could never convincingly state what their costs really were. Secondly, no government could have permitted a fares increase which might have resulted in such a large rise in the living costs of so many people. A third solution was to withdraw from the suburban passenger service. Some railways did move a little in this direction but, again, so many people would have been adversely affected that, through different ways in different countries, governments persuaded the railways to continue to carry loss-making suburban passengers. In the USA after World War II it was the financial burden of commuter services that drove at least one major railroad into bankruptcy, and others were so impoverished by them that they could not find the capital to improve their other services. Nor had they any incentive to invest in new suburban trains so, instead of reaping public appreciation for the sacrifices they were making for their commuters, they were criticized loud and long for their poor facilities.

In America and Europe, despite the low fares, the postwar commuter was glad to desert the train in favour of his own car. City governments in the 1950s and 1960s were only too glad to spend the taxpayers' money on wide expressways to accommodate the peak-hour automobile traffic. But the novelty soon wore off, the expressways soon seemed to be less grandiose than they once were, and city populations soon realized that even if the whole town area were razed and asphalted there would always be demand for more roads and more parking space. Road-building had not been entirely unwelcome to the railways; their commuter trains lost traffic but local governments, proud of their new expressways, became more willing to allow the railroads to drop passenger services. So when, in the late 1960s, it was realized that a single railway track could carry as many passengers as a 10-lane highway, there were not many railroad commuter services left. The railways could be usually obliged to continue loss-making services but there was no way to force them to reinstate them once they had been withdrawn.

Subsidization and co-ordination of services

Local governments therefore began to enter into agreements with railways by which the latter would operate commuter services and be recompensed in one way or another by the taxpayer. In Britain, passenger-transport authorities were set up in several urban areas to co-ordinate railway and bus services and to pay the railways for the services provided. In the USA, as early as 1966, the Urban Mass Transportation Administration was set up to channel federal subsidies to similar schemes, and in 1973 a step was taken which ten years previously would have been unthinkable: the Federal-Aid Highway Act made it possible to transfer to railway schemes money already allocated for inter-state highways. In continental Europe the change was less dramatic, for a more rational approach had never quite been abandoned even at the height of the enthusiasm for expensive city highway schemes. In Germany, especially, the S-bahn concept was long established, in which the state railway operated city commuter services in close co-ordination with the short-distance tram, bus and underground services run by the city transport departments. But even in Germany the past decade has witnessed a considerable increase in the funds made available for introducing new S-bahns, as in Munich, Cologne, and Stuttgart, and for improving existing S-bahns. In the Netherlands, where almost all internal services have a commuting clientele, the government was quick to acknowledge in 1967 that it was worthwhile to maintain a frequent, fast and attractive service of trains even at a considerable loss, for the benefit of removing cars from the roads was worth more than the losses made by these trains.

In American suburban services, just as there is a great variety of equipment, so is there a variety of subsidizing agreements. The three biggest city transportation authorities (New York, Philadelphia and Chicago) contract to purchase certain services from the railroads while setting the fares, deciding the schedules, and using a federal subsidy to help cover the loss. In other cases an authority may simply pay a grant to the railroad. Another device, which sometimes seems more palatable to the taxpayer, involves city ownership of trains, tracks, and stations. However, these ways to reinvigorate suburban rail service have as yet only slightly alleviated the urban-transport problem. Less than one per cent of American workers travel to their jobs by rail, although this figure increases to eight per cent in the case of New York and Philadelphia. In New York, the Long Island Railroad, always virtually a commuter railroad, is now owned by New York State, and represents the biggest commitment by a non-federal public body to suburban rail transport. In other American cities the old-style, unloved commuter train still lingers on. San Francisco has a single commuter route towards San Jose. It makes great losses but the Southern Pacific Railroad receives no subsidies and continues to operate it only because local legislation prevents its withdrawal.

Some current systems

Toronto

One of the best-planned and most successful of the new subsidized commuter services is that of GO (Government of Ontario) at Toronto. Situated on the north shore of Lake Ontario, Toronto's suburbs expanded on either side of the city along the Lakeshore until, by the mid-1960s, there were almost 400,000 residents in those suburbs—more than four times the pre-war population.

Rush-hour traffic began to choke the highways, and when expressways were built they soon reached maximum traffic levels. The highway commuter found himself spending an increasing proportion of his time sitting in traffic hold-ups or searching for a city parking space. Fortunately, the main line of the Canadian National Railways also paralleled the Lakeshore, so a better and more intensive commuter service seemed a convenient solution. At the time the CNR was operating a handful of commuter trains along the route but these were of the traditional kind and were unlikely to attract automobile owners. One difficulty was that until a good service was provided it was impossible to know whether it would be a worthwhile investment; that is, the number of commuters who would decide to leave their cars at home and take the train could not be determined, so a risk had to be taken. The Government of Ontario felt it had the resources to take such a risk and in 1965, with the CNR, it began to plan a 96 km (60 mile) commuter service using CNR tracks through Toronto, between Hamilton in the west and Pickering in the east. A fairly cautious appraisal suggested that enough passengers would be attracted to cover slightly less than half the operating costs. The government accepted this, as well as the 18 million dollars of initial capital investment, in the knowledge that just a mile of new urban expressway would cost 15 million dollars.

In 1967 the service began. The trains were operated by the CNR but were not of standard CNR design. Built by Hawker Siddeley of Canada to the order of GO, the coaches were largely of aluminium, unpainted, and weighed only 35 tonnes, very light by American standards. They were softly lit, provided with piped music, and offered 94 bucket-type seats. Assembled in eight or ten-car formations, they were push-pull operated, the car furthest from the locomotive having a driving cab. The locomotives were also specially built, and although operated by the CNR carried the green insignia of GO. With their 3,000 horsepower, they could offer 7 hp per tonne of train when eight-car formations were used. This was perhaps less than some electric trains but nevertheless permitted rapid acceleration to speeds of up to 113 km/h (70 mph) between stations. For off-peak services nine railcars with 330 hp Rolls-Royce diesel engines were provided. Initially there was a train every twenty minutes in the rush hour, and hourly at other times, with the first train leaving at 6 am and the last at midnight. Fares were fixed at a level to make it cheaper to leave the car at home. The results exceeded the expectations; the anticipated number of daily passengers was exceeded within three months, as the word spread, and continued traffic growth meant that the GO operation became rather bigger than the service originally planned.

The GO services did not use the main city station as a terminus but worked right through from one suburban terminus to the other. This reduced congestion at the busiest point; the line through Toronto is the CNR's most intensively used section. Adding a third track at stations, and introducing two-way centralized train control, obviated interference with the Railways' normal traffic.

Paris

Cross-city suburban services like GO are becoming increasingly common elsewhere, for the same reasons of convenience. In Paris, for example, several cross-city links are being built. With high-density new towns being developed on the edge of the city, short-distance traffic has begun to expand, and to promise even greater expansion, beyond the level that extensions of the Metro rapid-transit system can handle. Moreover, without relief the existing commuter termini in Paris would reach intolerable levels of congestion. The first cross-city route is a 5.5 km (3.4 mile) east to west tunnel from the suburban termini of Nation and Auber, that hitherto handled trains to the suburbs of Boissy and St Germain en Laye respectively. The new link has five stations, including one at the main-line Gare de Lyon and another at Châtelet. At Châtelet there is a junction with two other extended suburban lines: the Sceaux line from the south, formerly terminating at Luxembourg, is extended to Châtelet, and the Marne la Vallée line from the east also feeds into the system at Châtelet. Thus the beginning of a Parisian network has been created from four independent commuter lines. Eventually it is expected that seven of the ten Paris commuter railway termini will have been converted into through stations. Châtelet seems destined to be the world's busiest interchange station with 55,000 passengers passing through in each direction in the peak-hour.

A section through the new Châtelet interchange station in Paris. On the lower level, the SNCF uses the two central tracks, being flanked by Sceaux and cross-city lines. Line 4 of the Paris Metro has two platforms, seen at the extreme left of the upper level. The excavation made for this station was the largest ever carried out in Paris. Wide platforms and circulating areas enable the station to handle 55,000 passengers per hour at the peak period.

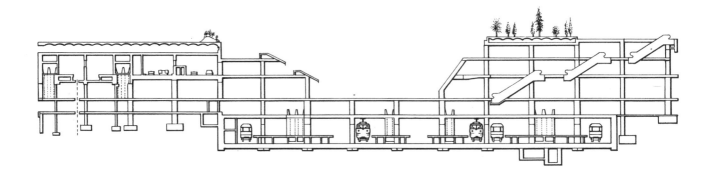

With two tracks carrying 144 trains in the peak hour, there is a headway between trains of rather less than one minute, which is more than conventional signalling methods can handle. Automatic driving of trains in the central area, with supervision by computer, is part of the solution, and another is a more sophisticated block system in which short blocks enable a train slowly to enter a station platform as the preceding train is pulling away. In the stations, the two tracks become a four-track layout, so that arriving trains stop at alternate platforms.

Although investment elsewhere in France does not match that of Paris, where magnificent stations like Châtelet (seven tracks, 34 escalators) have been built, provincial commuters have not been entirely neglected. Some local authorities have agreed to invest in SNCF improvements and have thereby given birth to new short-distance services like 'Metrazur' (Cannes–Menton), 'Metrodune' (Calais–Dunkerque) and 'Stelyrail' (Lyons–St Etienne). In 'Stelyrail', the local authority bore the entire cost of providing new passenger vehicles.

Stuttgart

In Germany, the new S-bahn at Stuttgart will run beneath the centre of the city but in the first stage of the project, after running on the surface as far as the main station, trains will go underground for a short distance to pass along a line which loops round and returns them back towards where they came from. One of the stations on this underground section, Stadtmitte, is unusual in that it is built to serve as an atomic-blast shelter for citizens and has massive radiation-proof doors at each end. Eventually the Stuttgart system will have a 165 km (103 mile) network. In general, it resembles existing German S-bahn systems, notably that of Munich, but its equipment and especially its train control system is more sophisticated.

Sydney

A terminal loop is one of the features of the Sydney suburban system; trains arriving at Sydney from the west and south continue past the main station towards the harbour. Some of them cross the Harbour Bridge (whose railway tracks are purely for commuter service) to serve stations to the north but the majority loop back at Circular Quay and return to where they originated. This layout was completed as recently as 1956, although it had been talked about and sporadically worked on for half a century. The extension being built to Sydney's eastern suburbs is a natural development from this although that, too, has taken longer to discuss than to build. The other big Australian suburban network, at Melbourne, is building a similar arrangement of a loop line in a tunnel at the city centre from which another new line will lead out towards the eastern suburbs.

British Rail's Great Northern line

Congestion of a main-line terminal by suburban trains was one of the factors taken into account in the planning of the Great Northern electrification scheme of British Rail. This suburban project, opened in 1976 (for the inner suburbs) and 1977 (for the outer), resulted in all the inner suburban trains terminating not at the main-line Kings Cross terminus but at Moorgate on the London Underground system. For this reason the trains are equipped to take current both from the overhead 25,000 V lines of British Rail and from the 600 V third rail of the Underground. The Moorgate terminus is closer to the centre of the

City, and even before the new scheme a proportion of the diesel multiple-unit trains used in suburban service ran to that station. In the peak period the new service provides eighteen inner suburban trains an hour from Moorgate towards Hertford and Welwyn Garden City; outer suburban trains towards Royston still leave from the main-line Kings Cross Station, with six trains an hour in peak periods, and the last train leaves at 23.50. Some stations, closer to London, have an all-night service, still quite unusual for suburban railways. These trains are mainly intended for railway staff servicing late-night or early-morning trains, but are open to the public too. The results of the new service have so far been promising. Because the project was discussed for more than a decade before work started, the previous services were equipped with rather uninviting rolling stock: aged diesel multiple units and the last locomotive-hauled non-corridor passenger cars used by British Rail. Thus there were fears that passengers who had forsaken the train in disgust would never be attracted back. But in fact, even though the opening days of the service were chaotic because the new timetable was introduced with massive publicity before enough trains had been built or enough crews trained, traffic climbed steadily. After a year's operation the new trains were carrying 16 per cent more passengers than the old.

Britain's Passenger Transport Authorities
The Great Northern scheme, in which £63 million of capital was invested, was not a local-government venture. It was purely a British Rail project although the central government, which supplied the capital, was closely involved. In Britain there are several Passenger Transport Authorities which co-ordinate suburban and urban passenger services. The first four of these were for the Manchester area, Merseyside, Tyneside, and West Midlands. In Manchester, for example, the PTA is responsible for fares, finance, and quality of service while British Rail looks after day-to-day operation and management. At the time this organization was established, in 1972, there were 26 rail-commuter services in the Greater Manchester area whose total deficit was about £5 million per annum. In accepting responsibility for this deficit the local government was not taking as great a risk as it seemed, because the central government was offering a 90 per cent grant towards the losses of unremunerative but socially necessary rail services. The big advantage of the PTA form of organization is that it places bus and train services under the same body, thereby facilitating the co-ordination of services. Hitherto, unlike continental European cities, there was little tradition in Britain of city buses running in connection with train services. With PTAs, not only were timetables co-ordinated, but tickets could be issued valid for both kinds of transport. In nearby Liverpool, the Merseyside PTA rescued and financed several train services which British Rail had wished to abandon. On Tyneside a new transit system on modern lines is being created. The latest PTA scheme is the new cross-Birmingham commuter service established by the West Midlands PTA and British Rail. This, operated by refurbished diesel multiple-unit trains, runs over existing main-line trackage from Sutton Coldfield in the north-east to Longbridge in the south-west with occasional trains running from Lichfield. The service was opened in May 1978 in the hope that it would reduce congestion of the parallel main road. A number of new stations were built and bus connections were provided at certain stations. A good service was provided; with four trains an hour in off-peak periods, would-be passengers could feel that they could just walk along to the station and would not

have long to wait. By British standards, the operating day was quite long: the first train left Longbridge at 06.35 and the last at 23.10.

It is too early to judge how successful this Birmingham scheme will be. Regular commuters are quite slow to break old habits and it may be several years before a new service can build up its clientele to a worthwhile volume. What seems certain from British and European experience is that for these schemes to be successful big thinking is required. A local authority must be prepared to bear heavy losses for several years and must not succumb to the temptation of reducing its services. Train-service cuts, though they might be very tempting when certain trains carry only one or two passengers, make the overall service less attractive. Frequency of service, reliability, and fares which seem no more than the costs of travelling by private car, are the main elements of an attractive scheme. There have been several such suburban projects which have not succeeded. One example is the short length of line between Derby and the industrial suburb of Sinfin. The Derby council negotiated with British Rail for a diesel-train service on this line. After some bickering the two bodies reached agreement, the line was improved, a couple of simple stations built, and a train service announced. However, although in the initial week or two a satisfying number of passengers tried the new trains, most did not come back for more. Apparently the frequency of service was quite unattractive; with only a handful of trains the would-be passenger found he had to plan his activity around the train schedule, which is irksome to those who are used to a frequent bus service or to their own cars. Also, the trains were provided simply by extending the run of diesel multiple units arriving at Derby from elsewhere. Thus the new commuter service was operated by trains which might be late because of delays encountered earlier and might be dirty from previous use. The first reaction to declining passenger numbers was to reduce the service still further, and that could only reduce the number of passengers. In retrospect, it would seem that this service, which was quite sensible in its aims and its means, failed to gain impetus because economy was given precedence over service.

Japan, India and Russia

Some of the most massive commuter operations take place in Japan, India and Russia. A common characteristic of these three countries is the sheer size of the passenger traffic and the running of tightly crowded trains. In the Tokyo suburban service there are the legendary people-pushers, specially-hired men who push the passengers into the tightly packed trains so that the doors may be closed. In India, the Bombay and Calcutta commuter trains are probably as heavily loaded as those in Tokyo; Indians do not need to be pushed into the trains, because if there is no more room they are prepared to hang on the outside and the doors are therefore usually kept open. The standard electric multiple-unit train in the Bombay and Calcutta service is of nine cars, and is officially reckoned to carry 1,800 passengers when standing passengers are dense enough to touch, but not dense enough to crush each other. In reality, such trains often carry 3,000 or more travellers. Inside, they are so tightly packed that even pickpocketing is impossible. Outside, passengers hang on to projections along the sides and between the vehicles and there are some brave spirits who ride on the roof, carefully watching the movement of the overhead conductor wire. Even at off-peak periods there is severe overcrowding, enough to mean that for the old and weak, unable to fight their way on to the trains, there is in effect no service. How this situation might be alleviated without enormous capital expenditure has been occupying the planners of the two cities for two decades but apart from the start of a rapid-transit system in Calcutta, which should relieve the railway of short-distance riders, not much has been done. The train service is already as dense as line capacity will allow; the trains are already as long as the station platforms, and double-deck cars are difficult to introduce because of the low clearance beneath the catenary. The problem seems therefore likely to get worse, if that is possible. It was reckoned in the early 1970s that the Bombay suburban lines (essentially sections of the two main lines out of the city) were carrying two-million passengers daily, and the population of Bombay may well have grown by three times by the end of the 1980s. A dense train service covers the traffic: on just one line, from 04.28 to 01.00, 150 trains leave Bombay for the suburbs. On the other two big Indian commuter networks, the entirely-steam Secunderabad lines and the mainly-steam Madras lines, the situation is a little easier, though uncomfortable.

The shifting of responsibility for suburban services on to local governments is not new. In the 1920s in the young Soviet Union the city Soviet of Baku was allowed to take over the suburban line out to the oil refineries at Sabunichi. This line, operated by old locomotives and cars, provided such a slow and unreliable service that its worker passengers were very discontented with it, and showed it. The city Soviet appealed to the commissariat of railways to electrify this line but the commissariat refused; it had more important things to think about and, besides, there were no electric railways in Russia to provide experience. The Soviet, after taking over the line, successfully electrified it but when, some years later, the commissariat did electrify one of its own lines, it was the latter which was claimed to be the USSR's first electrified railway.

In 1975, of the Soviet Railways' 3,470 million passengers, about 90 per cent were commuters. Moscow and Leningrad account for about two thirds of this traffic but this proportion may decline now that other large cities are receiving modern electric multiple-unit trains. As in India, rapid urbanization has provided ideal conditions for the growth of suburban rail services; this is a reversal of the more traditional situation in which it is the railway which stimulates the growth of residential suburbs. When, after the mid 1950s, the housing backlog began to be tackled in the USSR, it was not houses with gardens which were provided but high-density blocks of flats, with high-density residents inside them. This meant that the new populations on the city outskirts were concentrated, so that everybody could be within walking distance of a station. Another advantage of Russian suburban lines is that there is not such a pronounced peak period as in other countries. With widespread shift-working, Sunday and evening shopping, passenger flows tend to be well spread over the whole day. This means that most equipment can be utilized most of the time and does not need to stand idle for long periods. Expressed differently, it is more worthwhile to spend money on new equipment.

One of the biggest commuter operations is that from the Yaroslavl terminus in Moscow. This line was the second line to be electrified in the USSR and the busiest section is the 18 km (11 miles) out as far as Mytishchi. To accommodate this stretch three tracks lead from the terminus: one track is for long-distance trains and the other two for suburban services. The last train of the day leaves at 01.21.

This section passes over 250 commuter trains per day and it is envisaged that in future some lines may have train densities of 300–400 trains. Such densities are difficult to handle, so the Soviet Railways, probably more than any other railway, have built experimental multiple-unit trains in an effort to find the best prototype for series production. The aim is to produce a train which will relieve line capacity as much as possible, either by carrying more passengers, or moving faster, or spending less time at stations. In the 1970s 10-car sets predominated, seating 1,056 passengers and having an acceleration of $0.6\,\text{m/sec}^2$ ($2\,\text{ft/sec}^2$). A promising prototype to replace these has only eight cars, but these are longer, and the train exactly fits the standard 210m station platforms. It has regenerative braking which, perhaps optimistically, is claimed to provide eight per cent of the line's energy requirements. It provides 972 seats and its sixteen 220kW motors accelerate it at a rate of $0.7\,\text{m/sec}^2$ ($2.3\,\text{ft/sec}^2$). The Baltic Railway has been using a combined contact/battery electric train. It picks up current from the overhead wire for most of its journey but on the outer, non-electrified, section works from a battery. Such a train can run about 50km (31 miles) between charges, at an average speed of 44km/h (27mph).

Current designs, features and innovations

The design of bodies is quite important in commuter trains. If aluminium can be used, the trains' lightness means that the traction motors can accelerate it faster which is an important consideration. The door arrangement is also crucial. The benefit for line capacity of fast acceleration can be lost if trains spend too much time at stations so quick loading and unloading of passengers is valuable. Since with open-plan cars additional doors tend to reduce the number of seats, a compromise has to be reached. Russian research has shown that three doors on each side of the coach is best, an extra central door encourages standing passengers to distribute themselves more evenly inside the car and at the same time enables them to board and disembark faster. With such three-door cars station time could be reduced by at least one third, thereby decreasing the journey time by ten per cent and increasing the line capacity by ten per cent. However, the old-fashioned British-style commuter car, with six-a-side seating in compartments and with a door at each end of the compartment, was probably the most efficient from this point of view. Such doors may still be encountered on the Southern Electric services of British Rail although they are increasingly regarded as old fashioned. For the new electric multiple-unit trains built for its Great Northern scheme British Rail decided to dispense with self-opening doors since, among other reasons, it was pointless opening all the doors of a train on a cold winter morning at a station where only one or two passengers wished to board or disembark. Rather sophisticated sliding doors were provided but it was weeks before the passengers learned how to handle them. Moreover, the operation of these doors, in which the movement was power-assisted, depended on a fairly delicate mechanism which was soon out of action. The modification of these doors was one of several expensive and time-consuming tasks which had to be done while the new service was settling down.

Most commuter trains have a busy and wearing life, and in addition recent progress in electronic control has made them obsolescent. In the late 1970s, therefore, many commuter vehicles introduced in the 1950s and 1960s were being replaced by new equipment. In Holland, the NL has been trying out prototypes of its new *Sprinter* suburban trains. These are two-car units which can be combined into trains of up to eight vehicles. Designed especially for the high-density traffic lines, where stations are near to each other, these 1,500 V units have a 215 hp motor driving each axle, giving an acceleration of 1 m/sec² (3.2 ft/sec²). There are regenerative as well as air-operated disc brakes. Each two-car set has 112 second- and 32 first-class seats, and there are 26 tip-up seats. As in many modern suburban sets the first-class sections are little different from the second-class, the main distinction being the colour and material of the upholstery. No toilet facilities are provided, for they would occupy part of the space now available for 140 standing passengers. Each vehicle has three doors on each side, the Dutch evidently sharing the Russian preference for this arrangement.

The Dutch *Sprinter* can reach 125 km/h (78 mph) in 80 seconds from a standing start. Another modern commuter train, the Swiss RABDe 8/16, whose prototype was on trial in 1974, has an acceleration enabling it to reach the same speed in 71 seconds. Intended initially for the Zurich suburban service, this four-car train (two outer powered cars and two intermediate trailers) can seat 304 passengers. Unlike other suburban trains, it provides toilets but compensates for the resultant loss of seating space by having only two doors on each side of the cars.

A rather different approach to the ideal suburban train is that of the SNCF, and of the DR in the German Democratic Republic. Relying on a century-old tradition, these two railways have exploited the possibilities of double-deck rolling stock. Such double-deck trains are locomotive hauled, usually in a push-pull arrangement: this enables diesel or electric traction to be used according to circumstances. It is also claimed by the SNCF, less persuasively, that use of locomotives eliminates the traction equipment which otherwise would occupy space used for seating. The SNCF trains, which began to enter service in 1975, can be assembled as seven-, eight- or nine-vehicle sets. The vehicle at the locomotive end has a luggage compartment while the other end of the train has a driving cab. The intermediate vehicles can seat 175 passengers (with standing room for another 132) when only second-class accommodation is provided. A car carrying first and second class, in which the seating is 2+2 (that is, two passengers on each side of the central aisle), instead of 3+2, carries proportionately fewer. With 307 passengers on its two decks, a second-class car might be expected to present problems at stations with heavy traffic. However, the SNCF claims that in tests 300 passengers can unload in 90 seconds even though only two doors are provided each side. Admittedly these doors are wide yet with so many passengers, many of whom have also to negotiate stairways, 90 seconds seems an unduly optimistic figure, and the casual observer can only wonder whether the SNCF's experimental collection of passengers really represented the cross-section which a genuine test should have used. The trains have a maximum speed of 140 km/h (87 mph); their acceleration depends, naturally, on the horsepower of the locomotives assigned to them.

Another variant of double-deck stock is that used for the New South Wales suburban services. The New South Wales Government Railways for many years operated a few double-deck vehicles, typically placing one such vehicle in each train of ordinary stock. This lengthy trial period presumably enabled a really practical appreciation of their faults and virtues to be made. Evidently the double-deck idea was satisfactory, for more such cars were produced, and entire trains began to be formed of them. Moreover, in the early 1970s new and more comfortable double-deck trains were introduced on outer suburban services to Gosford and Penrith. Finally, a modern type of double-deck train was introduced for the ordinary commuter services. Based on a prototype with electrical equipment supplied by Mitsubishi, it was delivered by the Commonwealth Engineering Company from 1972. An interesting feature of these trains is that the power cars are sheathed in corrugated stainless steel whereas the trailer vehicles have aluminium bodies.

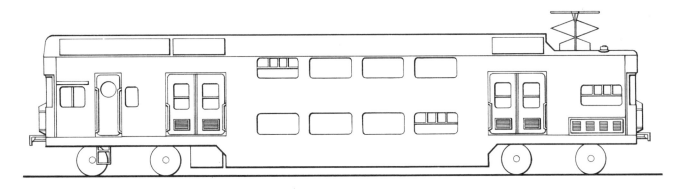

One of the world's largest commuter railroads, the Sydney suburban lines of the New South Wales Public Transport Commission (formerly New South Wales Government Railways) are also notable for their large-scale use of double-deck trains. This is a double-deck power car built by Comeng, a Sydney engineering company.

A number of railways, instead of ordering new equipment, have preferred to refurbish old stock. British Rail, which because of past profligacy has a surplus of diesel multiple-unit trains, made a good and economical job of renovating old trains for, among others, the new cross-Birmingham service. Such refurbishing includes re-covering of seats, fitting of more pleasing fluorescent lights, cleaning or replacing plastic wall covering, re-covering floors and redecorating driving compartments to make them better places in which to work. A more substantial renovation might also include replacing the seats entirely, fitting carpets and modifying the engines to make them more suitable for suburban work.

A distinctive renovation was achieved by the CIE in Ireland. As part of its plans to develop suburban services around Dublin, it withdrew a number of old diesel multiple units. These former main-line trains had their worn-out engines removed, were redecorated, and re-entered service as locomotive-hauled push-pull trains, handled by locomotives which were themselves elderly, re-engined, machines.

In the USA, commuter trains vary from shabby wooden-bodied stock, both in the form of electric multiple units and of locomotive-hauled trains, to the modern double-deck ('bilevel') vehicles of the Burlington and the Chicago & North Western railroads, and to modern 'Metropolitan' and 'Cosmopolitan' electric multiple units built by General Electric for the Long Island and New Haven lines. Some of the 'Cosmopolitan' trains on the New Haven provide a snack service, a reminder that commuting distances are rather longer in the USA than in Europe. This is usually the case for, ever since the days of steam, London office workers have commuted from places like Brighton (82 km or 51 miles). It is said, too, that since the introduction of High Speed Trains a commuting traffic has developed between Bristol and London (190 km or 118 miles). Thus the definition of a commuter has little to do with the distance he travels. True, a US Federal court did declare that New York to Philadelphia trains were not commuter trains, and therefore could only be operated by Amtrak, which is an inter-city transport organization. Amtrak duly runs them, but this does not prevent commuters from travelling on them.

Freight Transport

by Michael Harris The history and features of freight
operation, together with accounts of national systems.

From the earliest days railways have succeeded because they are uniquely good at performing one major task: that of moving bulk loads in consistent quantities; loads which require a minimum of handling and which travel more than a few kilometres. This remains the foundation of rail freight today. Railways compete for other categories of freight traffic but this is where they are most vulnerable and where profitable operation is less certain. In particular, much highly-rated, valuable traffic has been lost to road in most of the industrialized countries. Even so, freight operations on rail are largely profitable whereas only a very small percentage of the world's railways can boast of passenger services which consistently pay their way.

History

Three principles established during the early history of commercial freight operation now provide severe obstacles to competitive performance. The principle of a railway as a common carrier compels the operator to accept all types of traffic offered whether or not profitable. In many cases, railways have been compelled to maintain their common-carrier obligation and to provide a system-wide service for customers, even at a heavy loss.

Charging 'what the traffic will bear' was a relevant method of fixing freight rates in the absence of effective competition. Yet increasingly the method has left the railways to carry bulk traffic at low rates—traffic in which other freight operators are not interested. Attention has, therefore, been diverted from competition for high-value and profitable freight. As labour costs and operating costs have risen adherence to an unrealistic charging system, which is not based on the actual cost of moving freight, has prevented rail freight rates from achieving profitability. Government intervention in the fixing of freight rates during the 19th century, and subsequently, has saddled many railways with a service run at an uneconomic cost. In more recent times, public and customer resistance prevents increases to a realistic charge.

Consequently, railways throughout the world have been trying to escape the stranglehold of past legacies. The ideal solution has been the emergence of a freight policy which allows the railway to choose what traffic to carry, to fix special rates related to operating costs and to concentrate on those traffics which are most profitably carried by rail—bulk freight for long-distance transport.

By the late 1860s and early 1870s, a whole range of opportunities and influences set the picture for freight operation. Expansion of the railways throughout the world benefited existing systems: Britain exported 15,000 tonnes of rails to the United States in 1867 and 515,000 tonnes four years later. More powerful and efficient locomotives were increasingly matched by more satisfactory wagons.

By 1890, the United States' railroad network was virtually complete. Through freight loadings made long-distance rail shipment competitive and successful. In 1893, US Federal law made the fitting of automatic couplers to wagons compulsory—halving, incidentally, the number of accidents to shunters. Towards the turn of the century, American practice was in the forefront of railway development. British and European railways sent staff to study the systematic control of train working, the collection of statistics and types of high-capacity wagon. Railways became more businesslike in controlling their freight traffic and identifying costs. Some were hampered by outside influences: British railways found it difficult to modernize their own wagon stock when the bulk of coal wagons were owned by colliers loath to

Previous pages: Large international-standard containers being transhipped between highway and railway in Munich, West Germany. Overhead gantries are used for this purpose at most of the bigger container terminals, even though they are very expensive to buy and to install. For smaller terminals, handling smaller containers, simpler lifting equipment is sometimes used.

adopt higher-capacity wagons or to appreciate the advantages of vacuum brakes in place of the outdated 'pin down' variety.

World War I saw the world's railway systems stretched to the limit with war freight. At the same time, war experience proved the value of the lorry. Railways were still expanding, however, particularly in countries like Canada. Total rail-borne freight was still increasing.

In Europe, railways reacted to road competition by working with or buying out road-haulage companies. Schemes of road/rail co-ordination frequently worked to the disadvantage of rail. This happened in Northern Ireland where the combination of railway-owned and private road haulage was disastrous for rail freight. By the late 1930s, the old rigid freight-rate structure was a serious embarrassment to effective competition with road transport.

In the postwar period, the pattern of freight operation began to change radically in the face of road competition—although, in nearly all countries, the over-all volume of traffic carried by rail increased. Rail's share of the total freight movement in most industrialized countries started to fall by the mid 1950s. In 1962, rail was responsible for handling 43 per cent of freight in the USA, 46 per cent in Germany, 64 per cent in France, 37 per cent in Japan and 52 per cent in Sweden. During the next two years, rail's freight share had dropped still lower in each case.

Types of freight train

The well-established rail-freight service consists of the movement of individual wagons—in *wagonloads*. Almost everywhere, the traditional wagonload service relies on a large number of local railway-owned depots throughout the network—usually with collection and delivery by railway-controlled road services. The commercial basis is a quotation for individual consignments on the basis of published rates. The railways make up wagonloads or part-loads in their depots. The wagons are collected on local 'pick up' or 'trip' trains and moved between marshalling yards in 'rough' or unmarshalled trains.

All the wagons are 'common user' and none is designated for particular services. Until the application of computerized systems, there was little reliable control over the whereabouts of wagons in transit. Within yards, trains were made up on a 'first come, first served' principle. Consequently, railways were unable to guarantee the precise arrival of the wagon to the consignee—unless special monitoring procedures were observed. Universally, such services are regarded as obsolete and are loss-makers. The reasons are that the making up of wagonloads in many small depots leads to below-optimum payloads and loss of control over the wagons. Because these are common-user wagons, they can spend much time awaiting traffic and wagon turnround is, consequently, poor. Every time a wagon is 'handled'—placed in a yard or coupled or un-coupled to a train—costs increase because movement and shunting charges are high. Transhipment at depots to road vehicles is expensive and frequently leads to damage or pilfering. Such freight services cannot compete with road transport unless the road-haulage system is subject to government-imposed restrictions.

In the past ten years railways have rationalized the traditional wagonload service by closing small, inefficient freight depots and by cutting out part-loads. Railways have tried to opt out of the common-carrier principle by refusing traffic that cannot cover costs.

Freight services have been concentrated by restricting depots to main centres, by making up complete wagonloads and by delivering or collecting

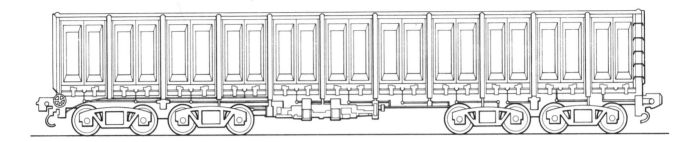

traffic by road in a radius of between 30 and 50 km (20 and 30 miles). Trains of economic payload can then be made to run between yards or the depots themselves.

Efficient traffic-information facilities have been introduced using either the telex or computerized systems. Marshalling yards have been modernized and automated to reduce handling costs. However, marshalling yards, even the most efficient, represent a break in transit that lengthens journey times. The trainload working in combination with rationalized wagonload services is, therefore, becoming more and more widespread.

Increasingly, railways have moved towards trainload or inter-block services. These are scheduled services operating, so far as possible, as complete blocks of wagons. Instead of remarshalling in yards, sections or blocks of wagons are coupled and uncoupled often without entering major yards at all. This service is becoming the pattern in Britain, Japan, Denmark and France. The wagons are loaded and unloaded in private sidings managed by companies and within their own works. The principle is to concentrate on door-to-door services between factories and to avoid expensive road/rail transhipment. The block trains are operated at fast speeds and are completely restricted to suitable wagons. Fully computerized information ensures control over wagon location at all times. Often the wagons are permanently allocated to a particular service or customer to reduce turnround times.

Unit trains are often company trains designed to carry one commodity for one customer: high-density, bulk movement quite often over distances of 50 to 70 km (30 to 43 miles) of, typically, coal, iron ore, cement and phosphates. The trains act as a conveyor belt between mine and port, steelworks, major manufacturing plant or power station. The name 'unit train' is significant in that this designation permits the railway to quote a special competitive rate based on the movement costs of a given tonnage or shipment. The wagons are often owned by the customer, restricted to the particular type of service, and designed specially for it.

To maximize use of the wagons, special loading and unloading facilities are normally provided and the wagons are not remarshalled but are frequently permanently coupled. Some unit trains load and unload on the move; this is known as 'merry-go-round' working in Britain and Canada. This railway operation is competitive with pipeline or shipping (rather than road) for such movements.

Inter-modal services combine road and rail, lorry or truck trailers being loaded on to low, flat wagons. The system is known as piggyback (in France, as *kangourou*). This type of traffic has developed considerably in North America, Germany and France providing long, fast transits, often with a network of

In order to obtain the advantages of very-high-capacity mineral cars without the high axleweights so destructive of track, the Soviet Railways use increasing numbers of eight-axle open cars. This example has a capacity of 125 tonnes, more than double that of a conventional four-axle car, yet the axleweight is similar. One disadvantage found in practice is that empty four-axle cars running among eight-axle vehicles are liable to derail at the higher speeds. On the new BAM railway in Siberia it is expected that only eight-axle cars will be allowed in main-line service.

special services. In Europe, where strict control over permits for international lorry movements is in force, piggyback services are allocated a special quota to encourage road hauliers to use road/rail facilities. Rail rates are competitive for hauliers in the face of increased oil prices. Other combinations such as roadrailers, in which the vehicles have road and rail wheels, enjoyed short-lived popularity in the 1950s to 1960s but were often inefficient in operation.

Container trains are a system of special trains of flat wagons for 7m (20 ft) and above freight containers which run between specially-built road/rail transhipment depots. The trains are operated at 120 km/h (75 mph) maximum. Pioneered in Britain this system has been followed in a number of countries such as Japan and on an increasingly expanded network throughout Eastern Europe. A European network of trains between special terminals in major industrial centres is operated by Intercontainer, a company set up by 23 European countries. Such trains are known as TEC—Transports Européens Combinés. Containers are also moved in ordinary long-distance fast freight trains particularly when only maritime containers are handled.

Freight services—worldwide

The 12,900 km (8,000 mile) Trans Siberian Railway (TSR) is one of the most remarkable feats of railway construction and a massive challenge to train operation because it covers such a wide range of geological and geographical conditions. Apart from the eastern section beyond Irkutsk, the TSR is electrified. The potential of the TSR within the Soviet Union for transcontinental operation has always been obvious but the container revolution in deep-sea trade has seen the TSR develop as the central section of a major rail/sea route between the Far East and Europe. The Siberian landbridge operation was planned in the 1960s to secure a share of the growing general merchandise traffic between Japan, Eastern Europe and inland points to Western Europe. Russian and Japanese container ships provide the sea link from Japan to Nakhodka, north-east of Vladivostok, the eastern terminal of the TSR. More recently, a new container port has been constructed at Vostochny. Traffic is predominantly westbound from Japan, the imbalance being three or four to one. Despite this disadvantage and all the problems of empty working of container trains, traffic has grown from 1,000 7m (20 ft) container equivalents in 1971 to some 60,000 in 1975. At present, only dry cargo is accepted for TSR shipment but specialized traffics will be handled in due course. The journey time via the 12,900 km (8,000 mile) TSR is some 30 days over a typical sea/rail haul such as Yokohama to Western Europe. What is remarkable is that the Siberian landbridge, which offers a short transit time combined with low freight rates, is fully competitive with many throughout-sea transits. The TSR also carries heavy flows of conventional rail freight, mostly minerals, as well as passenger services. Growing transcontinental traffic, together with planned exploitation of rich coal and mineral resources in Siberia, has led to the construction of a new 3,200 km (2,000 mile) railway known as the Baikal–Amur line which will be completed in 1982. This will cut several hundred kilometres off the TSR route for container traffic passing through the Russian Pacific ports and will make the Siberian landbridge an even more formidable competitor for maritime shipping.

The potential of the TSR for other flows of container traffic is also being exploited, particularly for the growing Japanese to Middle East trade. This movement has risen steeply in the past year or so particularly in cars from Japan to Iran.

The North American continent has also looked towards the development of a landbridge. The Canadian Pacific 5,220 km (3,350 mile) route between Vancouver in the west and St John could provide a four-day transit for container traffic moving between Japan and North America or Europe. Although no sizeable volume of containers has yet moved by this route, much work has been done to develop a system in which the transfer between ship and rail through a container port is smoothly achieved. Current scheduled freight services across Canada already provide an impressive facility and usually consist of a mixture of boxcars, road trailers on flatcars and containers loaded on flats. The sight of one of these trains made up of over 100 wagons hauled by three large diesel locomotives moving at passenger-train speeds across the prairies of Saskatchewan or Manitoba underlines the capability of rail for long-distance freight. Train 902 of the Canadian Pacific is typical of these services. Leaving Vancouver at 10.50 pm on day 1, train 902 runs through to Toronto (4,320 km–2,700 miles) via Calgary, Medicine Hat, Winnipeg and Thunder Bay to give an arrival in Toronto at 3.35 pm (local time) on day 3—a transit time of 83 hours, at an average speed of 52 km/h (32.5 mph) including 6½ hours for traffic stops. From the container port at St John, New Brunswick, complete container trains are run to Montreal conveying through maritime containers from Europe and the US mid-west. In the United States, the Missouri Pacific and Union Pacific railways handle a large traffic in maritime containers moving from Japan to the mid-west for on carriage to Europe via east-coast US ports.

In Australia it has taken time for through freight transits across the continent to develop into an integrated service. This is because of variations in the track gauge between the seven railway systems. Only since the 1970s have Sydney, Perth, Brisbane and Melbourne been linked by standard gauge. Interstate freight traffic has only really built up in comparatively recent years. During 1973, interstate rail freight from the eastern states to Western Australia increased by about 15 per cent. Unfortunately wagon shortages have affected the growth of this traffic—an average shortage of about 3,000 modern bogie wagons.

Through freight transits by rail across Europe and the Middle East to Asia are difficult because of breaks between railway networks. The United Nations Organization has, however, encouraged the concept of a through Europe—Asia—SE Asia rail route for some time. From 1971, a standard-gauge rail/ferry link between Iran, Turkey, the Mediterranean Coast and Central and Western Europe has been in existence. The route is through Tabriz, Razi, Van and Tatvan using the Lake Van and Bosphorus train ferries which avoids the previous transhipment problems caused by the break between the standard-gauge Iranian and 1,524 mm (5 ft) gauge Russian systems. The link through Turkey was made possible by the construction of a new impressively-engineered railway between Sharifkhaneh (Iran) and Van (Turkey). As yet, the limited capacity of the Lake Van ferries restricts capacity for through freight but direct rail transits from Europe to Iran via Turkey take some 30 days. Growing traffic between Europe and the Middle East has led to such huge increases in lorry movements that it is vital for rail to develop attractive services. Plans for development exist but have been shelved—a line along the shore of Lake Van will probably be delayed for 10 years.

Within Europe, close co-operation in providing through freight transits has existed since the 1900s on the mainland and since the 1920s by train ferry between Britain and continental Europe. Because of differences in gauge, no

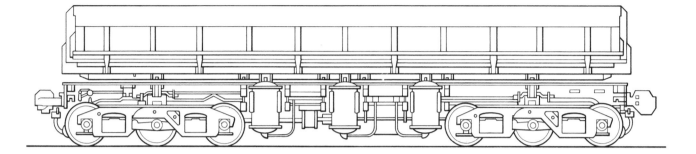

A heavy-duty six-axle mineral car designed and built in Poland for export to the USSR. Intended for ores, stone, and sand, it can carry 105 tonnes. The three cylinders in the centre are for tilting the body, which can move through 45 degrees to assist unloading.

train ferries have operated between Ireland and the rest of Britain, although there have been through container services since the late 1960s. Many of the technical problems between European railways have been simplified by the close co-operation of railway administrations through the work of the UIC (International Union of Railways)—standardized wagon dimensions—and RIV (Regolamento Internazionale Veicoli)—wagon design standards. Within the past two decades, European railways have worked together to develop rail links between countries. To exploit rail's advantages for container movement, Intercontainer was founded in 1968 as the agency for more than 20 European railways' container services. This has led to the development of a network of Trans-Europe Container Expresses such as those between Paris and Cologne and Rotterdam and Paris. In addition, there is the longer-established system of Trans Europ Express Marchandises (TEEM) trains. These are made up of ordinary wagons but also convey container traffic. An earlier co-operative agency in Europe is the Interfrigo company, founded in 1949, which manages perishable refrigerated traffic for over 20 railways and which has its own fleet of more than 7,000 refrigerated wagons.

More generally, the European railways have worked together through UIC towards an efficient uniform railway network providing fast inter-city passenger services, greater carrying capacity and direct freight routes between the main centres of population and industry. The outcome of a series of studies was the UIC Master Plan for the development of the European network published in 1973. Apart from identifying traffic bottlenecks for elimination the Master Plan emphasized the need for a new standard-gauge line between the Spanish/French border, Madrid and Barcelona—an important development for freight in view of the considerable traffic which now originates from Spain even with the present break of gauge between Spain and France. One further aspect of the development of an improved rail network in Europe is continued interest in the Channel tunnel; despite abandonment in early 1975, the European Economic Community has supported the development of better rail links between member countries and has recently published a proposal for EEC financing of infrastructure improvements. This proposal could hasten realization of the UIC Master Plan and, possibly, the Channel Tunnel itself.

Some international freight links across Europe have experienced vast increases in traffic over the past 20 years, interrupted only by the recent industrial recession from 1974 to 1976. In particular, there are the international routes via Switzerland's north–south St Gotthard, Simplon and Lötschberg

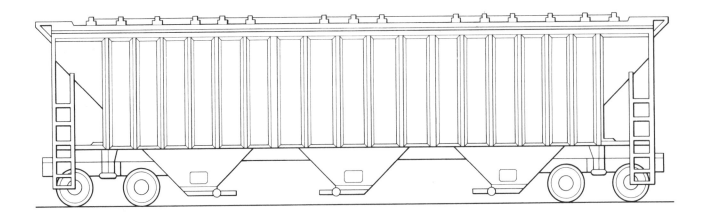

lines—most of the traffic being in transit to and from Italy. By 1969, 45 m tonnes of freight was being moved across the Alps in a year—rail taking some 41 per cent or 19 million tonnes. Between 1968 and 1969 alone, traffic grew by 10 per cent. The Swiss Federal government accordingly drew up a major plan for improving the Trans-Alpine routes involving the construction of a new Gotthard base tunnel, new cut-off routes and double-tracking schemes. Between 1974 and 1975, because of the world-wide recession, freight traffic fell by 30 per cent removing the need for immediate improvements. Plans for the improvement of the Lötschberg route are expected to go ahead at some time in the future.

Eastern European railways have also been planning major improvements for international freight traffic—rail has the major share of all land freight movements in the Comecon nations. Co-operation has progressed through Comecon to improve the capacity of major routes by electrification, increased dieselization, streamlined transhipment facilities at the breaks of gauge with the Russian system, and the introduction of international container trains. Better integration is being achieved by wagon pooling and computerized freight-traffic management.

The major advantage of rail for transporting goods over long distances is underlined by the determined efforts of governments and railways to improve international rail links the world over. Apart from breaks between the railways of neighbouring countries, other difficulties exist such as changes in track gauge, transhipment differences in loading gauges and the need to provide satisfactory transhipment facilities. Many of these problems are emphasized by the success of road freight in taking advantage of major growth in trade, by its greater flexibility and by absence of many limitations.

National systems—Europe

Throughout the European Economic Community and Western Europe generally, rail freight has grown steadily—although rail's share of all freight has been falling—and widespread investment, modernization and rationalization has taken place. In Belgium, there was a dramatic increase in solid fuels, ore, metal products and oil traffic—about 9 per cent per annum in the early 1970s—and further electrification is planned to improve freight. The Netherlands moves a comparatively small amount of freight by rail—with a recent decline because of the closure of the national coal mines. Rail has a 50 per cent

A high-capacity covered hopper car built for American railroads by Pullman Standard. Suitable for dry bulk goods, like grain, it has a capacity of 134 cu m (4,750 cubic feet). Three hopper doors guarantee fast unloading. High-capacity cars have been only slowly adopted in the USA, partly because the Interstate Commerce Commission, over-ready to believe that railway-freight rate cuts are 'unfair competation' against other forms of transport, has been reluctant to approve the lower charges which use of such cars permits.

share of freight traffic in France and a third of the traffic is international. Particular effort has been put into container, piggyback and import/export services. Private sidings have been opened at a rate of one per day over the 1973–75 period. Freight service handling is becoming fully computerized. West Germany introduced a transport policy—the Leber plan—in the late 1960s to divert freight traffic to rail. Much effort has been put into service modernization and the construction of private sidings. Deutsche Bundesbahn has enjoyed considerable recent success in carrying more container traffic in 1976 than ever before, in establishing a piggyback block-train network for transporting heavy lorries in 1,500 tonne trains and now operating some of the heaviest freight trains in Europe—5,000 tonnes. Britain carries a comparatively small amount of its freight by rail (20 per cent) but British Rail has recently launched a major freight drive by building on its successes with company trains, improving private sidings and expanding ferry wagon traffic to Europe. Rail freight has gained much of the North Sea oil traffic and will benefit from the development of the proposed Selby coalfield. Wagon control has been fully computerized. Italy is rationalizing its conventional freight services, developing its international freight traffic—likely to benefit by new 'cut-off lines'—and since 1975 has built up a wagonload liner-train network. Typical of recent modernization is the major marshalling yard at Alessandria with a capacity of 3,200 wagons daily. Eire is in the process of centralizing and rationalizing its conventional freight traffic and developing the growth of unit trains. Eire's target is to maintain the present volume of trade with a third of the existing wagon fleet.

Outside the European Economic Community, Austrian railways have seen continuous growth in rail freight but future expansion depends on route modernization across the Alps. In Switzerland, international freight traffic growth (despite the downturn in 1975) is the main target for improvement—helped by the recent construction of major marshalling yards such as Basle, Lausanne and Zürich. Thirty-seven new or improved marshalling yards will gradually take over the work of ninety existing ones. The 1977 railway modernization plan in Spain is based on phenomenal freight traffic growth since the early 1970s which outstripped the plan target. By 1980, the volume of traffic will be three times that of 1972. Although already moving more than 50 per cent of the country's freight, Spanish railways actually increased their share of the total market in 1972. By contrast Portuguese railways have had only a modest growth in traffic since the 1950s—Portuguese freight is still very largely moved in wagonloads. Some 3,000 wagons have recently been ordered for delivery over five years.

In the Scandinavian countries the most impressive developments in rail freight have been in Finland and Sweden. The Finnish railways have been considerably modernized since the 1950s and the upgrading of lines has particularly benefited freight. Traffic has grown at about 5 per cent per annum since the mid 1960s and this is expected to continue. Major effort has been put into improving long-distance freight traffic with the USSR. A new marshalling yard at Vainikkala (the border with USSR) is being built to handle two-thirds of the eleven million tonne import/export traffic and will coincide with electrification of the through route. In Sweden freight traffic by rail has benefited from severe restrictions on long-distance heavy goods vehicles imposed since 1974. A quadrupling of rail traffic with East Germany through Trelleborg has led to greatly increased train-ferry capacity. In Denmark, a fifteen-year plan aims to concentrate all general freight into a network of block trains. In

Norway, there are plans to move North Sea oil by rail over a new 240 km (150 mile) railway from Narvik to Tromsø, which would then be the most northerly terminal of the European standard-gauge network.

The railways of Eastern Europe all carry a substantial share of their countries' freight and although statistics are lacking, this share averages out at 45–75 per cent. Rail is especially suited to the heavy industrial bias of many of the Comecon countries and their own modernization contributes considerably to the volume of freight traffic.

The giant of all rail-freight systems is the USSR. The expected achievement —to carry half of the world's freight by 1975—seems to have been exceeded as the 1975 plan target was met one year early.

More than three million million tonne/kilometres of freight were carried in 1974. Some 4,800–6,400 km (3,000–4,000 miles) of new routes were constructed from 1971 to 1975. Electrification has been imperative for heavy freight working on many lines where freight trains of 9,000 tonnes operate. The maximum speed is 80 km/h (50 mph) for most services but some operate at up to 120 km/h (75 mph). Apart from the new Baikal–Amur line in Siberia already mentioned, a 720 km (450 mile) railway was opened in 1973 to serve the Siberian oilfields. An extensive container train service is operated.

The railway's share of freight movement in Czechoslovakia is probably the lowest of any country in Eastern Europe—along with Yugoslavia. The Czech rail-freight volume is increasing slightly, although much less than in the 1960s. A great deal of investment is going into a container-service network. There is similar emphasis on containerization in East Germany where there has also been much investment.

National systems—North and South America

The importance of railways in moving long-distance freight, particularly bulk traffics, is well demonstrated in Canada. The two main railway systems—Canadian National and Canadian Pacific—together with the various state and private administrations move a large proportion of Canada's freight. Major new lines for freight have been built in recent years such as the Great Slave Lake Railway to tap Canada's vast resources of minerals and coal. The volume of traffic has increased by some 10 per cent annually in recent years. Most of the major expansion has occurred in coal movements—export coal moved by Canadian Pacific increased by nearly 200 per cent in 5 years in the west. Forecasts suggest that there will be a five-fold expansion of export coal moved by Canadian National over the next five years and the railway plans to invest heavily in new equipment and facilities. Some of the traffic is moved by 'merry-go-round' trains. Recent studies by Canadian National demonstrate that a new railway from Alberta to the Mackenzie river delta would compete economically with a pipeline in transporting oil and natural gas. The railway could move two million barrels of oil per day and three billion cubic feet of gas transported in trains of 225 tank wagons hauled by as many as seven 3,000 hp locomotives.

Transcontinental freight has grown so much in recent years that major schemes of doubling and upgrading main lines across the Prairies and in the Rockies are in progress by both national railways. Future increases in traffic have led to major studies advocating electrification of 13,000 km (8,000 miles) of railway across the Prairies and in the Rockies over the next 25 years. Merchandise freight movement has contributed a large increase in revenue and a number of marshalling yards have been re-equipped. One of the most notable developments has been the growth of piggyback loadings over long distances. US to Canada fast freight services have been introduced—such as that between Montreal and Washington—some 1,200 km (750 miles). Both railways operate a large mileage of uneconomic branch lines in the Prairies serving wheat-growing areas and, as part of a rationalization programme, both railways want to close about 6,500 km (4,000 miles) of track out of the present 30,000 km (19,000 mile) rail network.

Rail freight operations in the United States are fittingly on a massive scale. The US railroads are predominantly freight carriers—over 97 per cent of the 309,600 km (193,500 miles) of line are freight only. US government statistics show that two-thirds of rail freight movement is carried over a fifth of the network. In general, the US railroads do not have an impressive productivity record—wagon turnround in days is nearly four times worse than West Germany, for example, and the traffic moved per motive power unit is under half that of the French railways. The problem is the large number of independent railways, duplication of services and a multiplicity of marshalling yards. Even so, the railways carry 40 per cent of all freight moved in the US. Coupled with strict control over freight rates imposed by Federal regulation these factors have spelt bankruptcy for a number of major companies.

US railways have generally found it difficult to attract new investment and much of the rolling stock, track, signalling and yards have become obsolete particularly in the north-east. Between 1961 and 1970, seven major railways went bankrupt in all, operating 43,200 km (17,000 miles) of track. The US government accordingly has set up a new independent corporation with the stock held by the Federal government. The corporation, known as Conrail, will control 24,000 km (15,000 miles) of railway in the north-east, and is expected to cut the present $300 million loss by half in five years by more efficient working and by reducing the mileage by one quarter.

This is the gloomier side of the picture. Many railways are profitable—such as the huge Union Pacific Railroad, the Southern Pacific and the Southern. Major investment is going into new equipment, particularly into rolling stock and facilities for the current and projected growth in coal traffic. Rail moves some 65 per cent of all US coal produced and from carrying 388 million tonnes in 1974 will hope to increase tonnage to 650 million by 1985. Most of this will be moved in unit trains made up of 60–110 wagons of around 100 tonnes capacity at speeds of 64–96 km/h (40–60 mph). It is expected that the railways will need to buy about 8,000 more locomotives and 150,000 wagons in the next ten years.

Other solutions to achieve greater efficiency are being found in the construction of new marshalling yards and national boxcar pools. The proposed St Louis yard would handle 10,000 wagons daily and replace 63 existing marshalling yards operated by 19 companies. The boxcar pool entered into by 40 railways will acquire 10,000 units and achieve more efficient working by the operation of a national fleet.

Until the early 1970s the railways of Central and South America seemed set for stagnation if not decline, bankruptcy and abandonment. One problem was the isolation of national systems, isolated lines within countries, different track gauges and outworn equipment. Many of the countries, particularly in Central America, operate railways of comparatively localized importance, often owned by overseas companies and restricted to particular traffic such as fruit. In South America, there had been a period of rapid expansion in the 19th century leading to fairly intensive networks, particularly in Argentina and

Uruguay, but with a record of traffic becoming increasingly transported by road in recent years.

Recently this picture has changed dramatically. After expanding the road network in the 1960s, the government in Brazil decided to recast its transport policies in favour of railway modernization to exploit the huge mineral resources and open the inland areas for industrial development. A major plan was drawn up in 1973 to cover railway improvements and traffic developments over the next 25 years. The more ambitious proposals have since been modified or deferred but the Brazilian railway strategy, largely calculated to boost rail freight, is one of the most impressive testimonies to the potential of railways in the world.

National systems—Asia

The value of a railway system in contributing to the growth of a developing economy can be seen in the dramatic growth of India's rail freight. The volume of traffic grew by 80 per cent between 1953 and 1961; in the next fifteen years it rose by 65 per cent and, between 1975 and 1989, the increase will be 100 per cent. Eight basic bulk commodities dominate Indian rail freight: coal, iron and steel products, ores, limestone, cement, fertilizers, grains and petroleum products. Most of these traffics move in heavy flows on a dozen or so major routes. This is ideal for rail to exploit its advantages. Such movements involve relatively low speeds—about 80 km/h (50 mph) maximum—and are suitable for transport in large-capacity bulk wagons which can then be worked as unit trains. Indian Railways aim to improve the railway infrastructure—signalling, track, running loops and motive power—so as to work most of it in 4,500 tonne air-braked trains. More efficient working and the replacement of steam by diesel and electric traction has enabled the Indian Railways to keep pace in traffic. Compared with 1950, traffic volume has doubled but only 30 per cent more locomotives have been added to the fleet.

India's railways are administered as nine zonal systems and consist of a mixture of broad- and metre-gauge lines. Work is in progress to convert the most heavily-used lines to broad (1,676 mm or 5 ft 6 in) gauge to cut out transhipment problems and increase capacity. Other problems revolve around freight rates since, as with so many railways, there are statutory controls on rates which mean that traffic is carried at uneconomic charges. Examples are food grains for famine areas and industrial coal. For this reason, despite moving the bulk of the nation's freight, Indian Railways have to fight to retain high-rated merchandise traffic.

New railways are being built such as the Banspani–Jhakpura line for mineral-ore traffic in Orissa. At the end of 1974, for example, over 320 km (200 miles) of new railway had been approved for construction and nearly 960 km (600 miles) of new construction or major reconstruction of existing lines was in progress. Industrial systems in India such as those serving steelworks are major railways in themselves. A good example is the Bokaro steelworks system in Bihar which has 256 km (160 miles) of track and handles 40 million tonnes of traffic annually with its fleet of 70 locomotives.

Pakistan, too, has seen much the same pattern of expansion in industrial traffic as India although on a smaller scale. The new massive marshalling yard under construction at Pipri will be able to handle as many as 2,500 wagons daily.

In Bangladesh 'consultants'' studies in 1973 indicated that the railway would be the most important form of transport in the Chittagong to Dacca corridor moving about 45 per cent of all land freight. A major programme of upgrading and investment is in progress.

The railway system in China is the major carrier of surface freight with the heaviest traffic consisting of coal, grain, cotton and pig-iron. Evidence suggests that, during harvests, the railways work at full capacity to move the millions of tonnes of grain. The railways are still thinly spread over the huge landmass. Since the Cultural Revolution, major railway construction has taken place: some lines like the Chuchow to Kweiyang line are to open up the interior and others such as the Chengtu to Kunming line are to tap natural resources—in this case shale-oil.

Many of the problems of freight operation faced by railways in industrialized countries afflict Japanese National Railways. The JNR freight services lost Y405,200 million in 1975 and efforts are being intensified to stem losses by closing marshalling yards and freight depots and by reducing services. A major plan launched in 1973 is aimed at reorganizing the freight business and concentrating on services that the railways can do best. There is a successful network of block container trains modelled on the British Freightliner system. Wagonload services have been remodelled making extensive use of computer control of wagon movements. Marshalling yards have been extensively modernized. Over 30 per cent of freight tonnage moves in single-commodity unit trains carrying coal, limestone, petroleum products and cement. Overall rail-freight volume has remained stable, rail steadily losing its share of the total freight business.

One of the most remarkable and least known railway systems is in Mongolia, nearly 14,400 km (9,000 miles) in length and constructed between 1938 and 1955 to the Russian 1,524 mm (5 ft) track gauge. The 1,152 km (720 mile) main line from north to south forms part of the main USSR–China link. Freight traffic over the whole system has quadrupled between 1955 and 1967 and includes much timber and coal.

In the Middle East, after a long period of neglect, improvements are in hand on a number of rail systems to develop through freight.

Existing lines are being upgraded or new lines built for bulk freight in Iraq, largely for sulphur and oil traffic, and in Jordan, for phosphates. Major development plans are in being or are planned to provide new links between principal towns and cities and ports in Iran, to Bandar Shahpour, in Israel and Saudi Arabia. High-capacity lines are being created from existing routes by upgrading in Iran, Iraq, Syria and Turkey. The result should be that by the late 1980s a collection of previously under-invested and declining systems will provide a modern infrastructure for through freight—having benefited from investment from Middle Eastern oil revenue. A major international loan is being used to develop the Egyptian Republic Railways as a major carrier of agricultural products. There is also a plan for a 560 km (350 mile) phosphate-export railway to a new port on the Red Sea. One most interesting prospect is the proposal for linking the Sudanese and Egyptian systems.

National systems—Africa

African railways are developing rapidly from the fragmented pattern of lines running in from major ports to the interior, principally for trading products. The exceptions to this pattern were in the north and south where more complete networks were built. Since the 1950s major new railways, principally for freight, have been built right across the continent. There has been a virtual explosion in railway construction since the mid 1960s with extensive railways

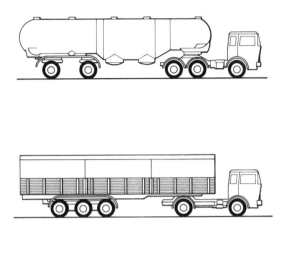

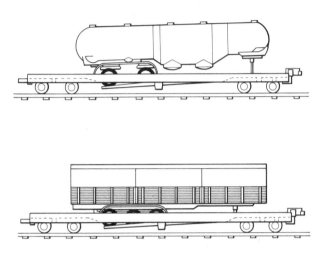

constructed or planned in Cameroun, Gabon, Guinea, Malawi and Morocco. The most spectacular and significant development is the Tan-Zam Railway opened in 1975. This railway, built with Chinese assistance, would appear to inaugurate a new era in African railways by directly connecting the east and central African markets and by providing a major new outlet to the sea.

This development has also proved correct the vision of railway administrations, for the World Bank doubted that the 1,866 km (1,160 mile) railway linking land-locked Zambia and Dar es Salaam would be an economic proposition. Less than 300,000 tonnes of traffic per year was anticipated after construction. Within a year of opening, the line carried one million tonnes of freight. African countries have recognized that the lack of an integrated railway network inhibits economic development and have established the Union of African Railways to explore ways of unifying the African railway networks, among other major tasks.

As in the case of other developing countries, major African railway projects are tapping the vast resources of raw materials. A 320 km (200 mile) section of the Trans-Cameroun railway was opened in 1974. A 320 km (200 mile) railway with standard 1,435 mm (4 ft 8½ in) track gauge is under construction in Gabon and is expected to carry 1 million tonnes of traffic annually, mainly timber. A 1,200 km (750 mile) system is being built in Guinea for bauxite and iron exports.

Of the railways in the north, the systems of Algeria, Morocco and Tunisia are experiencing record traffic levels, particularly of iron ore and phosphates. Other notable bulk traffic railways include the Lamco Railroad in Liberia which moves 13.5 million tonnes of iron ore annually over 274 km (170 miles) in its 12,000 tonne trains. The Mauritanian national system has a 640 km (400 mile) line which transports 12 million tonnes or iron ore each year in some of the heaviest freight trains in the world.

Many railways have had a phenomenal growth rate in freight business in recent years. Nigeria doubled its traffic between 1974 and 1976; Algeria doubled its volume in four years and the Ivory Coast is expecting freight tonne

The Piggyback system, or TOFC ('trailer on flat car'). This system flourished, especially in North America, before containerization became popular. Those railways which introduced it still, in the main, use it; this drawing shows a continental European operation in which high-capacity highway semi-trailers are loaded on to flatcars for the trunk segment of their trip. In this way the tractor units, with their drivers, are released for further hauls of semi-trailers. Unlike the container system, no cranes are required at the interchange terminals. On the other hand, the chassis of the trailer occupies valuable space even when, as illustrated, a 'kangaroo' pocket is provided in the floor of the flatcar to accommodate the wheels.

kilometrage to have tripled between 1970 and 1990.

South African railways have an established 32,000 km (20,000 mile) system. It is planned to increase the electrified network by 80 per cent between now and the early 1990s by which time 80 per cent of freight traffic would be electrically hauled. As in the case of the United States, Japan and India, considerable effort is being put into moving bulk traffic in unit trains principally to carry iron ore and coal. With the imminent containerization of maritime traffic to South Africa, a major container-train network is being built up. Wagonload business is being modernized by the use of computerized information systems, terminals rationalization and the modernization of marshalling yards. Current investment in freight is about three times that of passenger-service re-equipment. Two major new freight routes have recently been or will shortly be completed: a 480 km (300 mile) line, partly new, partly reconstructed, from Vryheid (Transvaal) to Richards Bay (near Durban) for coal exports and an entirely new 896 km (560 mile) export iron-ore line in Cape Province running from the ore field at Sishen to a new port at Saldanha Bay. The Richards Bay line has the annual capacity for some 30 million tonnes of coal exports to be moved in 5,500 tonne trains.

National systems—Australia and New Zealand

Australian railways' general freight problems have been discussed earlier. One of the most interesting developments has been the construction of new high-capacity mineral railways. The most spectacular of these is the Hammersley Railways largely built in 1965–66 and now extending over 384 km (240 miles) from the iron-ore fields at Paraburdoo and Mount Tom Price to Dampier in Western Australia.

The heaviest trains are 23,000 tonnes gross and 1,750 m (1,800 yards) long. Annually the line at present carries some 22 million tonnes of traffic, expected to increase to 40 million tonnes in the future. The three major iron-ore railways owned by mining companies in Western Australia—including the Hammersley Railways—carry about 62 million tonnes of freight a year over nearly 1,280 km (800 miles) of railway—a striking example of railway productivity. Other major bulk-freight operations are in Queensland—coal and phosphates—and New South Wales, mainly coal. Freight traffic is booming in New Zealand where in 1975–76 the system carried more freight than ever before and a successful container-train operation for export/import traffic has been built up.

Throughout the world, distinct trends are evident in rail freight. In Europe and Japan a determined effort has been necessary to rationalize conventional freight services to make them competitive with road and to pay their way. This has been done by withdrawing from the very general, small-load merchandise business and concentrating on building up block wagonload services, container-train networks or piggyback facilities. In North America, many of the rationalization processes are only just beginning. In developing countries the expansion and modernization of freight railways is seen as integral to economic development. In Africa, South America and Asia efforts are being made to build up a continental network of lines so that railways are more fully effective in their role as long-haul carriers. Universally, the opportunities for rail to provide conveyor-belt movements of coal and mineral traffic are being optimized so as to ensure that railways will continue to be an indispensable part of national transport systems throughout the rest of the 20th century and into the 21st.

New Construction

by John Westwood The most important
new railway projects since 1945.

Although it may have become fashionable in Europe and North America to regard the railway as an outdated means of transportation, in fact ever since the railway age began the world's trains have been operating over a steadily extending network. The shrinkage of the railway networks of the USA, Britain and a handful of other countries has been compensated by the opening of new lines elsewhere. And even in countries showing a general decline, there have been one or two new lines built to tap raw material resources or to shorten existing routes. Even in Britain it is not unknown for a short line to be built to reach a new stone quarry or mine. In the USA a number of quite long branches have been built in the past decade to bring new coal mines into connection with main-line railroads, and electric companies have built their own lines to link power station with pit-head. In the USA, also, there have been cut-off lines built and realignments of existing track. Even the Cajon Pass, the scene of legendary hill-climbing exploits by locomotives of the Santa Fe Railroad, has been affected by this, with the old twisting main line replaced by a straighter route.

The USSR

With the largest territory in the world, much of it hundreds and even thousands of kilometres from a railway, it is not surprising that in recent decades it has been the USSR which has laid the most new track. In its early years the Soviet regime completed projects started by the tsarist government. Notable among these was the Turkestan Siberia Railway which dropped southwards from a junction on the Trans Siberian Railway to the heart of Soviet Central Asia. Later, new high-capacity lines were built to reach resources of metal and coal. Among these was the Pechora Railway extending into the Arctic from a junction with the Northern Railway. This 1,563 km (971 mile) line was finished in harsh conditions during World War II, having been built by involuntary labour; it is one of those lines that are, literally, laid over the bones of its builders. In recent years construction has been mainly in Central Asia and Siberia, still in connection with mineral deposits. During the present five-year plan 3,400 km (2,112 miles) of new line are expected to be built. Among the most important projects are the Baikal Amur Railway (BAM) and the North Siberia Railway. The latter, built near Tyumen, already extends for 1,000 km (621 miles). Construction has been particularly difficult because of the swamps, which do not freeze even in 50 degrees of frost. On average, the builders have to shift 70,000 cubic metres of soil per kilometre (146,500 cubic yards per mile).

But the difficulties of the North Siberia Railway seem trivial in comparison with the problems faced by builders of BAM. The latter is not only the most important railway project in the USSR but has also been nominated as one of two 'Great State Construction Works', a status which gives it a certain priority in obtaining materials and labour, and also assures it of continuous publicity. BAM is a 4,400 km (2,734 mile) line which is to run from the Trans Siberian line from west of Lake Baikal right to the Pacific. Its alignment is north of the Trans Siberian. However, its purpose is not merely to provide a second rail route to the Pacific, somewhat more distant from the frontier with China: its main task is to carry raw materials out of central and eastern Siberia to the Pacific coast, where they can be exported or processed.

The idea of building this line is an old one, and a start was made before World War II. In fact, surveying continued during the war even though a section of the route already laid was lifted in order to provide rails for an

Previous pages: Japan's New Tokaido Line, the Tokyo–Osaka section of which was opened in 1964, is an outstanding example of the modern made-to-measure railway. Limited to fast passenger services, and built to its own particular gauge, it made good use of new constructional techniques. This picture shows one of its 'Bullet Trains', bound for Osaka, crossing a long reinforced-concrete bridge.

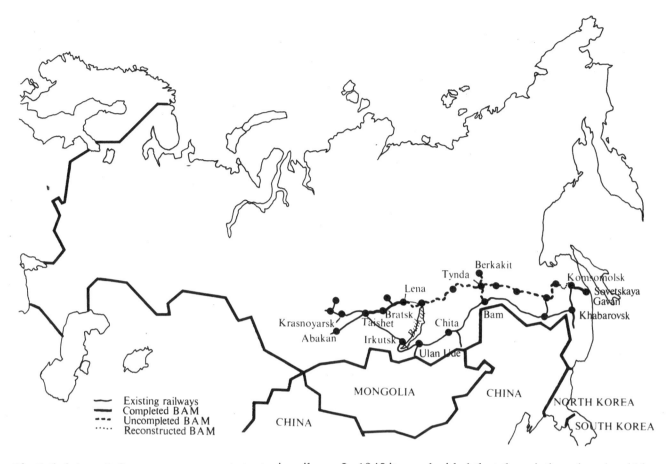

Existing railways
Completed BAM
--- Uncompleted BAM
····· Reconstructed BAM

The Baikal Amur Railway, showing completed work and construction still in progress. (The largest land area shown is that of the Russian Republic, part of the USSR.)

urgent strategic railway. In 1945 it was decided that the existing plan should be updated to permit diesel-locomotive operation and the use of larger freight cars. Also, the earlier engineers had apparently not taken sufficient account of the earthquake, low-temperature and flooding problems; it would seem that they felt that they had to produce an optimistic scheme whatever the circumstances. In the late 1950s the western section, from the Trans Siberian to Lena, was completed although a part of it had later to be relaid because it passed through land scheduled to be inundated by the Bratsk hydro-electric scheme. At the other end, the line inland from the Pacific harbour of Sovietskaya Gavan to the settlement of Komsomolsk on the Amur river was also finished. So the BAM project, announced with a flourish in 1974, was really the long and very difficult central section: 3,162 km (1,965 miles), together with the 'Little BAM' which goes from south to north from the new station of BAM on the Trans Siberian, across the 'Big BAM' at Tynda, and further north to mineral deposits at Berkakit. This 'Little BAM' was the first to be started for it gave access to Tynda which, being about half-way along the 'Big BAM', was a suitable construction base enabling construction to proceed both eastwards and westwards.

It had at one time been intended to lay a pipeline instead of a railway because the main reason for starting the line was to provide an outlet for Siberian oil production. However, it was decided that a railway would not cost significantly more than a pipeline and would do what a pipeline could not do: open up the country along its route and in particular permit the exploitation of greater timber and mineral reserves. The oil is to be sent by pipeline to the western end of the line then transhipped to railway tank cars which will take it to an oil terminus near to the Pacific. Here it will move by another pipeline to be processed at the refineries.

Completion of the line is scheduled for 1983. It will be interesting to see not only whether this can be achieved but also to what extent the natural obstacles will be overcome. Frequent earth tremors are one peril and they can cause landslides as well as weaken the roadbed. The condition of permafrost, in which the ground below the topmost layer is frozen throughout the year, also causes construction problems. For example, a bridge pier sunk into such frozen ground might conduct warmth which over the years will melt its foundation. Ground ice—water which oozes upwards, spreads deeply and widely, and then freezes hard—is another difficulty. Ground fissures, caused by differential freezing or thawing, are an obvious danger for the permanent way. And then, apart from all these, there are the difficulties of annual floods and of mountain terrain. Seven mountain ridges are to be crossed with the help of 24 km (15 miles) of tunnels and 3,700 bridges and culverts.

The planners are perhaps optimistic in their expectation of a 1983 opening, and even more so in their belief that the natural obstacles will undoubtedly be overcome. But even if the line is only partly successful in fulfilling expectations it will still rank as one of the greatest of the world's railway undertakings. There will certainly be extra costs associated with the physical conditions, and it may well be that in conventional accounting terms the railway will never pay for itself. But in terms of social benefit it will achieve no less than the opening up of a huge region which up to now is hardly inhabited. The line itself, though modern in its conception, is not highly sophisticated. Existing standard equipment is to be used, although there is a possibility that because it is being built to wider clearances than usual it will be worthwhile to build big tank cars especially for 'captive service' on the line. Nor has a final decision been reached about motive power. For the heavy trains planned, passing over long steady gradients, electrification would be the best answer in operating terms but it would demand heavy expenditure. The gas-turbine locomotive also thrives under such conditions and, the converse of a diesel, it does better at high altitudes where the air is thinner. However, the Soviet planners apparently do not feel that Soviet experimental gas-turbine locomotives are sufficiently well proven to be used on this line. What is most likely is that powerful diesel locomotives will be allocated to the line but that an early start may be made in electrifying the western part of the route, where tunnels and gradients will be most severe. The line is to be single track (although structures are engineered to provide space for a second track in future), so electrification might also be beneficial through the extra line capacity which it creates.

Canada

Outside the USSR, the most daunting conditions faced by modern railway builders are to be found in Canada—another country where construction is still proceeding. Canadian railways started as east to west main lines with occasional branches to serve the prairies and US connections. It is only in recent decades that expansion northwards has become a main concern. The 708 km (440 mile) Ontario Northland Railway from the Canadian National Railways main line at North Bay to the southern shore of Hudson Bay was finished in 1932 but this was exceptional in that its completion was hastened by the government's need to provide work at a time of severe unemployment. Another line to Hudson Bay—the Hudson Bay Railway, part of Canadian National Railways—had been finished in 1929 enabling a port to be built at Churchill from which, during the brief summer season in 1931, the first grain

The evolution of the rail in western Europe.
1: French bullhead-section rail as used on the Mediterranean, Rhone and Loire Railway in the mid 19th century.
2, 3, 4: Reversible rails as used by the Paris–Strasbourg (2), Paris–Lyon (3), and Ouest (4) railways. These could be found in use in the mid 19th century but in practice the idea of turning the rails upside down after the top surface had worn out was not successful.
5, 6, 7: By World War I most of the French railways were using American-style flat-bottomed rails. The Est Railway's flat-bottomed rail (5) was soon too light for heavy-traffic lines and was replaced by heavier designs similar to the 36 kg/m (72 lb/yd) rail of the Bourbonnais line (6) and the 37.4 kg/m (75 lb/yd) of the Nord (7).
9: The Est Railway's 44 kg/m (89 lb/yd) flat-bottomed rail was typical of French main-line rail in the early 20th century.
10: Outstanding, both in careful design and weight, was the 62 kg/m (125 lb/yd) rail used by the PLM Railway on its heavy-traffic route south from Paris.
13, 14, 15: Present-day SNCF standard rails, the 46 kg/m (93 lb/yd) rail for light traffic lines (13), the 50 kg/m (101 lb/yd) section for intermediate lines (14), and the 60 kg/m (121 lb/yd) UIC design used for SNCF main lines (15).
8, 11, 12: The evolution of the British rail section. Iron bridge-rail (8) as used in the early years of the Great Western Railway. Standard bullhead rail (11), favoured by British railways until the mid-20th century. Flat-bottomed rail (12) used on British Rail's main lines.
16, 17: Early 20th-century rail sections used in Germany. The standard rail for south German railways (16). The Prussian State Railways standard (17).
18: The German (DR) inter-war standard rail section.
19, 20, 15: Present-day German (DB) rails. The 49 kg/m (99 lb/yd) rail for lightly-used routes (19). The intermediate 54 kg/m (109 lb/yd) rail (20). The UIC 60 rail of 60 kg/m (121 lb/yd), as used by the DB (15).

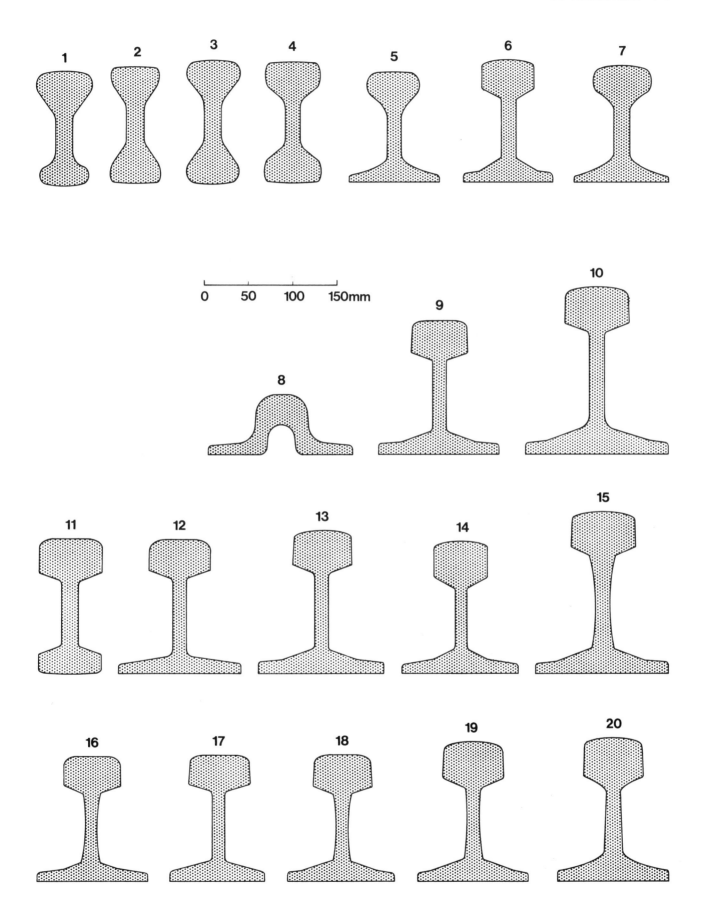

exports were shipped. Since then ocean ships have continued to visit Churchill, much to the satisfaction of westerners whose agitation for the building of the railway had been largely prompted by a desire for an outlet for their products which would be independent of the commercial interests of eastern Canada. The Railway also runs a passenger service which is increasingly used by tourists who relish the chance to view a sub-Arctic landscape through the window of a sleeping car.

The 820 km (510 mile) Hudson Bay Railway was built over harsh terrain, and the engineers experienced especial difficulty in its northern section which runs through a region of permafrost. When branches were built from the line subsequently, in order to tap mineral resources, the same kind of obstacle daunted many contractors. When the 232 km (144 mile) mineral branch from Sherridon to Lynn Lake was begun in the 1940s, 27 contracting companies asked for plans of the line, five came to look over the terrain, and finally only three submitted bids. Building a line in country consisting of nothing but rock, water and trees (and even the trees were too stunted to be used as crossties), where there was no human habitation, no roads and no usable waterways, was not an enticing prospect at a time when contractors could find plenty of other more agreeable work.

The construction of this Lynn Lake line had to be started from a single railhead and there was a 32-month deadline for completion. With temperatures of 55 degrees below zero during winter, construction had to be carefully planned for some work was impossible in such low temperatures while other work could only be carried out when the ground was frozen; transport of materials by tractor-drawn sleighs was one of these latter functions. The alignment of the line had been mapped out by two survey parties totalling about 40 men, helped by aircraft observation, and it was the resultant map, distinguishing the areas of solid rock, wet muskeg (swamp) and thick moss, which so discouraged the prospective contractors. The first drillings through the rock began in the autumn of 1951 and in that following winter enough tools and materials were deposited at selected points along the route to permit six months' work during the warmer season. When clearance work started, it was found that machine razing was less effective than hand labour so extra clearing teams were organized. Timber bridges were prepared before the track-bed and earthworks were started, because pile-driving equipment could be moved over the soft muskeg only in winter. Portable boilers supplied steam to thaw the ground so that the pile-drivers could do their work. Rapids had to be blasted during the winter so that when the thaw came there would be no floods to disturb the work. The absence of serious mountain obstacles and the generous use of explosives enabled the ruling gradient of 1.75 per cent (1 in 57) to be adopted. However, in order to keep down the first cost of the line, curves up to 15 degrees were accepted. The line was finished in late 1953, and soon afterwards the flow of nickel concentrates moved south from the Lynn Lake Mine. This was a heavy-duty transportation service which only a railway can perform but there were some side benefits too: freight rates to Lynn Lake dropped from the 60 dollars per ton of the sleigh operators to an average of four dollars a ton by Canadian National Railways. The miners immediately went on a buying spree, but this burst of acquisitiveness soon faded away when it was realized that the railway meant all-the-year transportation; no longer would there be shortages for the three months of spring when the frozen-hard terrain changed into a mess of flood-water and even aircraft could not function.

A train of empty ore cars on the Mount Newman Railroad in Western Australia, arriving at Mount Newman mines from the coast. Easy gradients permit these trains to be hauled by a single diesel unit.

The British Columbia Railway is unusual among new railways in owning a steam locomotive for excursion trips. This locomotive is No. 2860, formerly belonging to the Canadian Pacific Railway. One of the Royal Hudson class, its previous duties were the haulage of the Canadian Pacific's best-known passenger trains.

China, for perhaps two decades or even longer, has been the first or the second (after the USSR) railway-building nation. This picture shows the forbidding terrain through which many of the new lines have been built. It was taken on the Hsiangyu trunk line, completed in 1973 between Hsiangfan (Hupeh province) in the east and Chungking (Szechwan province) in the west. This new line has no fewer than 405 tunnels in its length of 916 km (569 miles).

Another mineral-carrying freight railway, the Hamersley Railways of Australia. As with most such railways, the operation is geared to one task—the haulage of ore from inland mines down to the nearest port. Having only one purpose, these railways can be operated more efficiently than conventional common-carrier railways.

In Alberta, an extensive system of new railways has been built in the north of the province. These form the Northern Alberta Railways, owned by the province but jointly operated by Canadian Pacific and Canadian National. In 1965 a new 611 km (380 mile) extension was built by the CNR for this system. This was also primarily to tap mineral sources, in this case the lead and zinc found on the south shore of the Great Slave Lake.

Another branch of the Northern Alberta Railways joins with the British Columbia Railway, thereby providing a link with Pacific ports. The British Columbia Railway has had a long and chequered history but in recent years has prospered and grown so that it is close to achieving the designs of its original promoters. The latter included businessmen with links with the Great Eastern Railway in England, which is why the railway until recently was known as the Pacific Great Eastern or PGE ('Past God's Endurance' to its enemies and 'Progressively Growing Earnings' to its friends). Owned by the provincial government, it provides a link between Vancouver and the interior lands of the north-east. Between 1921 and 1949 the extension of this railway, even the vital link between its few kilometres of line from Vancouver and the start of its main route northwards from Squamish, was unfinished. However, in 1949 a more business-orientated government restarted its development and in 1953 the important settlement of Prince George, already on the Canadian National's route, was reached. Three years later, built expensively on the side of steep cliffs, the 64 km (40 mile) connection between Squamish and North Vancouver was completed. Further expansion has continued and in the late 1960s the valley of the Rocky Mountain Trench was entered by a line which is being extended via Dease Lake into the Yukon. When the planned extensions are complete, the Railway should have a mileage of about 3,200 km (2,000 miles). Its main trunk line is busy with the haulage of raw materials, especially timber, to processing plants and to the ports of Vancouver and (via the connection with the CNR) to Prince Rupert. But although traffic has been increasing very fast the line is unprofitable in accounting terms, although the financial benefits it brings to the Province are many times greater than its book loss. It also runs a passenger service on the southern part of the route and in recent years has attracted attention by running steam excursions behind its only steam locomotive, a Royal Hudson acquired from the Canadian Pacific.

On the other side of Canada, Quebec and Labrador have been provided with several new railways designed to bring ores from the interior down to the St Lawrence River. In 1950 the Quebec, North Shore and Labrador Railway was started. This 573 km (356 mile) iron-ore line runs northwards from the new port of Seven Islands to the mining settlement of Schefferville. Heavy ore trains are operated, usually of about 135 cars, and they take fifteen hours for the southbound trip. As each car can carry 85 tonnes of ore the capacity of this line is very high, especially as modern devices like centralized traffic control are used. At peak periods more than 100,000 tonnes of ore can be moved each day, and there is also a three-times-a-week passenger service. The railway is owned by the mining company. Not far away the 1962 Cartier Railway, 306 km (190 miles) performs a similar operation for the iron ore of Lac Jeannine.

It is likely that railway construction in Canada will continue for many years. As in Russia, there are vast areas deprived of any means of bulk transportation but which possess rich reserves of one raw material or another (and usually several). New lines to such places do face the economic problem that more than nine-tenths of the traffic is in one direction so there are unprofitable

A heavy ore train moving towards the St Lawrence River on the Cartier Railway in Quebec, Canada. Single-purpose railways like this, owned by a company interested in the extraction of raw materials, are not a new concept, for the logging railway dates from the 19th century. What is new, however, is the size and modernity of these new mineral railways.

long hauls of empty freightcars, but this is balanced by the steadily increasing value of raw materials. Canadian National Railways alone is expecting to lay about 772 km (480 miles) of new line between 1975 and 1985, including iron-ore lines in northern Ontario and northern Quebec, and a 435 km (270 mile) line north from Terrace in British Columbia.

Australia

Another country of wide open spaces, Australia, has also been building new railways in order to bring minerals to market. In Queensland and New South Wales lines have been built in recent years to carry coal to east-coast ports whence much of it is shipped to Japan. The Western Australian Government Railways (Westrail) has been building lines to assist new mineral-sands mining ventures. Also in that province are several new lines owned by mining companies. The Mount Newman Railroad and the Hammersley Railways both own more than 320 km (200 miles) of route, served by 50 or so diesel locomotives. The Hammersley Railways attracted attention recently by acquiring a famous British steam locomotive, *Pendennis Castle,* with the intention of using it on excursion trains.

A major construction project has been undertaken by Australian National Railways in South Australia and the Northern Territory. This is an 831 km (516 mile) line which leaves the Trans Australian Railway at Tarcoola and is being laid northwards to Alice Springs. At present Alice Springs is served by a 1,067 mm (3 ft 6 in) gauge line from Port Augusta; the new line will provide a shorter route, a standard-gauge link and a more modern type of operation. Whether the new line will be extended through the hot and barren Northern Territory to Darwin is still under discussion but it seems possible that it will.

China

China is yet another country where there are wide areas, especially in the west, which are untouched by railways. A feature of the very ambitious plan for railway building has therefore been the emphasis on the far west, with links for Tibet and Sinkiang provinces. The south-west, rather mountainous, has also been provided with new lines. Notable among these is the Chengdu–Kunming line which has 427 tunnels in its 1,065 km (674 miles) of route. In the five years 1971–75 it is said that about 10,000 km (6,200 miles) of new line were built, and this rate, apparently, is being maintained.

The Middle East

The Middle East seems likely to witness a great extension of rail transport in the 1980s. In Israel a line of great strategic and political importance is being built southwards to connect Eilat, on the Gulf of Aqaba, with the rail network. In Syria the 742 km (461 mile) line from the port of Latakia to Aleppo and then along the Euphrates Valley is very advanced. It is of standard gauge and is being built with Russian assistance; its trains are hauled by Russian-built diesel locomotives. Egypt has a new line of 348 km (216 miles) laid south-westward from Helwan.

Developments in some oil-producing countries

However it is the countries enriched by increases of oil prices which have drawn up the most ambitious plans. Iran plans to increase its rail network from 4,500 km (2,800 miles) to 14,000 km (8,700 miles). Among the first lines to be built are a 700 km (435 mile) line through the desert to the Gulf port of

Bandar Abbas, and a 580 km (348 mile) line to the east which is to link up with the Pakistani Railways at a break-of-gauge station near the frontier. On another frontier, a rail link with Turkey has been in operation for some years. However, indications in the late 1970s that the Iranian plan was over-ambitious will probably result in the postponement of some of the projects. In Iraq a high-speed standard-gauge line is to be provided down the Tigris Valley, from Baghdad to Basra (850 km or 528 miles). There is also to be a standard-gauge line to connect with the Syrian railways. Presumably the narrower-gauge lines of Iraq and Syria will eventually disappear. In Venezuela it is intended to increase the rail mileage from 175 km (109 miles) to 3,700 km (2,300 miles) by 1990. In yet another oil-producing country, Nigeria, there is a plan already in action to replace the present 1,067 mm (3 ft 6 in) gauge network with a partly new, partly re-gauged system of 1,435 mm (4 ft 8½ in) gauge lines.

Developments in Africa

Elsewhere in Africa scattered new lines are being built, usually to tap virgin country. In South Africa a 204 km (127 mile) line is being built from Vryheid to Empangeni, to serve a new harbour being built at Richards Bay. The South African Railways also now operate the new ore-carrying line from Sishen to Saldanha (860 km or 534 miles), built by the South African Iron & Steel Industrial Corporation and noteworthy as a large-scale application of the new 50,000 V electrification system.

A new African railway of special economic and political importance is the Tanzania Zambia Railway, the 'Tan Zam'. This 1,860 km (1,156 mile) line was finished in 1975, linking the Tanzanian port of Dar es Salaam with the copper-fields of Zambia. This line had great attraction for Zambia, whose other rail links with the outside world passed through countries which could not be regarded as politically reliable. Tanzania also benefited for the line passed through her south-western region where there were mineral deposits which could not be properly exploited without railway transport. Half of the line is in Zambia and half in Tanzania, but as the railway systems of these two countries have different gauges a difficult decision had to be made. This was decided in favour of Zambia, since through working of rolling stock was less important for Tanzania, given the lack of lines with which the new rail-way could connect. Construction of the 1,067 mm (3 ft 6 in) line was financed by a loan from China, used to pay for Chinese help in building and equipping the route. Chinese-built rolling stock has been imported. The initial motive power was a batch of 102 diesel-hydraulic locomotives, said to be German in inspiration though Chinese by construction. The passenger stock has a dis-tinctly Russian appearance, because the Chinese car factory in which it was built was once reconstructed with Soviet help. Trains use the air-brake, which means that certain Zambian locomotives are equipped with this brake in addition to the standard Zambian vacuum brake. Signalling includes colour-light installations, but also semaphores, rarely used nowadays in new rail-ways. This important line is one of the many which were discussed for decades before any action was taken. 1947 seems to have been the year in which the question was first raised. In 1952 a British survey reported that it was feasible but too expensive. In 1963 the East African Railways reconsidered the matter but proceeded no further. In 1964 the World Bank produced a report but its economists, then firm adherents of the rubber tyre, saw no future for a railway. In 1966 an Anglo-Canadian survey finally announced that the line would not only be feasible but economic as well. However, no offers of capital were made, except one by an investment company which demanded a monopoly of the copper shipments. In 1967 China offered to build and finance the railway and in 1968 Chinese engineers made their survey. An agreement was signed in 1970 and the line was finished five years later.

Yugoslavia

In Europe, outside Russia the most substantial new works have been in Poland and Yugoslavia. In the latter country the Belgrade–Bar main line was at last completed in 1976. Regarded as the final section of the Yugoslav trunk network, this line connects Belgrade with its nearest port, Bar, on the Adriatic. Apart from opening up territory hitherto isolated from the railway system, the line is expected to carry a heavy tourist traffic to the Adriatic coast as well as an increasing proportion of Yugoslavia's foreign trade. A ferry service from Bar to Bari will bring southern Italy into closer contact. The 476 km (296 mile) line was begun in 1952 but work was in abeyance from 1955 to 1966 because of a shortage of capital. A World Bank loan was finally obtained in 1968 enabling the work to go forward. The line crosses difficult terrain and the Slatibor mountains, in particular, were an expensive obstacle necessitating 18 km (11 miles) of tunnel. On the route as a whole there are 254 tunnels making a total length of 114 km (71 miles); that is, almost a quarter of the route is in tunnel. The steepest gradient is 2.5 per cent (1 in 40) and the bridge at Mala Rijeka is Europe's highest at 198 m (648 ft). Operated initially by diesel locomotives, electrification at 25,000 V was soon undertaken.

The crest of Yugoslav Railways; the name in Serbo-Croat is Jugoslovenske Zeleznice (JZ).

Poland

A rather different trunk route is under construction in Poland. Unlike the Belgrade–Bar line, this is not intended to aid or develop the territory through which it passes. It is a heavy-duty railway designed to expedite bulk haulage between Silesia and the Baltic. This Central Trunk Railway is expected to be completed in the early 1980s, although some sections are already in use. 563 km (350 miles) long, it runs northwards from Zawiercie to the port of Gdansk, by-passing Warsaw. Electrification on the Polish 3,000 V system is taking place as construction proceeds. An interesting feature of this route is that the heavy 5,000 tonne freight trains will have to share tracks with frequent passenger services because it will provide a shorter and faster route from Warsaw to the cities of central and southern Europe. It is intended to operate passenger trains at 160 km/h (100 mph) and in order that the speed differential between freight and passenger trains should not reduce line capacity unduly it is hoped to operate express freight trains and container trains at up to 120 km/h (75 mph).

France

Elsewhere in Europe, although some short lines have been built, including some DSB lines in the Copenhagen area and two Netherlands Railways lines to Schiphol Airport and Zoetermeer, the big projects are the high-speed lines being built in Germany, France and Italy. Work has already started on these and some railwaymen regard them as the first segments of a future European high-speed network.

The French scheme is the Paris–Sudest line. This will connect Paris with Lyons and is scheduled for completion by 1980. The traditional rail route between these two cities, the PLM main line, is already intensively used and, since traffic between Paris and south-east France has been increasing steadily, some relief works would have been necessary in any case. But instead of investing capital to improve the bottlenecks of the existing railway, a completely new line is to be built. This will be for passenger trains only and will probably have no intermediate stations. Diversion of the long-distance passenger traffic on to this line will enable the old line to handle freight and local passenger services with capacity to spare. It is expected that 120 passenger trains will be operated on the new line daily. These will be built to the same dimensions as standard SNCF stock so that trains will be able to utilize the existing trackage between the ends of the new line and the two existing main-line stations; the expense and disruption of carrying the new line into the centres of Lyons and Paris is not acceptable. Also, most trains will in any case proceed to points beyond Lyons over the traditional railway. By using the new line, for example, a train for Marseilles will spend only two hours on the Paris–Lyons segment thereby reducing the overall time from the capital to the Mediterranean to less than five hours. Conventional track is being used but the alignment is such that 300 km/h (186 mph) will be the safe maximum. In practice, at least at first, the maximum speed will probably be around 250 km/h (155 mph). The trains will probably be modelled after the TGV 001 gas-turbine prototype which has been on trial for several years, but it is expected that they will be electric rather than gas-turbine powered.

The French government approved this line after alternative solutions had been examined. Quadrupling the remaining double-track section of the PLM line was not expected to be a good long-term solution; it could relieve the strain for a few years but it would not attract the extra traffic which a high-speed line might be expected to gain. STOL aircraft like the already-existing *Mercure* would have a higher cost per passenger and moreover would probably, for aesthetic reasons, be forbidden to terminate close to built-up areas. The French aerotrain would have been very expensive, as it could hardly be used unless its track was carried into the centres of both cities. Moreover, passengers for further destinations would have to change at Lyons.

Italy

The Italian high-speed lines, of which the first stage is the Rome–Florence *Direttissima*, are rather less spectacular because ordinary trains will use them. As with the Paris–Lyons route, increasing north-to-south traffic made greater capacity urgently necessary and it was decided to achieve this by constructing a new line more or less parallel to the old. The new line is straighter and shorter, and capable of accepting locomotive-hauled passenger trains running at speeds up to 200 km/h (125 mph). At various points connections are made with the old line. This will make it possible to switch trains from one route to the other according to circumstances. In turn this implies that the new line will not be reserved for high-speed passenger services but may be used, at least for part of their journey, by freight and slow passenger trains. Other north–south improvements, connecting with the Rome–Florence project, include provision of two more tracks between Florence and Milan and the doubling of the Bologna–Verona line. The latter will connect with a new route northwards through the Brenner Pass, as the existing railway is to be substantially realigned.

West Germany

Overloading of north–south routes was also the reason why the German Federal Railways (DB) decided to build new lines and upgrade others. Both the line from Hamburg through Hanover to Nuremberg and the Rhine route from Cologne through Frankfurt to Munich were working at more than their optimum capacity and forecasts told of a continuing growth, especially of passenger traffic. One project is a 280 km (174 mile) line to relieve the bottleneck south of Hanover, running from that city to Gemunden. The line from Hamburg to Hanover, and from Gemunden to Nuremberg, will be upgraded; on the new section 300 km/h (186 mph) will be the maximum speed, and 200 km/h (125 mph) on the upgraded sections. Meanwhile the Cologne to Frankfurt route will be relieved by a new line from Cologne to Cross Gerau (180 km or 112 miles) and from Mannheim to Stuttgart. The intervening length of line between Cross Gerau (which is near Frankfurt) and Mannheim will be upgraded. At a later stage there will be a continuation of the new line beyond Stuttgart to Munich. A few connecting lines will also be upgraded so that high-speed trains can run from one of the new north–south routes to the other. It will be possible, for example, to operate a high-speed train from Hanover to Frankfurt on a 2 hr 15 min instead of the existing 3 hr 15 min timing. It is expected that fast passenger trains (TEE, 1C and D-trains) will be the main users of the new routes, with the slower E-trains, local trains and freights using the traditional lines. But a few fast freight trains will be scheduled over the new lines.

Japan

Inspiration for many of the new high-speed lines came partly from the success of the Japanese *Shinkansen* network. Japanese planners began seriously to study the possibility of an entirely new standard-gauge railway system in the late 1940s. Twenty years later the necessary legislation was passed and in 1964 the first 1,435 mm (4 ft 8½ in) gauge route, the New Tokaido Line, was opened. The high-speed 'bullet' trains which hurtled along this passenger-only connection between Tokyo and Osaka attracted international attention and were one of the factors aiding the Japanese railway-manufacturing industry in its assault on export markets. After ten years some of the defects of the system became apparent although these were never serious enough to outweigh the advantages. Some difficulties, indeed, were the price of success; the phenomenal increase of traffic meant that maintenance work fell behind schedule with the result that the condition of the track and structures after ten years was not as good as it should have been. The use of steel-girder bridges, together with the high speeds, caused a noise problem which attracted the hostility of environmentalists. From the Japanese National Railways' point of view, a more serious development was that as the line was extended, increases of passenger traffic became less impressive; above a certain distance, say 480 km (300 miles) the airliner retained most of its attraction against the train (helped by a fare structure which was not always in favour of the railway). Thus the planned extension of the system will probably be carried out more cautiously than had been anticipated. The current projects are lines from Tokyo to Morioka, to be extended eventually further north through the new Siekan Tunnel to the island of Hokkaido; a short spur from Tokyo to the new Narita airport, and a longer spur to connect Tokyo with Niigata. Engineering standards are to be higher; reinforced concrete will replace steel girders, and the maximum permitted speed will be 260 km/h (160 mph) instead of the previous 210 km/h (130 mph). When these lines are finished the existing 1,067 mm (3 ft 6 in) gauge lines which parallel them will be devoted to freight and slow passenger services only.

A characteristic of the lines under construction is the large number of tunnels, necessitated by the requirement of gentle curves and slight gradients through country which is often very mountainous. Japan already occupies first place in the world for the number of long railway tunnels, and when the Seikan Tunnel under the Tsugaru Strait is finished she will have the world's longest tunnel. Intended to carry power cables, a gas pipeline and telephone cables as well as a railway, this tunnel will be 54 km long (33 miles) of which 23 km (14 miles) will be under water.

Regauging railways

Already in Japan the pre-*Shinkansen* network, which is still the most important part of the railway system, is termed 'the narrow-gauge lines' and ultimately, after the *Shinkansen* network is completed, those older lines which are not redundant will be converted to standard gauge. The regauging of railways, almost always from a narrower to a broader gauge, is a fairly inexpensive way of increasing railway capacity and speed of service. Apart from Nigeria, which has plans to convert its entire network to standard gauge, India and Australia have ambitious regauging programmes.

In India it has for decades been a declared policy of the government to convert the extensive metre-gauge system to the standard broad gauge (1,676 mm or 5 ft 6 in). Since the metre gauge represents about half the Indian mileage this is very much a long-term ambition, given the shortage of capital in India. However, some important conversions have been made. These are usually of short metre-gauge lines lying between broad-gauge lines whose conversion enables a long broad-gauge route to be created. Or sometimes it is a metre-gauge line whose capacity is overtaxed; re-gauging is in such a case a better alternative than track-doubling. At present an important metre-gauge main line, that from Delhi to Ahmedabad, is being regauged for that reason. An encouraging feature of the regauging plan is that it seems to be quite unaffected by the pressures of politicians; because Indian communities seem to feel that those living on the metre gauge are in some way second-class citizens, aspiring politicians frequently include regauging among their election promises. But it is hard to find any instance where such promises have caused Indian Railways to change their plans.

In Australia, after decades of argument, a substantial step towards a nation-wide standard gauge was achieved in 1970, when the first standard-gauge trains ran between Sydney and Perth. The Trans-Australia line had always been standard gauge, as had the railways of New South Wales, but South Australia and Western Australia, also part of the coast-to-coast route, used 1,600 mm (5 ft 3 in) and 1,067 mm (3 ft 6 in). The introduction, for the benefit of trans-continental services, of the standard gauge in those provinces seems to promise a further extension of that gauge as time passes. Indeed, in Western Australia a substantial programme of regauging has continued ever since 1970. Lines linking sources of heavy freight traffic with the transcontinental route have had first priority and it seems likely that Western Australia will be the first province, after New South Wales, to be entirely standard gauge. In Queensland the standard gauge appeared in 1930 when the New South Wales line up to the border was extended as far as Brisbane. In Victoria, where 1,600 mm (5 ft 3 in) was the standard, a standard-gauge line was built from Albury, on the border with New South Wales, to Melbourne. This was finished in 1962, enabling freight to be despatched to Sydney or Brisbane without transhipment.

Signalling and Train Control

by John Westwood   From the time of hand signals to the current automatic and electronic features of train control.

The early days of signalling

In the beginning, signalling systems were devised simply in order to prevent rear-end collisions. Head-on collisions, on single-track lines, could not be prevented by signalling until the development of the electric telegraph, which fortunately became practicable soon after the start of the railway age. In those early years before the telegraph the collision problem was eased by the provision of double-track lines and the regulation of train departures from stations in order to preserve a time interval between successive trains.

Hand signals of the traffic-police type soon gave way to various kinds of mechanical device, of which the semaphore variant eventually predominated. Meanwhile the telegraph, even in its most elementary form, enabled a station to exchange news of train movements with the next station along the line. Hitherto, movements on single-track lines had either been unregulated, on the 'one engine in steam' principle (a totally safe and still existent method), or, where traffic required more than one locomotive, regulated by strict adherence to a timetable which showed where trains would cross each other. The latter system was sometimes quite inadequate, because any unscheduled delay to a train meant either that all traffic came to a standstill or that someone had to take the responsibility, and the risk, of authorizing an infringement of the timetable.

The telegraph and train-order system, still used on many lines in the USA, retained the timetable but accommodated modifications by means of train orders handed to locomotive crews at stations. The controller, or despatcher, at one station would be in touch by Morse telegraph with other despatchers and could therefore write out orders specifying a change of crossing station. Extra trains would be provided with special orders to regulate their movements. Three-aspect semaphores at the stations informed locomotive crews that they must stop and sign for orders (the semaphore arm in the horizontal position), or that they could pick up less important orders without stopping (the arm raised 45 degrees) or that they could proceed freely (vertical arm). In most of Europe the system was rather different, with semaphore signals indicating stop or proceed and with no use of train orders. But everywhere the old system of a time interval between trains had given place to the safer distance interval. In America a following train could only enter the section between stations at reduced speed if there was another train still in that section (and not at all if passenger trains were involved) while in most of Europe so-called block sections were delineated by signals, and a signalman did not open a block section by pulling off its semaphore until he heard by telegraphic code signal from the next station along the line that the preceding train had cleared that section.

Human error, however, could still cause a collision and so could mechanical failure, to a gradually reducing extent. One great advance was interlocking, which was a device preventing a signalman from setting up a conflicting sequence of signal and switching positions. In its original and simplest form this was a purely mechanical arrangement that, for example, locked a signal lever until a point or switch lever had been moved to a position in conformity with the proposed signal change. On single-track lines not worked on the train-order system the staff or tablet method was introduced. In this a locomotive could proceed only if its crew possessed a token of permission. This was a staff or tablet, and was one of several stored in an electro-mechanical

Previous pages: *Modern train-control apparatus used by London Transport for its underground services. The miniature levers are the modern equivalent of the heavy man-size levers used in traditional wire-operated semaphore signalling systems, and the operator is helped by illuminated track diagrams which show the positions of trains. With this kind of installation, the main task of the signalman, or controller, is no longer the maintenance of safety (which is supervised automatically) but the making of decisions to assure punctual running.*

machine which released a token only if no token were still at large in the hands of the locomotive crew of an opposing train.

Electric signalling

In the inter-war period refinements of the existing systems were put into service in accordance with the various railways' capacity to replace obsolescent, but not worn-out, equipment. Operation of switches and signals was increasingly power assisted, which in turn meant that small levers or switches could replace the heavy manual levers. With operation made so much easier and quicker, it became possible to arrange the electric-operating circuits in such a way that a single lever movement would initiate a series of changes, setting and opening a complete route through a junction. At such junctions, or other very busy stretches, the signalmen or despatchers could be provided with an illuminated diagram showing all the lines under their control and the positions of trains on those lines.

Track circuiting

These diagrams were a product of the technique of track circuiting. This concept, first developed in the 1870s to automate signal operation, involved the passing of low-voltage currents from the signal box (interlocking tower) down one rail of a block section. Each block section was insulated from the next and when a section was empty the current, on reaching the entry of the section, was passed through a signal control coil that, when thus energized, held the signal at green. When a train entered the section the current was short-circuited, passing through the wheels and axles immediately to the second rail and returning directly to the battery. The signal, deprived of its stimulating current, thereupon changed to red. It was not technically difficult to devise a train-describing diagram actuated on the same principle in which the presence of a train in the section would be indicated by a light.

In signalling there has always been a long interval between the development of a new technique and its widespread application but track circuiting is now very widely used both as an informative medium and as the basis of automatic block signalling.

Multi-aspect signalling

Conventional block sections have to be at least as long as the braking distance of the heaviest and fastest trains using them. A locomotive crew is informed of a closed block ahead by an advance, or 'distant' signal (usually yellow). This distant signal is, typically, placed at the entry of the block preceding the block whose situation it indicates; frequently it is placed on the same post as the red 'stop' signal of the preceding block. With the manual system, blocks become longer as trains become faster but the longer the block sections the fewer the number of trains which can run on a route. One solution is multi-aspect signalling, most easily applied with colour-light signals. In this an advance warning is conveyed not only of the situation in the following block but also of the block, or blocks, after that. Thus a train can be warned to slow down while it is still more than one block away from the obstruction and a section can be shorter than braking distance. In a very congested area a section need be little longer than a train length.

Colour light signals are now replacing semaphores. They come in many varieties; in the USA, for example, neighbouring railroads may employ different types. A main distinction is between those which have three or four lenses and those with a single 'searchlight' lens, the colour of the light being determined by a filter near the bulb. By using a four-light signal, two yellow lights can indicate the situation of the second and third signals along the line, and the addition of a flashing system for these two lights can provide even more flexibility.

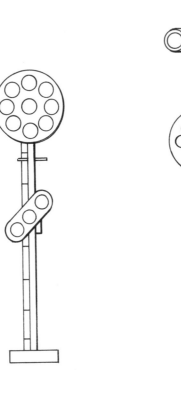

Train control

Between the wars automatic train-control devices were introduced on many main lines. These comprised a line-side actuator which, usually by electro-magnetic means, caused a given response on a receiving apparatus carried by the locomotive. In practice what happened was that if a train passed a distant signal at its warning aspect and the crew took no action, the brake would be automatically applied. In most systems there was also a warning indication in the cab, which told the crew what the signal was indicating; this was an invaluable aid in thick fog when a signal might be invisible. In Britain the Great Western Railway was well to the fore in applying this system which was partly responsible for its good safety record. In the USA railways were encouraged to use this equipment by a 1947 ICC ruling that raised the maximum permitted speed on equipped lines above the 125 km/h (80 mph) normally imposed.

American colour-light signals. Extreme left: Three-lens type. Green is usually the top lens. Some railroads arrange the lenses horizontally or even as a triangle. Centre left: position-light signal. Lenses are of the same colour and indication as given by a straight line of three illuminated lenses; that is, by horizontal, vertical, and two diagonal positions. The Pennsylvania RR additionally uses an O-form indication to request electric locomotives to lower their pantographs and an X-form as a take-siding signal. The lower 3-light bar is added to some signals to provide additional local instructions. Centre right: A colour-position signal introduced by the Baltimore & Ohio RR in the 1920s and giving more combinations than the simple position light signal. Extreme right: The more modern 'Searchlight' signal, in which a lens is moved in front of the lamp. This is very efficient, giving 1·6 km (one mile) visibility with a 5-watt lamp, the beam being highly concentrated. Also, false or obscure indications caused by direct sunlight falling into the lens are eliminated with this type.

Centralized train control

As soon as electric power replaced muscle power in the operation of signals, it became technically possible to extend one man's area of control beyond the limit imposed by lever and wire actuation. In some circumstances this was desirable and in others not. When there was a fairly heavy use of single-track line the centralization of control over a long stretch of route could be very valuable because the single controller, watching the lights representing trains move along his track diagram and having all the signal and switch controls at hand, could plan ahead the crossing places of these trains. If crossing loops were made long enough, it was possible to cross two trains without either of them stopping. On double-track lines the increase of overall train speeds and of line capacity was less dramatic, but nevertheless often worthwhile, and the extension of centralized train control (CTC) has been a feature of postwar railway operation. One of its benefits is the replacement by one centre of dozens of signal installations, each requiring three shifts of increasingly scarce signalmen.

A typical example of the benefits offered by CTC is presented by the Florida East Coast Railroad, whose entire operations are controlled by one despatcher sitting in the CTC office at New Smyrna. This man controls not only main-line trains but also activity on branch lines and the operation of three lift bridges over waterways. The Railroad has been able to convert its double track into a mainly single-track route, with lengths of second track left in place so that the despatcher can arrange for opposing trains to make 'running meets', that is, pass each other without stopping. The despatcher is in radio touch with all trains and is additionally helped by a uniform maximum speed for all trains of 96 km/h (60 mph). At intervals along the track automatic devices scan passing trains to detect hot axleboxes, loose wheels, train breakages and shifted loads.

Automatic train control

While centralized train control can do much to increase line capacity, especially where single track predominates, it can do little to ensure that local speed restrictions are observed. Where loads are heavy and gradients severe, and where perhaps train crews are inexperienced or unused to self-discipline, modern versions of automatic train control (ATC) are useful. On the Lamco Railroad in Liberia, for example, heavy ore trains move over a hilly route and for safety reasons ATC has been installed. One of several systems was chosen which uses both permanent and electric magnets on the track. The polarity of these can be changed and receivers on the locomotives can distinguish such changes. The magnets are placed at signals and at temporary or permanent speed restrictions. To check on a train's speed two magnets are used, the distance between them depending on the speed limit desired; if the train, judged by the time it takes between the magnets, is moving too fast the apparatus on the locomotive applies the brake. Similar emergency brake applications are made for passing signals at danger and the brakes can only be released by the controller, who sends a special code message by radio link.

Radio and electronic systems

Railway signalling is essentially concerned with the transmission of information between a stationary office or controller and a moving train. Over the decades this transmission has moved, in stages, from visual and written media (line-side signals and train orders) to more complex methods, including radio and electronic systems. Radio communication between train crews and controllers has long been feasible, but has also been handicapped by the many blind spots on a railway route in which radio signals are blocked by tunnels, hills and other obstructions. In the postwar period the microwave radio, with repeater stations along the route, has been used for train control by several railways. The Hammersley Railways in Western Australia provides a good example of this technique. This line, 388 km (241 miles) long, runs from the Indian Ocean at Dampier to mines in the interior. It is almost entirely single track, although there are long double-track sections where trains can pass. Typically, nine ore trains are operated daily; these may be of 154 or 184 100 tonne cars, depending on whether two or three 1,800 hp diesel locomotives are used. With the radio network the train controller at Dampier can schedule train meets without causing delays, arrange the path of each train precisely and in the event of failures quickly arrange for assistance. In the storm season he receives reports from train crews about conditions on the railway and when maintenance of track is being carried out he can, thanks to his constant communication with train and permanent-way crews, arrange 'windows'— periods in which work can be carried on without hindrance by passing trains. Because trains are manned by just a driver and an observer, both at the head end, radio is also valuable in reporting hot boxes from the lineside. Since a train may be 1,800 metres (1,950 yards) long, line-side workers are just as likely to spot a defect as the train's observer. All this is achieved by three microwave terminals and six line-side repeaters.

Radio communication in West Germany

Microwave systems are used, typically, on long lines with infrequent trains and widely-spaced stations. Radio communication between controller and train is equally beneficial on intensively-used railways. In West Germany the DB plans to have 15,000 km (9,300 miles) of its route equipped for such communication by 1980. It has already completed the installations for more than half of this target; all electric stock had been equipped by mid 1978. The apparatus is operated by push-button, and messages which are commonly used can be transmitted simply by pressing the button with the appropriate symbol; the receiving apparatus thereupon illuminates its corresponding symbol. A controller can call any particular train without other trains in the area being affected, and he can if necessary make an announcement to passengers over the train's public-address system. Train conductors can use the train-driver's apparatus to pass messages and to switch into the DB's telephone system. Senior operating officials, by dialling the appropriate number on their telephones, can address simultaneously all train drivers on a given section of track. According to the terrain, and especially according to the number of tunnels, repeaters are spaced along the line at intervals from 2 to 10 km ($1\frac{1}{4}$ to $6\frac{1}{4}$ miles).

Radio communication and British Rail

An advanced system of radio communication is under study by British Rail. This was stimulated by the need to evolve a system good enough to be standardized by European railways; the Channel Tunnel was expected to require a good system but since the postponement of that project research has continued because a thoroughly reliable system is a prerequisite of automatic (that is, one-man) train operation. A section of the new Great Northern suburban electrification scheme has been chosen for experimentation because it includes a considerable mileage in tunnel; it is electrified on the 25,000 V ac system—which is notorious for the problems of interference it poses—and its rolling stock is unlikely to be transferred to another area after being expensively equipped with the new apparatus. With this system the controller, or signalman, of a given area has a radio channel of four uhf frequencies while his neighbouring controllers have different channels. On the train, the receiver locks on to the first strong signal it encounters but should the signal strength deteriorate it once more begins to search for a better signal on one of the three other frequencies. Having found this, it locks on to it. Line-side transmitters are distributed along the track to provide continuous reception but in tunnels a new technique of radiating cables is used.

This technique is under intensive study by British Rail, and a special test coach, *Iris*, is almost permanently engaged in the work of measuring field strengths. The essence of the system is the use of a special line-side coaxial transmission cable whose outer sheathing allows a slight leakage of energy in the form of radiation at a frequency usable for radio communication. Radio signals are fed into one end of the cable and these leak out all along its length. With suitably designed receivers, this leakage can be picked up within 10 metres (11 yards) of the cable and is thus receivable by trains. Such cables can transmit both coded and speech messages and one cable can serve two, and perhaps four, parallel tracks.

Whatever method is used, control-to-train radio communication is expensive and to be acceptable needs to provide much more assistance than the telephone traditionally located at signals, by which a train crew can communicate directly with the signalman or controller (usually to ask what has gone wrong). In fact, such radio systems do give many more possibilities although often they are possibilities that are not really required. The early and very rewarding use of radio communication was at marshalling yards, where a lot of time-consuming message-running could be eliminated. On railways where trains were $1\frac{1}{2}$ km (1 mile) or more in length, radio was useful in providing communication between the locomotive crew and the rear-end conductor. The new generation of radio systems can improve efficiency (that is, fit frequent trains into a busy section of track without wasting capacity or delaying traffic), can provide more advanced warning of difficulties, can so improve the operation of overloaded single lines that double-tracking becomes unnecessary, and can provide train description information in advance thereby helping, for example, station announcers. In the future, it is also a step towards one-man train operation; in other words, to the automatically-driven train.

The pulse system

A forerunner of automatic driving was the automatic train control used on some lines before World War II, in which brakes were applied automatically should the train pass a distant signal at danger without the driver himself applying the brake. The accompanying visual or sound indication in the cab was similarly a forerunner of modern cab signalling but it was somewhat limited in the amount of information it could provide. This is why, in the inter-war period, the pulse system was developed. In this, electric pulses are sent down a rail and picked up by an apparatus on the locomotive. By varying the frequency of pulse a variety of messages can be conveyed; for example, the situation of many sections ahead of the train can be communicated. It is also possible for an approaching train to transmit its presence ahead in the same way; for example it can actuate the sequences necessary to set up a route to pass a junction or operate the flashing lights or barriers at a highway crossing.

Transponders

Another step towards automated train operation will probably be the wide use of transponders. The world's oldest main line, from London to Birmingham, is now equipped experimentally with about 150 transponders and a laboratory car, *Test Coach Mercury*, is regularly attached to London–Birmingham trains to test the system. The transponders—electronic devices enclosed in a light casing—are fixed between the rails. Their special virtue is that they require no batteries or electricity supply; all the power they need is derived from the inductive energy created by the passage of a train overhead. This energy is then used to transmit a signal back to receivers on that same train. Each individual transponder has its own code emission, sealed in at time of manufacture. Thus a train passing overhead can receive a set signal initiating, for example, the speed restriction necessary at that point, or indicating the precise location of the train both to the driver and, in the case of automation, to a computer or other controlling device. Three of British Rail's Advanced Passenger Trains are to be fitted with a speed-control system based on transponders. The simplest system is to use successive transponders, each coded to give a speed indication relevant to their particular section of route—indicators which are automatically obeyed by the train. Alternatively, a train could carry a computer store of information about its scheduled running and this schedule could be checked for proper fulfilment as each transponder was passed.

Computers

With growing emphasis on the informative aspects of train control, with efficiency of operation as the goal now that accident-avoidance has been satisfactorily achieved, the computer has become increasingly useful. Moreover, with the development of the mini-computer, apparatus suitable for on-train use has become available. In the initial applications of computer technology the railways, like the airlines, found that laborious operations, like those handled by an army of clerks in reservation offices, were the most eligible, especially as computers of that generation were large and heavy. A later, but not dissimilar, application was in car control. The problem which a railway management could face in locating a given freight-car or shipment was well known in all countries and especially by shippers whose goods had been 'mislaid' in transit. Not only this, but because a railway administration could never know precisely where its different vehicles were, and which of them were empty, it often had difficulty in assembling cars of a certain type for a given shipment. This in turn meant that local managers held on to empty vehicles so as to have a reserve at their disposal.

With a computer there are no technical (as opposed to human) obstacles to the establishment of a constantly updated store of information which includes the serial number of all vehicles, their classification into types, their load at any given moment, their position, their point of origin and their point of destination. With such information literally at their fingertips, railway managers can not only tell shippers the precise location of their goods and the expected time of arrival but they can quickly assemble in advance the types of freight car which they expect to need shortly. This ability reduces the number of vehicles required or, put differently, enables a given vehicle to make more loaded trips per year with a resultant saving of capital and maintenance costs. However, some of the early systems suffered from the poor quality of the reporting procedures; if local personnel failed properly to report the details of the vehicles passing into or out of their area the result could be in accordance with the 'nonsense-in nonsense-out' principle. On South African Railways, for example, it was found that if an intermediate reporting point failed to report the passage of a given vehicle, then information of its passage from the next reporting point along the line would be rejected by the computer; since it had not been reported passing point A, the information from point B could only be nonsense so far as the computer was concerned.

Probably the most successful but not the most sophisticated system of car control is that known as TOPS (Total Operations Processing System). This was developed by the Southern Pacific Railroad and then adopted by British Railways in the early 1970s. It has since been chosen by the Spanish National Railways too. The British installation is centred in London, where two computers are located; one of these is operational while the other is a reserve that also stores information about past performance. Linked with the central operating computer are the approximately 150 input/output terminals at the main freight centres of Britain. The computer not only knows the different characteristics of the various car types but also the correct sequence of sorting yards for any given transit, and can instruct railway staff accordingly. One of its most noteworthy procedures is the immediate despatch of vehicles which have just been unloaded. Instead of leaving these cars to accumulate on sidings until called for, the computer routes them to where they are best placed to find a new load.

The TOPS system can also handle locomotive operation, devising and issuing instructions for workings which make the best use of the units within the limits set by train schedules and the need to receive maintenance at set times and places. It is not, however, the only way in which computers can be utilized for more efficient railway operation. The German Federal Railways (DB) have been developing an ambitious programme of computer control. A so-called 'cybernetic island' was set up in the Hannover area to develop and test new ideas which included computer control of both commercial and operating tasks. In 1977 it was decided to invest in a system-wide application of the new techniques, to be collectively known as Integrated Transport Control. Thus the experience over several years of the Seelze marshalling yard, which is almost entirely automatic, is embodied in a new yard near Hamburg. Computer control of a section of line (Hannover to Verden), which carries both passenger and freight trains, began in 1975 and this too will be applied elsewhere.

In this system the computer stores the train-service timetable in its memory. A train entering computer-controlled territory has its number reported to the computer by a human controller in the first signal box. As the train proceeds, its position is reported by rail contacts to the computer. The latter then compares the timetabled progress of the train with its actual progress. It is expected that on the basis of this comparison, and other stored information, it will soon be possible to adopt a system in which the computer can make decisions to cope with late running. On the experimental line, as the train's position is reported the computer devises a route for it and instructs local signalmen to set the appropriate points and signals. However, there is no technical reason why the human element should not be eliminated, except where intervention is required to cope with unforeseen or especially complicated problems. By 1980 it is expected that a hierarchy of computers will be in service and all the important main-line trains will have their progress monitored by, for example, print-outs of the train running situation so that the human managers have an up-to-the-minute picture of what is going on.

Underground Railways

by John Day   The history and features of underground and rapid-transit railways, and statistics of the world's systems.

History

The idea of putting urban railways in tunnels underground originated in London some time in the 1830s. It simmered, fairly quietly, until 1851, when a scheme of Charles Pearson's to build a wide road from King's Cross to Farringdon Street, with six standard-gauge and two broad-gauge tracks in a tunnel below, was examined by a committee before being put to, and accepted by, the Common Council of the City of London.

Charles Pearson, City Solicitor, and John Hargrave Stevens, Architect and Surveyor to the City (Western Division) were the two men who fought hardest and longest to establish urban underground railways. Although Pearson's own scheme was cut and mangled by others—and emerged, a shadow of its original self, as part of an underground, mixed-gauge line from Paddington to Farringdon Street via King's Cross—Pearson was the undoubted father of the urban rapid-transit, or underground, railway. The railway which owed its origin to Pearson was London's Metropolitan Railway, opened on 10 January 1863, the prototype in style and name of 'Metros' throughout the world. Pearson himself died a few months before the line opened, but he must have lived long enough to see some of the work and to know that his brainchild was coming to birth.

After abortive trials by the Metropolitan's engineer, John Fowler, with a specially-built locomotive (*Fowler's Ghost*) which depended on hot bricks to keep up steam in the tunnels, so eliminating smoke, the Metropolitan was worked from its inception by Great Western Railway broad-gauge loco-motives and stock. These were banished when, following a quarrel, the GWR withdrew its trains at short notice and forced the Metropolitan to borrow standard-gauge locomotives and rolling stock from the Great Northern Railway and rolling stock from the London & North Western Railway, until such time as the Metropolitan could acquire its own equipment.

The Metropolitan was a great success despite the smoke and steam. It was mainly a cut-and-cover line, built just beneath the surface, and was followed by the similar Metropolitan District Railway—intended as a partner but later, for a time, a bitter rival. These two cut-and-cover lines, greatly expanded, formed the main sub-surface (as opposed to 'Tube') network of London Transport.

The first 'underground' to be built elsewhere in Europe was $3\frac{3}{4}$ km ($2\frac{1}{3}$ miles) long and ran mainly under one of Budapest's main thoroughfares. Opened in 1896, it too was sub-surface. In the USA a Bill was introduced into the New York state legislature in 1864 to allow a 'subway'—or underground railway—to be built to the designs of A. P. Robinson. The Bill did not succeed but when, from 1900 on, the main New York subway system was built, some of Robinson's routes were followed.

New York did have a subway, however, as early as 1867. It was only 90 m (100 yards) long and was built secretly by Alfred Ely Beach from the basement of a building on the corner of Broadway and Murray Street. Beach had permission to build two small tunnels, only 1,371 mm (4 ft 6 in) in diameter, in which to experiment with pneumatically-driven freight vehicles. But he ignored that, designed his own shield and built a 2,743 mm (9 ft) diameter tunnel with a pneumatically-driven passenger car, which carried people up and down his little experimental line for some months. Beach could not get permission to build more deep subways but he was given authority to build some subways for use by steam trains. These were never built; perhaps the success of Charles Thompson Harvey's 'subway in the sky'—the Elevated

Previous pages: *A view of the Washington underground railway in the USA. Despite the great expense of construction and operation, underground railways are being built in more and more cities. Since the automobile ousted the streetcar systems and electric trams, and then multiplied so as to make streets impassable at peak periods, the inner-city rail vehicle has been modernized and put underground. The Washington D.C. system is relatively short but is one of the best examples of modern mass-transit techniques.*

Railway—spoiled Beach's chances of success. The 'EL', though not an underground railway, operated in a similar manner on similar routes. Its incursion into the tomato-growing Bronx in 1886 at once extended the area of New York, and at the height of its career its steam-hauled and electric cars were carrying a million people a day.

The 'EL' in New York, and in Chicago, set out to do the same job as that performed by underground railways from the beginning to the present day—to carry passengers swiftly under (or over) streets crowded with people and vehicles. Old photographs of most cities show clearly that the imagined leisurely days of horse-drawn vehicles were really nothing of the sort. The streets were packed with such vehicles and congestion was as bad as, if not worse than, it is in the streets of today. For traffic engineering, except in a rudimentary, rule-of-thumb style, was an unknown science.

Advantages of underground railways

What, then, does an underground railway offer which makes it, though very expensive, so desirable that every great city on earth either has one, is building or designing one, or is thinking (in varying degrees of urgency) about the need for having one built? Its main benefit—as has always been the case—is its ability to move workers, shoppers, pleasure-seekers, tourists and all ordinary people engaged in their ordinary pursuits swiftly about congestion-free, private tracks under the heart of a city, ignoring what is happening on the roads. Its second major advantage is that underground lines need take up no surface space (apart from staircase wellheads at stations). Lines can be built over and kept out of sight and, to the man in the street, out of mind. They are electric, so they cause no pollution. With modern equipment, at least 40,000 people can be carried in one direction in one hour—on some lines half as many again may be possible.

Motorways to carry this number (and more than fifty per cent of commuter-hour motor cars tend to contain only the driver) would need so many lanes that they would spread into a concrete tangle, stifling the life from any city, as planners in the very home of the motor car—the USA—have now come to realize. On a more personal level, you cannot read the news on the way to work in your own car, but to the average commuter, adept at folding his newspaper, it is simplicity itself when riding in the train—and, while you read, the train keeps going when snow, fog and traffic jams turn the world above into a driver's nightmare. By its unobtrusiveness, the underground can save the historic centre of a city steeped in tradition and still give access to all its delights.

Features of the modern underground

Undergrounds are not always underground. The modern tendency is to dive underground in the congested centre and then rise, possibly, to an overhead structure for the section immediately beyond the centre, running down to ground level as soon as the lie of the land permits.

Only about a third of London's Underground is actually underground (including the characteristic, but unusual, deep tubes built in that ideal tunnelling medium, the London blue clay) and San Francisco's new 121 km (75 mile) system for the Bay Area will have only just over a quarter below ground (or water, since there is a $6\frac{1}{2}$ km (4 mile) tube on the bed of the Bay). One of the best of the new ideas—seen in Chicago, San Francisco and Japan, for example—is to run the tracks in the median strips of motorways.

Underground railways exist very largely to carry considerable numbers of people into cities in the morning on their way to work and out again in the evening on their way home. For this task they need: a full complement of trains; stations designed (especially in the central area) to pass great numbers of people through quickly, and a considerable staff. Before, between and after these peak hours it would probably be possible in most cities to use only half the trains, half the staff and much smaller stations to deal with the greatly reduced volume of traffic. One cannot, however, bring men and women to work for three or four hours in the early morning and then send them home until they are needed again in the evening; or this can be done only to a limited extent. It is this contrast between peak and off-peak services, with the need to build and supply everything to cater for a maximum number in a short period of time, which makes not only underground railways but all forms of public-transport operation expensive—a steady load throughout the working day would make things much easier.

To carry these loads the use of clean, smokeless electric trains is now virtually universal, at least on in-town sections of lines, and nearly all railways use cars with steel wheels running on the familiar steel rails. In Paris, however, experiments were carried out in the early 1950s with rubber-tyred trains and Line 11, which runs from Châtelet to Mairie des Lilas, was fitted out completely for this stock by the end of 1957 and three lines now use these trains. The track is rather complicated, as are the wheel arrangements. Briefly, the rubber tyres run on two concrete beams laid along the tunnels, the tyres being kept on the beams by another, horizontal set of pneumatic-tyred wheels, which run on guiding rails or beams at the side of the track. At points and switches where the trains have to transfer from track to track, the side guides cannot be kept continuous, so there are standard-gauge, steel rails laid all long the tunnels next to the concrete beams and there the flanged steel wheels are mounted co-axially on the cars with the rubber-tyred wheels. At points the concrete beams fall away and the train runs over normal, rail-type switches on its flanged wheels. Should a tyre burst in normal running, the axle concerned will drop only until the steel wheel reaches the steel rail below and the train can then carry on.

In tunnels, this rubber tyre has certain advantages of adhesion and—some say—of noise reduction, but the improved adhesion also demands more power and therefore produces more heat to disperse, so that the tunnels tend to get hotter and hotter and need better ventilation or cooling. In the open air, where frost and snow can cake the running surfaces, the pneumatic tyre is at a decided disadvantage. In Paris, the latest stock to be ordered is once again steel-wheeled although another conversion has now begun. Nevertheless, the system has spread, under French influence, to Montreal, Mexico City, and now, Santiago.

Other types of underground railway are possible. For light work there is an American system—so far not installed in any city but at a very advanced stage —in which small coupled or single cars with pneumatic tyres travel over a flat concrete track on which they are guided by wheels running horizontally on each side of a central rail. Thought is also being given in the USA to long-distance high-speed tube lines which will have some form of pneumatic propulsion.

Monorails are sometimes claimed to be suitable for underground railway work, and they could be so used for the short centre section of a monorail line, the rest of which is on the surface, but the monorails' special rail(s) and equipment would involve making the tunnels much bigger (and therefore more expensive), so their use is unlikely.

With modern materials, it might be possible to go back to the pneumatic-propulsion system advocated in Britain by Brunel, among others, in the 1840s but electric propulsion is so advanced and efficient that changes seem unlikely —except for the possible adoption of transistorized control for the motors, with which experiments are going on all over the world. The linear motor, a most important development because of its lack of moving parts and conse-

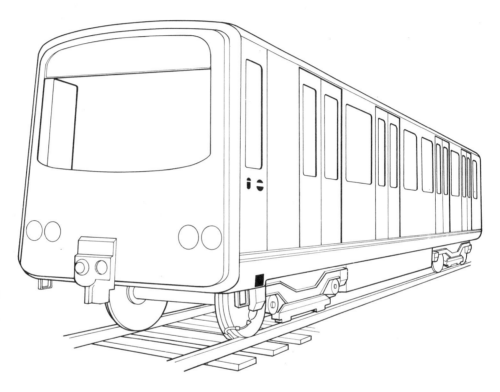

One of the newest underground railways is that of Brussels, which is still being developed. This is a prototype vehicle, on which the standard trains are modelled. Such vehicles can be combined in formations of from two to five cars, each car providing room for about 200 passengers (mainly standing, although most cars have 40 seats). However, a train is reckoned to carry 850 passengers at the peak, which means that 25,500 passengers can be passed over a single line in one hour. The cars have two motors, and maximum speed is 72 kph (48 mph). There is a high accelerative capability, very necessary as the average distance between stations is only 600 metres (656 yards).

quent frictionless drive, would seem at present to be more suitable for use on high-speed main-lines or in specialized cars than in an underground railway system.

Comfort on trains is a matter of several trends going in different directions at the same time. In smaller cities, or those with underground railway networks of limited size, only basic passenger comforts tend to be catered for— e.g. somewhere to stand with a support to hold, heating and lighting. Newer, longer-distance lines, however, have more comforts, and in the USA where the problem is not only to carry passengers but firstly to lure them away from their private motor cars, a high degree of comfort and air-conditioning are considered vital necessities. In other cities, with medium to busy routes, the aim is to give a fair number of comfortable seats which will accommodate most of the travellers in off-peak hours and passengers have to accept that in the central area, at least in the peak hours, half or more of them will have to stand and this, like many compromises, is probably the most sensible solution.

The need for air-conditioning depends on the ambient temperature of the city served. A totally-underground line in moderate climates can probably be kept at an acceptable temperature by tunnel- and station-ventilating equipment without any need to air-condition the trains themselves. The problem, since electrical equipment and passengers themselves generate quite a lot of heat, is more often to remove heat than put it in. The picture changes considerably, of course, if in-town sections in tunnels are short and the trains spend much of their time in the open air. The problems then become much the same as those of main-line railways in the area—and, indeed, of architects, builders, shop-owners and all others responsible for premises or vehicles used by the public. If there is general acceptance of air-conditioning as a commonplace of life in a given city, an underground railway must fall into line if it is to fulfil its purpose. Air-conditioning means much more than heating. It also means cooling when needed and a reasonable amount of humidity control.

Any modern, underground railway which is deeper than a few feet below the surface must have banks of escalators to take passengers up and down to platform level. Long flights of stairs discourage passengers as does the 'block' movement, with spells of inactive waiting time, associated with lifts. The 'no-waiting' aspect of escalators is an incentive to travel, as are the bright, well illuminated, functional but attractive stations, which are a feature of modern systems and are recognized as an ideal to be achieved as quickly as possible in the modernization of other lines. Stations are designed today with the results of passenger-movement studies at hand, so that even walking flow is made continuous by the presence of adequate widths of passageways and stairs. At busy periods, closed-circuit television helps with crowd control.

Another delaying factor for passengers which must be overcome is that entailed in buying tickets. The sensible, regular commuter buys himself a season ticket, thus saving both time and money, but the casual traveller, or anyone who does not use a regular daily route, must buy his ticket somewhere —usually at a station ticket office—where he is likely to have to queue, or from a machine for which he either needs the right money or coins for which the machine will give change. On systems with flat fares automation to save ticket delays is easy. The only necessity is to make sure that a passenger pays that flat fare. In the simplest method he does so by dropping a coin into a slot to release a turnstile. Because coins can be bent and jam machines, an alternative is to ask him to buy a ticket—or more often a number of tickets—which will operate the machine. Tickets of this type are often bought from book-sellers, tobacconists, etc., rather than a railway office and it is only necessary to put one into a suitable gate mechanism to have the gate opened for access to the trains. Such tickets can have punched holes, codes, magnetic backings, metallic-tape insertions, or quite a number of other identification points which will enable the gate to recognize them. With flat fares it is not necessary to check outgoing passengers. When a system has a large number of graduated fares and many different types of ticket, a much more sophisticated form of coding, generally involving punched holes or coded magnetic backing, is required and the gates need a considerable 'memory' system to recognize them all. Because of the complexity, tickets for such a system can rarely be sold by anyone but the underground railway itself and the scope for buying in advance is limited. In systems like this, tickets must be checked at the beginning and end of the journey. Apart from the season ticket, the best, time-reducing possibility for such railways is the 'stored-fare' ticket, which may cost, say £2 or £4 (or any other figure according to individual needs). When such a ticket is put into a gate to open a way to the platforms, it is impressed by the gate with coded information giving the station name, date, etc. At the destination the outgoing gate 'reads' this information, calculates the proper fare, deducts it from the total and returns the ticket, now worth the price of the journey less than when purchased. The value remaining in the ticket can be checked by putting it into a 'reader' which will display the value in hand. Such tickets are the subject of much experiment and may one day be the ideal ticket for underground railways which have a common fare structure with the city's buses, trams, ferries, etc. It could be used on any of them and, unlike the season ticket, requires no pre-selection of route. It could be a great timesaver.

The other main field of underground railway automation today is in automatic driving. There is a tendency to think that automatic driving of trains is in itself a good thing, but this is only partially true. It does enable all trains to be driven in a standard manner—the best manner—and thus saves current and evens out running-time fluctuation due to individual styles of driving. But its main use is to enable a train to be operated either without a crew or with only one man on board who, freed from driving duties (though a qualified driver for emergency purposes) can concentrate on other aspects of running the train, such as opening and closing the doors at stations (helped by closed-circuit television to see the parts of the platform obscured from direct vision by passengers) setting the automatic driving equipment into action, monitoring the performance of the train, driving it into and out of the depot and reversing it at the journey's end, as well as making announcements to his passengers if needed. Most, if not all, of these functions could be performed automatically or by some source outside the train. For example, a man on a station platform could close the doors and start the train on its way and open the doors of the next train from external switches or by inductive controls from a platform console, but the many underground railways which are experimenting with or adopting automatic driving agree that despite automatic lifts and other unattended equipment, passengers as a whole are not ready for completely unmanned trains. Especially in the case of two-track tunnels where access to a stalled train is easy, however, there seems no reason why this should not come.

Automatic driving can be achieved by two methods. In one—adopted in London—local trackside controls give coded instructions to trains about the safety aspects of the track ahead, controlled by feedback from the last train to pass, while other trackside controls, carefully positioned after theoretical and practical tests, tell the train where to start coasting and where to brake to travel at a pre-selected speed and finally to stop in the right place at the platform. The other main system, used in San Francisco, gives continuous feedback of information from all trains to a central computer, which issues instructions to every train when to start, what speed to run at, and so on. There are numerous variations, including trains with on-board computers, which give instructions to the train according to a preset programme when the train has travelled pre-arranged distances.

This short chapter can only touch the fringe of the possibilities of underground railways for passengers, but the world as a whole is experiencing a great upsurge of interest, with dozens of cities—in Europe, the United States, Canada, Central and South America, and Russia, where underground railways are already well established, as well as Australia, New Zealand, China, and other countries where such railways are new—preparing to join the list of those which already have underground systems. Soon it may well be truly said that the underground, or rapid-transit, railway is the hallmark of a great city.

Major underground and rapid transit systems

City	Length of route		Length in tunnel		No of lines	No of stations	Passengers carried (mill. per year)	Date first line opened	Remarks
	km	miles	km	miles					
Amsterdam	18.0	11.2	3.5	2.2	1	17	13	14.10.77	
Atlanta	11.4	7.1	4.7	2.9	1	17	—	12.1978	
Baku	18.5	11.5	16.0	9.9	1	10	41	1967	Being extended
Barcelona (all lines)	85.8	53.3	50	31.0	6	91	400	1863 (Section which then formed part of surface steam railway)	Being extended
Berlin (W)	97.5	60.6	72.0	44.7	8	105	285	18.2.1902	Being extended
Berlin (E)	25.5	15.8	22.5	14.0	2	34*	61		*Plus 11 not in use
Boston	62.0	38.5	15.0	9.3	5	48	95	1901	Being extended
Brussels	11.7	7.3	5.5	3.4	2	7	—	20.9.1976	First pre-Metro lines converted to full rapid transit
Bucharest	8.0	5.0	8.0	5.0	1	7	—	1.8.1978	
Budapest	4.0	2.5	3.5	2.2	1	11	150	1896	Original line
	13.7	8.5	12.5	7.8	2	11		4.4.1970	Modern system, being extended
Buenos Aires	32.1	20.0	32.1	20.0	5	57	400	1913	Extensions in hand
Chicago	143.1	88.9	17.1	10.6	9	154	104	1892 (Elevated) 1943 (Subway)	
Cleveland	30.0	18.6	0.6	0.4	1	18	13	15.3.1955	
Glasgow	10.5	6.5	10.5	6.5	1	15	15	14.12.1896	Being reconstructed
Haifa	1.8	1.1	1.8	1.1	1	6	6	6.10.1959	
Hamburg	89.9	55.9	31.6	19.6	3	79	188	15.2.1912	Being extended
Kiev	18.2	11.3	12.7	7.9	1	14	178	22.10.1960	Being extended
Kharkov	17.9	11.1	12.1	7.5	1	13	—	1975	
Kobe	13.6	8.5	13.0	8.1	1	11	11	5.7 km opened 3.1977	
Kyoto	3.5	2.2	3.5	2.2	1	4	—	—	Being extended
Leningrad	56.0	34.8	55.2	34.3	3	27	400	11.1955	Being extended
Lisbon	12.0	7.5	12.0	7.5	1	20	70	30.12.1959	Extensions planned
London London Transport (owned)	383.0	238.0	156.0	97.0	8	249	601	10.1.1863	Being extended
(run over)	410.0	255.0				279			
British Rail	2.4	1.5	2.4	1.5	1	2	—	11.7.1898	
Lyons	11.4	7.1	11.4	7.1	2	11	55	2.5.1978	Being extended
Madrid	66.0	41.0	60.2	37.4	7	99	530	17.10.1919	Being extended
Marseilles	9.0	5.6	6.0	3.7	1	12	18	26.11.1977	

City	Length of route		Length in tunnel		No of lines	No of stations	Passengers carried (mill. per year)	Date first line opened	Remarks
	km	miles	km	miles					
Mexico City	40.8	25.4	30.8	19.2	3	48	437	5.9.1969	Being extended
Milan	28.5	17.7	26.5	16.5	2	41	120	1.11.1964	Being extended
Montreal	36.1	22.4	25.6	15.9	3	28	148	14.10.1966	Being extended
Moscow	172.7	106.8	141.4	87.9	8	107	2136	15.5.1935	Being extended
Munich	18.7	11.6	13.9	8.6	2	19	60	19.10.1971	Being extended
Nagoya	38.1	23.7	35.6	22.1	3	41	179	11.1957	Being extended
New York NYCTA	371.2	230.6	220.6	137.1	32	461	1100	27.10.1904	Being extended
New York PATH	22.4	13.9	12.6	7.8	2	13	40	1908 (As PATH, 1.9.1962)	Extension proposed
Nuremberg	9.3	5.8	—	—	1	—	—	1.1978	
Osaka	70.2	43.6	60.0	37.3	6	56	683	5.1933	Being extended
Paris Metro	183.4	114.0	169.1	105.1	15	276	1250	19.7.1900	Being extended
Regional	92.1	57.2	32.0	19.9	3	53		12.12.1969	Being extended
Peking	22.4	13.9	22.4	13.9	1	16	20	1970	Being extended
Philadelphia	62.8	39.0	30.9	19.2	4	65	112	4.3.1907	Extensions planned
Prague	11.7	7.3	11.7	7.3	1	16	—	9.5.1974	Long-term plans for 125 km (78 miles) system and 144 stations
Rome	11.3	7.0	6.0	3.7	1	11	22	9.2.1955	Second line under construction
Rotterdam	17.0	10.6	3.2	2.0	1	8	28	1968	Being extended
San Francisco (BART)	120.7	75.0	37.0	23.0	4	34	53	11.9.1972	
Santiago	16.7	10.4	11.3	7.0	2	16	—	1977	
Sao Paulo	17.2	10.7	15.0	9.3	1	23	176	14.9.1974	Being extended
Sapporo	24.2	15.0	19.4	12.1	2	23	—	1972	Rubber-tyred system
Seoul	9.5	5.9	8.8	5.5	1	9	175	15.8.1974	Being extended
Stockholm	104.0	64.6	57.0	35.4	2	96	186	1950	Being extended
Tashkent	16.2	10.1	16.0	9.9	1	9	—	7.11.1977	Being extended
Tbilisi	12.6	7.8	10.2	6.3	1	11	75	1965	
Tokyo	175.3	109.0	149.0	92.6	9	157	1700	1927	Being extended
Toronto	51.7	35.9	44.2	27.5	3	57	170	30.3.1954	Being extended
Vienna	3.1	1.9	3.1	1.9	1	5	—	25.2.1978	Short open-air section operated from 8.5.1976
Washington	34.0	21.0	25.0	15.5	2	29	65	29.3.1976	Eventual system 157.2 km (97.7 miles) with 86 stations
Yokohama	11.6	7.2	11.6	7.2	1	11	25	12.1972	Being extended

Railway Preservation

by John Westwood Railway museums,
enthusiast activities and tourist lines.

Railway museums

Over the past two decades the steam tourist railway has become so common that it is often forgotten that railway preservation did not start with museum lines but with museums. The static exhibition of railway relics began in the late nineteenth century, when, in various places and according to no particular plan, items from the early days of railways were put aside by foresighted or sentimental men, rather than being abandoned or sent for scrap. It is such men to whom we should be grateful, for example, for the preservation of so many early colliery locomotives.

Nowadays the static railway exhibit is usually inside a railway museum, or forms part of a technical museum, or is a lone exhibit at, typically, a railway station. There are exceptions: there is a Prussian 4-6-0 near Hanover attached to a dining car to form a novel restaurant; there is another 4-6-0 inside a kind of temple in Moscow, celebrated as the locomotive which hauled Lenin's funeral train; there are a pair of 4-4-0s marking the spot where the last spike of America's first trans-continental line was driven home.

The first museum devoted purely to the railway seems to be that of Hamar, in Norway, which had its beginnings in 1896 and is one of the world's most beautifully situated museums. It has the collections of documents, pictures, track and signals, passenger cars and locomotives which are the usual stock of such museums. The locomotives, in common with many such museums, include early British examples, demonstrating the leading role of Britain in early railway technology.

United Kingdom

Britain's own railway museums have had a chequered history. A few railways at certain times decided to retain old equipment, but all too often a keen new broom of a management decided to get rid of what it regarded as scrap metal. The case of the old locomotives at Swindon, once preserved by the Great Western Railway, is a little different for there the vandals were themselves locomotive engineers who, it seems, had little appreciation of the work of their predecessors.

In Britain the most creditable role in railway museum history was played by the North Eastern Railway. This company had a strong sense of corporate identity and, faced with enforced amalgamation, founded a museum at York of selected items of equipment including locomotives. In the inter-war years a few items were also acquired from other railways, including the Great Western's *City of Truro*, the Brighton's *Gladstone* and two of the famous Great Northern Atlantics. After nationalization British Railways decided that the premises at York were too small and that a larger collection was desirable. In those days, London was still considered to be the heart of Britain so a site in the capital, at Clapham, was chosen and a list drawn up of items which should be preserved rather than scrapped. The staff at the Clapham Museum were able to mount a splendid display, and their restoration of old items was superb and immaculate. But before long it was decided to transfer the exhibits to York where a new National Railway Museum would be established. This new decision was well executed. The museum was not housed in the old North Eastern offices like the old York Museum but in a refurbished locomotive depot. A more suitable site for an exhibition of rolling stock could hardly be imagined and the planners of the museum took full advantage of their good fortune. The new

Previous pages: Evening Star, the last steam locomotive built for British Railways, is now preserved. It is sometimes used for excursions, although its long wheelbase, unsuitable for negotiating some recent main-line trackwork, may limit its future activity. It is of an exceptionally successful class; with a 2-10-0 wheel arrangement, the class was intended for heavy freight work, but its balancing was so good that it could be seen hauling fast passenger trains at peak periods in the last years of British steam traction.

National Railway Museum has received many more visitors than expected and seems likely to continue as a great tourist attraction as well as a rich source of interest for the serious student of railway history. Not all the museum's larger exhibits are shown at the same time; one novel and imaginative feature is the loaning of locomotives to steam tourist railways, where they are used to haul trains.

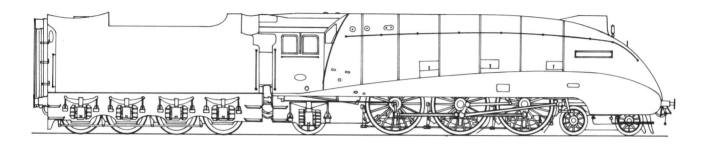

The A4 Pacific, one of the most celebrated inter-war British locomotive designs. Several of these fast engines have been preserved, including Dwight D Eisenhower *in the USA. Designed by Gresley for the London & North Eastern Railway, they hauled trains like the* Coronation *and* Flying Scotsman. *In 1938* Mallard *of this class reached 202·8 kph (126 mph), which is regarded as the world speed record for a steam locomotive.* Mallard *is on view at the National Railway Museum at York, and there are three others of the type preserved in working order in Britain.*

Other notable British museums include the Science Museum in London, which exhibits a Great Western Castle and the prototype Deltic diesel locomotive—as well as Stephenson's *Rocket*, Hedley's 1812 *Puffing Billy* and Hackworth's *Sans Pareil*. Another Hedley locomotive is at the Royal Scottish Museum in Edinburgh while Stephenson's *Locomotion* for the Stockton & Darlington is at York. British regional railway museums include the Museum of Transport at Glasgow, specializing in Scottish locomotives, and the Transport Museum at Belfast which has, among other things, a collection of Irish locomotives of various ages and gauges. At Swindon there is the Great Western Museum, in which *City of Truro* and four other GWR engines have found a final home.

North America

The Baltimore & Ohio Railroad in the USA occupies a similar place among pioneers of the preservation movement as the North Eastern in Britain. The museum at Baltimore contains not only B & O locomotives but also some notable antiques from elsewhere. However, the oldest (and still operable) American locomotive is Stephenson's *John Bull* of 1831, built for the Camden & Amboy RR and now preserved in Washington. Other old locomotives are scattered around North America in various museums or are in store. Among these are Baldwin's *Pioneer* of 1836 at Chicago, Hackworth's *Samson* at New Glasgow in Nova Scotia, Hinkley's 1846 *Lion* at the University of Maine and Braithwaite's 1838 *Rocket* at Philadelphia. More modern locomotives are exhibited at the Railroad Museum at St Louis (a large railway enthusiast enterprise), at the Ford Museum near Detroit and elsewhere. In Canada the Canadian Railway Museum near Montreal is another ambitious and successful enthusiast venture which exhibits mainly Canadian locomotives but has also a few European items.

Europe

In continental Europe the Swiss Museum of Transport at Lucerne has a good collection of rolling stock; as might be expected, electric and rack locomotives are well represented. Not far from the Swiss frontier is the French railway museum at Mulhouse; like the British, the French decided that their capital was not the most suitable place for a national railway museum. The Mulhouse museum is still in course of putting its collection on display, but there is already a wide range of locomotive types on view including some of the pioneer compound locomotives for which the French railways were so noted. A fair amount of other rolling stock has also been preserved. Somewhat longer established than the French museum is that of the Netherlands Railways. This is situated in a disused station at Utrecht, the headquarters city of the Railways. Among the locomotives are several of the Beyer, Peacock types which were so common in Holland, as well as some German- and Dutch-built machines. Steam trams, once familiar in the Netherlands, are also prominent. The Belgian railway museum, like several others, is in temporary quarters and most of its locomotives are in store awaiting proper exhibition. Nevertheless the existing museum, in Brussels, is very well planned and does include a handful of early locomotives. In Germany, a notable display is at the railway museum at Nuremberg, which includes among its exhibits a Bavarian 2-4-0 of 1853, a pair of highly ornamented coaches built for the travels of King Ludwig II, a Crampton 4-2-0 of the Baden State Railways, a Bavarian Atlantic and the inter-war streamlined 4-6-4 which attained 201 km/h (125 mph) in 1936. At the Deutsches Museum at Munich the railway exhibits include pioneer diesel and electric locomotives as well as one of the celebrated three-cylinder Pacifics of the Bavarian State Railways. The Neuenmarkt-Wirsberg museum also has many locomotives.

This is only a selection of the world's railway museums, for there are many more. In Australia, for example, the enthusiast organizations in the different states have created their own museums to display a remarkably complete range of local locomotive types. A railway museum opened recently at Delhi. Austria, Hungary, Spain, Poland, Sweden, and Denmark all have interesting collections. In the USSR, although there is not yet a museum housing full-size exhibits, a number of locomotives are on display at various stations. Italy also has a good collection of locomotives and stock at the Leonardo da Vinci Museum in Milan.

Enthusiast activities and tourist lines

From the point of view of railway and engineering historians, the static museum is an adequate means of preserving the past. Not least of its virtues is that the exhibits do not wear out and are properly looked after. But there is another side to railways, namely, the appeal to the emotions of 'rain, steam and speed' which has attracted artists since the earliest days and which still attracts a general public. For this reason, the disappearance of live steam traction from the railways would have meant a great sensual loss which no museum exhibit could replace. Fortunately, the railway preservation movement has maintained the steam locomotive as a working machine. True, steam locomotives preserved for this kind of life inevitably wear out and new parts have to be substituted for the original; but this is a feature of any railway and ensures that the preserved line is not static but constantly changing in one small way or another.

There are not many countries in the northern hemisphere where it is impossible to see a steam engine at work at some place or time each year. There are the railway enthusiast organizations that have devoted themselves to the renovation of lines abandoned by the main-line railways and to their operation by restored steam locomotives. There are commercial organizations that, sometimes with enthusiasts' help, perform very much the same function with the object of making a profit from tourist traffic. And, increasingly, there are the main-line railways themselves that from time to time either operate their own steam trains in the hope of making a little extra passenger revenue, or allow enthusiasts' organizations to run locomotives over their tracks.

United Kingdom

The earliest of the enthusiast projects was the Talyllynn Railway in Wales. This narrow-gauge slate line had survived decade after decade of dwindling traffic. By 1948, so decrepit had it become and so hopeless as a commercial venture that it was not absorbed by British Railways at the time of nationalization. Its owner was determined to keep some kind of operation going and after his death a specially-formed enthusiast company took it over. After thousands of man-hours had been spent by volunteer labour it became possible to open the line for tourist passenger traffic in the early 1950s. Passengers did come, in large numbers, and the Railway has prospered ever since. Not far away the famous Festiniog Railway, once the standard-bearer of the narrow-gauge champions, was reopened on similar principles. This too has done well. Several other Welsh narrow-gauge ventures have appeared since then, of which the Welshpool & Llanfair is perhaps the most notable. Traversing un-spectacular but agreeable scenery, this friendly little line, because of its proximity to the well-populated Midlands, has been able to attract both volunteer labour and tourist traffic. Like the Talyllyn and Festiniog lines, it has been able to start work on extending its route. While the Festiniog is extending eastwards (to its original terminus at Blaenau Festiniog) the Welshpool & Llanfair is doing the same, intent on re-entering Welshpool.

All three of these railways have had to supplement their original equipment with items acquired from other, defunct, narrow-gauge railways. Thus the Festiniog, even though it still uses one of its original Fairlie 'double-enders', has an American tank locomotive originally built for the Western Front of World War I as well as a pair of engines which once worked a quarry at Penrhyn in north Wales. The Welshpool & Llanfair, in its search for equip-ment to handle increasing traffic, has acquired narrow-gauge locomotives from Germany, the West Indies and west Africa. Another major Welsh narrow-gauge line, the Vale of Rheidol, is still self-sufficient. Part of British Rail, it operates its service with the three tank locomotives inherited from the Great Western Railway at the time of nationalization.

Reopening of standard-gauge lines required more resources than the narrow-gauge enterprises but this did not deter pioneers who reopened the Bluebell Railway in 1960. This, a branch line in Sussex, was closed by British Railways and, after some initial skirmishing, amicably transferred to the enthusiast organization. With its varied collection of operable steam loco-motives, and its proximity both to London and to south-coast resorts, this line was an early success and, like the Talyllyn, inspired a host of worthy imitators. So much so that the number of steam tourist lines in Britain is too large to enumerate here in detail. Moreover, the number has been increasing, although this expansion may soon come to an enforced halt. It has long been said, as each new venture was announced, that too many lines were being opened, thereby spreading the essential tourist patronage too thinly. Yet while lines once condemned as hopeless have survived, the supply of steam locomotives is approaching exhaustion. For years a steel scrap company in south Wales, which acquired hundreds of British Rail's last steam locomotives, has been selling the soundest units to enthusiast societies. But by 1978 viable locomotives remaining at this yard were very few indeed. But now that old diesel locomotives are acquiring an antiquarian attraction, some lines are introducing selected examples of that type of motive power.

Some of the more ambitious British undertakings are the Severn Valley, the Torbay and Dartmouth, the Keighley and Worth Valley, the North Yorkshire Moors, the Nene Valley and the Great Central. All these have their own particular flavour. The Severn Valley is a former secondary line of the Great Western Railway which passes through pleasant surroundings from Bridgnorth to Bewdley. It possesses a wide range of locomotives, some still awaiting restoration, and leans towards Great Western and LMS practice. The Torbay and Dartmouth runs over a former GW branch line and for the most part manages to retain the atmosphere and equipment of the Great Western. The North Yorkshire Moors, running over striking terrain, is the home of two former North Eastern Railway locomotives among others. The Keighley and Worth Valley, by now one of the oldest and most successful of the tourist lines, runs through Pennine scenery associated with the Brontë family and is accordingly well placed to attract tourists. It has a variegated locomotive stock but emphasis is on the LMS Railway, once the owner of this line. The Nene Valley Railway at Peterborough is unique in several ways: it was blessed with great co-operation from the local authorities; it has a regular freight traffic, and its structures can accommodate foreign locomotives, of which it has several examples. The Great Central, based on Loughborough, runs its trains over a former main line, that of the old Great Central Railway.

The crest of the Keighley & Worth Valley Light Railway.

The 'live museum' concept is also practised in Britain. This involves a stock of operable steam locomotives that have only a limited length of track on which to move. Steamtown at Carnforth is a good example of this; it consists of a large locomotive shed once used by British Rail. In this are kept the exhibits, except for one or two units which are kept in steam during visiting hours and which can move up and down the yard tracks. Tyseley, a former GWR locomotive depot in Birmingham, is similar in principle. Didcot locomotive depot, near Oxford, is the home of the Great Western Society, which keeps its large stock of GWR locomotives there and operates a steam-hauled train along a short length of line alongside. Another large collection of operable locomotives is at Bressingham in Norfolk. Like several other British collections, it includes a non-British locomotive—in this case an American-built 141R 2-8-2 of the SNCF. Locomotives at Carnforth, Tyseley and Didcot include some which have been approved by British Rail for use on long-distance steam excursions.

Steam-hauled trains on British Rail restarted in 1971 after a period in which the management banned steam traction. A few routes were named as open for excursions organized by societies and tour operators, and a handful of preserved locomotives were accepted for their haulage. These trains ran at certain weekends in the spring and autumn. In 1978 a new feature was the organization by BR of its own steam excursions—regular services behind steam traction to attract summer holidaymakers. These services ran from York and from Carnforth, making use of locomotives preserved at those places. How these 'official' steam services would affect the traffic of the neighbouring tourist railways was a matter of some concern for the latter. Another railway which decided to take advantage of the tourist boom was the Derwent Valley

Railway, an industrial short-line. In addition to its daily diesel-hauled freight train, this company began to run a steam-hauled passenger service behind a former British Railways 0-6-0 tank locomotive. Not only this, but the freight also began to be handled by the passenger service so that on days of light freight traffic a steam-hauled mixed train replaced the daily diesel freight, and all for sound commercial reasons.

In Northern Ireland the Railway Preservation Society has been operating steam trains during the summer. These include a regular excursion train from Belfast hauled by the Society's 2-6-4 tank locomotive. Two other engines, an old 0-6-0 and the more modern 4-4-0 *Slieve Gullion*, are used on longer excursions which often run over the border in Eire.

Europe

In continental Europe there are many tourist lines, typically operating only at summer weekends and using 0-6-0 and 0-4-0 tank locomotives. The Netherlands has several of these of which the senior is the Hoorn–Medemblik line, which includes a tram engine in its motive power. Another Dutch line, the Goes–Borsele, uses the same kind of locomotive pulling vintage six-wheeled cars of Belgian and Prussian origin. In Germany several organizations possess rolling stock but no trackage, running their trains on Sundays over lines which are used by regular trains only on weekdays. Probably the biggest of the European voluntary organizations is Eurovapor which, although based in Switzerland, operates its trains in Austria and south Germany also. Although its trains are typically hauled by small tank locomotives, it includes a DB Pacific among its larger machines. In Austria the situation is unique because a number of local narrow-gauge railways, as part of their commercial business, operate steam tourist trains among their regular diesel services. Two of these enterprising lines also offer passengers a chance to drive the locomotive.

In Switzerland there are a few preserved steam railways. The Blonay–Chamby line is perhaps the best known of these. It has a short metre-gauge line but its locomotives also work trains over neighbouring conventional railways. In Scandinavia there are narrow-gauge steam lines in Sweden, Norway, Finland and Denmark, with standard-gauge activity also in Sweden and Denmark. The last-mentioned is in many ways the most active of the Scandinavian countries. Like the several enthusiast organizations, the state railway has a few steam locomotives which it uses to haul excursions on suitable occasions. The Danish Railway Club has nine standard-gauge locomotives to work its Lolland Railway weekend services and has begun to extend its activities to other lines.

In France railway preservation made a fairly slow start. For this reason the number of locomotives able to work main-line trains was until recently limited to a Paris–Orleans 4-6-0, the hard-worked 230G-353, although a US-built 141R 2-8-2 is now available. The tourist railways, though small in number, are of exceptional interest. Earliest among them was the Pithiviers line, a section of a 600 mm (2 ft) gauge sugar-beet railway which used steam traction right to the end. Resurrected by a group of enthusiasts to form both a museum and an operating railway, the line has been quite successful, partly thanks to its proximity to Paris. A more recent operation is between Richelieu and Chinon, in the Loire region, where an SNCF freight-only line is used on Sundays by the AJECTA organization to run three round trips behind steam traction. The pride of the line is a handsome 2-6-0 from the former Est Railway. AJECTA has a stock of other locomotives stored away awaiting restoration, so more interesting motive power may be expected on this line. An especially attractive metre-gauge line is the Vivarais Railway which operates part of the route of a defunct departmental railway between Tournan and Lamastre in the Massif Central. With a route of 33 km (20 miles) the organization used Mallet tank locomotives for its trains. These were part of the original equipment but have been supplemented by acquisitions from the now-closed metre-gauge lines of Brittany.

North America

The steam tourist line in North America has had a career more chequered than most. Lines have started up with great enthusiasm only to founder a year or two later. On the other hand there are enterprises which are surprisingly successful. One difference in the USA (as opposed, perhaps, to Canada) is that the unpaid labour of enthusiast volunteer workers is less available than in Europe. This is partly because the population pattern of the USA means that most volunteers would have to travel long distances in order to put in a day's work, and partly because the concept of doing something for nothing is less widely accepted in the USA. The key to successful operation is, therefore, the attraction of tourist traffic abundant enough to cover the operating costs. It is no coincidence that the most successful of the US lines are in districts which already draw tourists; passengers do not need to make a special journey to travel on these railways for the train trip is simply an extra in a trip made for some other purpose. Thus the Strasburg Railway in Pennsylvania, one of the earliest tourist lines, has been successful because it runs through the celebrated 'Dutch Country'. It is not an ambitious line nor does it stage those 'events' which horrify railway enthusiasts but which seem to attract tourists, yet in the summer months its modest station and handful of small locomotives are kept very busy. A well-known operation, the Silverton Train in Colorado, has a similar draw for it passes through mountain areas of high tourist attraction. This was an advantage from the very beginning for it meant that the project to save a long section of the 915 mm (3 ft) gauge line of the Rio Grande Railroad had the support of the state's tourist department. So for years now, every summer the Silverton Train has provided a daily service between Durango and Silverton, hauled by one of the original Rio Grande locomotives. The abundance of willing passengers, happy to relive the experience of America's past, enables this line to offer one of the longest runs operated by any tourist line — 72 km (45 miles). Length of run is normally one of the limiting factors in tourist-line operation, because tourists are usually unwilling to devote more than a couple of hours to savouring steam travel, nor are they willing to pay the high price which has to be charged for a longer-distance run. Or so, at least, is the theory. In practice a number of lines are extending their routes in the expectation of proving the theory wrong; the Festiniog Railway is extending its route in Wales, in Somerset the West Somerset Railways hopes to operate trains from its present terminus at Minehead to Taunton, and in Holland the Goes–Borsele line is also extending its service. If the experience of the Silverton Train is any guide, it is possible to tempt tourists with the prospect of a half-day or whole day's outing. After all, excursions over main-line railways are day-long events.

The 'fan trip' has a long history in America; what was apparently the first was arranged by Railroad Enthusiasts Inc. as long ago as 1934 over the Hoosac Tunnel & Wilmington RR, thereby anticipating by several years the British trip behind the single-driver locomotive No. 1 organized by the Railway

Correspondence and Travel Society. Obviously, the steam trip as such did not develop until the end of steam on American railroads. For some years thereafter several railroad companies retained one or two of their steamers in operable condition. These hauled occasional excursions that were sponsored either by the railroad or by an outside organization. But the expense of maintaining the locomotives became greater than the revenue that they could generate, so the number of available machines and willing railroads declined. One of the last surviving locomotives, happily, is No. 8444, an example of one of America's greatest locomotive types—the Union Pacific 4-8-4. The renovation and return to traffic of a Southern Pacific 4-8-4 and a Reading 4-8-4 to haul the US bicentennial train in 1976 may have marked a turning of the tide. It seems likely that in certain places the main-line steam excursion can be a paying proposition for the operating railroads and not merely a publicity gesture. In Canada the Canadian National Railways, after retaining a 4-8-4 for excursion traffic for several years, remained in the steam business even after its locomotive became due for very expensive repair. Instead of carrying out this repair, it reclassified the locomotive as a static exhibit and took down another static exhibit, 4-8-2 No. 6079, from its display stand in Alberta and renovated it for excursion service. Meanwhile, the British Columbia Railway has found it worthwhile to operate a regular weekly excursion train between Vancouver and Squamish (64 km or 40 miles), hauled by one of the celebrated Royal Hudson 4-6-4s formerly belonging to the Canadian Pacific Railway.

New Zealand

The New Zealand Railways since 1971 have been operating the *Kingston Flyer*, during the summer season, from Christmas to Easter. This is one of the best organized of the steam operations offered by main-line railways. Indeed, the *Kingston Flyer* is probably New Zealand's most famous train. Two units of the NZR's best-known locomotive class, the Ab Pacific of 1915, were renovated together with a set of wooden-bodied passenger cars and these run twice daily in season. Among the supporters of this venture perhaps the most satisfied were the inhabitants of Lumsden, because it assured the future of the branch line serving their township.

Australia

The *Kingston Flyer*, which is a studied resurrection of a period train, has much in common with the 'vintage train' concept of Australia. Several of the Australian state railways have assembled a train of nineteenth-century passenger cars which is used to provide railway participation in local events, typically centenary celebrations of townships on the railway's routes. Old locomotives are used to haul these trains, which normally include one or two tank cars behind the locomotive because locomotive watering facilities are now rare. In New South Wales a pair of 4-4-0 locomotives are retained for this work. Conventional main-line steam excursions in Australia reached a peak in the early 1970s, as steam was disappearing. With the total elimination of steam traction in normal service it has become more difficult to arrange these excursions. However, the state enthusiast organizations have succeeded in providing occasional trips behind one or other of the locomotives now in their possession. Steam tourist railways are uncommon in Australia. The only long-standing line is the so-called 'Puffing Billy' in the Dandenong foothills near Melbourne. This reproduces the flavour of Victoria's narrow-gauge lines and uses the original American-design 2-6-2 tank locomotives.

The future

In retrospect, it is clear that twenty years ago only the most blindly optimistic enthusiast could have envisaged the scope and the success of the railway-preservation movement in all its different forms. Everywhere in the developed world, wherever the steam locomotive has disappeared from regular traffic, it continues to exist and to satisfy public demand for whatever it is that makes it so satisfying a spectacle. The unpredicted extent of railway preservation makes it unwise to forecast the next twenty years. Although one or two trends seem inevitable what will emerge from the encounter of these trends is unforseeable. On the positive side it can no longer be said, as it once was said, that preservation projects, and in particular steam tourist railways, are not commercially viable. There must also be some questioning of a similar proposition: that the more lines that are opened the less traffic each will carry. It could even be true that a new line can help a neighbour merely by providing extra incentive for the tourist to visit that area. The association of the Welsh narrow-gauge lines in joint publicity ventures with the slogan 'The Great Little Trains of Wales' seems to support this.

Some limit may be placed by the unfortunate fact that steam locomotives wear out. It is true that a steam locomotive can be immortal in the sense that over the years every old part can be replaced by a new part. But this is very expensive, especially as nowadays every spare part tends to be a one-off job. It is not impossible that entirely new steam locomotives will be built. Already the Festiniog Railway has undertaken the building of a Fairlie locomotive partly using bits and pieces of old locomotives. The Great Western Society is planning to build a new locomotive to Churchward's Saint design using parts from other locomotives. Almost certainly, too, some static exhibits, of which there are several thousand in the world, will be taken from their pedestals and made operable.

In this kind of work, however, and in almost every other aspect of tourist railway operation, the unpaid labour of volunteers, many of whom have precious and fast-disappearing skills, is the key element. Without them the steam railway would be confined to a few operations of the Disneyland type and a few which are lucky enough to be situated in leading tourist areas. Whether volunteers will continue to come forward as before is unpredictable; a lot depends on how they are treated. Some have been offended, justifiably, when their labours have been exploited by commercial organizations. (There are several lines which are owned by commercial enterprises but which make use of unpaid workers; in such cases a very sympathetic and sensitive management is essential.) It must also be recognized that there will always be a conflict between those volunteers who want their railway to be a true replica of the steam age and managements that realize that the only way to entice the tourists on whom they depend is to offer them attractions of a kind quite out of keeping with railway tradition. But, whatever happens, at worst the gains of the past two decades can hardly be entirely lost and at best the prospects are as unimaginable as they were twenty years ago.

Index

Acknowledgements

The publishers would like to thank the following individuals and organizations for their kind permission to reproduce the photographs in this book:

W. J. V. Anderson 103 above, 292 below, 294; Association of American Railroads 278; R. Bastin 115 above left; The Bettmann Archive 23, 210; British Railways Board 197 above; The British Tourist Authority 42; Camera Press, London 1, 306–307; Canadian Pacific Ltd. 52, 197 below; J. Allan Cash Ltd. 159 above left; CCQ (T. B. Owen) 154 below; J. A. Coiley 240 centre right; The Cooper-Bridgeman Library 45 below; D. Cross 240 below; Deutsche Bundesbahn 159 centre, 234–235, 240 above right; Douglas Dickins 346–347; C. V. Gammell 43, 103 below, 155 above right, 289, 295 above, centre, below; The Guardian (Kenneth Saunders) 68–69; Victor Hand 48 below, 97, 100–101, 102 above, 104, 136–137, 153, 154 centre, 160 above left and below, 198–199 below, 200, 233, 238–239, 296; Japan Information Centre 338–339; J. M. Jarvis 292 above, 293 below; D. Jenkinson 159 above right; Chris Kapolka 262 above; La Vie Du Rail 44 below; London Transport 360–361; James Mackay 210–211; Merseyside County Museum 44 above; S. A. Mourton 293 above; National Railway Museum 240 above left, 240 centre left; L. A. Nixon 64, 180–181, 262–263, 284–285; O. S. Nock 158 below; Nordisk Pressefoto (Peer Lauritzen) 198 above; The Photographic Library of Australia 6–7, 8, 345, 350–351, endpapers; Photo Research International 211, 370–371; Popperfoto 262–263 centre; Quebec Cartier Mining Company (J. G. Moore Collection) 352; Railways of Australia 290–291; Rapho Agence de Presse 158 above; D. Rodgers 45 above, 48 above, 199 above; Ann Ronan Picture Library 245; Satour 155 below; The Science Museum, London (J. G. Moore Collection) 10–11, 41, 46–47, 109 above and below; SNCF 236–237; Spectrum Colour Library 2–3, (T. Boustead), 9, 60, 92–93, 386; Brian Stephenson 148–149, 154 above left, 159 below, 160 above right, 193, 196–197; Lu Sun-Hsiang 348–349; P. N. Trotter 154 above right, 198 below, 380–381; Westinghouse Brake and Signal Company Ltd. 35; John Westwood 56, 275, 276; J. S. Whiteley 45 centre, 102 below; Yugoslav Tourist Office 356; Zefa (Mohn) 4–5, (Th. Luttge) 322–323.

Colour artwork Lynn Brooks